VAMPIRE KNIGHT
Vol. 11
Shojo Beat Edition

STORY AND ART BY
MATSURI HINO

Adaptation/Nancy Thistlethwaite
Translation/Tetsuichiro Miyaki
Touch-up Art & Lettering/Rina Mapa
Graphic Design/Amy Martin
Editor/Nancy Thistlethwaite

Vampire Knight by Matsuri Hino © Matsuri Hino 2009. All rights reserved.
First published in Japan in 2009 by HAKUSENSHA, Inc., Tokyo. English
language translation rights arranged with HAKUSENSHA, Inc., Tokyo.

The rights of the author(s) of the work(s) in this publication to be so identified
have been asserted in accordance with the Copyright, Designs and Patents
Act 1988. A CIP catalogue record for this book is available from the British
Library.

The stories, characters and incidents mentioned in this publication are
entirely fictional.

Printed in Canada

Published by VIZ Media, LLC
P.O. Box 77010
San Francisco, CA 94107

10 9 8 7 6 5 4 3 2 1
First printing, December 2010

D0017877

www.viz.com

www.shojobeat.com

Matsuri Hino burst onto the manga scene with her series *Kono Yume ga Sametara* (When This Dream Is Over), which was published in *LaLa DX* magazine. Hino was a manga artist a mere nine months after she decided to become one.

With the success of her popular series *Captive Hearts* and *MeruPuri*, Hino has established herself as a major player in the world of shojo manga. *Vampire Knight* is currently serialized in *LaLa* magazine.

Hino enjoys creative activities and has commented that she would have been either an architect or an apprentice to traditional Japanese craft masters if she had not become a manga artist.

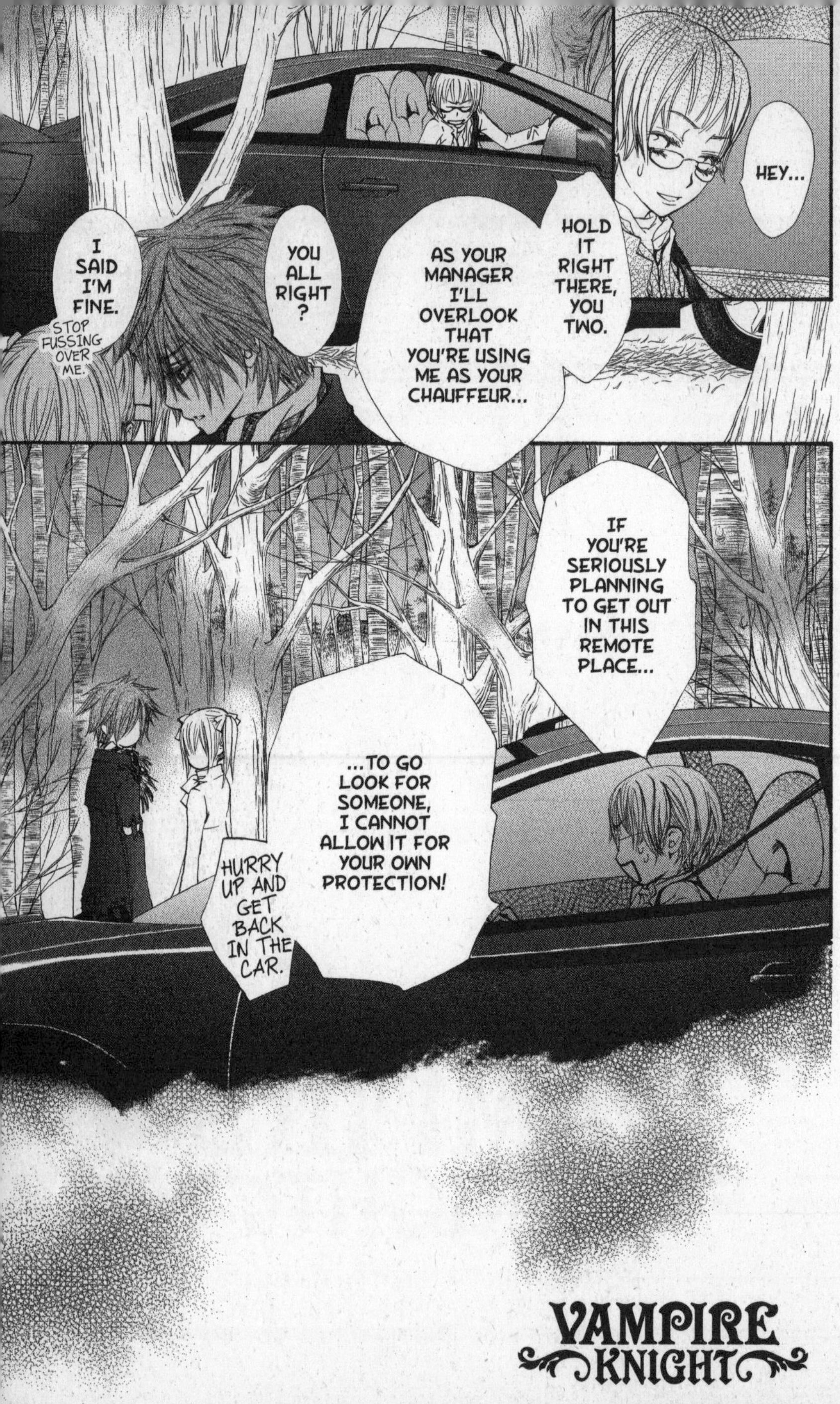
HEY...
HOLD IT RIGHT THERE, YOU TWO.
AS YOUR MANAGER I'LL OVERLOOK THAT YOU'RE USING ME AS YOUR CHAUFFEUR...
YOU ALL RIGHT?
I SAID I'M FINE.
STOP FUSSING OVER ME.
IF YOU'RE SERIOUSLY PLANNING TO GET OUT IN THIS REMOTE PLACE...
...TO GO LOOK FOR SOMEONE, I CANNOT ALLOW IT FOR YOUR OWN PROTECTION!
HURRY UP AND GET BACK IN THE CAR.
VAMPIRE KNIGHT

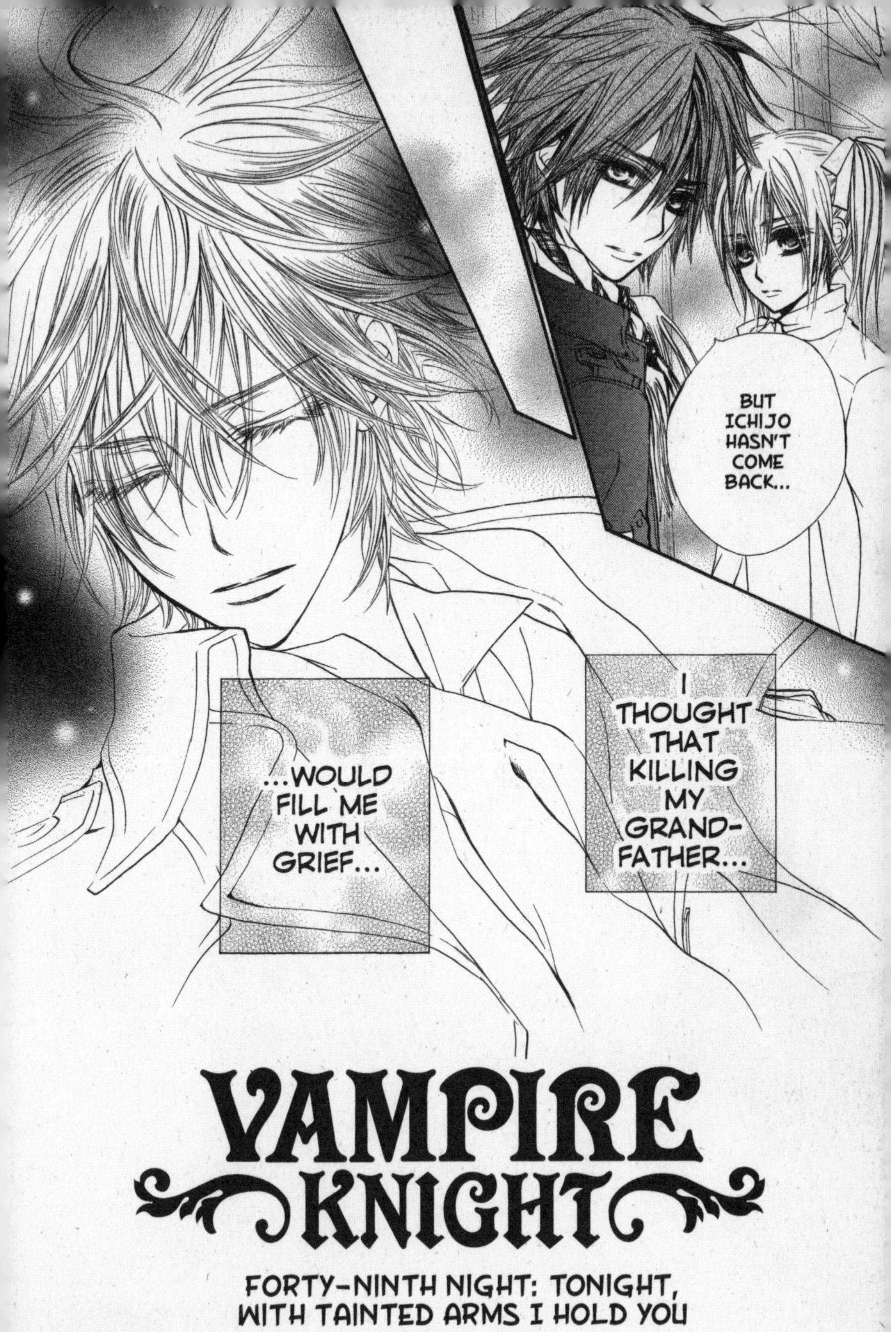
BUT ICHIJO HASN'T COME BACK...
I THOUGHT THAT KILLING MY GRANDFATHER...
...WOULD FILL ME WITH GRIEF...

VAMPIRE KNIGHT

FORTY-NINTH NIGHT: TONIGHT, WITH TAINTED ARMS I HOLD YOU

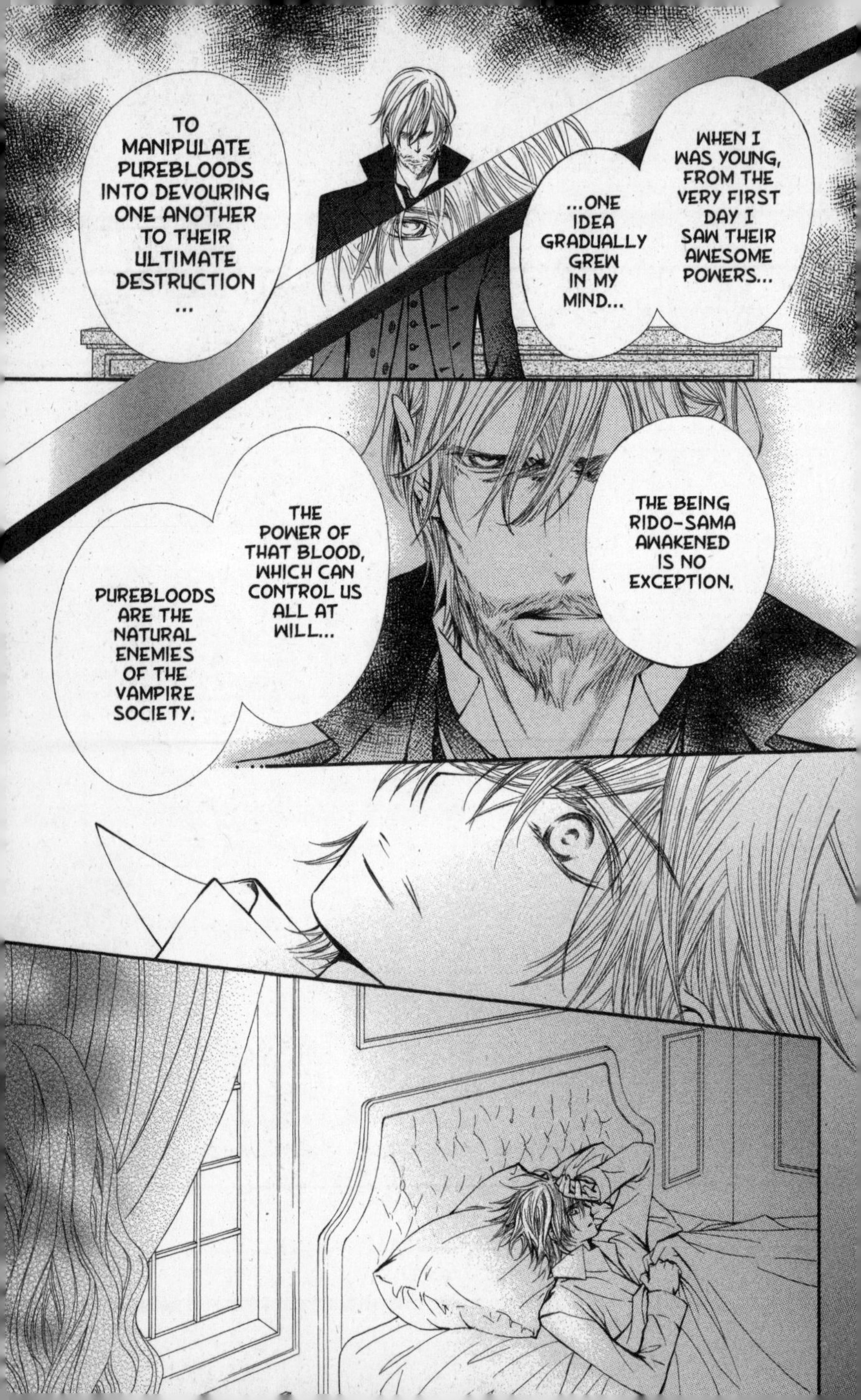
WHEN I WAS YOUNG, FROM THE VERY FIRST DAY I SAW THEIR AWESOME POWERS...
...ONE IDEA GRADUALLY GREW IN MY MIND...
TO MANIPULATE PUREBLOODS INTO DEVOURING ONE ANOTHER TO THEIR ULTIMATE DESTRUCTION ...
THE BEING RIDO-SAMA AWAKENED IS NO EXCEPTION.
THE POWER OF THAT BLOOD, WHICH CAN CONTROL US ALL AT WILL...
PUREBLOODS ARE THE NATURAL ENEMIES OF THE VAMPIRE SOCIETY.

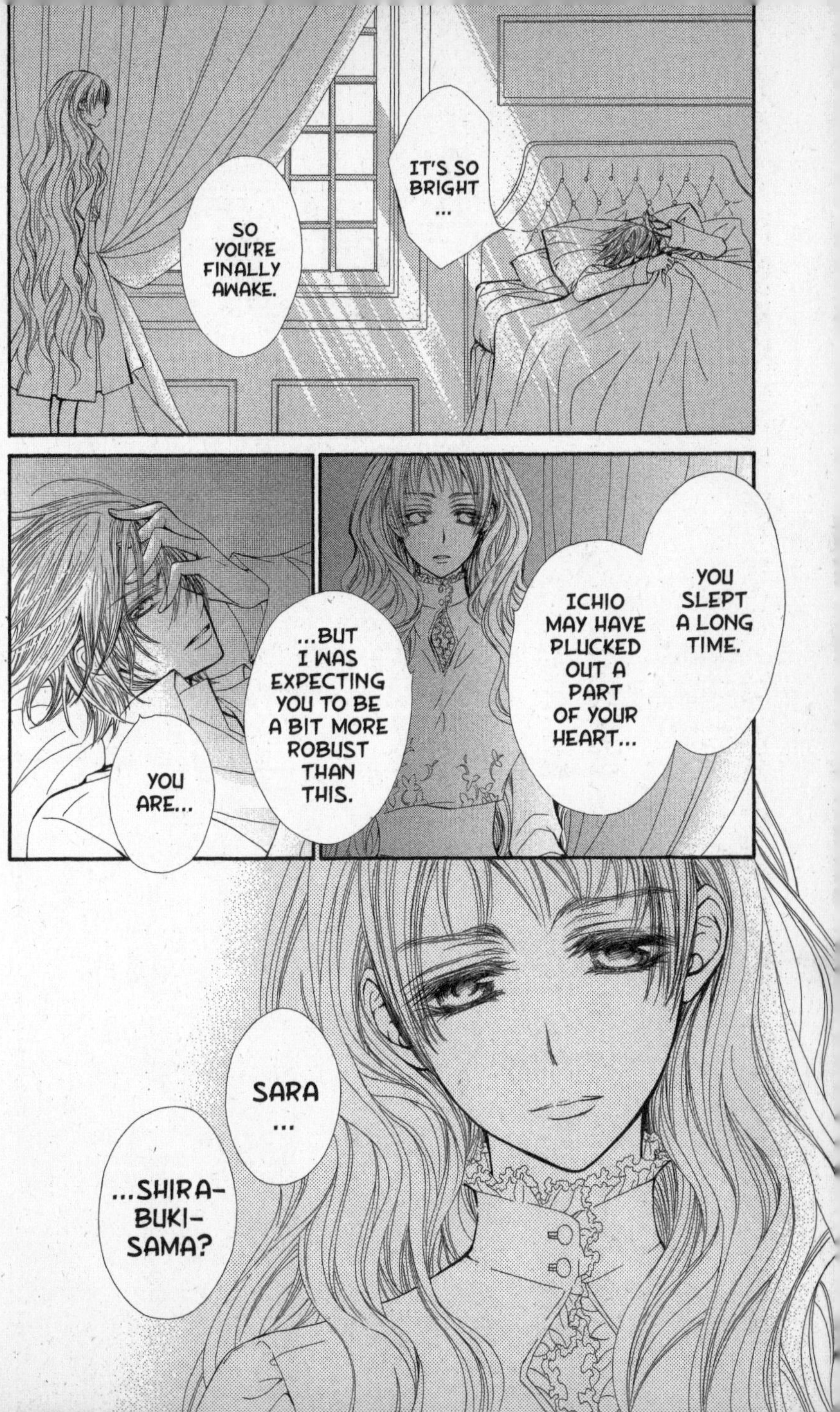
IT'S SO BRIGHT ...
SO YOU'RE FINALLY AWAKE.
YOU SLEPT A LONG TIME.
ICHIO MAY HAVE PLUCKED OUT A PART OF YOUR HEART...
...BUT I WAS EXPECTING YOU TO BE A BIT MORE ROBUST THAN THIS.
YOU ARE...
SARA ...
...SHIRA-BUKI-SAMA?

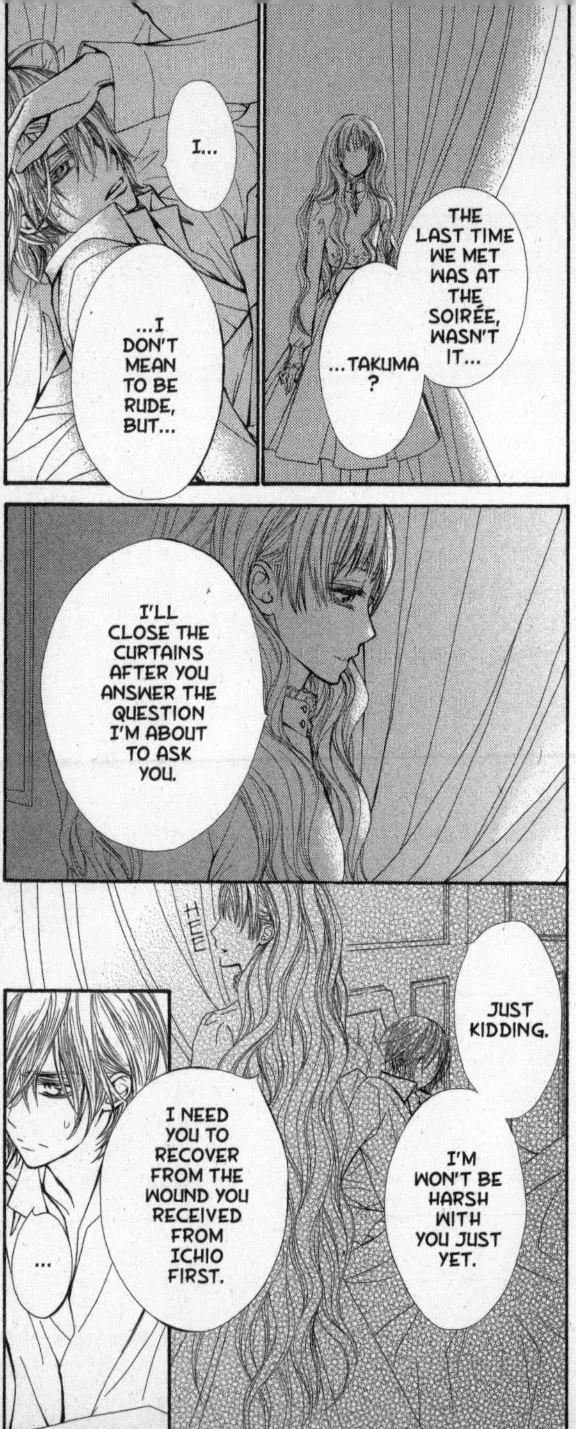
THE LAST TIME WE MET WAS AT THE SOIRÉE, WASN'T IT...
...TAKUMA?
I...
...I DON'T MEAN TO BE RUDE, BUT...
I'LL CLOSE THE CURTAINS AFTER YOU ANSWER THE QUESTION I'M ABOUT TO ASK YOU.
HEE
JUST KIDDING.
I'M WON'T BE HARSH WITH YOU JUST YET.
I NEED YOU TO RECOVER FROM THE WOUND YOU RECEIVED FROM ICHIO FIRST.
...

I

Hello!
I have been able to keep creating this series thanks to the continued support of the readers. This is volume 11.

A whole year passes in this volume, and I had some difficulty coming up with it. Yes... I can only say that I'll try to do my best! I really will!!

I cannot exactly say how many more volumes there will be, but starting from volume 12, my editor and I have agreed to create the most interesting piece of work I can with the hope of making the story fast-paced and enticing.

I hope you will all continue to support it.

So now...
Like I mentioned in volume 10, I would like to write about my impressions of Germany and the event I went to in March 2009. (continues)

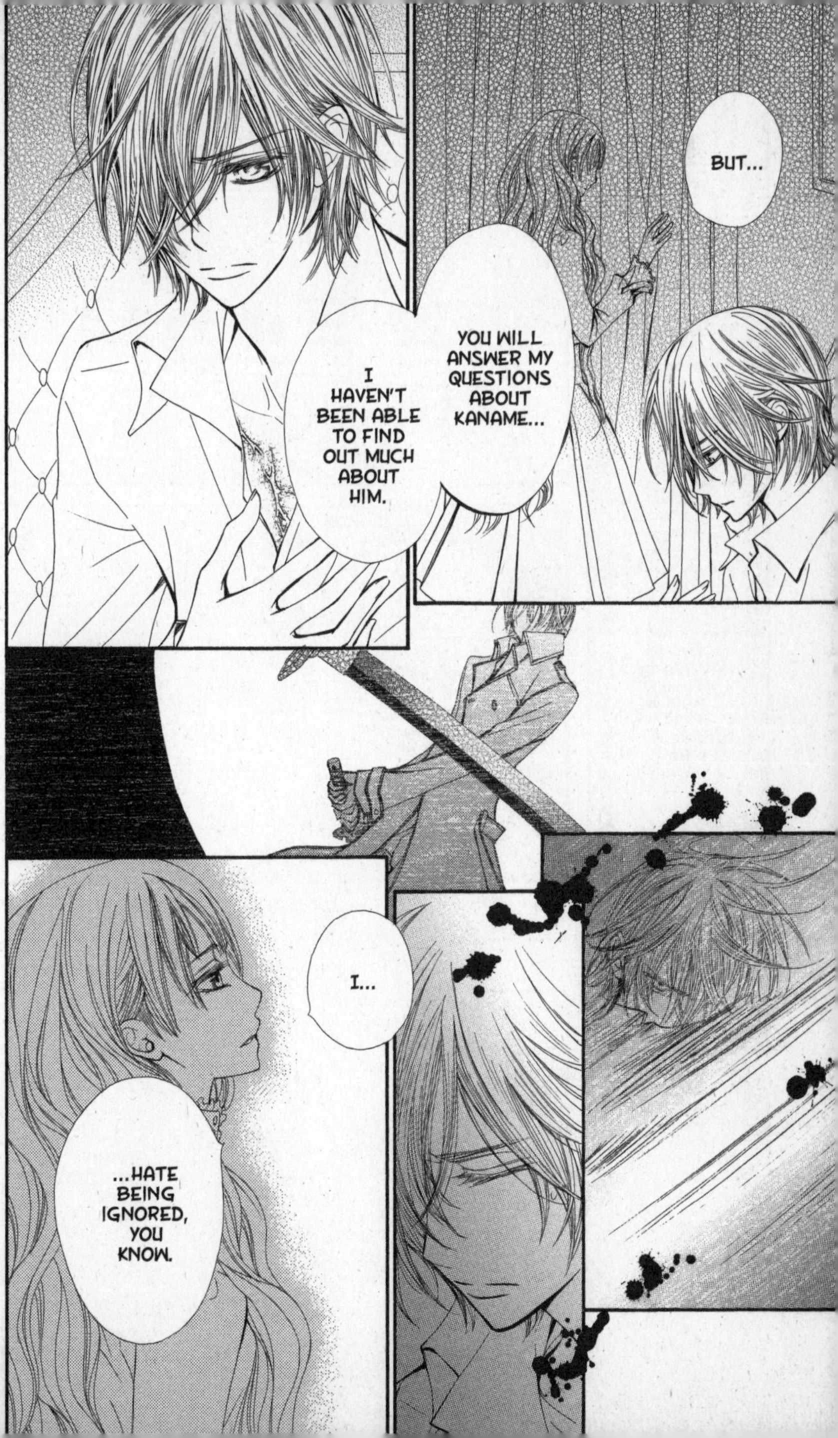
BUT...
YOU WILL ANSWER MY QUESTIONS ABOUT KANAME...
I HAVEN'T BEEN ABLE TO FIND OUT MUCH ABOUT HIM.
I...
...HATE BEING IGNORED, YOU KNOW.

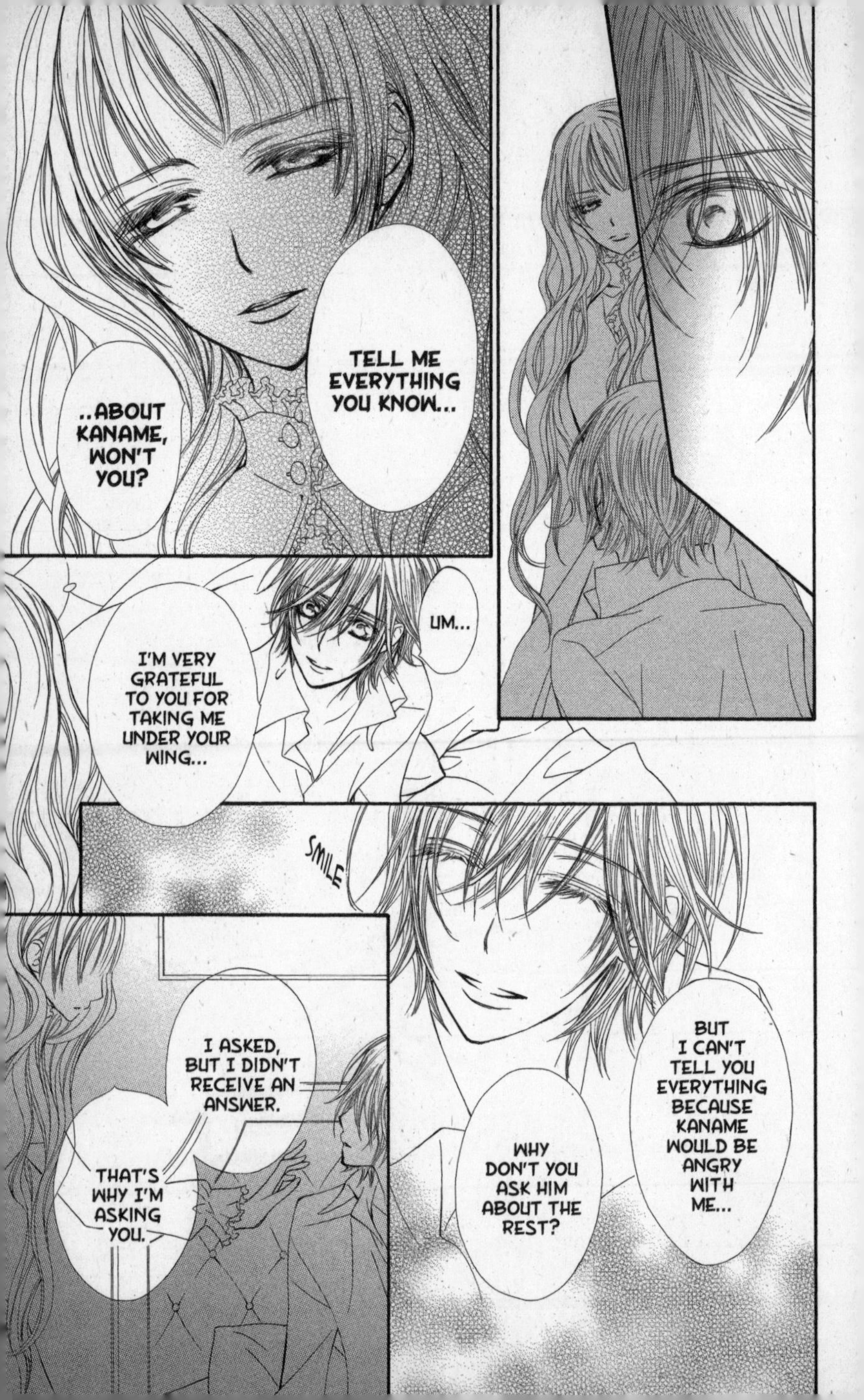
TELL ME EVERYTHING YOU KNOW...
..ABOUT KANAME, WON'T YOU?
UM...
I'M VERY GRATEFUL TO YOU FOR TAKING ME UNDER YOUR WING...
SMILE
BUT I CAN'T TELL YOU EVERYTHING BECAUSE KANAME WOULD BE ANGRY WITH ME...
WHY DON'T YOU ASK HIM ABOUT THE REST?
I ASKED, BUT I DIDN'T RECEIVE AN ANSWER.
THAT'S WHY I'M ASKING YOU.

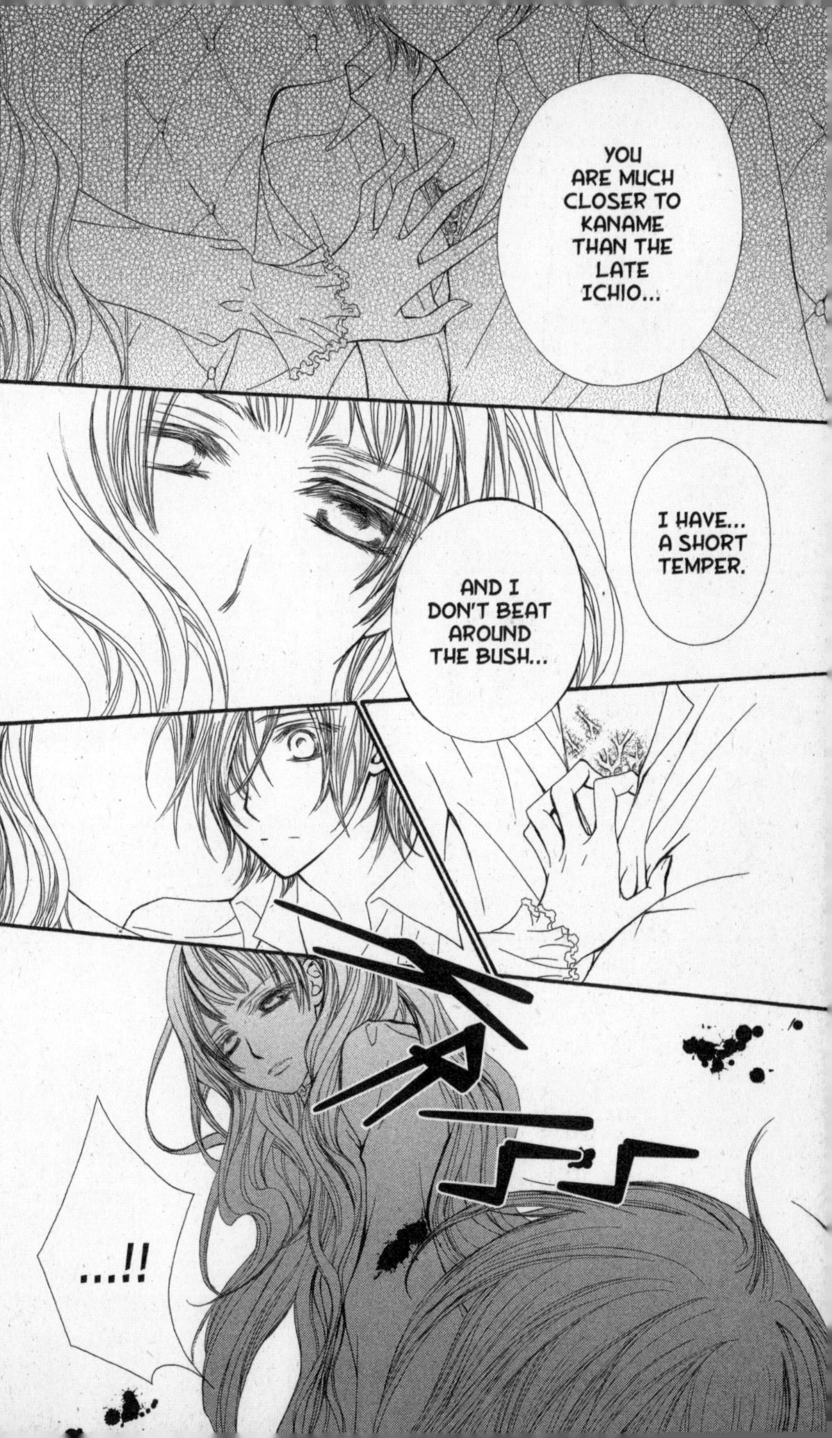
YOU ARE MUCH CLOSER TO KANAME THAN THE LATE ICHIO...
I HAVE... A SHORT TEMPER.
AND I DON'T BEAT AROUND THE BUSH...
...!!

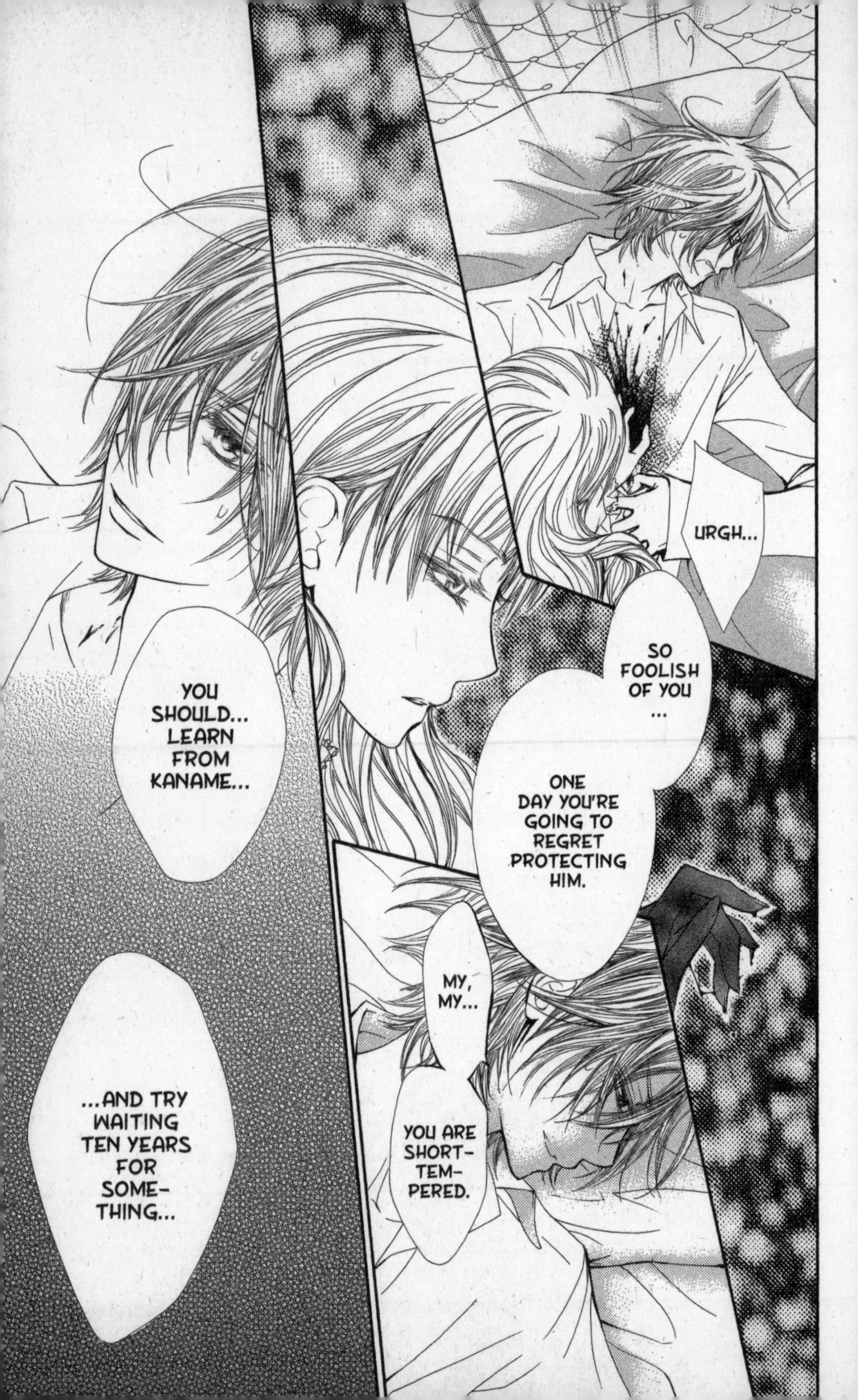
URGH...
SO FOOLISH OF YOU ...
ONE DAY YOU'RE GOING TO REGRET PROTECTING HIM.
MY, MY...
YOU ARE SHORT-TEMPERED.
YOU SHOULD... LEARN FROM KANAME...
...AND TRY WAITING TEN YEARS FOR SOME-THING...

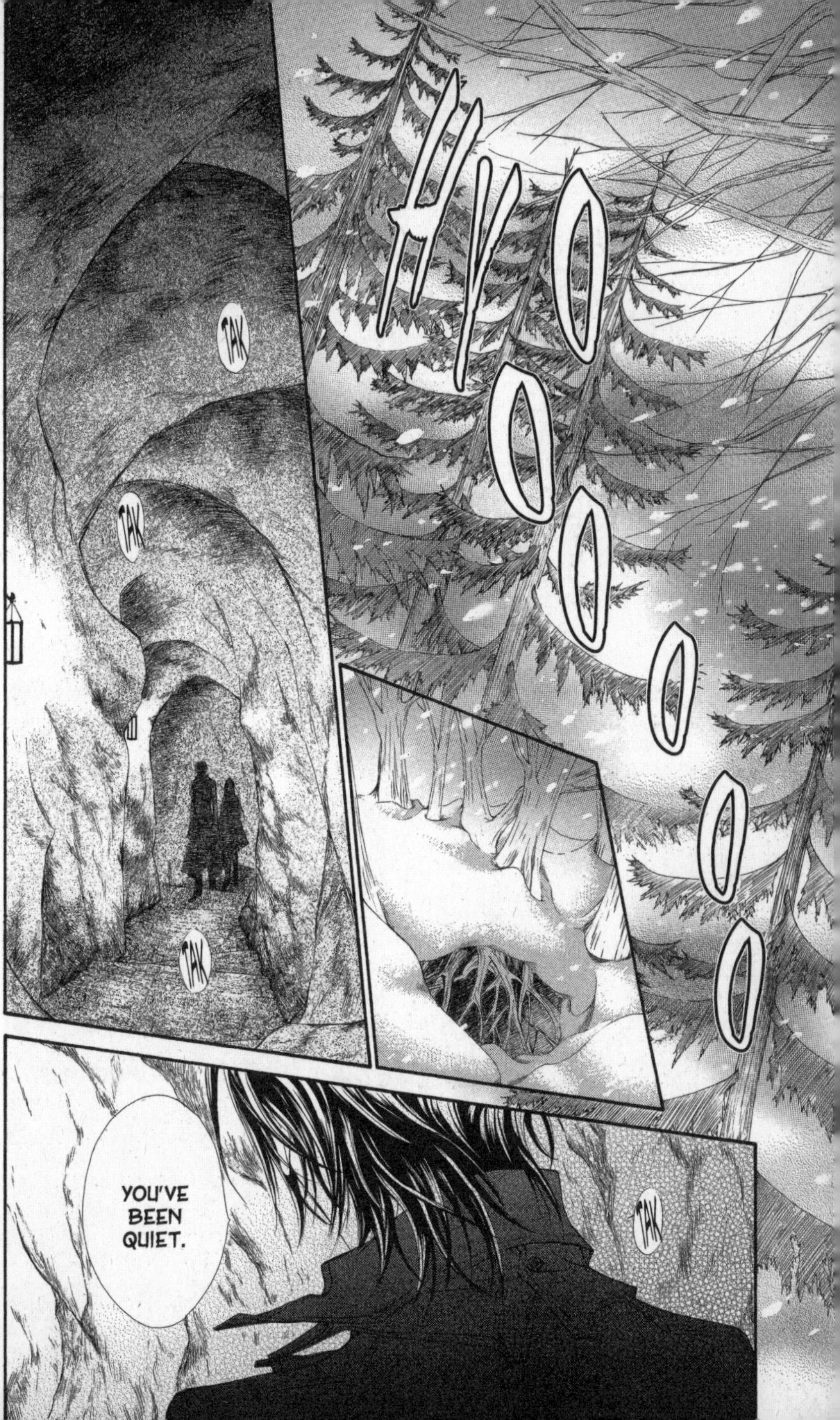

HYOOOOOO
TAK
TAK
TAK
TAK
YOU'VE BEEN QUIET.

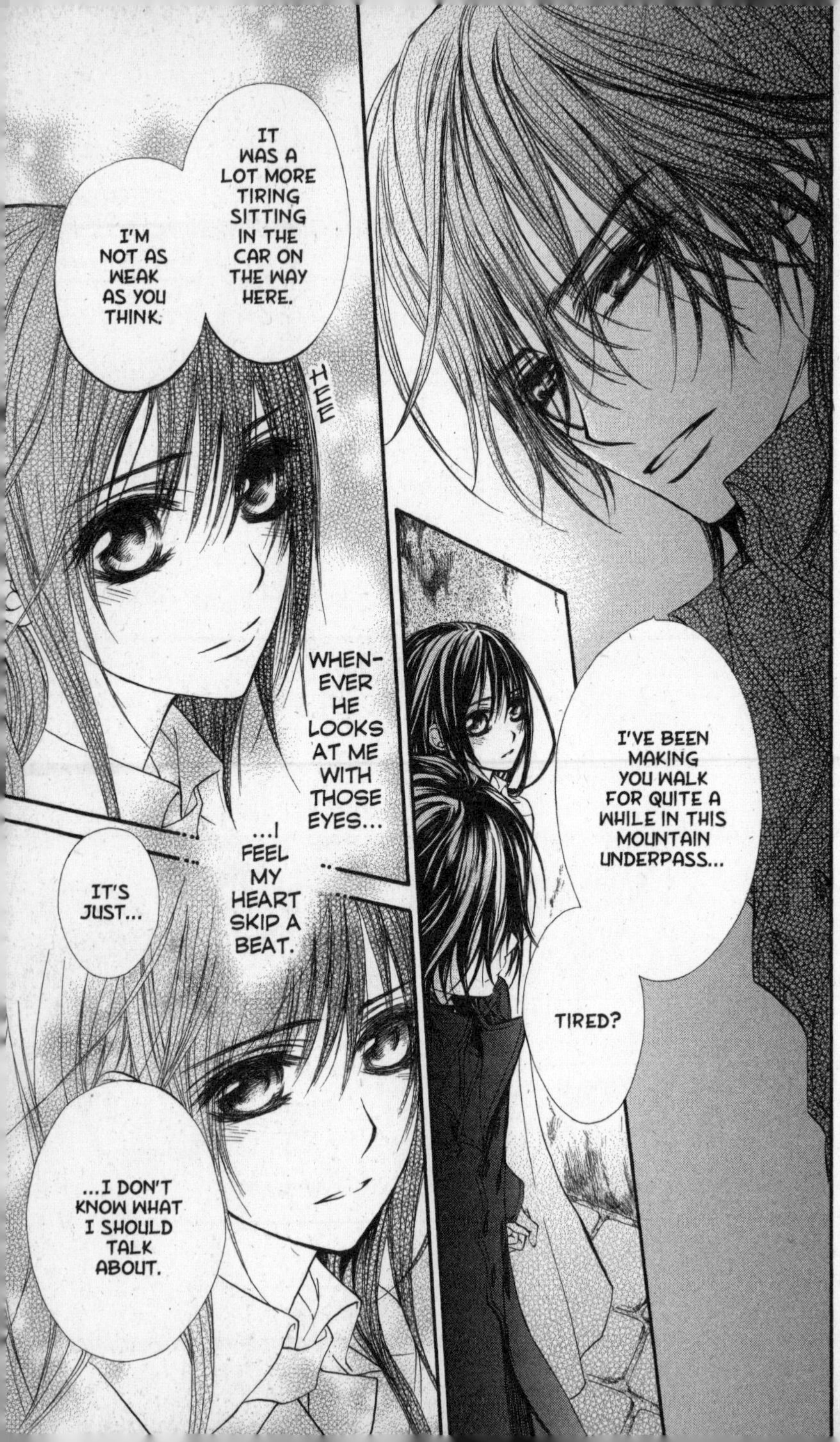
I'VE BEEN MAKING YOU WALK FOR QUITE A WHILE IN THIS MOUNTAIN UNDERPASS...
TIRED?
IT WAS A LOT MORE TIRING SITTING IN THE CAR ON THE WAY HERE.
I'M NOT AS WEAK AS YOU THINK.
HEE
WHEN-EVER HE LOOKS AT ME WITH THOSE EYES...
...I FEEL MY HEART SKIP A BEAT.
IT'S JUST...
...I DON'T KNOW WHAT I SHOULD TALK ABOUT.

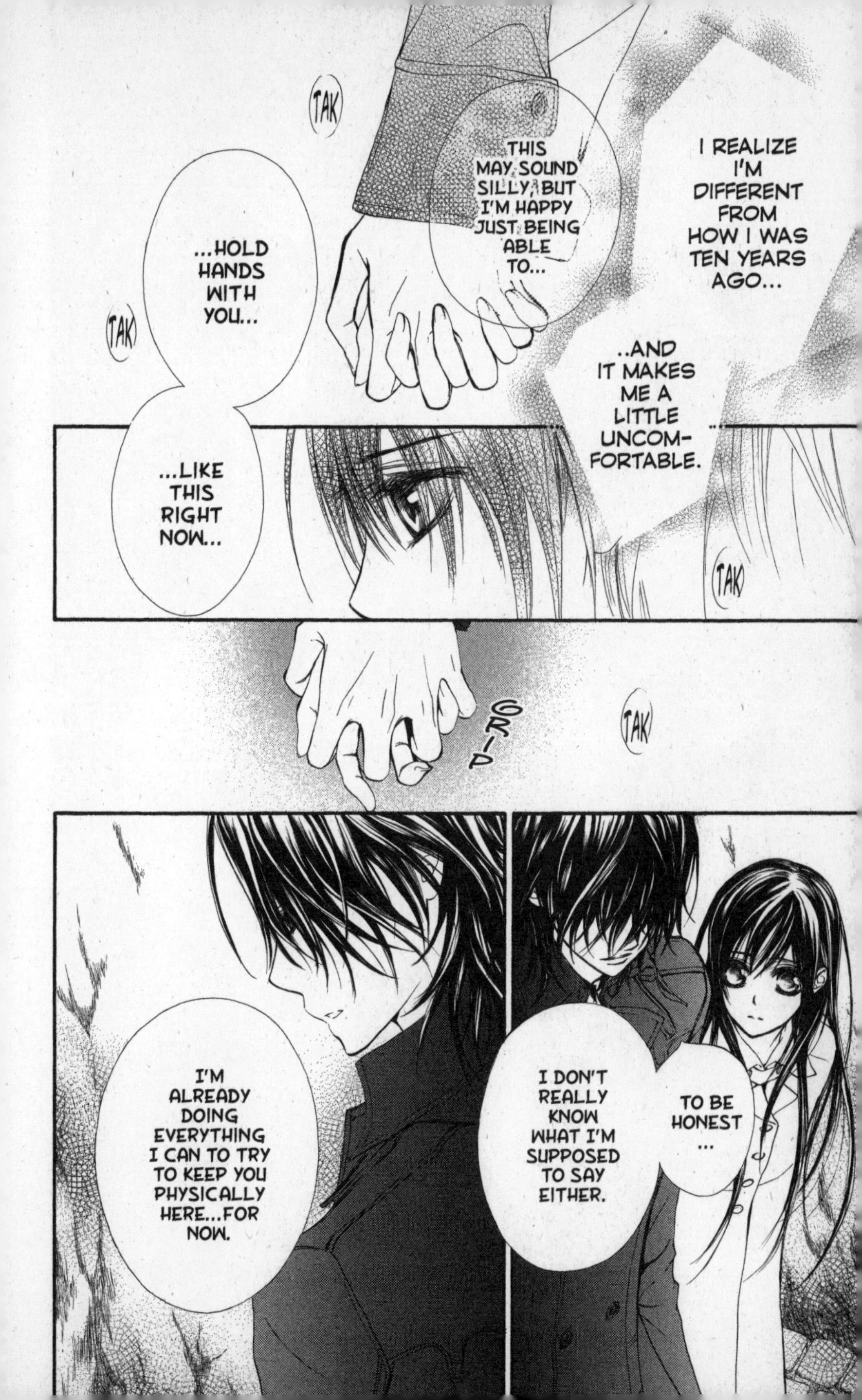
I REALIZE I'M DIFFERENT FROM HOW I WAS TEN YEARS AGO...
TAK
THIS MAY SOUND SILLY, BUT I'M HAPPY JUST BEING ABLE TO...
...HOLD HANDS WITH YOU...
TAK
..AND IT MAKES ME A LITTLE UNCOMFORTABLE.
TAK
...LIKE THIS RIGHT NOW...
TAK
GRIP
TO BE HONEST ...
I DON'T REALLY KNOW WHAT I'M SUPPOSED TO SAY EITHER.
I'M ALREADY DOING EVERYTHING I CAN TO TRY TO KEEP YOU PHYSICALLY HERE...FOR NOW.

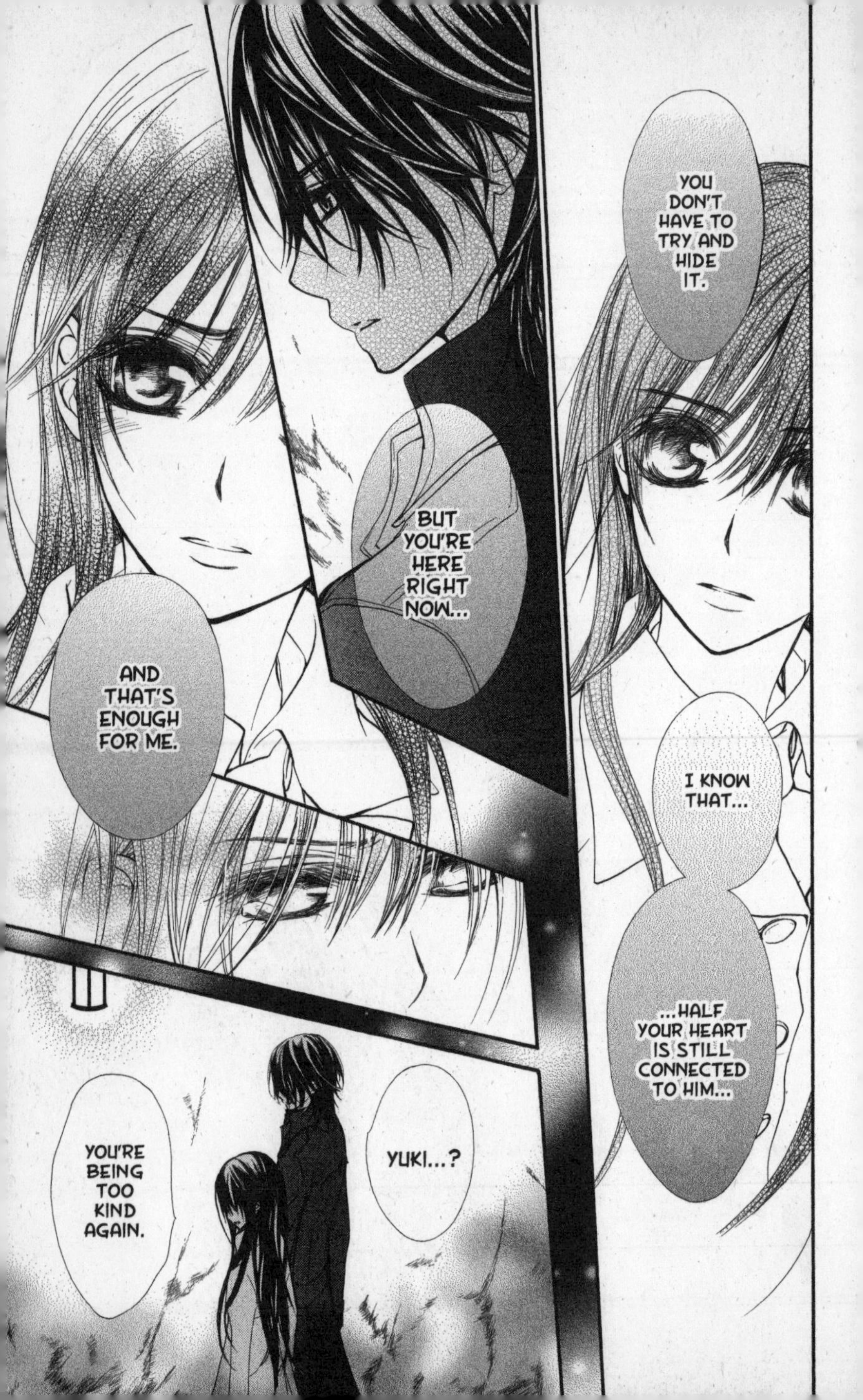
YOU DON'T HAVE TO TRY AND HIDE IT.
I KNOW THAT...
...HALF YOUR HEART IS STILL CONNECTED TO HIM...
BUT YOU'RE HERE RIGHT NOW...
AND THAT'S ENOUGH FOR ME.
YUKI...?
YOU'RE BEING TOO KIND AGAIN.

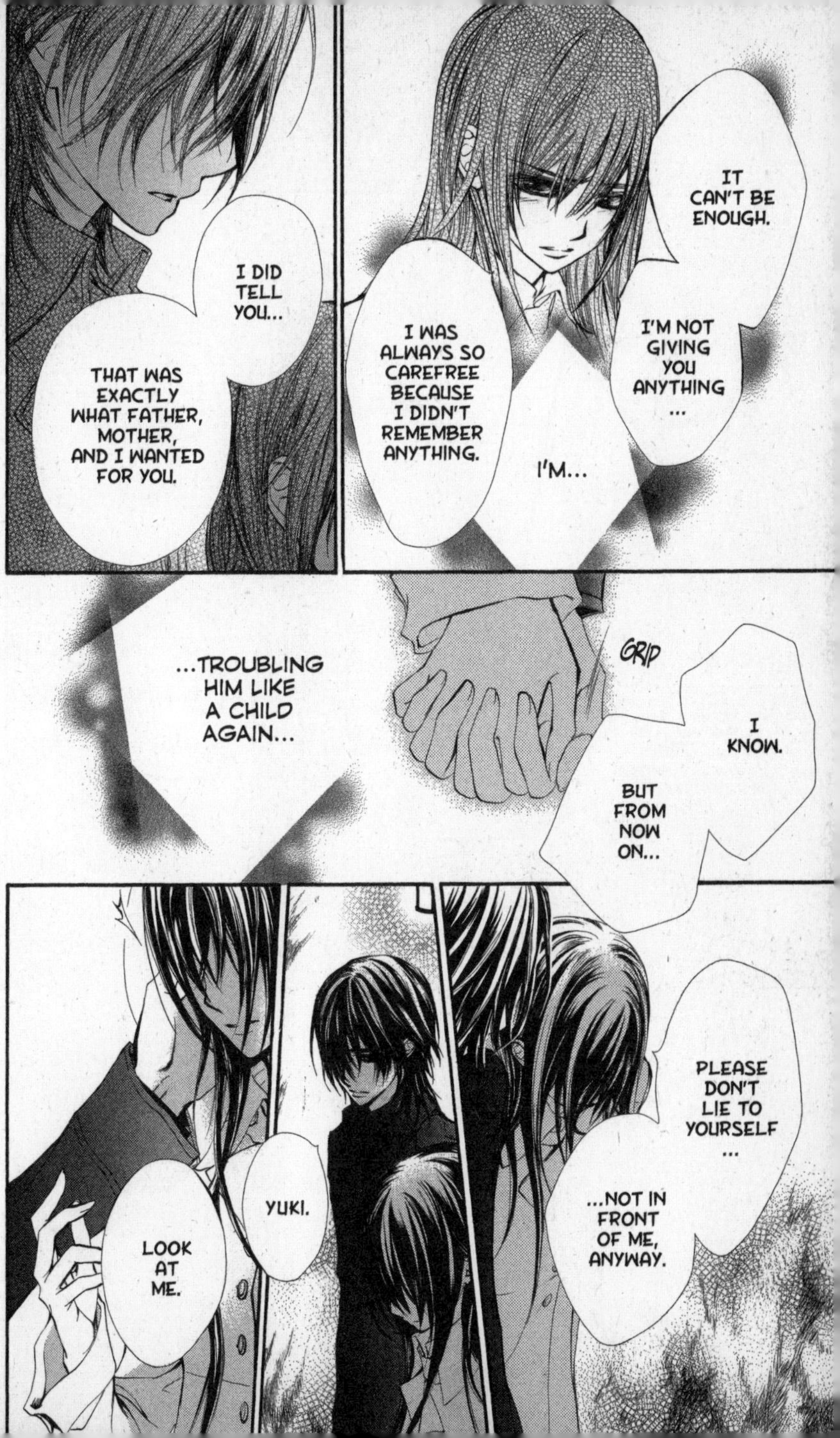
IT CAN'T BE ENOUGH.
I'M NOT GIVING YOU ANYTHING ...
I WAS ALWAYS SO CAREFREE BECAUSE I DIDN'T REMEMBER ANYTHING.
I'M...
I DID TELL YOU...
THAT WAS EXACTLY WHAT FATHER, MOTHER, AND I WANTED FOR YOU.
GRIP
I KNOW.
BUT FROM NOW ON...
...TROUBLING HIM LIKE A CHILD AGAIN...
PLEASE DON'T LIE TO YOURSELF ...
...NOT IN FRONT OF ME, ANYWAY.
YUKI.
LOOK AT ME.

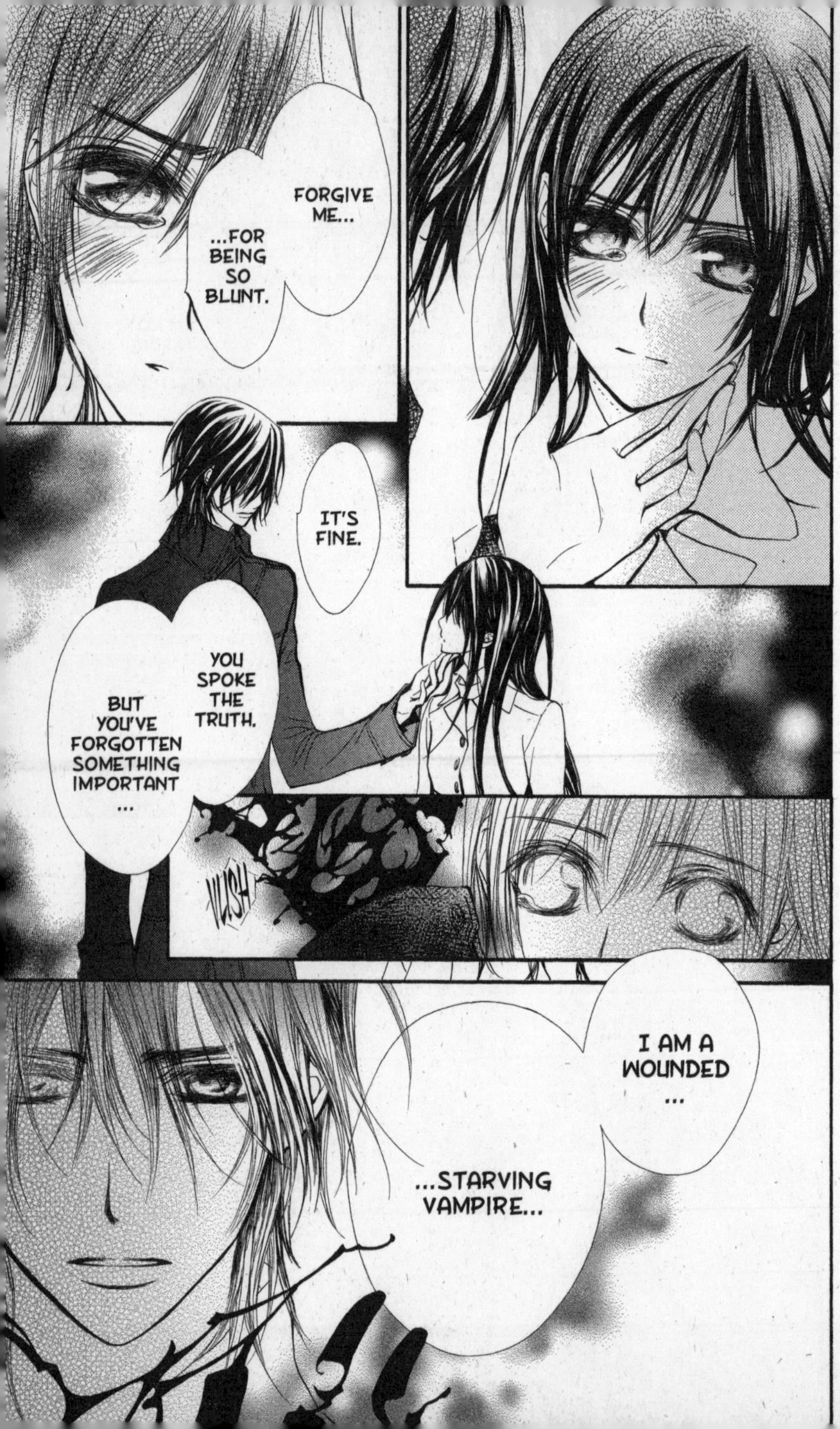
FORGIVE ME...
...FOR BEING SO BLUNT.
IT'S FINE.
YOU SPOKE THE TRUTH.
BUT YOU'VE FORGOTTEN SOMETHING IMPORTANT...
VUSH
I AM A WOUNDED...
...STARVING VAMPIRE...

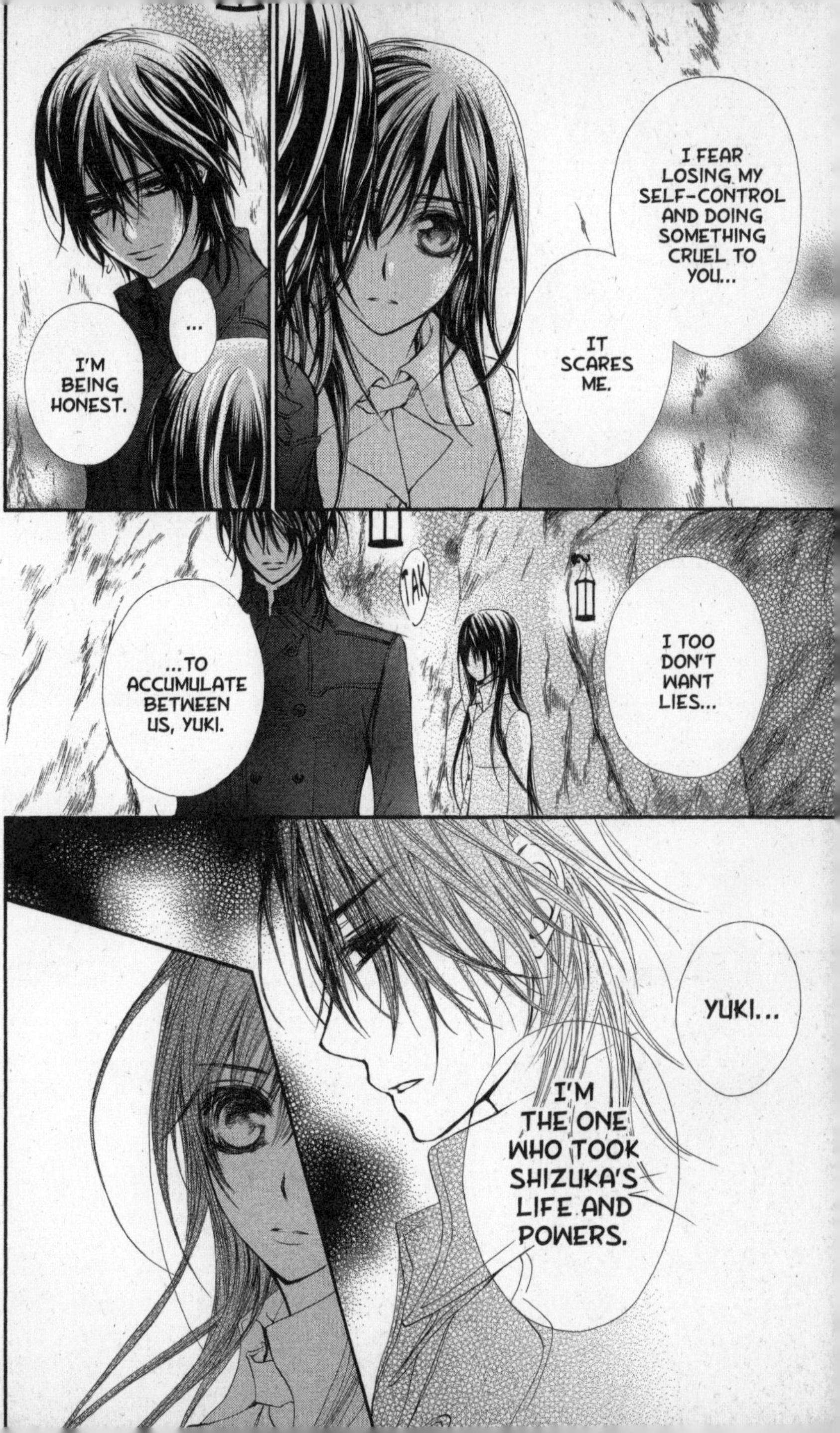
I FEAR LOSING MY SELF-CONTROL AND DOING SOMETHING CRUEL TO YOU...
IT SCARES ME.
...
I'M BEING HONEST.
I TOO DON'T WANT LIES...
TAK
...TO ACCUMULATE BETWEEN US, YUKI.
YUKI...
I'M THE ONE WHO TOOK SHIZUKA'S LIFE AND POWERS.

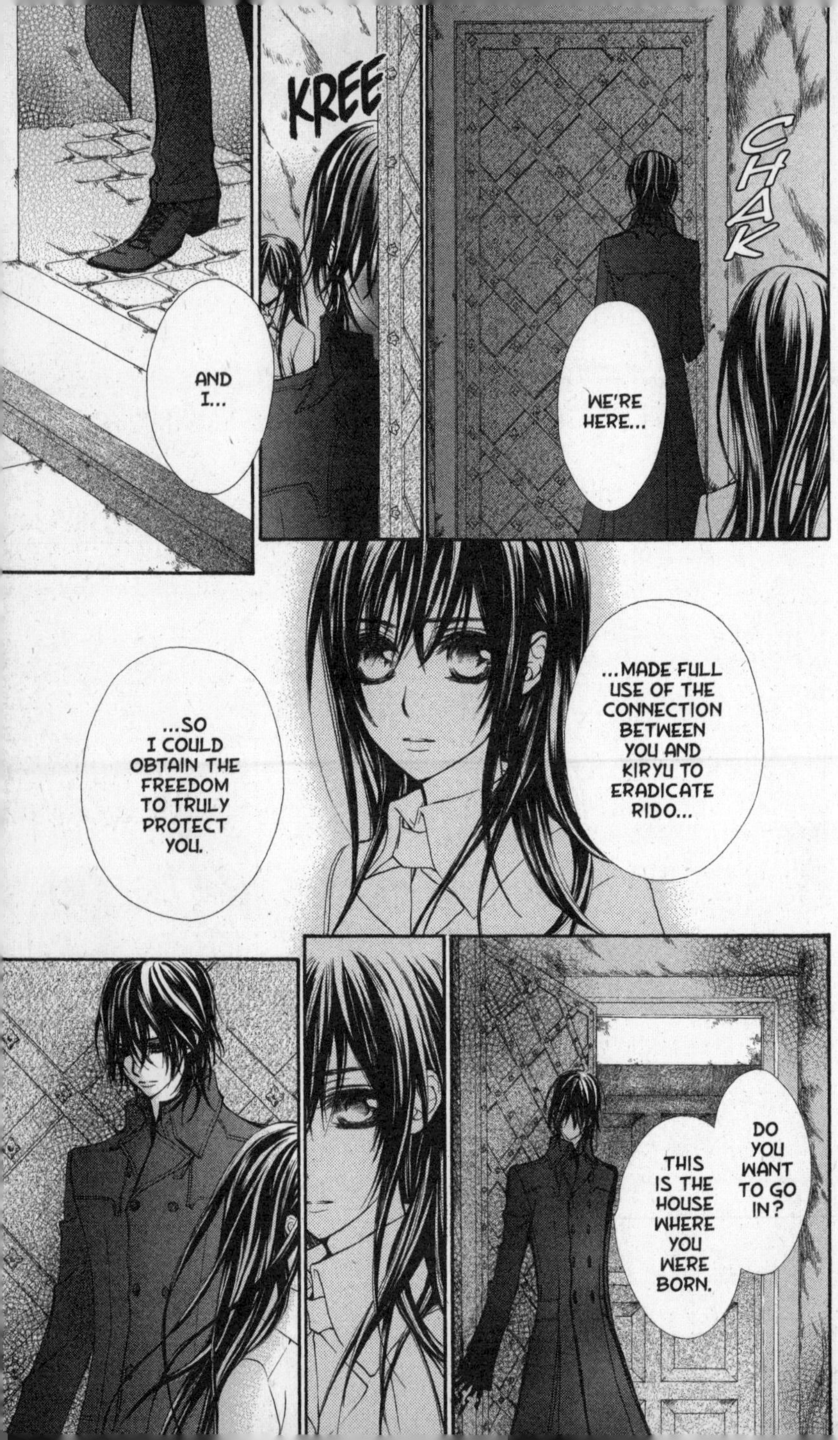
CHAK
WE'RE HERE...
KREE
AND I...
...MADE FULL USE OF THE CONNECTION BETWEEN YOU AND KIRYU TO ERADICATE RIDO...
...SO I COULD OBTAIN THE FREEDOM TO TRULY PROTECT YOU.
DO YOU WANT TO GO IN?
THIS IS THE HOUSE WHERE YOU WERE BORN.

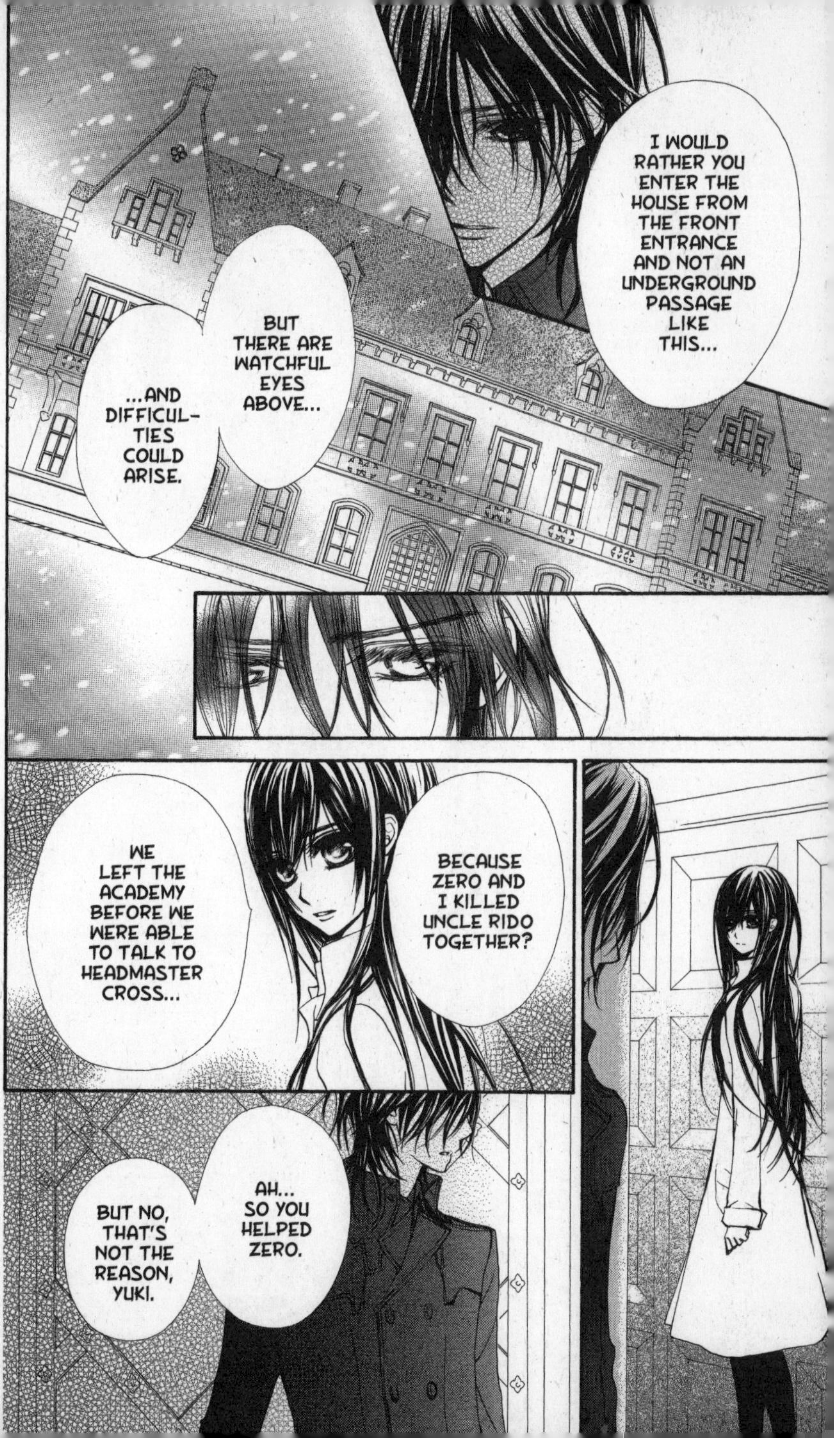
I WOULD RATHER YOU ENTER THE HOUSE FROM THE FRONT ENTRANCE AND NOT AN UNDERGROUND PASSAGE LIKE THIS...
BUT THERE ARE WATCHFUL EYES ABOVE...
...AND DIFFICUL-TIES COULD ARISE.
BECAUSE ZERO AND I KILLED UNCLE RIDO TOGETHER?
WE LEFT THE ACADEMY BEFORE WE WERE ABLE TO TALK TO HEADMASTER CROSS...
AH... SO YOU HELPED ZERO.
BUT NO, THAT'S NOT THE REASON, YUKI.

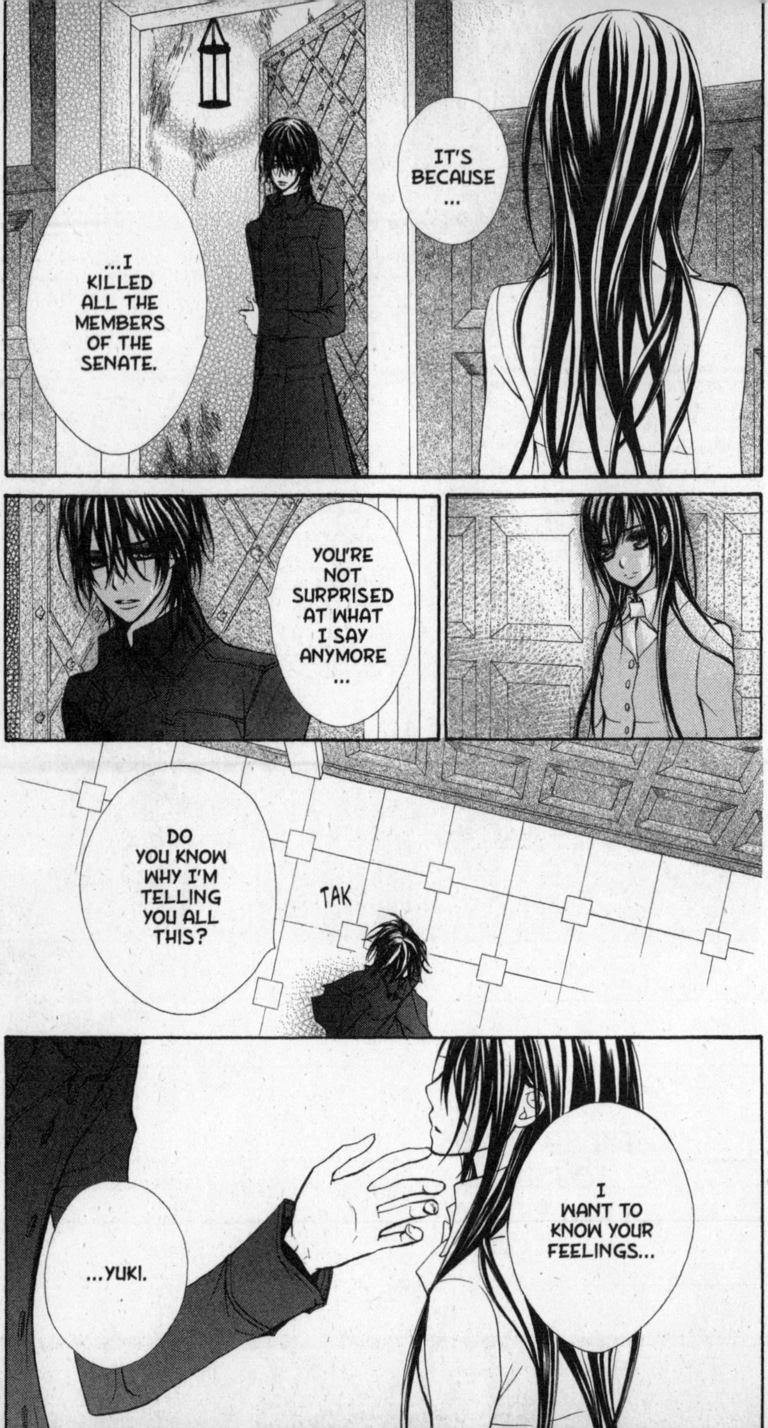
IT'S BECAUSE ...
...I KILLED ALL THE MEMBERS OF THE SENATE.
YOU'RE NOT SURPRISED AT WHAT I SAY ANYMORE ...
DO YOU KNOW WHY I'M TELLING YOU ALL THIS?
TAK
I WANT TO KNOW YOUR FEELINGS...
...YUKI.

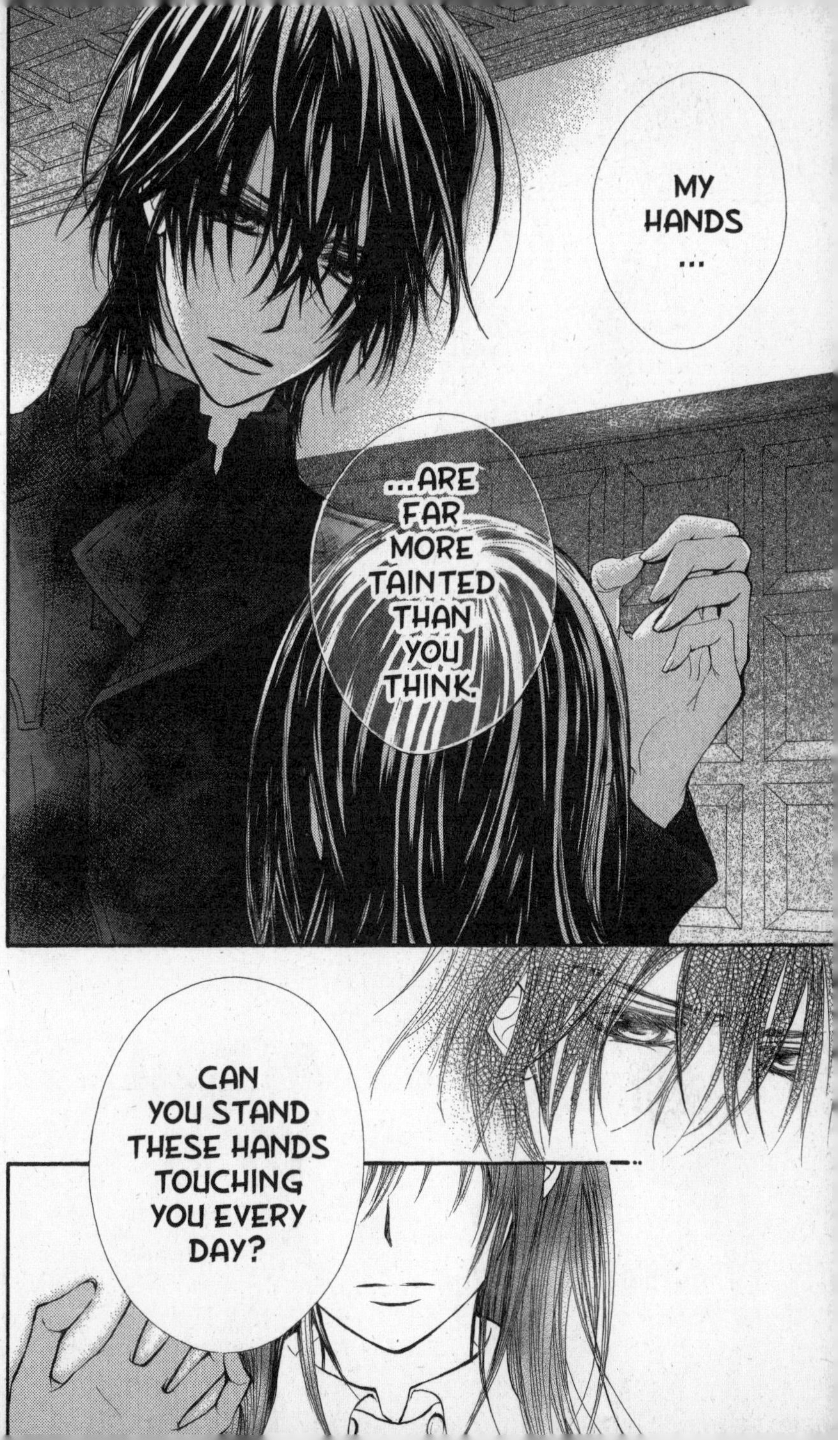
MY HANDS ...
...ARE FAR MORE TAINTED THAN YOU THINK.
CAN YOU STAND THESE HANDS TOUCHING YOU EVERY DAY?
—...

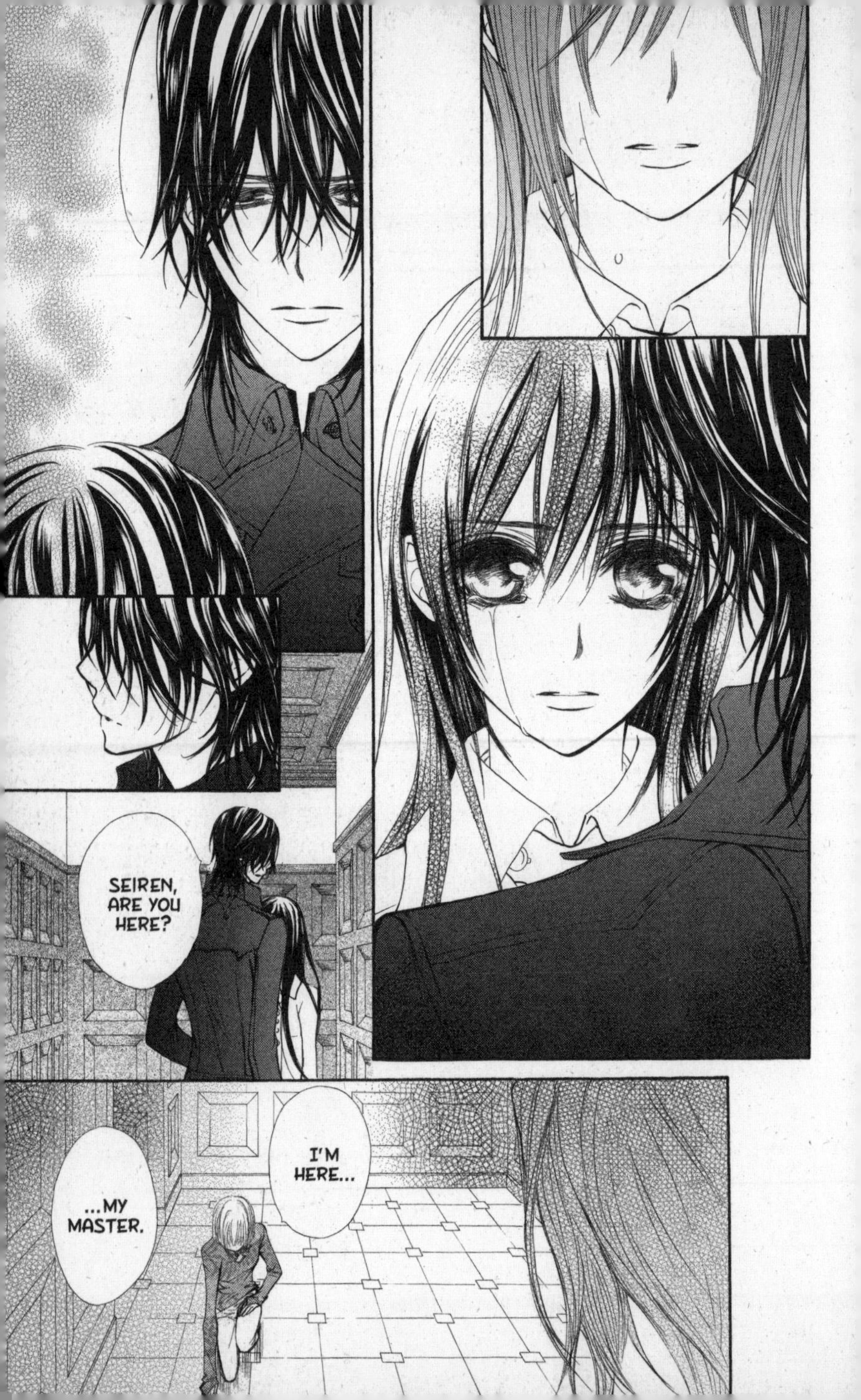
SEIREN, ARE YOU HERE?
I'M HERE...
...MY MASTER.

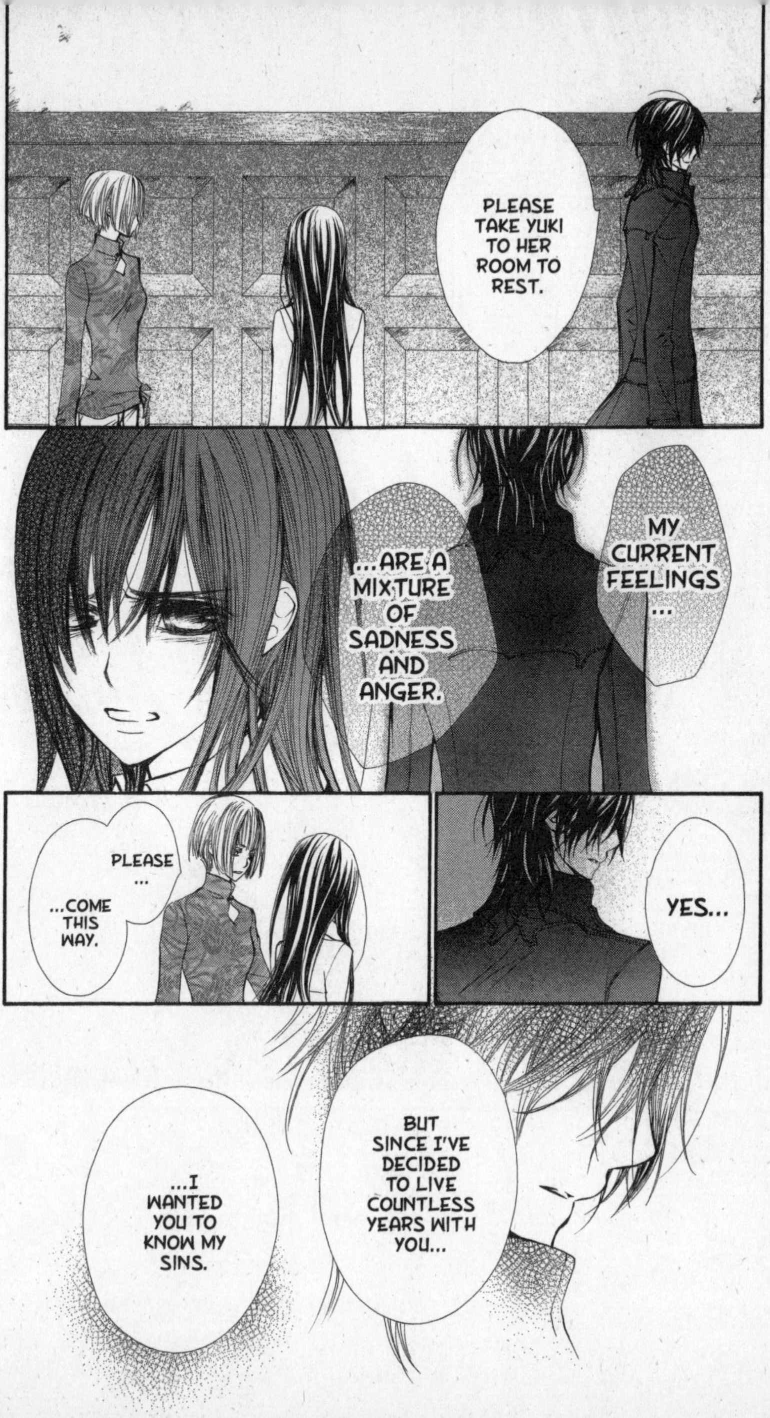
PLEASE TAKE YUKI TO HER ROOM TO REST.
MY CURRENT FEELINGS...
...ARE A MIXTURE OF SADNESS AND ANGER.
YES...
PLEASE...
...COME THIS WAY.
BUT SINCE I'VE DECIDED TO LIVE COUNTLESS YEARS WITH YOU...
...I WANTED YOU TO KNOW MY SINS.

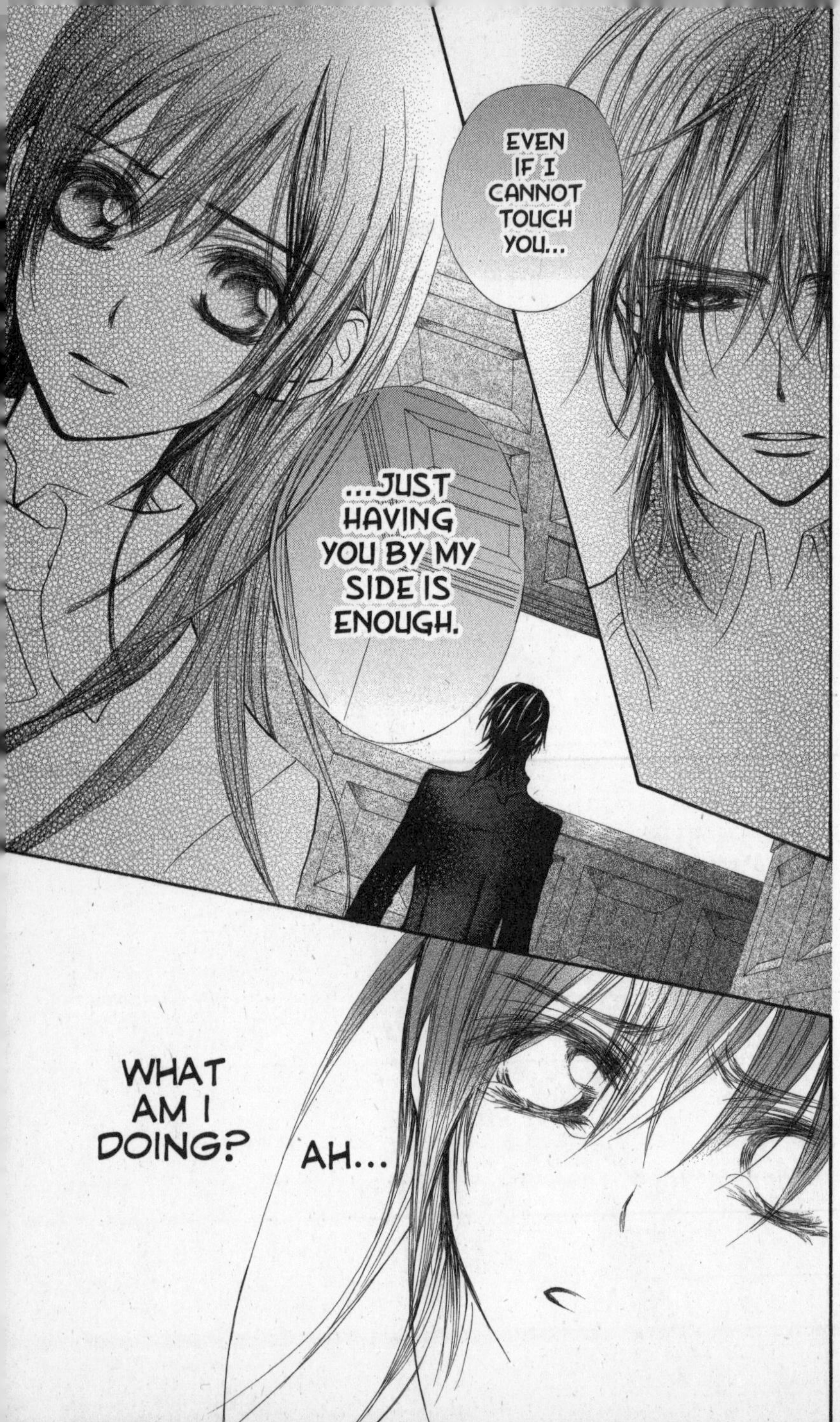
EVEN IF I CANNOT TOUCH YOU...
...JUST HAVING YOU BY MY SIDE IS ENOUGH.
AH...
WHAT AM I DOING?

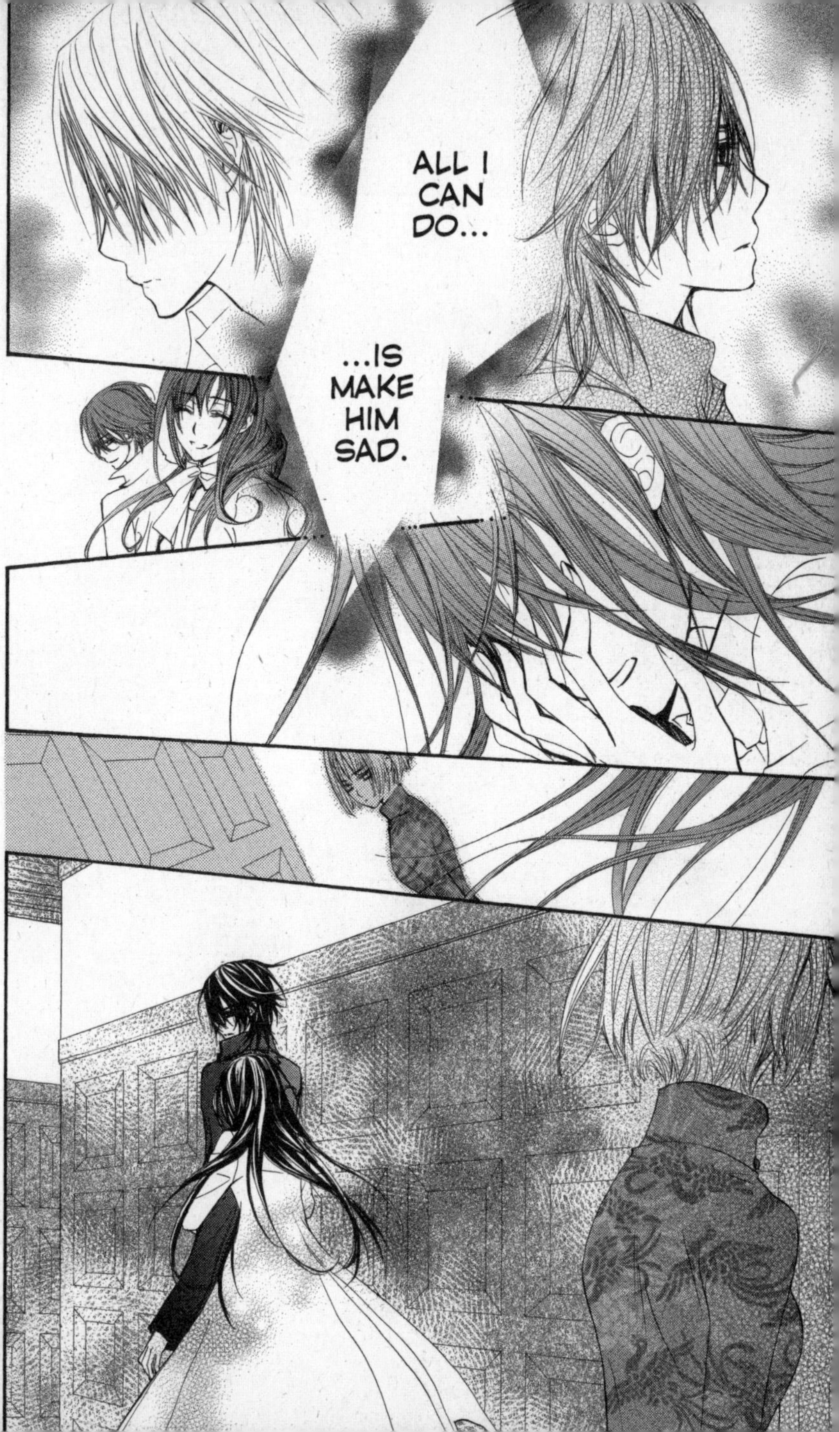
ALL I CAN DO...
...IS MAKE HIM SAD.

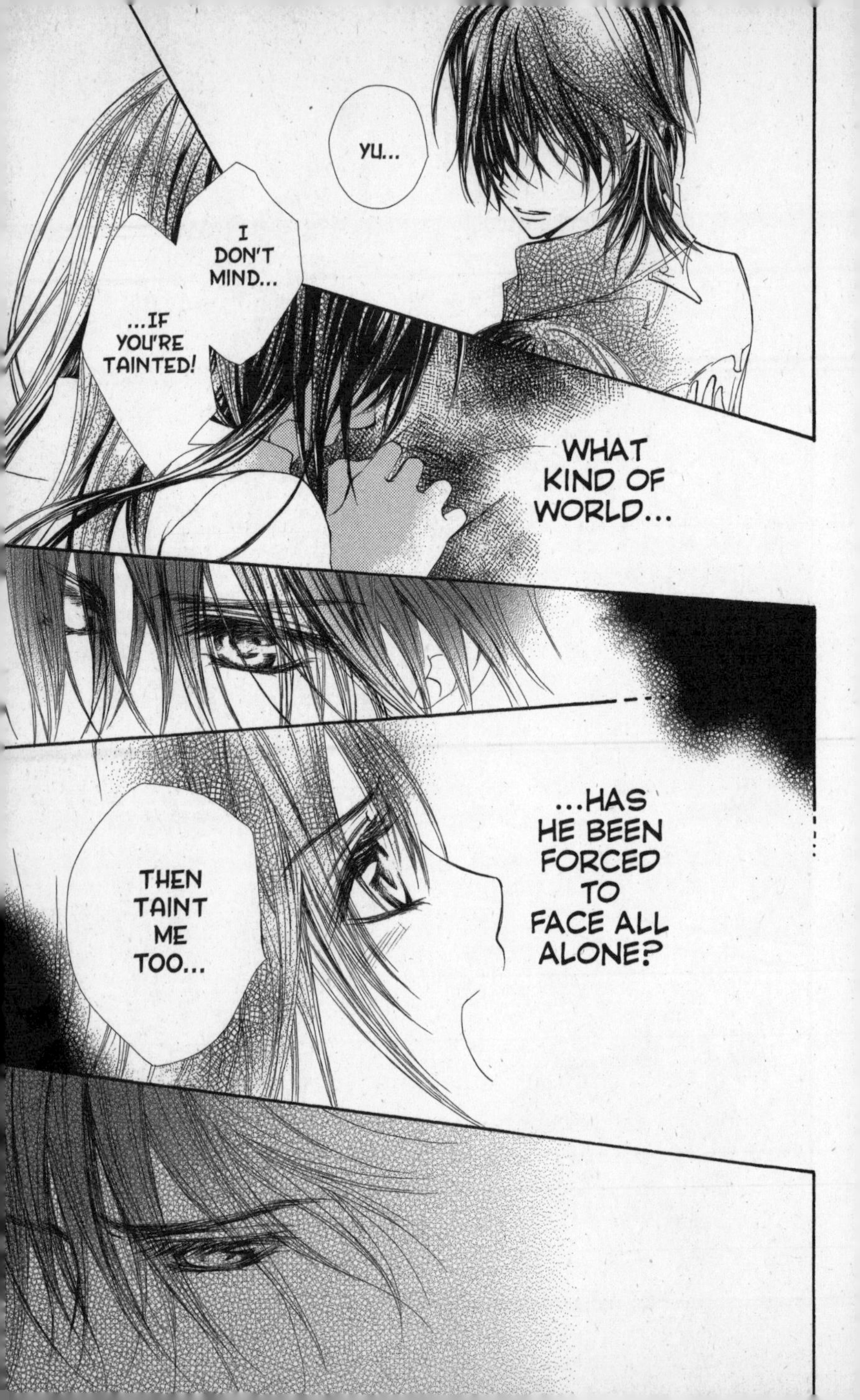
YU...
I DON'T MIND...
...IF YOU'RE TAINTED!
WHAT KIND OF WORLD...
...HAS HE BEEN FORCED TO FACE ALL ALONE?
THEN TAINT ME TOO...

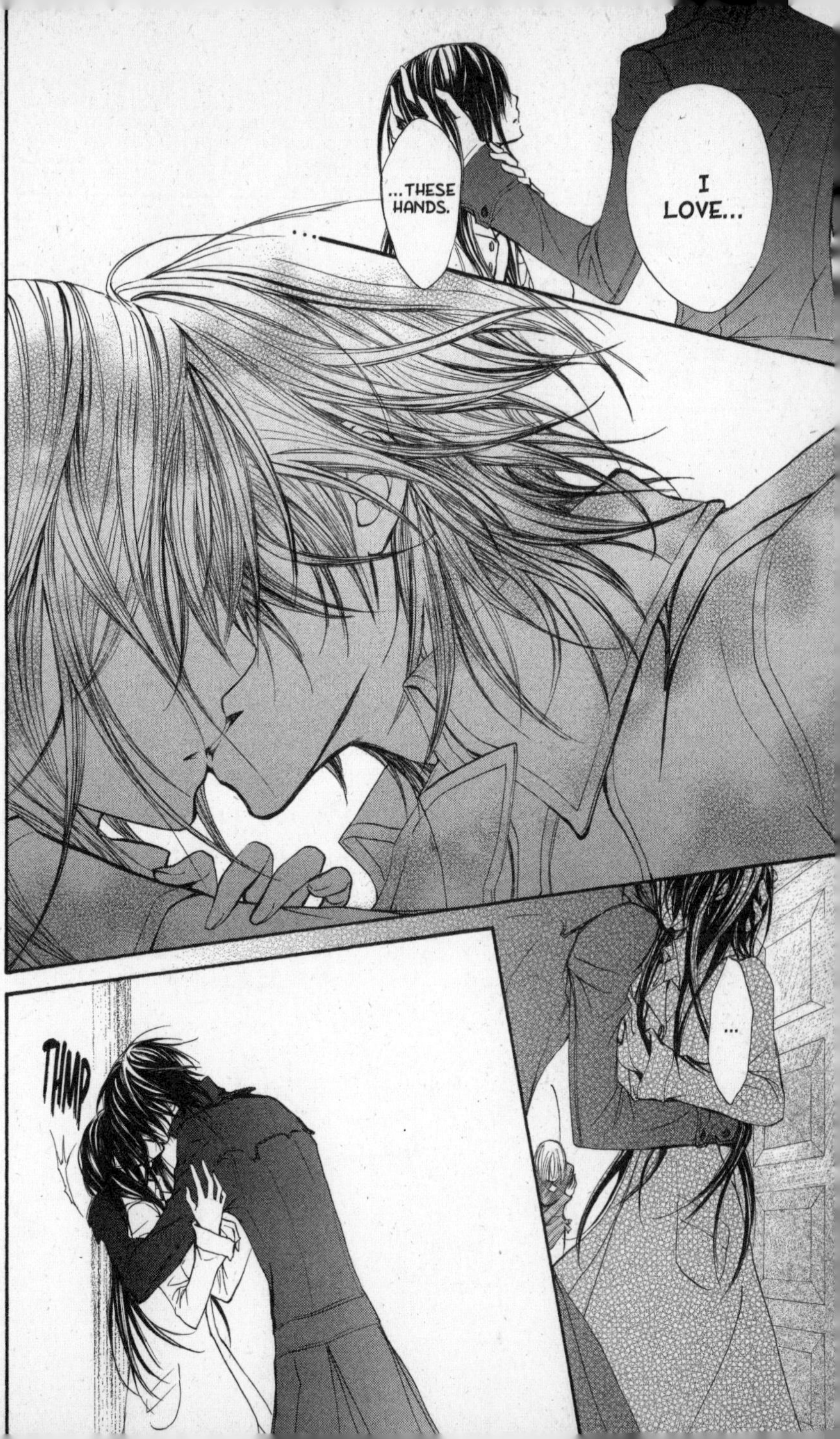
I LOVE...
...THESE HANDS.
...
...
THMP

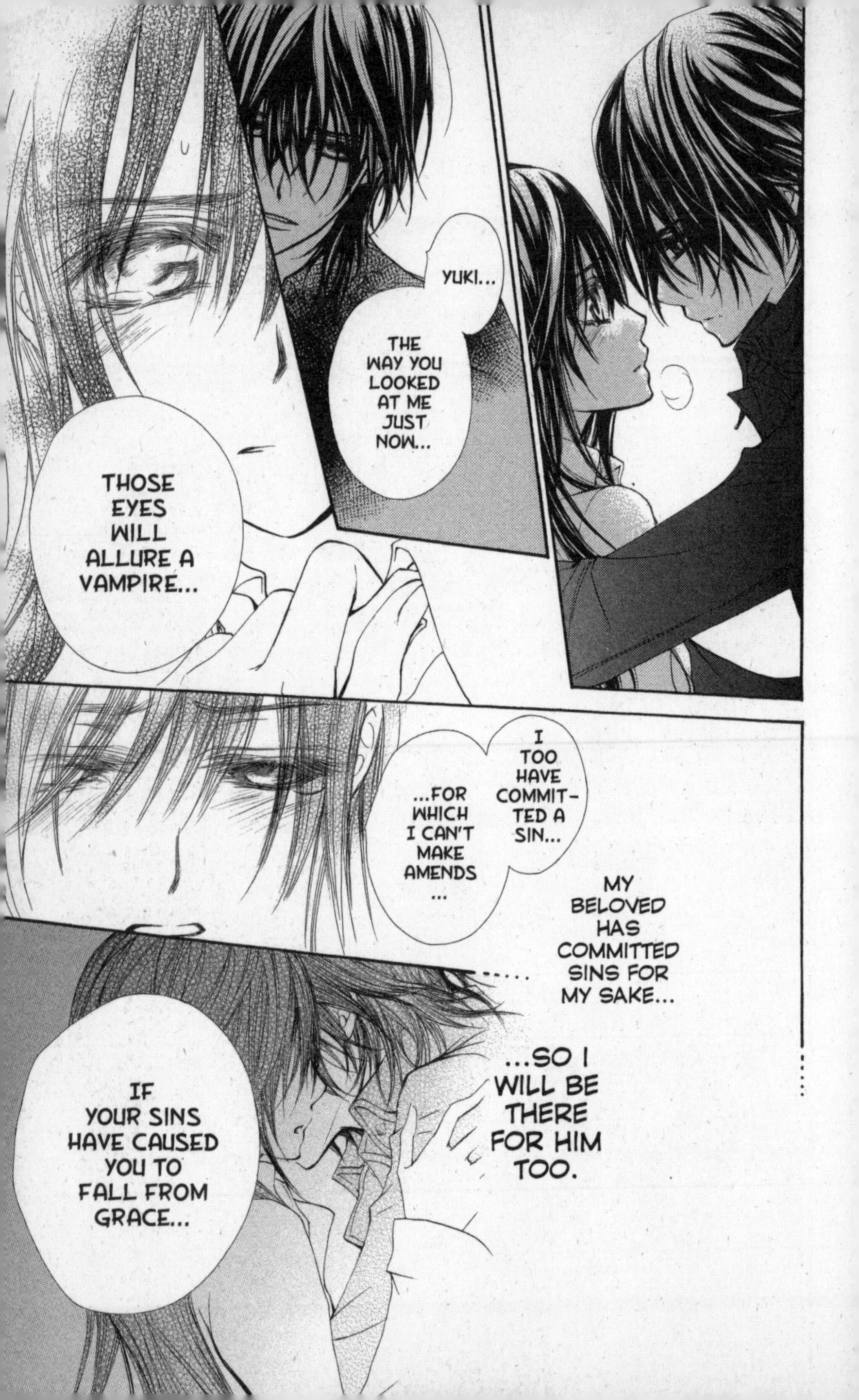
YUKI...
THE WAY YOU LOOKED AT ME JUST NOW...
THOSE EYES WILL ALLURE A VAMPIRE...
I TOO HAVE COMMIT-TED A SIN...
...FOR WHICH I CAN'T MAKE AMENDS...
MY BELOVED HAS COMMITTED SINS FOR MY SAKE...
......
...SO I WILL BE THERE FOR HIM TOO.
IF YOUR SINS HAVE CAUSED YOU TO FALL FROM GRACE...

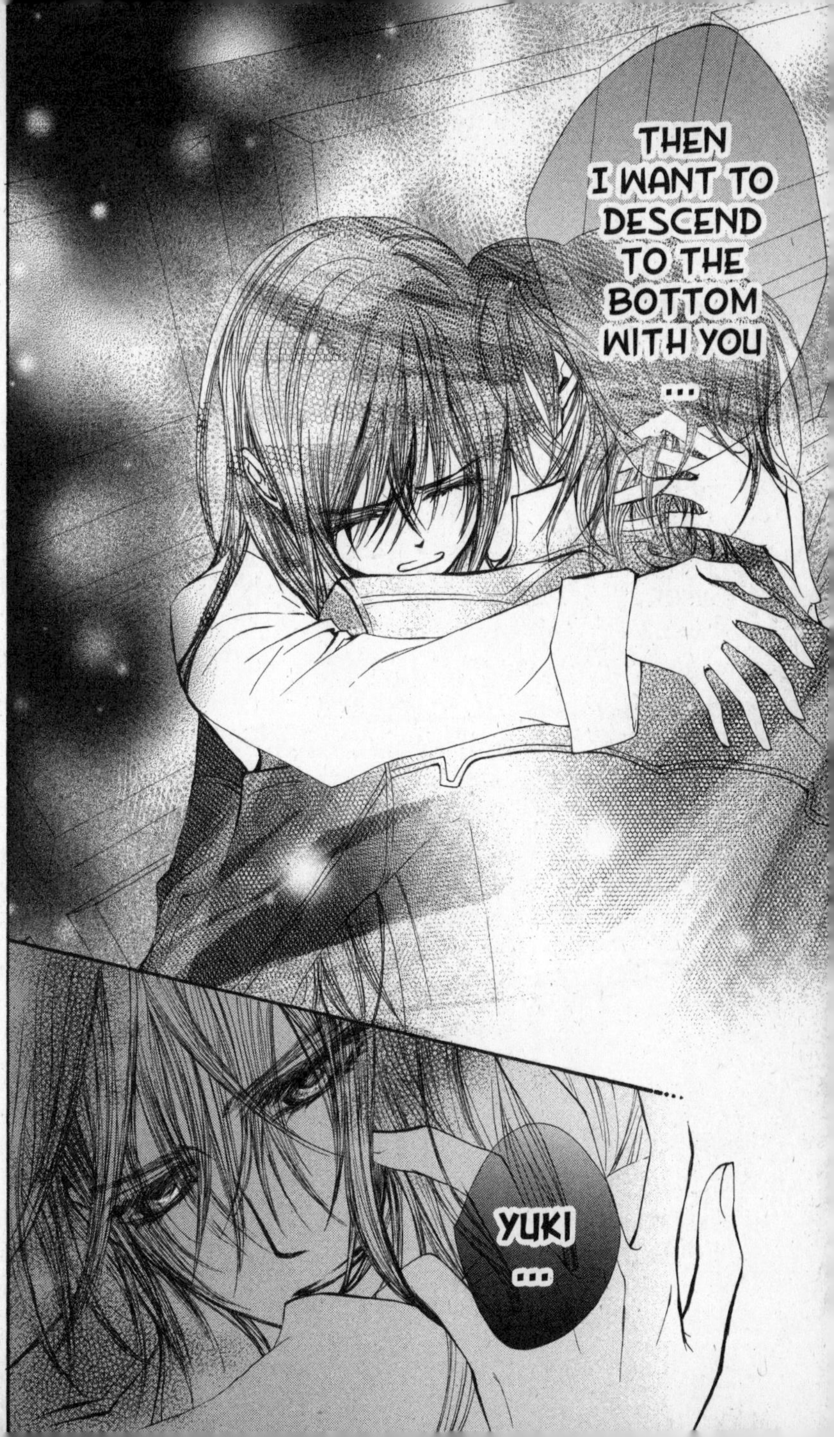
THEN I WANT TO DESCEND TO THE BOTTOM WITH YOU ...
.....
YUKI ...

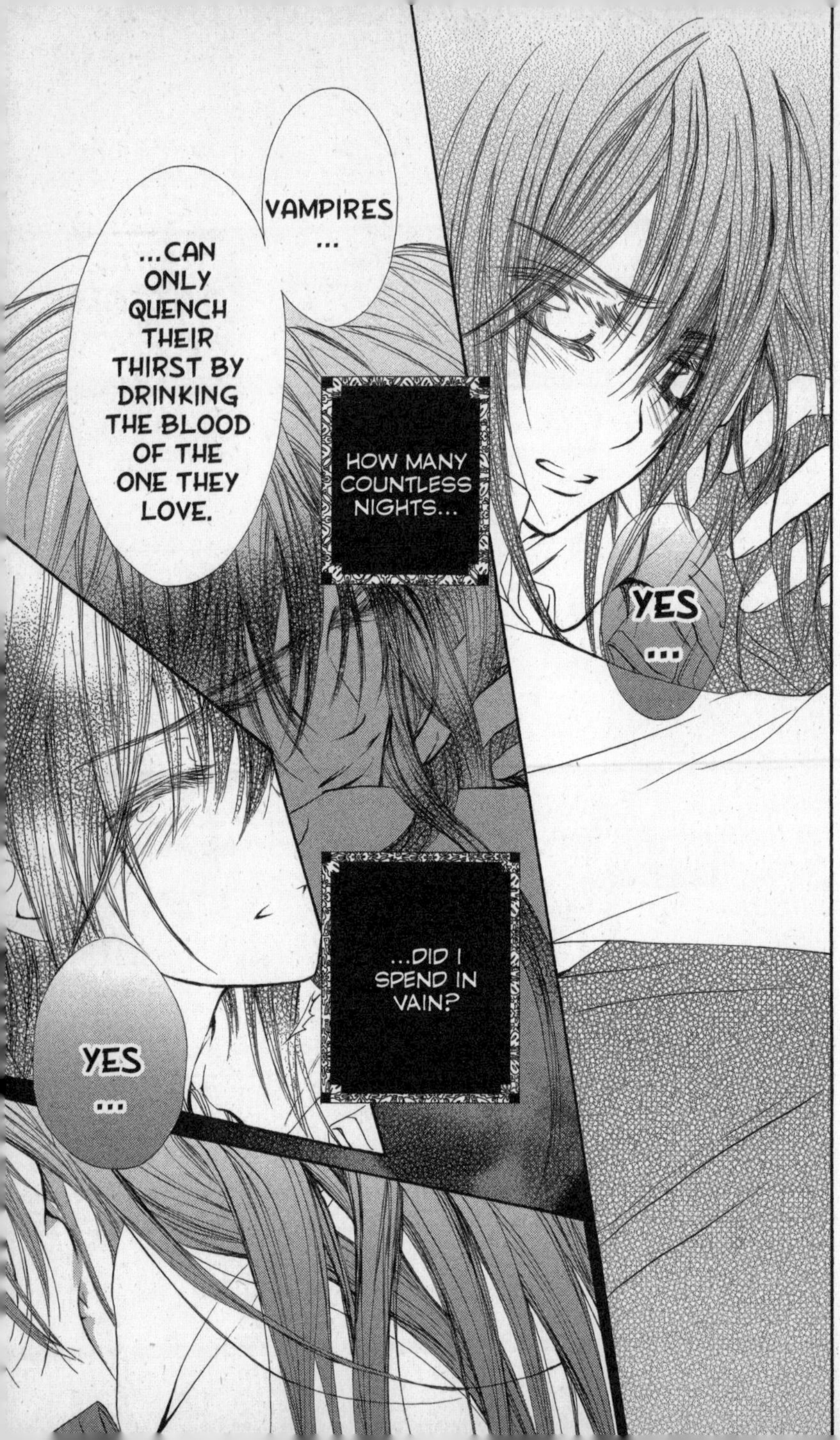
VAMPIRES...
...CAN ONLY QUENCH THEIR THIRST BY DRINKING THE BLOOD OF THE ONE THEY LOVE.
HOW MANY COUNTLESS NIGHTS...
YES...
...DID I SPEND IN VAIN?
YES...

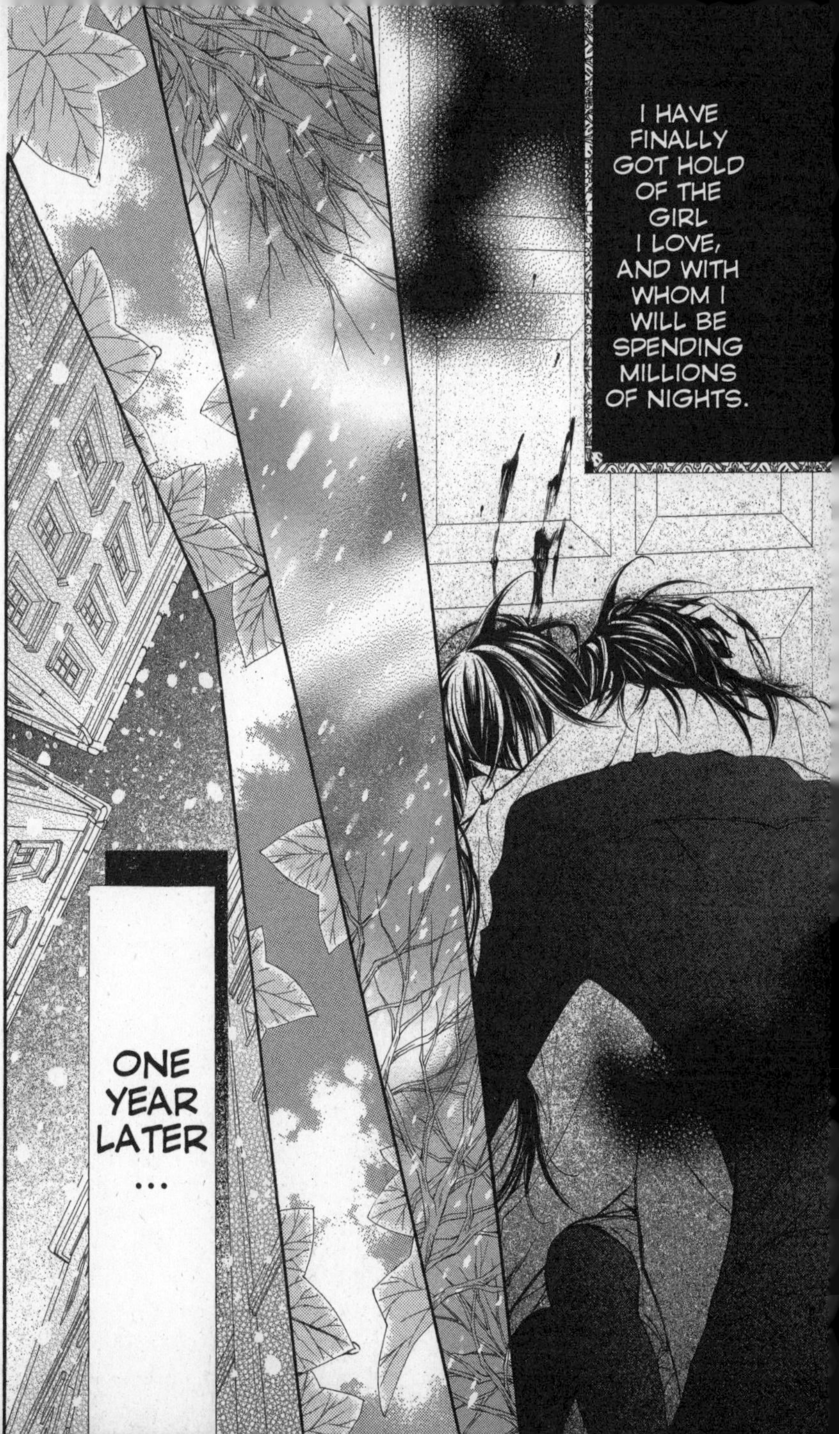
I HAVE FINALLY GOT HOLD OF THE GIRL I LOVE, AND WITH WHOM I WILL BE SPENDING MILLIONS OF NIGHTS.
ONE YEAR LATER ...

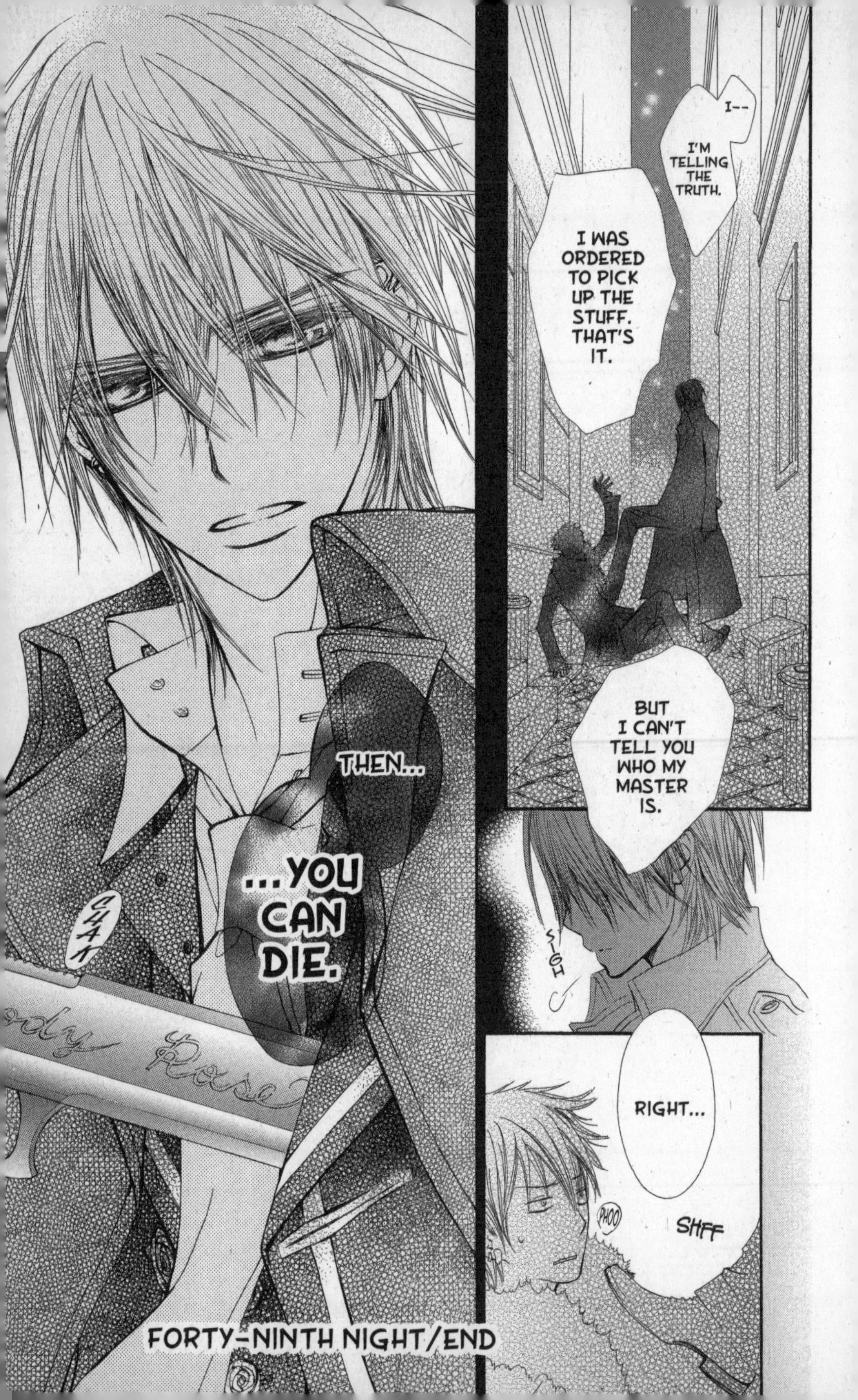
I--
I'M TELLING THE TRUTH.
I WAS ORDERED TO PICK UP THE STUFF. THAT'S IT.
BUT I CAN'T TELL YOU WHO MY MASTER IS.
SIGH
RIGHT...
PHOO
SHFF
THEN...
...YOU CAN DIE.
CHAK
FORTY-NINTH NIGHT/END

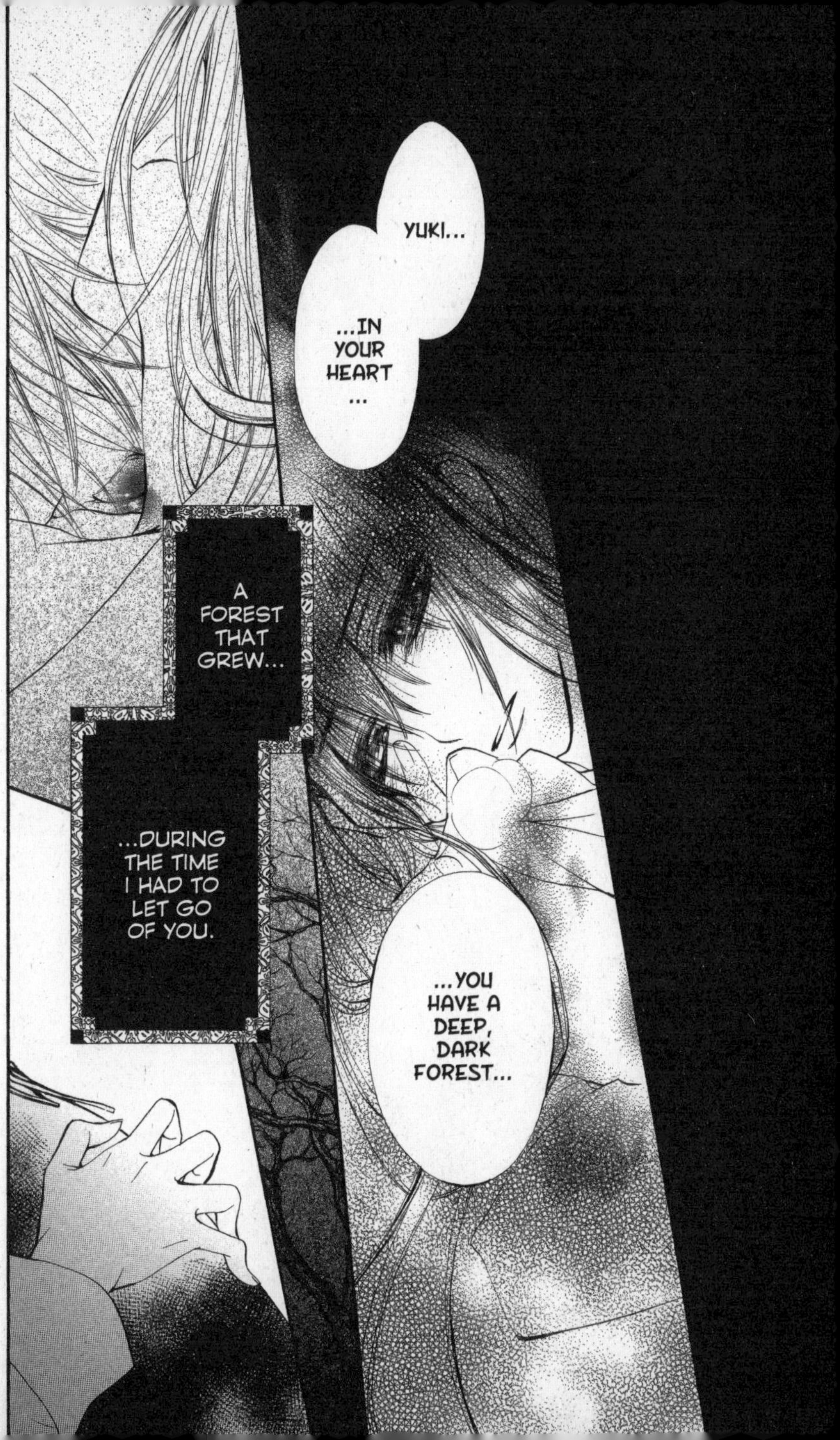
YUKI...
...IN YOUR HEART ...
A FOREST THAT GREW...
...DURING THE TIME I HAD TO LET GO OF YOU.
...YOU HAVE A DEEP, DARK FOREST...

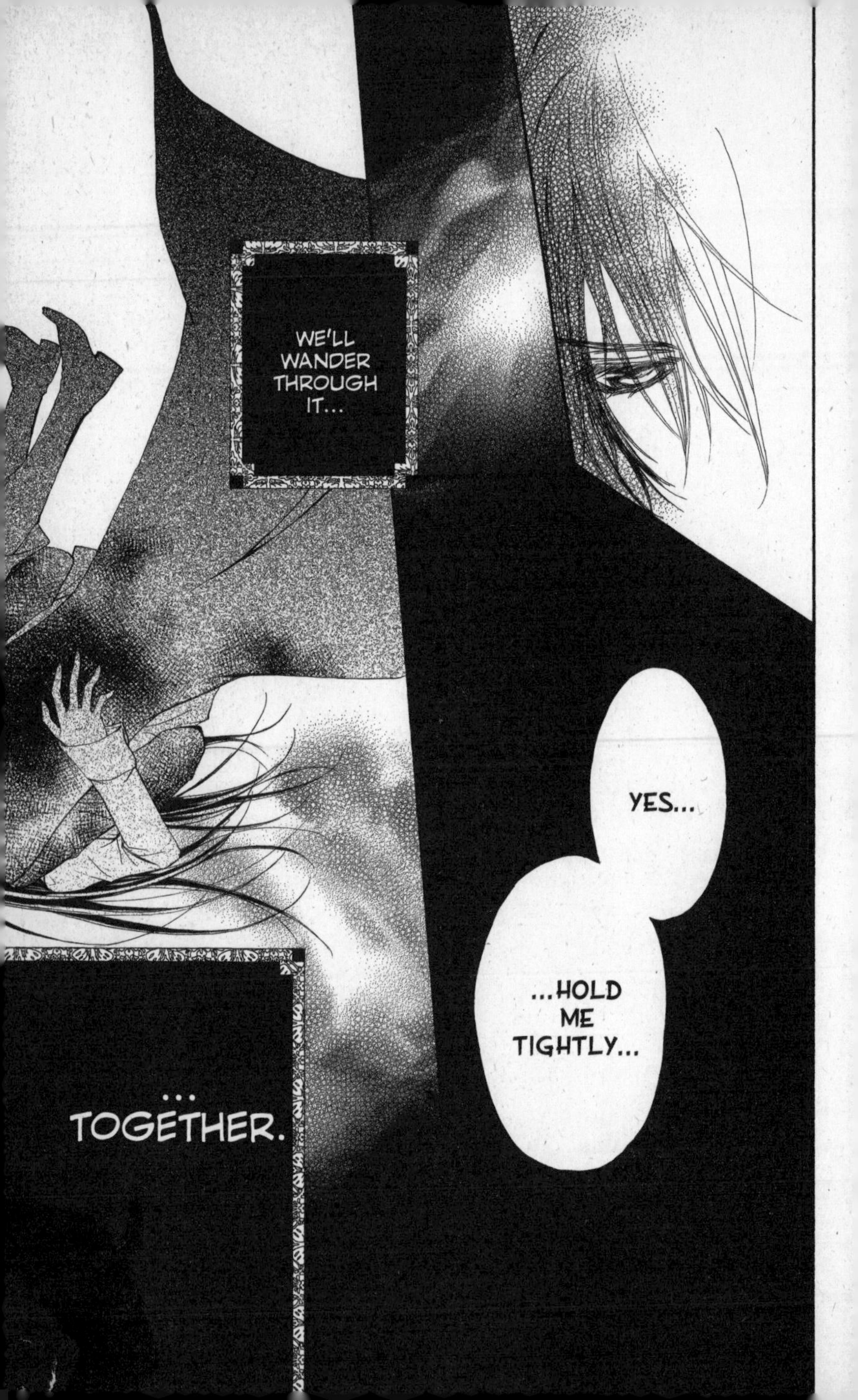
WE'LL WANDER THROUGH IT...
YES...
...HOLD ME TIGHTLY...
...TOGETHER.

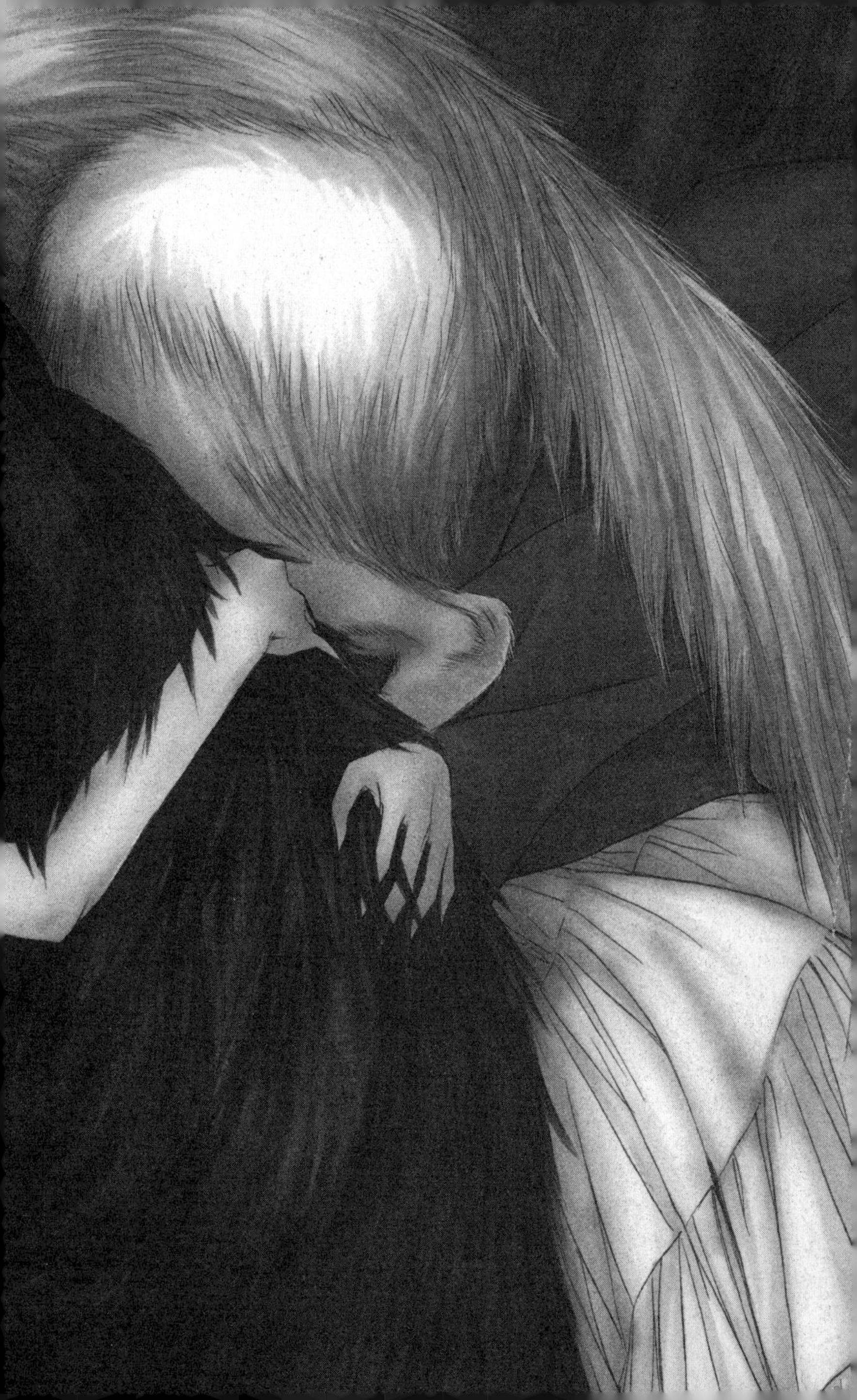

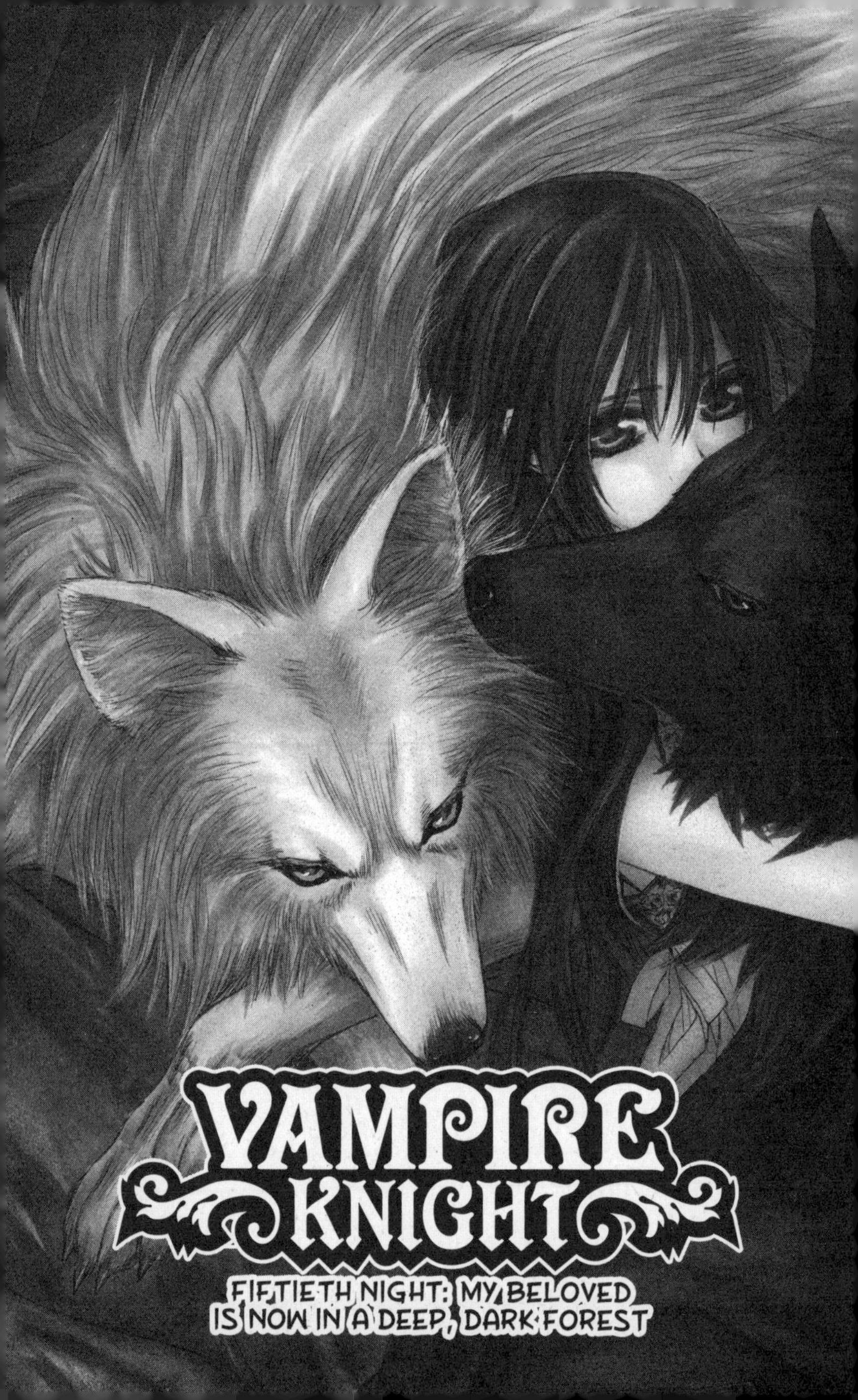
VAMPIRE KNIGHT
FIFTIETH NIGHT: MY BELOVED
IS NOW IN A DEEP, DARK FOREST

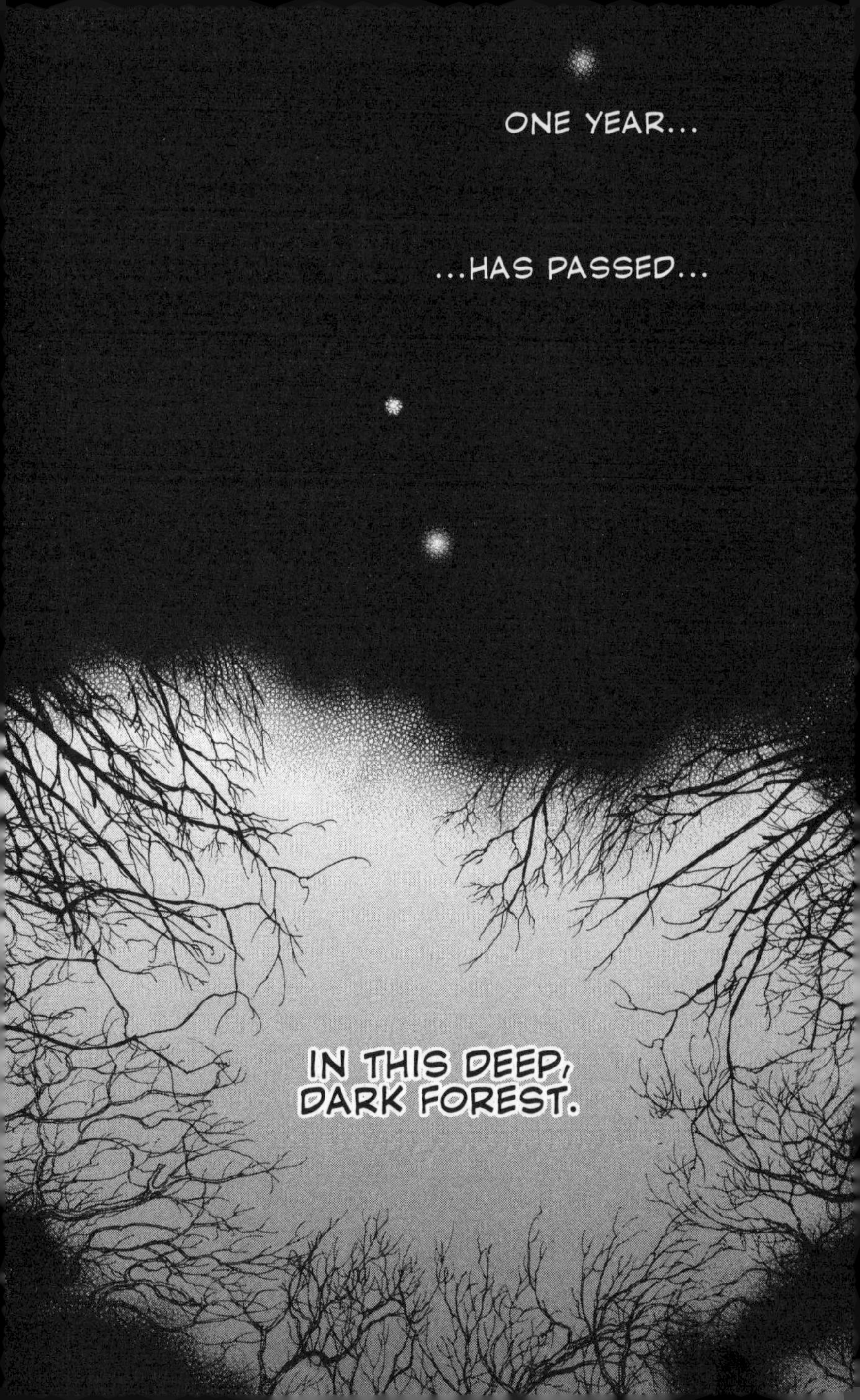
ONE YEAR...
...HAS PASSED...
IN THIS DEEP, DARK FOREST.

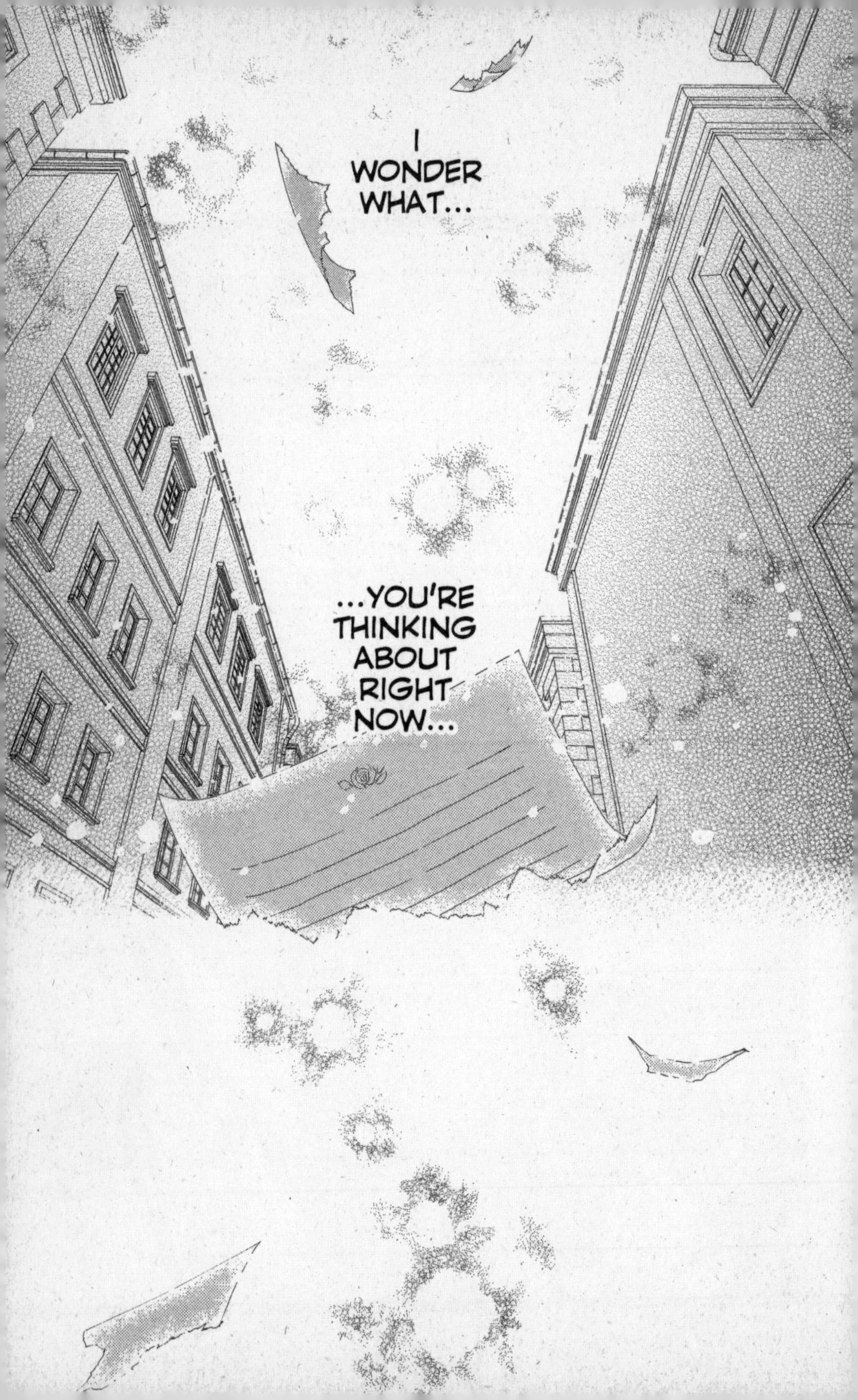
I WONDER WHAT...
...YOU'RE THINKING ABOUT RIGHT NOW...

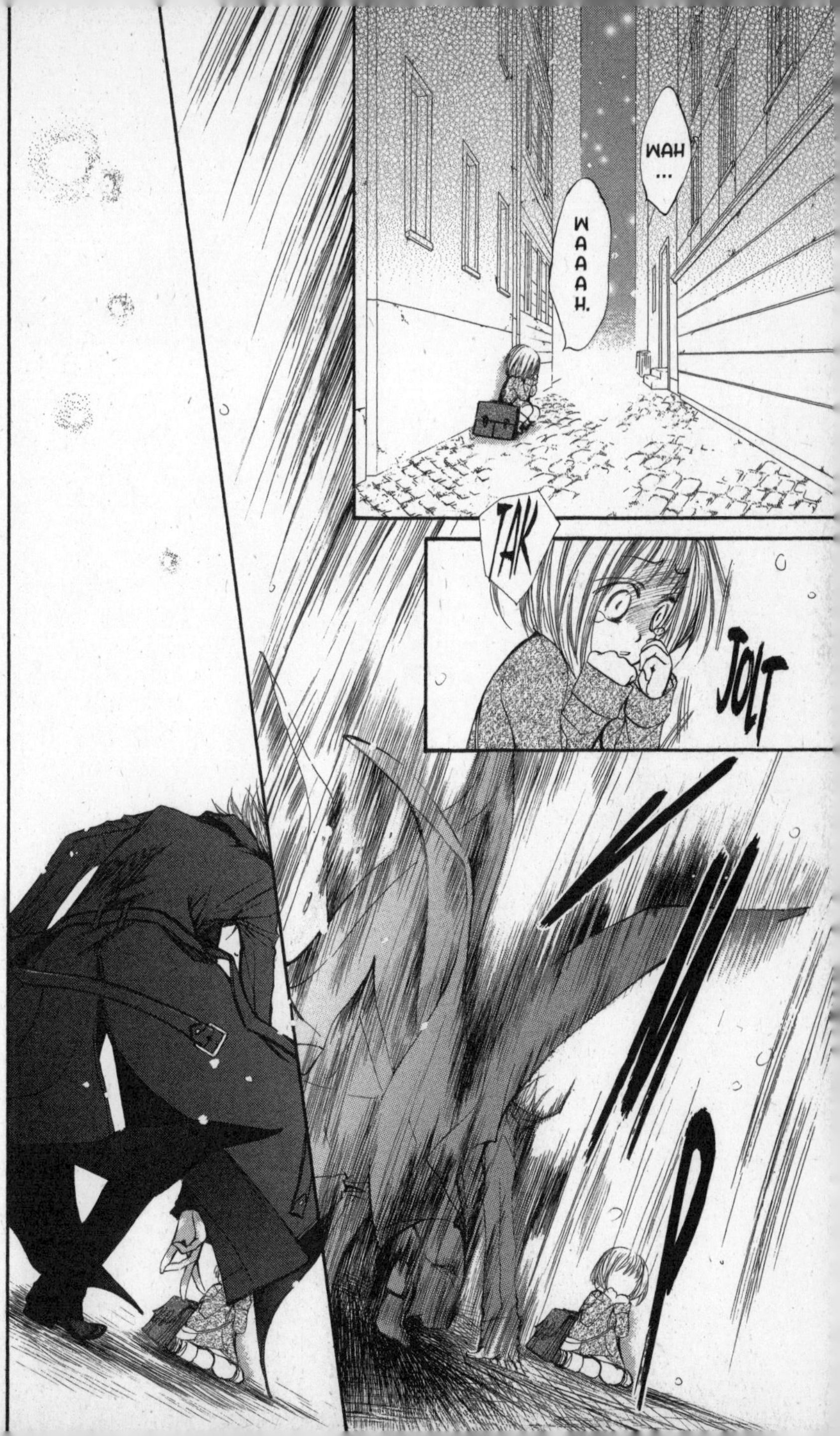
WAH ...
WAAAAH.
TAK
JOLT

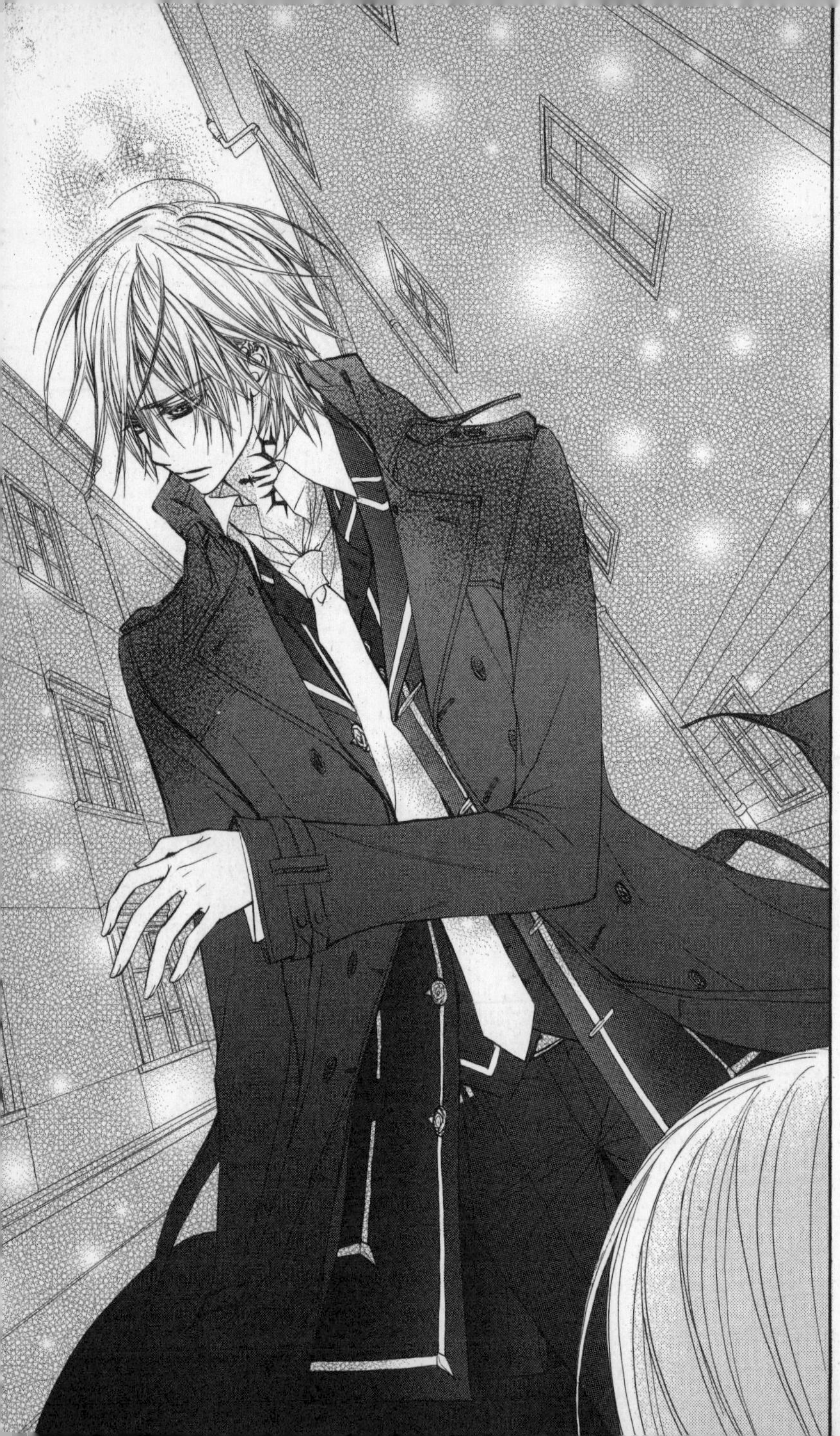

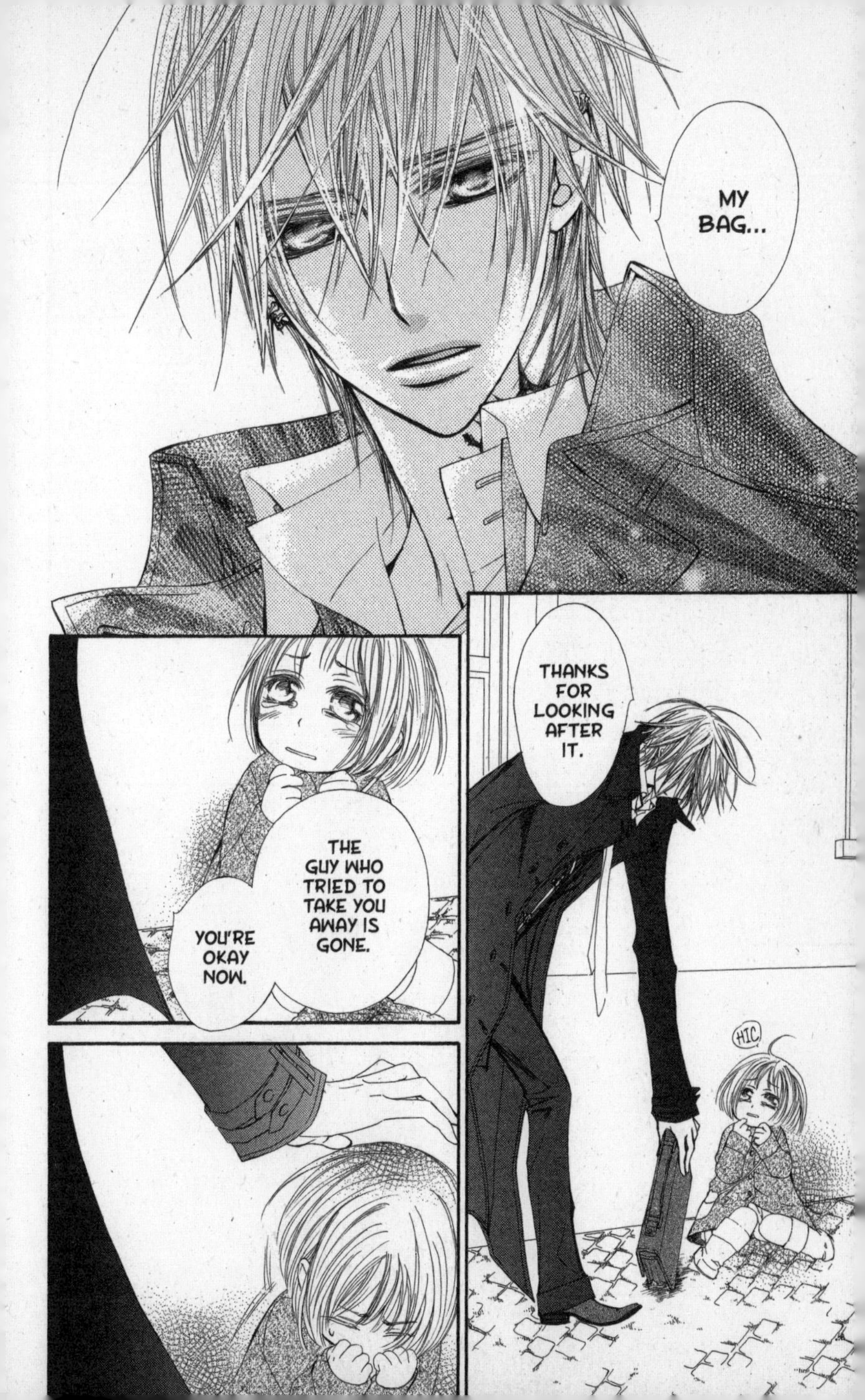
MY BAG...
THANKS FOR LOOKING AFTER IT.
HIC
THE GUY WHO TRIED TO TAKE YOU AWAY IS GONE.
YOU'RE OKAY NOW.

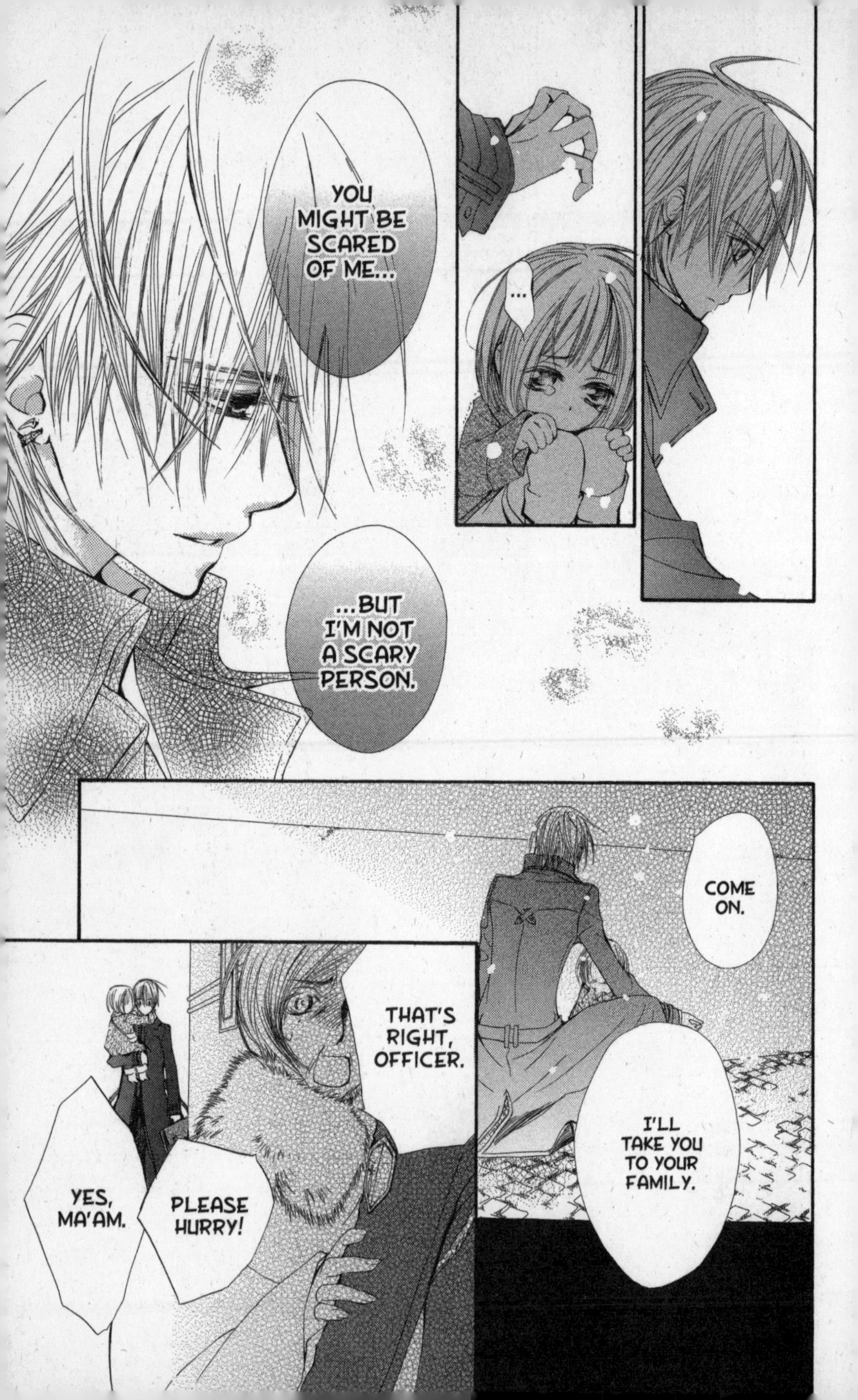
...
YOU MIGHT BE SCARED OF ME...
...BUT I'M NOT A SCARY PERSON.
COME ON.
I'LL TAKE YOU TO YOUR FAMILY.
THAT'S RIGHT, OFFICER.
PLEASE HURRY!
YES, MA'AM.

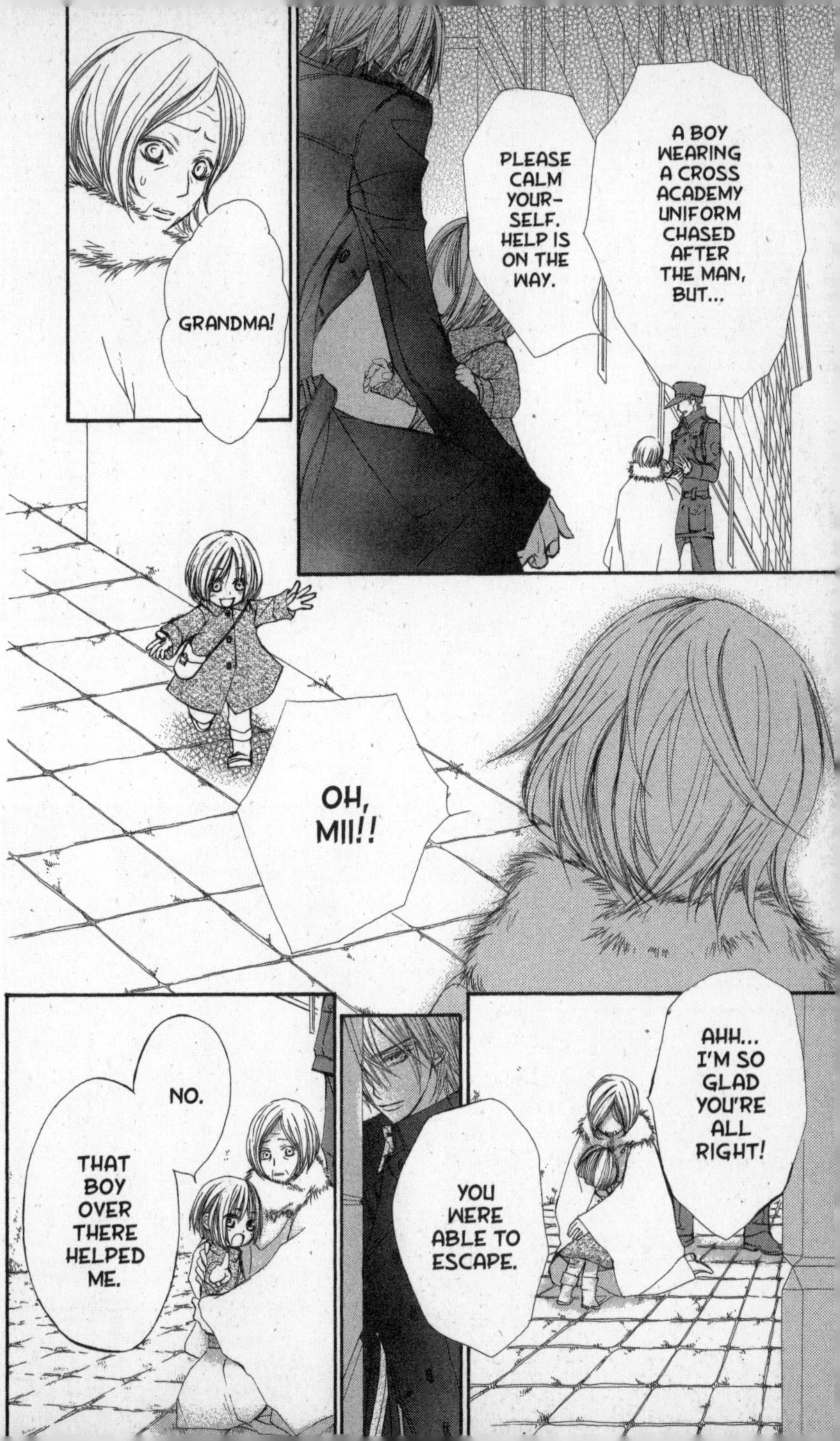
A BOY WEARING A CROSS ACADEMY UNIFORM CHASED AFTER THE MAN, BUT...
PLEASE CALM YOUR-SELF. HELP IS ON THE WAY.
GRANDMA!
OH, MII!!
AHH... I'M SO GLAD YOU'RE ALL RIGHT!
YOU WERE ABLE TO ESCAPE.
NO.
THAT BOY OVER THERE HELPED ME.

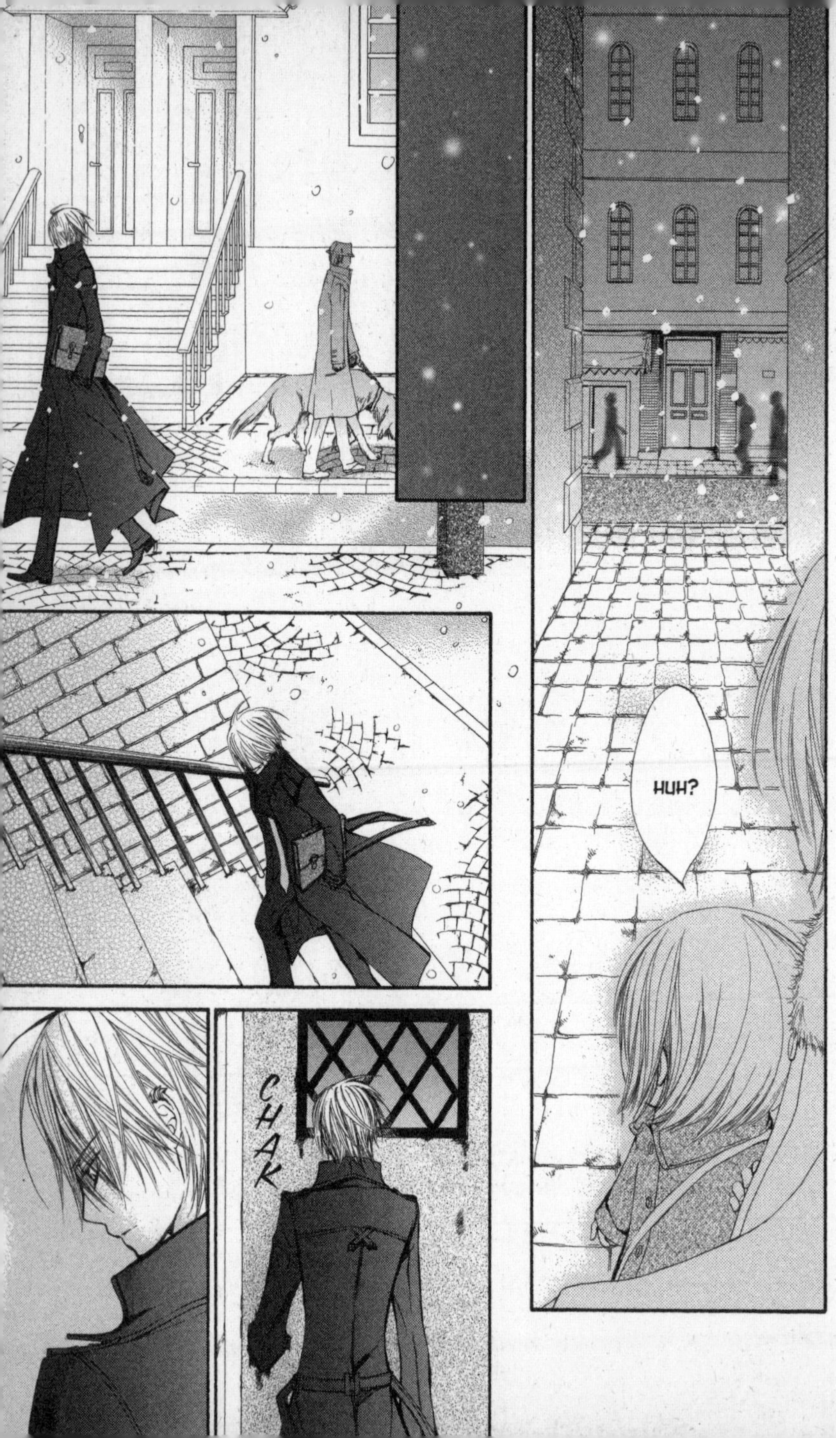
HUH?
CHAK

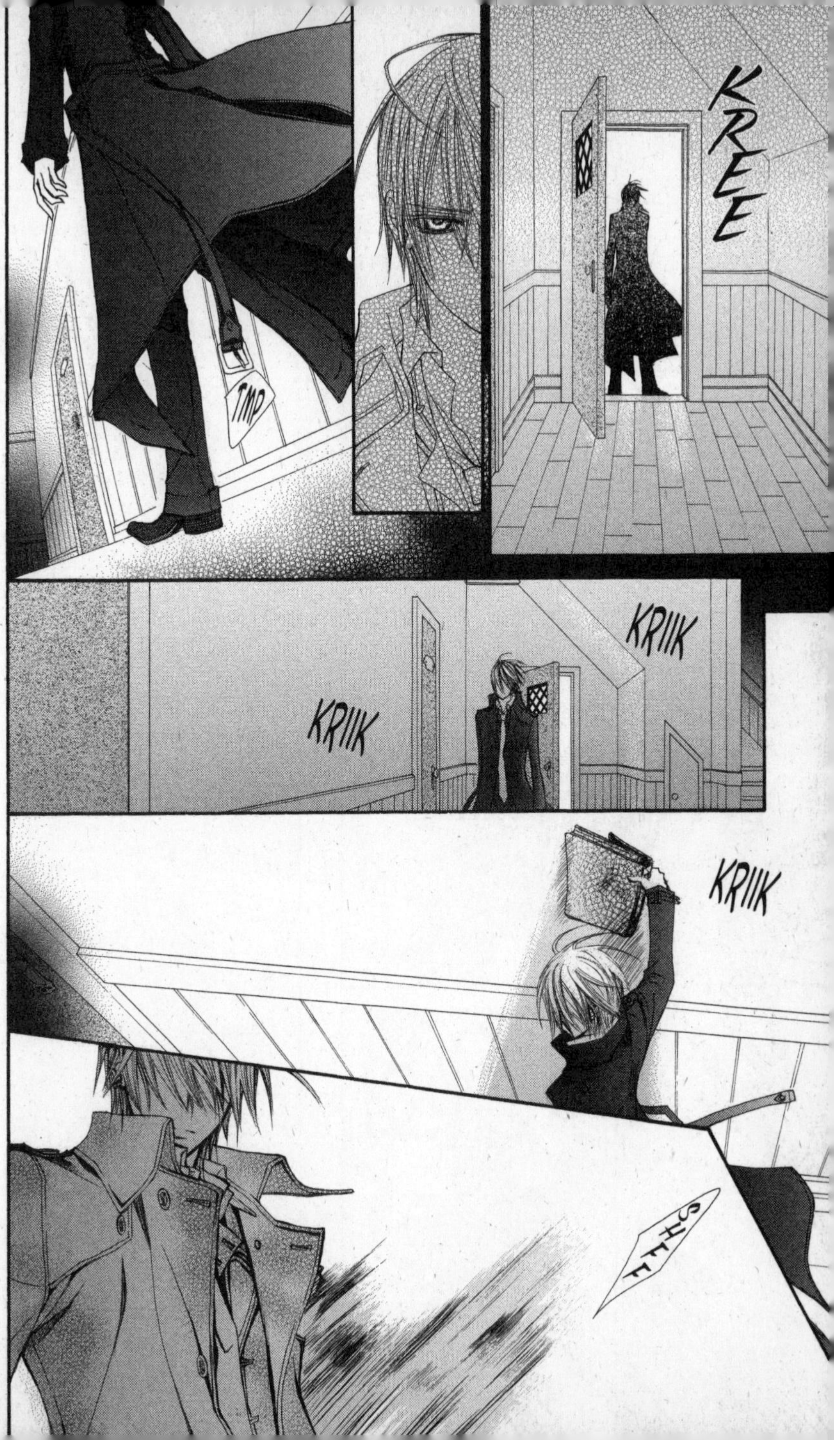
KREE
TMP
KRIIK
KRIIK
KRIIK
SHFF

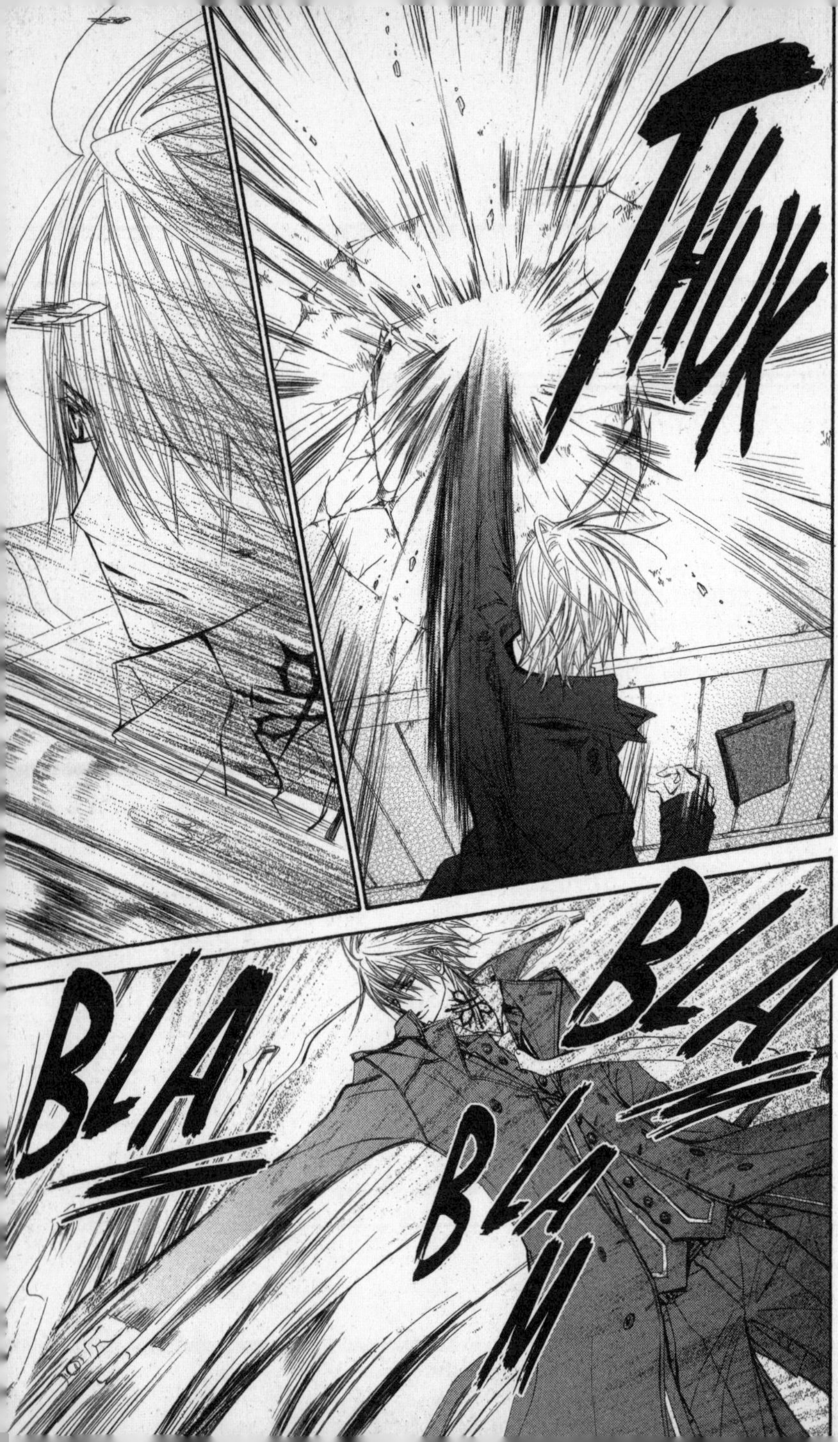
THUK
BLAM
BLAM
BLAM

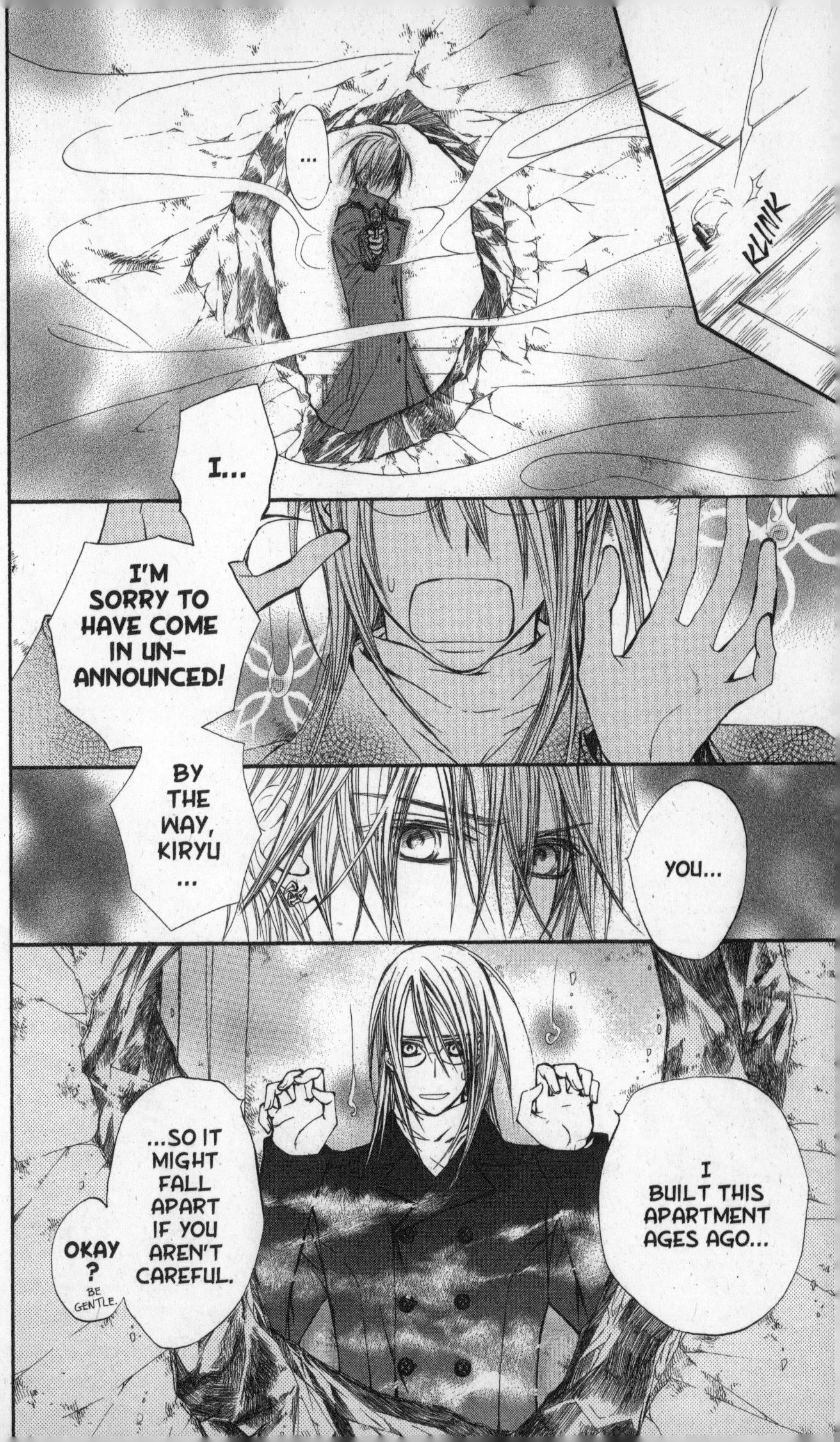
KLINK
...
I...
I'M SORRY TO HAVE COME IN UN-ANNOUNCED!
BY THE WAY, KIRYU ...
YOU...
I BUILT THIS APARTMENT AGES AGO...
...SO IT MIGHT FALL APART IF YOU AREN'T CAREFUL.
OKAY ?
BE GENTLE.

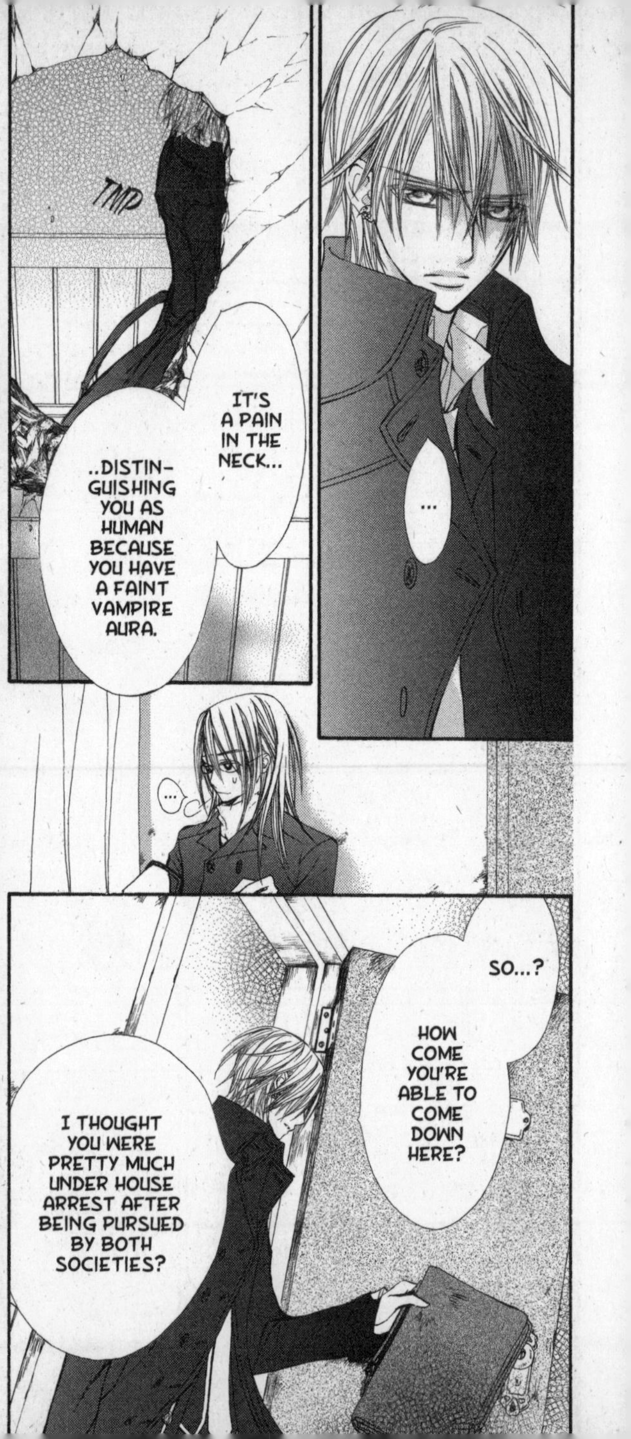
...
TMP
IT'S A PAIN IN THE NECK...
..DISTINGUISHING YOU AS HUMAN BECAUSE YOU HAVE A FAINT VAMPIRE AURA.
...
SO...?
HOW COME YOU'RE ABLE TO COME DOWN HERE?
I THOUGHT YOU WERE PRETTY MUCH UNDER HOUSE ARREST AFTER BEING PURSUED BY BOTH SOCIETIES?

II

The morning I was set to depart Japan... I was drawing the cover of the June edition of LaLa until 30 minutes before my departure. I hadn't slept or taken any rest for two days before that point. (I should have realized that this whole Germany trip was pretty reckless considering my schedule.) I was excited, but I was stressed about having to create the rough draft for the chapter title spread, so I was hardly able to sleep on the plane... That was how I entered Germany. I got on the connecting flight and reached the hotel after midnight. And I even woke up after three hours because I was so nervous. I was shocked when I saw myself in the mirror. The inner corners of my eyes were swollen, and I looked like a totally different person...!!

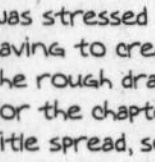

(I looked like this.)

So that was how my week in Germany started. For three days I woke up with swollen eyes and had to take three hours to calm them down with sports drinks, massages, and icing the area. Because the trip started out like this, I'd...

(→continues)

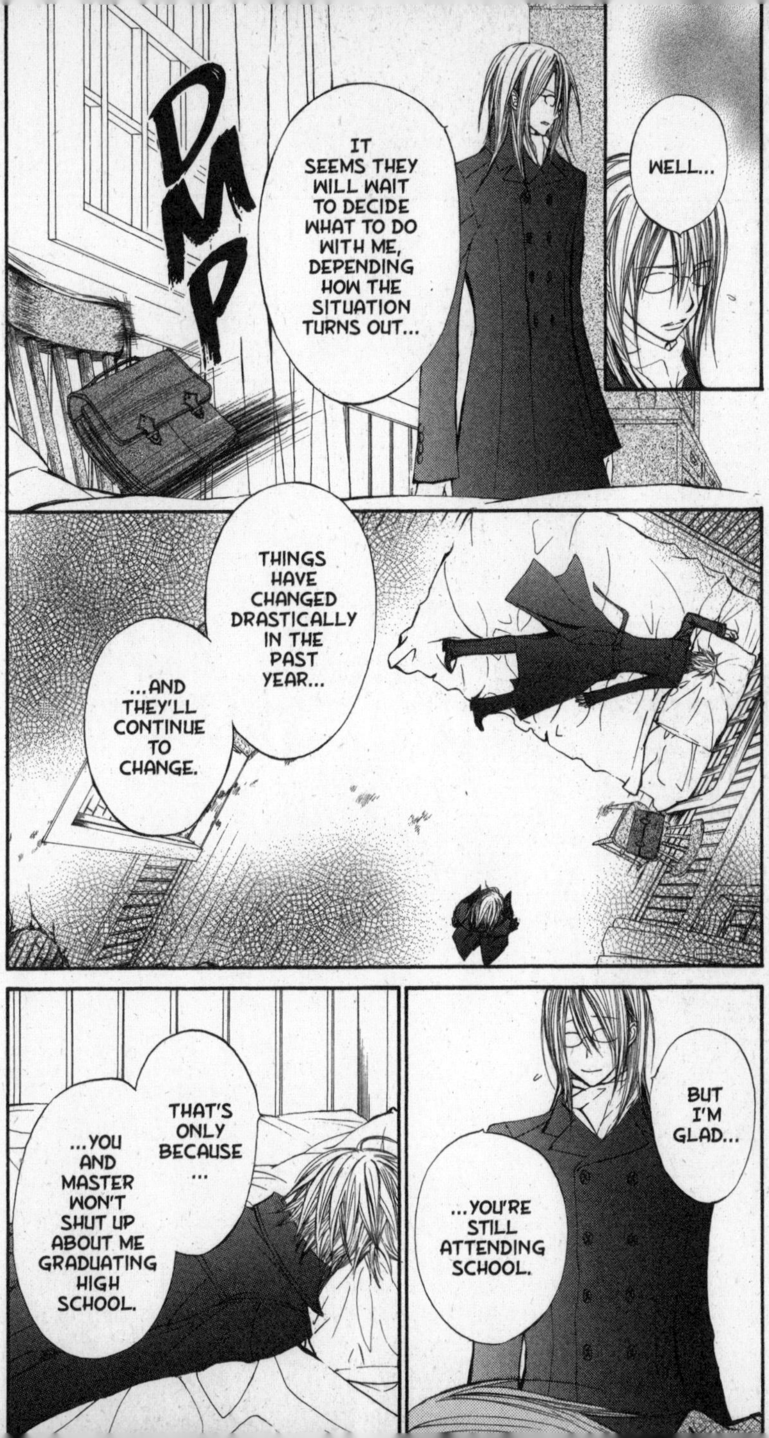
WELL...
IT SEEMS THEY WILL WAIT TO DECIDE WHAT TO DO WITH ME, DEPENDING HOW THE SITUATION TURNS OUT...
DMP
THINGS HAVE CHANGED DRASTICALLY IN THE PAST YEAR...
...AND THEY'LL CONTINUE TO CHANGE.
BUT I'M GLAD...
...YOU'RE STILL ATTENDING SCHOOL.
THAT'S ONLY BECAUSE...
...YOU AND MASTER WON'T SHUT UP ABOUT ME GRADUATING HIGH SCHOOL.

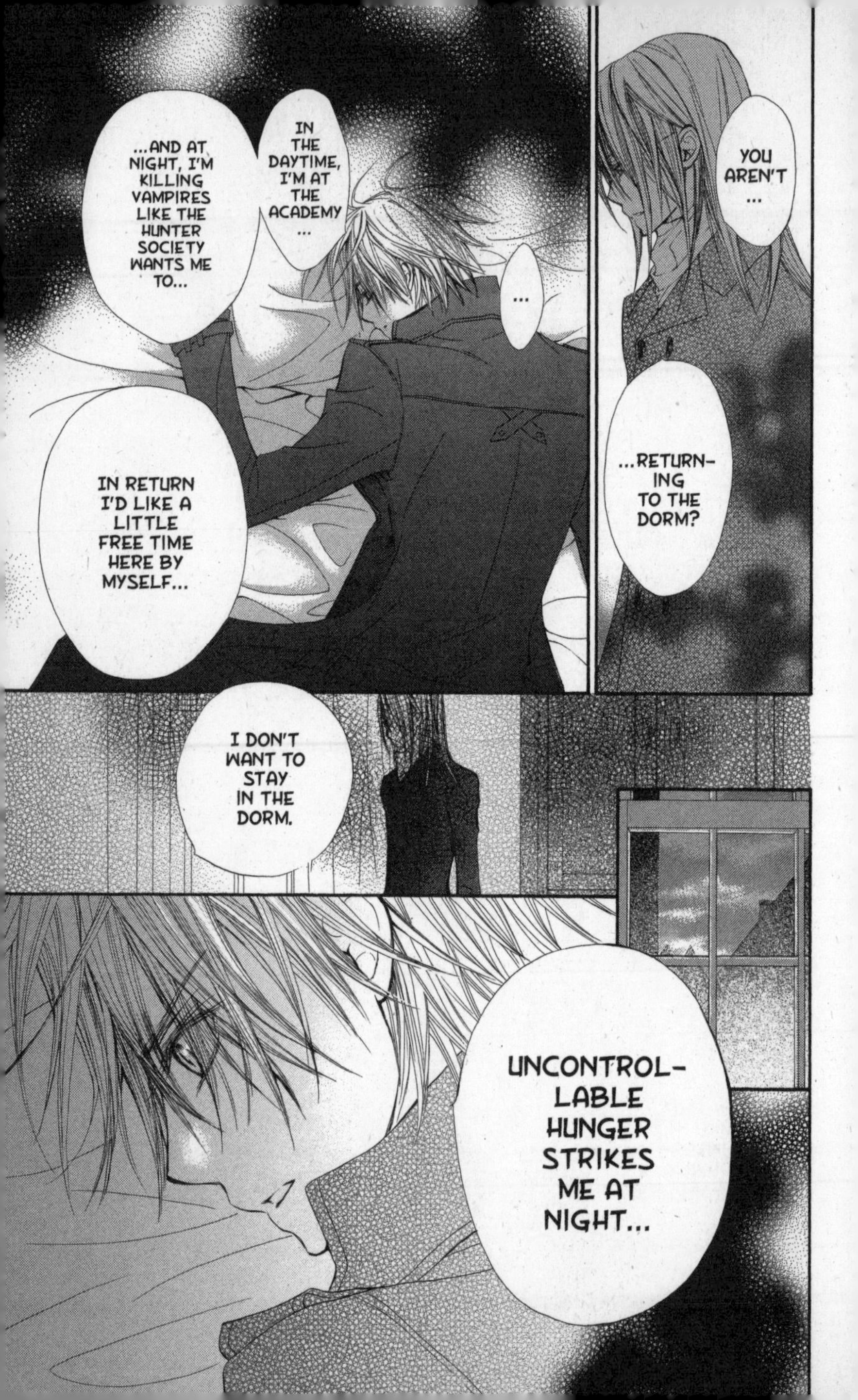
YOU AREN'T ...
...RETURNING TO THE DORM?
...
IN THE DAYTIME, I'M AT THE ACADEMY ...
...AND AT NIGHT, I'M KILLING VAMPIRES LIKE THE HUNTER SOCIETY WANTS ME TO...
IN RETURN I'D LIKE A LITTLE FREE TIME HERE BY MYSELF...
I DON'T WANT TO STAY IN THE DORM.
UNCONTROL-LABLE HUNGER STRIKES ME AT NIGHT...

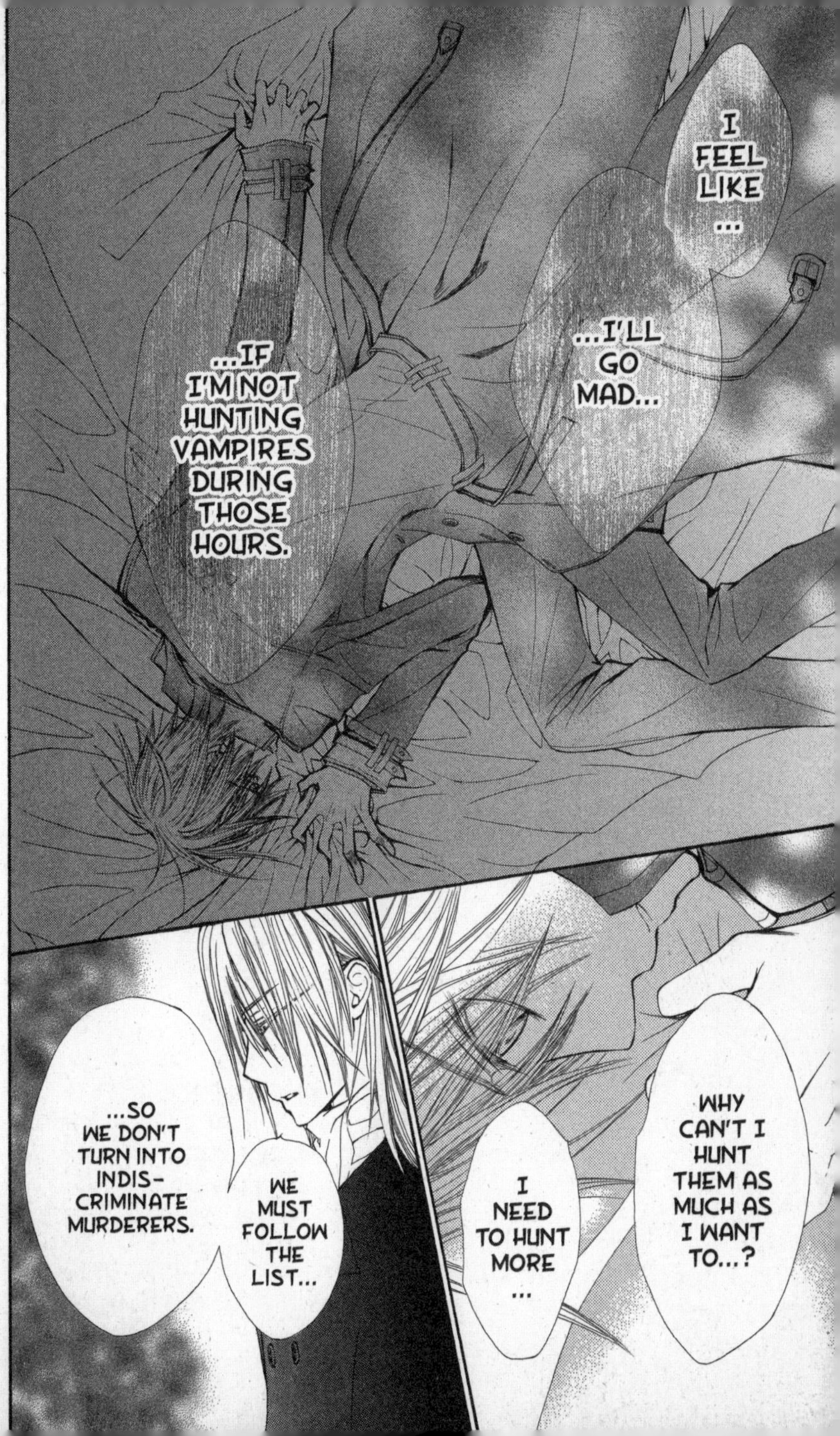
I FEEL LIKE...
...I'LL GO MAD...
...IF I'M NOT HUNTING VAMPIRES DURING THOSE HOURS.
WHY CAN'T I HUNT THEM AS MUCH AS I WANT TO...?
I NEED TO HUNT MORE...
WE MUST FOLLOW THE LIST...
...SO WE DON'T TURN INTO INDIS-CRIMINATE MURDERERS.

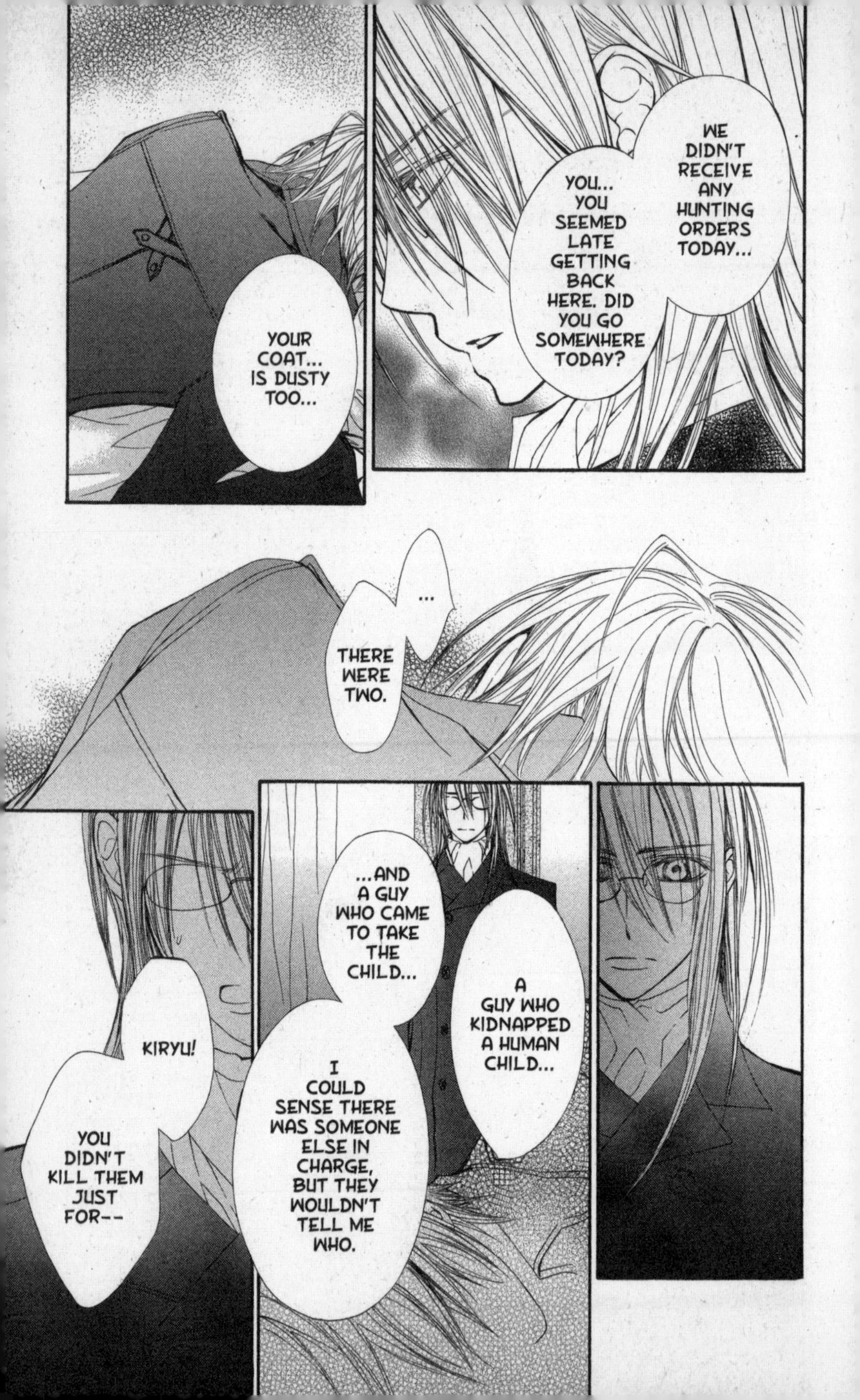
WE DIDN'T RECEIVE ANY HUNTING ORDERS TODAY...
YOU... YOU SEEMED LATE GETTING BACK HERE. DID YOU GO SOMEWHERE TODAY?
YOUR COAT... IS DUSTY TOO...
...
THERE WERE TWO.
A GUY WHO KIDNAPPED A HUMAN CHILD...
...AND A GUY WHO CAME TO TAKE THE CHILD...
I COULD SENSE THERE WAS SOMEONE ELSE IN CHARGE, BUT THEY WOULDN'T TELL ME WHO.
KIRYU!
YOU DIDN'T KILL THEM JUST FOR--

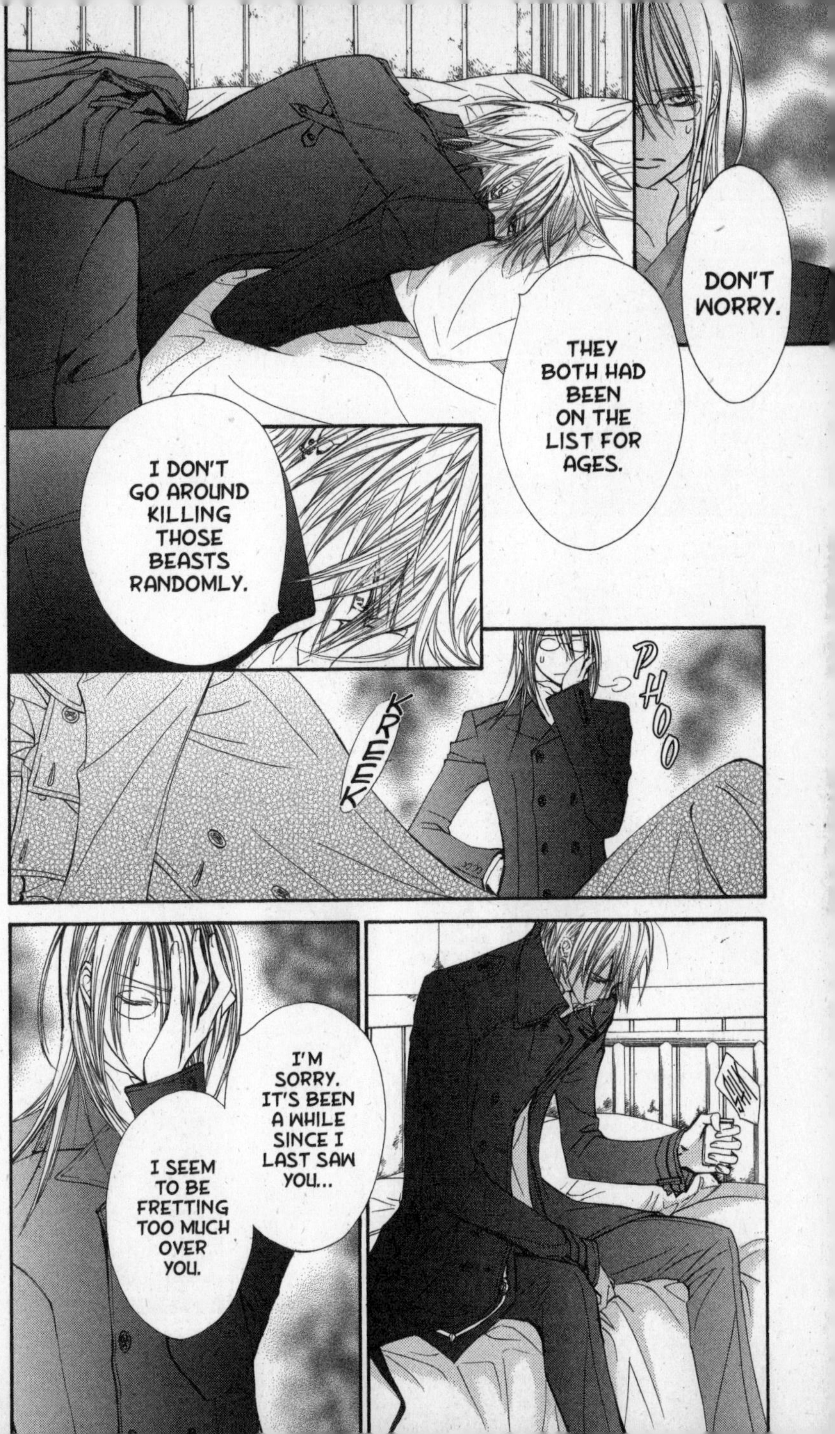
DON'T WORRY.
THEY BOTH HAD BEEN ON THE LIST FOR AGES.
I DON'T GO AROUND KILLING THOSE BEASTS RANDOMLY.
PHOO
KREEK
I'M SORRY. IT'S BEEN A WHILE SINCE I LAST SAW YOU...
I SEEM TO BE FRETTING TOO MUCH OVER YOU.

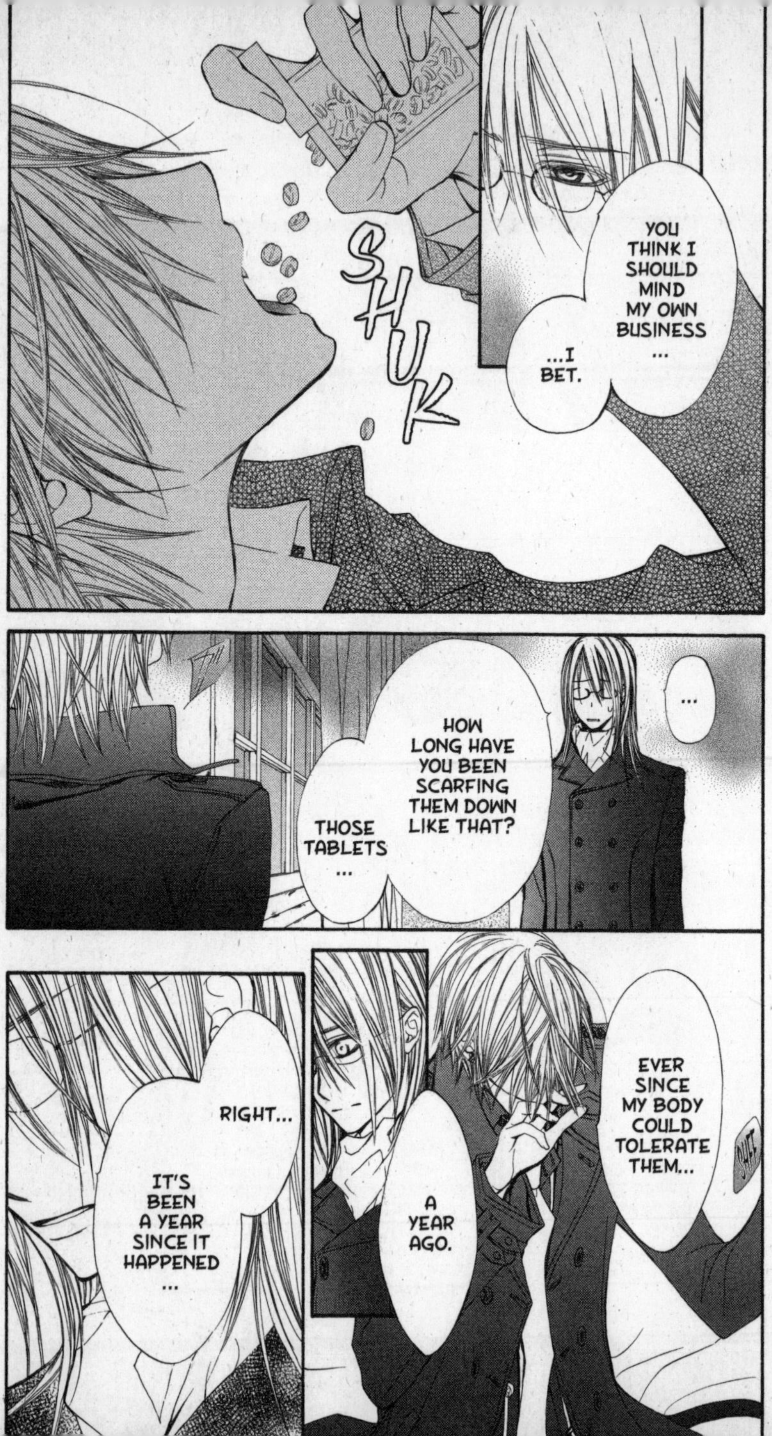
YOU THINK I SHOULD MIND MY OWN BUSINESS ...
...I BET.
SHUK
...
HOW LONG HAVE YOU BEEN SCARFING THEM DOWN LIKE THAT?
THOSE TABLETS ...
EVER SINCE MY BODY COULD TOLERATE THEM...
SHFT
A YEAR AGO.
RIGHT...
IT'S BEEN A YEAR SINCE IT HAPPENED ...

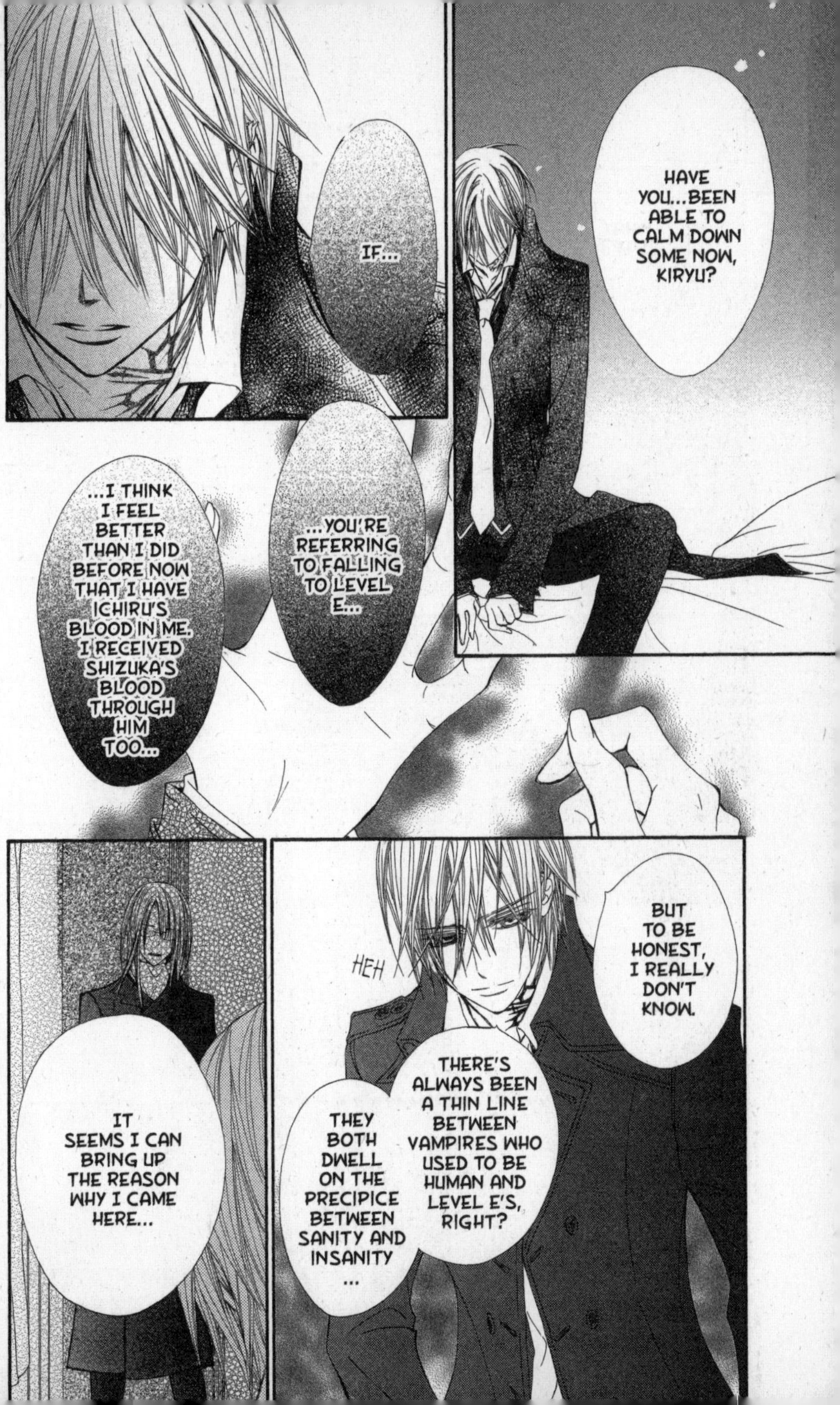
HAVE YOU...BEEN ABLE TO CALM DOWN SOME NOW, KIRYU?
IF...
...YOU'RE REFERRING TO FALLING TO LEVEL E...
...I THINK I FEEL BETTER THAN I DID BEFORE NOW THAT I HAVE ICHIRU'S BLOOD IN ME. I RECEIVED SHIZUKA'S BLOOD THROUGH HIM TOO...
BUT TO BE HONEST, I REALLY DON'T KNOW.
HEH
THERE'S ALWAYS BEEN A THIN LINE BETWEEN VAMPIRES WHO USED TO BE HUMAN AND LEVEL E'S, RIGHT?
THEY BOTH DWELL ON THE PRECIPICE BETWEEN SANITY AND INSANITY ...
IT SEEMS I CAN BRING UP THE REASON WHY I CAME HERE...

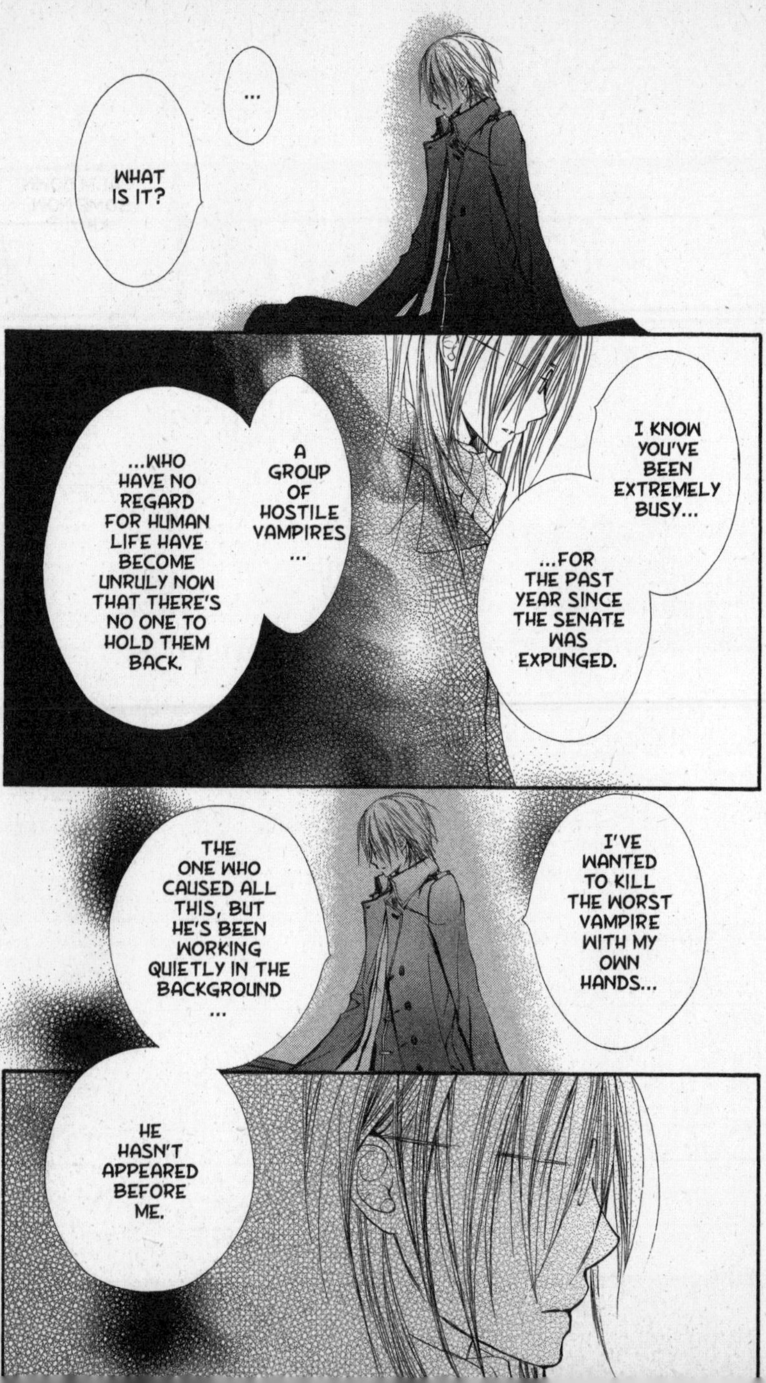
...
WHAT IS IT?
I KNOW YOU'VE BEEN EXTREMELY BUSY...
...FOR THE PAST YEAR SINCE THE SENATE WAS EXPUNGED.
A GROUP OF HOSTILE VAMPIRES...
...WHO HAVE NO REGARD FOR HUMAN LIFE HAVE BECOME UNRULY NOW THAT THERE'S NO ONE TO HOLD THEM BACK.
I'VE WANTED TO KILL THE WORST VAMPIRE WITH MY OWN HANDS...
THE ONE WHO CAUSED ALL THIS, BUT HE'S BEEN WORKING QUIETLY IN THE BACKGROUND...
HE HASN'T APPEARED BEFORE ME.

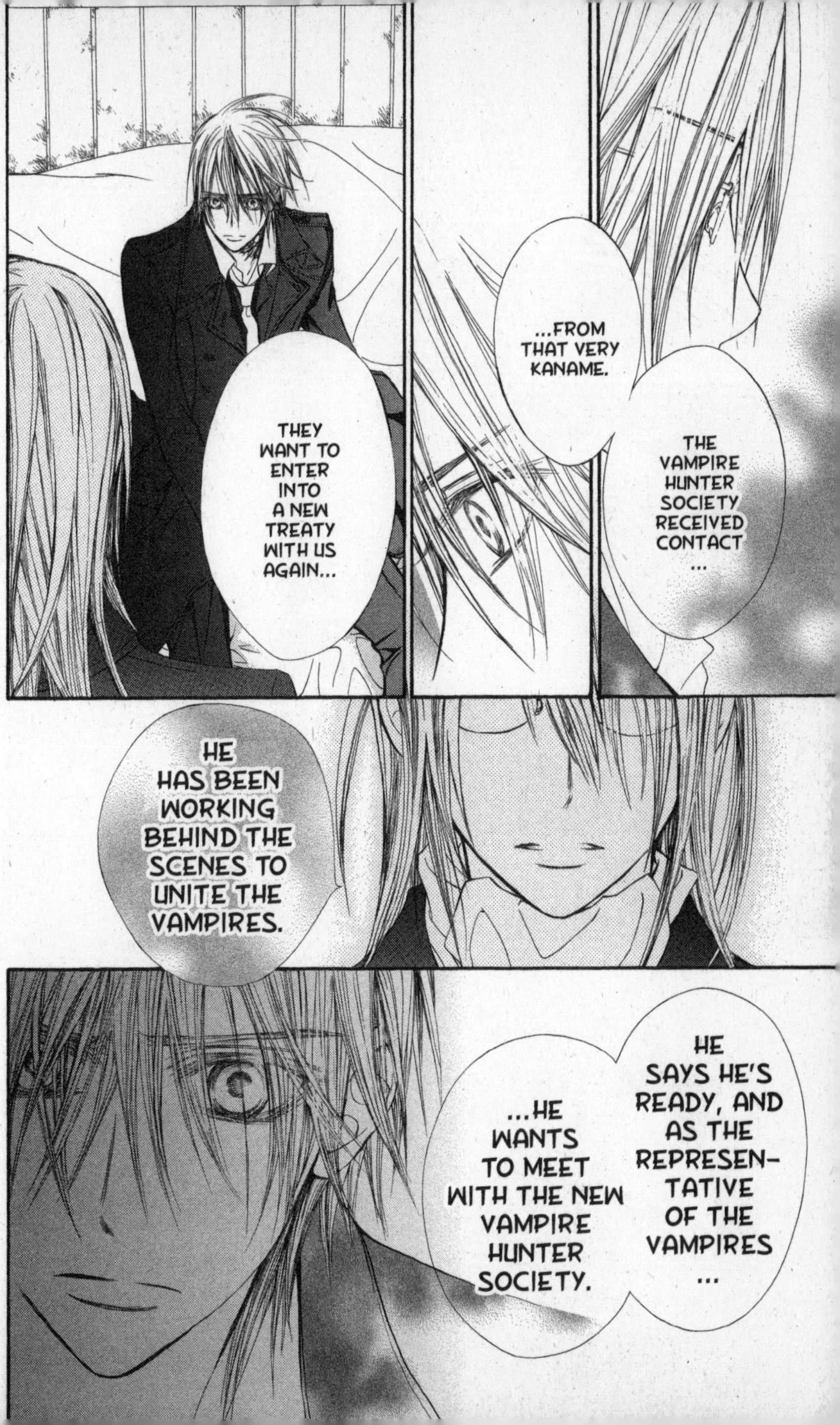
THE VAMPIRE HUNTER SOCIETY RECEIVED CONTACT...
...FROM THAT VERY KANAME.
THEY WANT TO ENTER INTO A NEW TREATY WITH US AGAIN...
HE HAS BEEN WORKING BEHIND THE SCENES TO UNITE THE VAMPIRES.
HE SAYS HE'S READY, AND AS THE REPRESEN-TATIVE OF THE VAMPIRES...
...HE WANTS TO MEET WITH THE NEW VAMPIRE HUNTER SOCIETY.

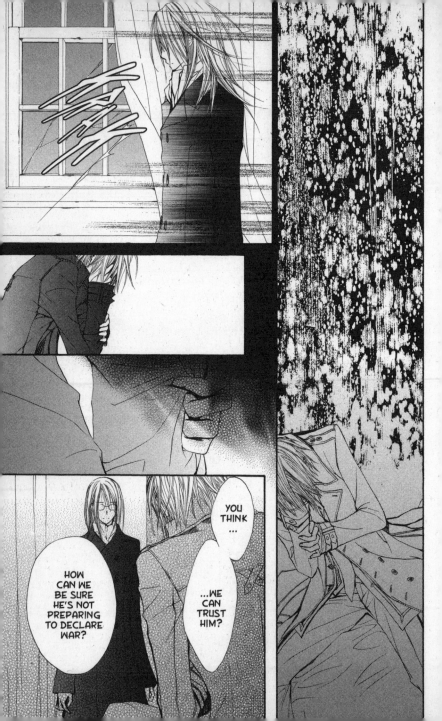

YOU
THINK
...

...WE
CAN
TRUST
HIM?

HOW
CAN WE
BE SURE
HE'S NOT
PREPARING
TO DECLARE
WAR?

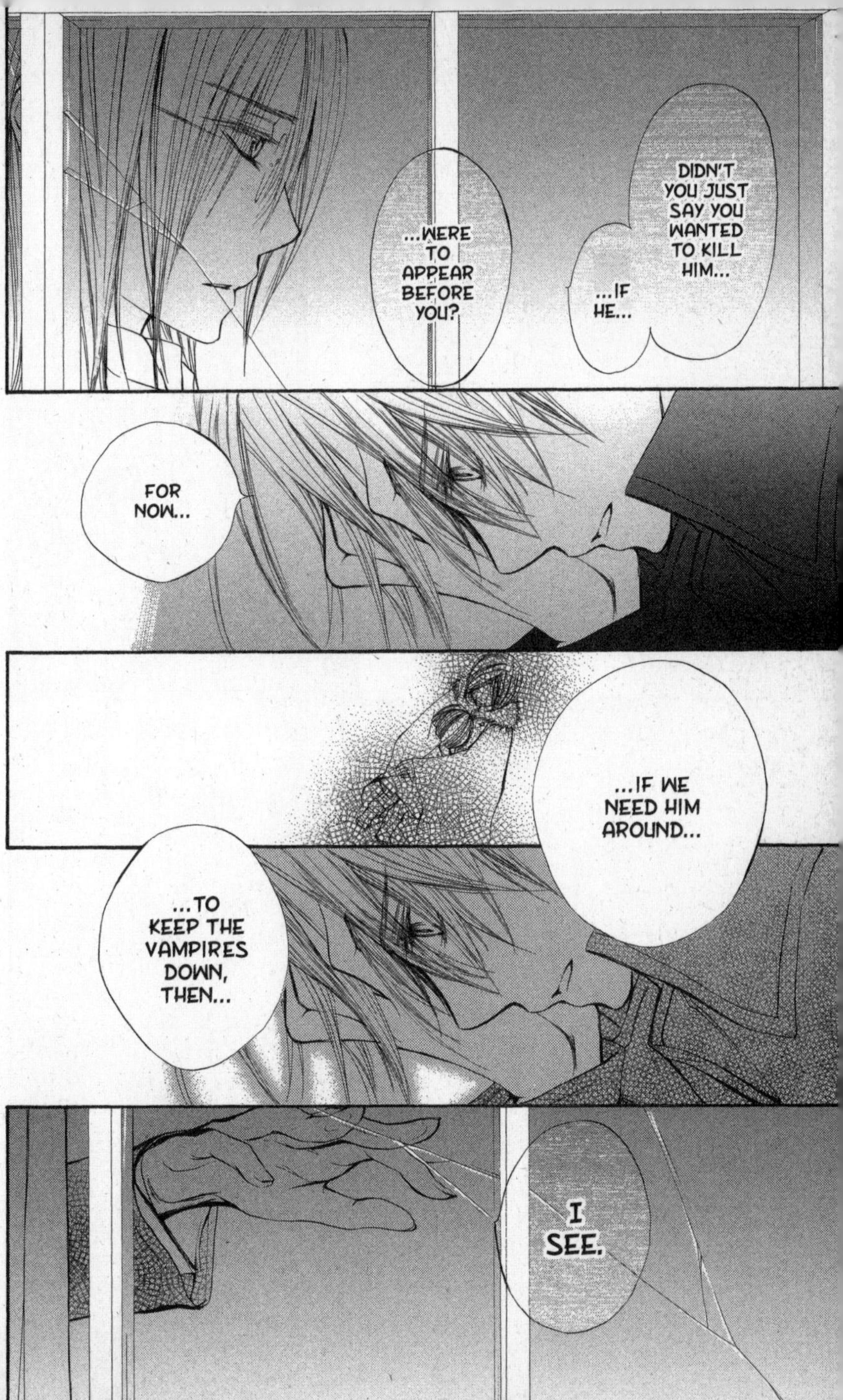
DIDN'T YOU JUST SAY YOU WANTED TO KILL HIM...
...IF HE...
...WERE TO APPEAR BEFORE YOU?
FOR NOW...
...IF WE NEED HIM AROUND...
...TO KEEP THE VAMPIRES DOWN, THEN...
I SEE.

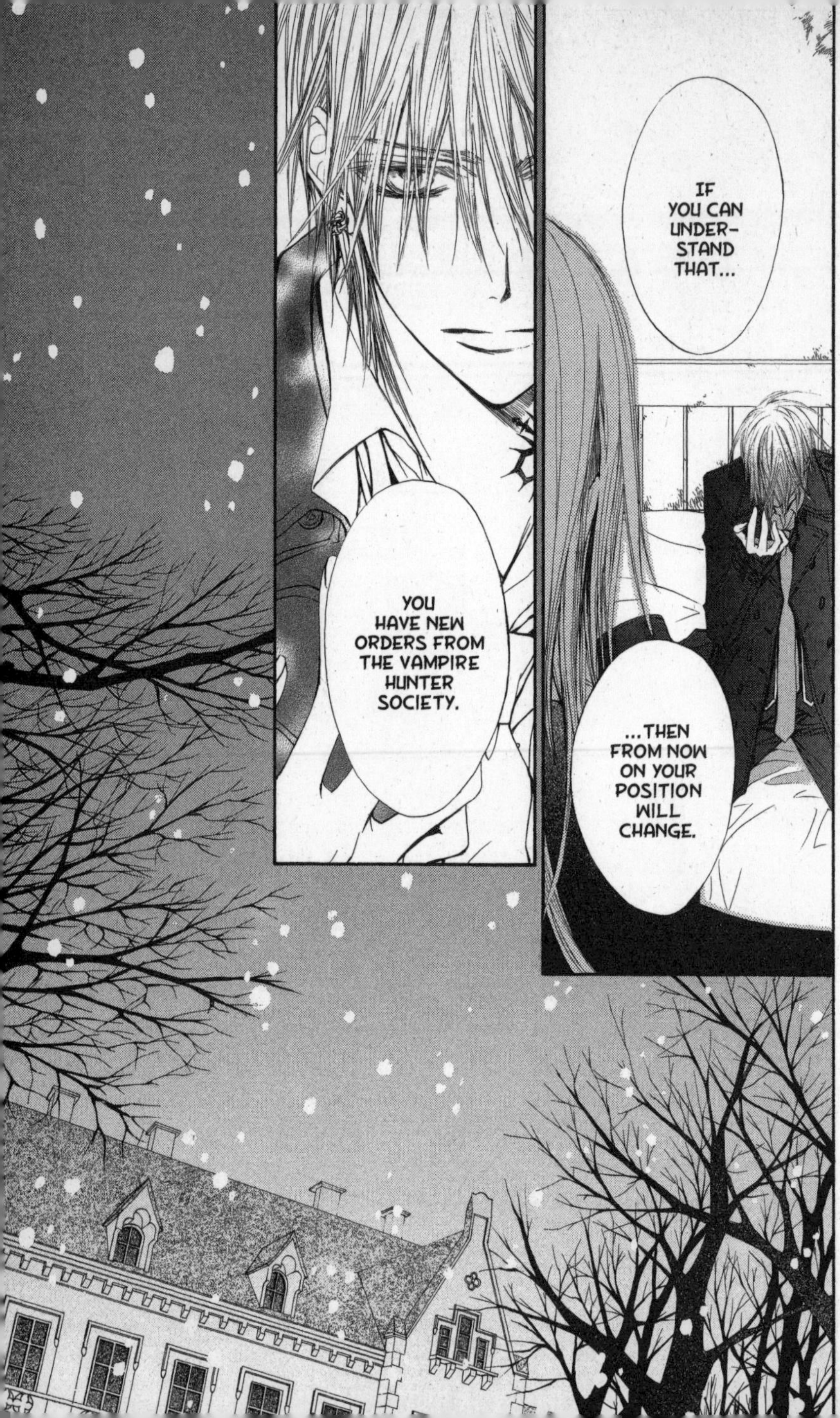
IF YOU CAN UNDER-STAND THAT...
...THEN FROM NOW ON YOUR POSITION WILL CHANGE.
YOU HAVE NEW ORDERS FROM THE VAMPIRE HUNTER SOCIETY.

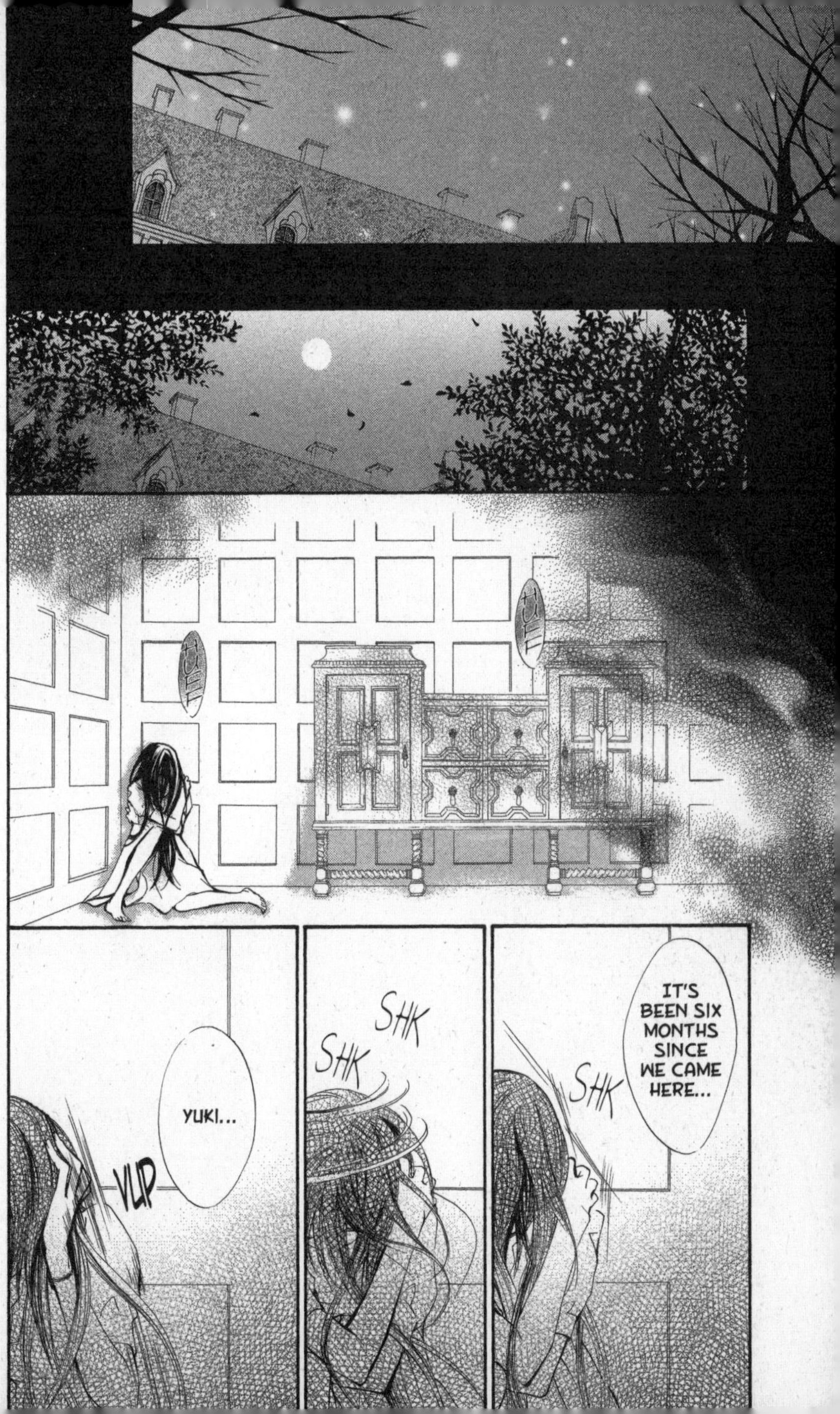
HUFF
HUFF
IT'S BEEN SIX MONTHS SINCE WE CAME HERE...
SHK
SHK
SHK
YUKI...
VLIP

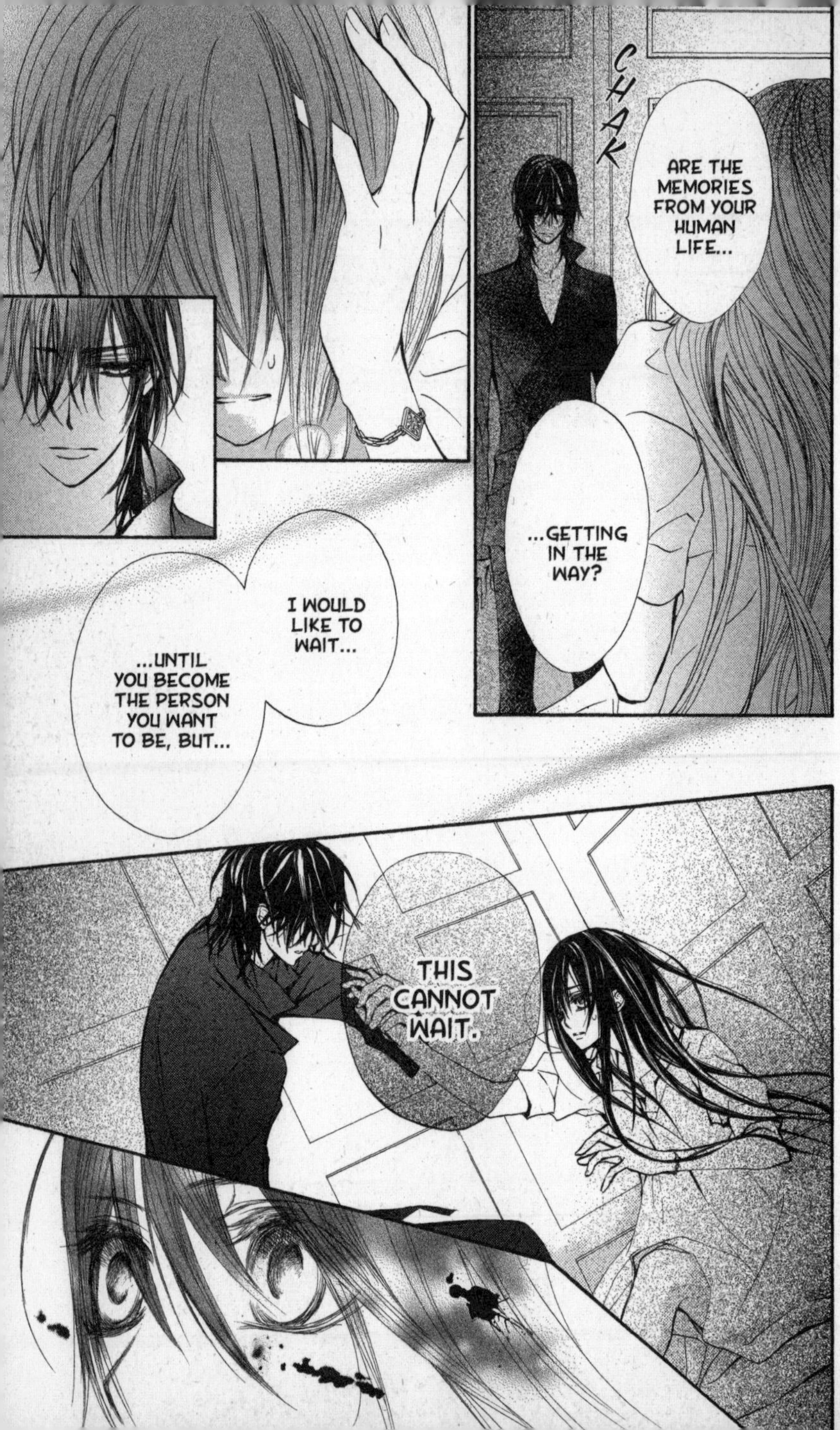
CHAK
ARE THE MEMORIES FROM YOUR HUMAN LIFE...
...GETTING IN THE WAY?
I WOULD LIKE TO WAIT...
...UNTIL YOU BECOME THE PERSON YOU WANT TO BE, BUT...
THIS CANNOT WAIT.

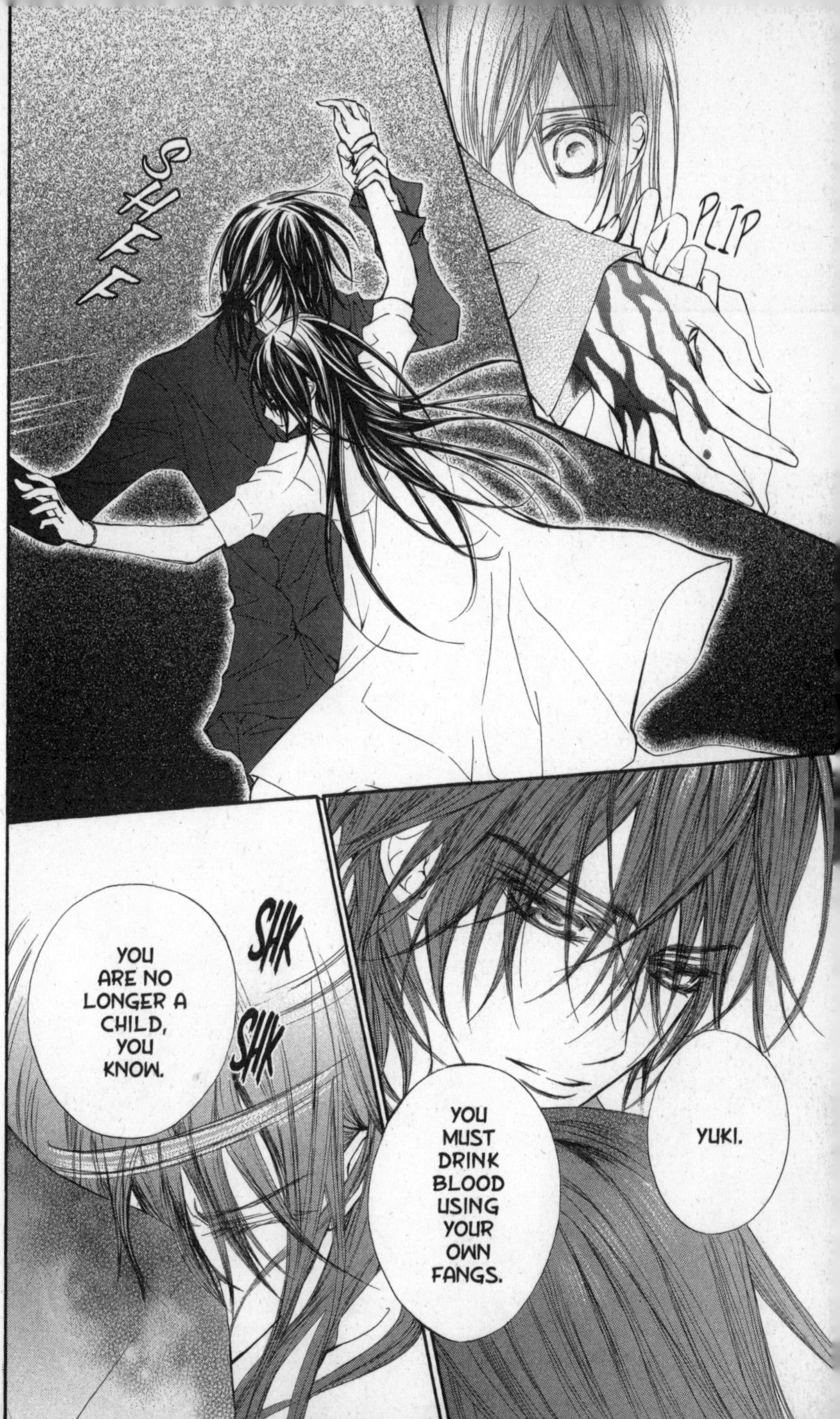
PLIP
SHFFF
YUKI.
YOU MUST DRINK BLOOD USING YOUR OWN FANGS.
SHK
SHK
YOU ARE NO LONGER A CHILD, YOU KNOW.

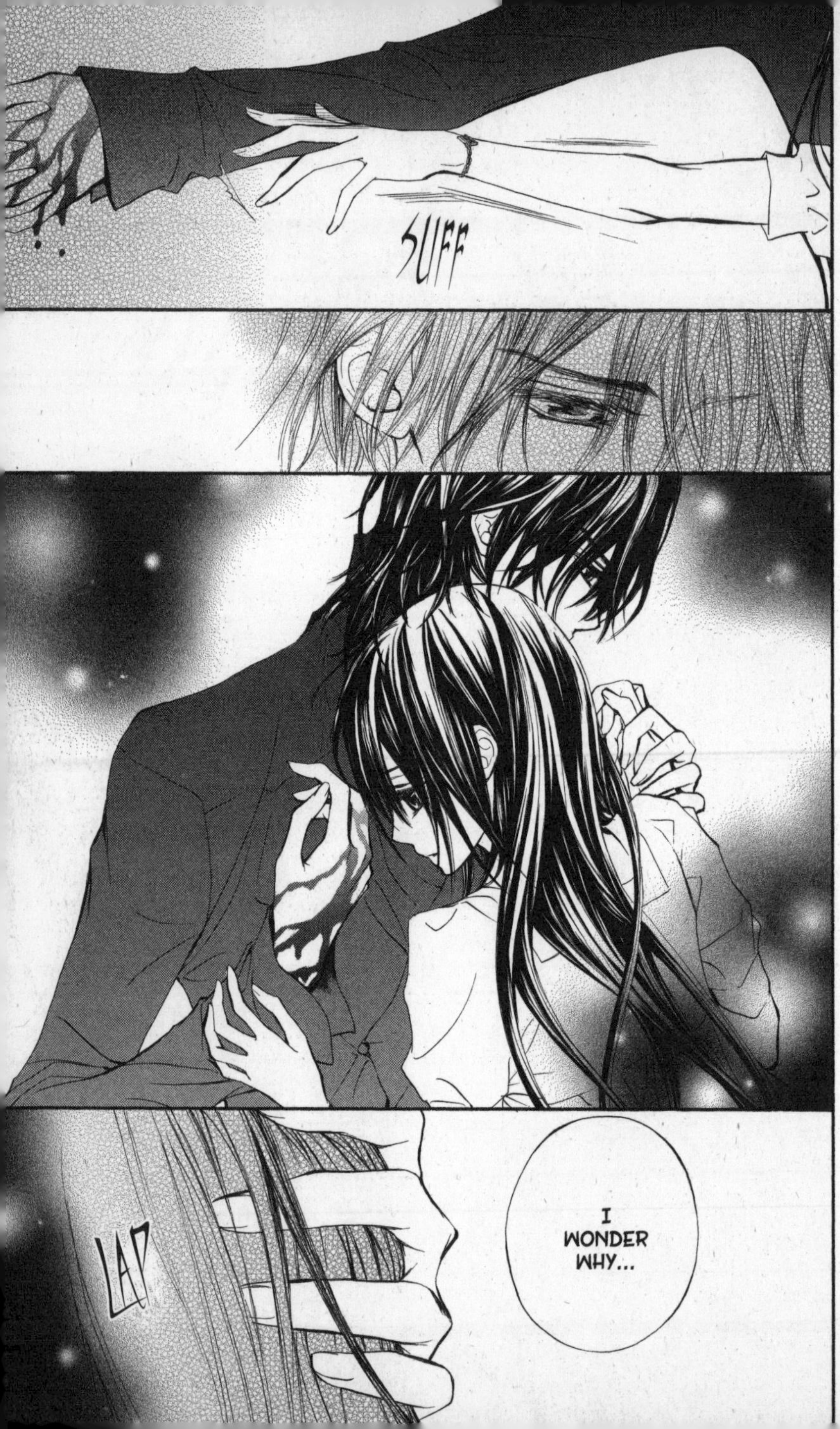
SUFF
I WONDER WHY...
LAP

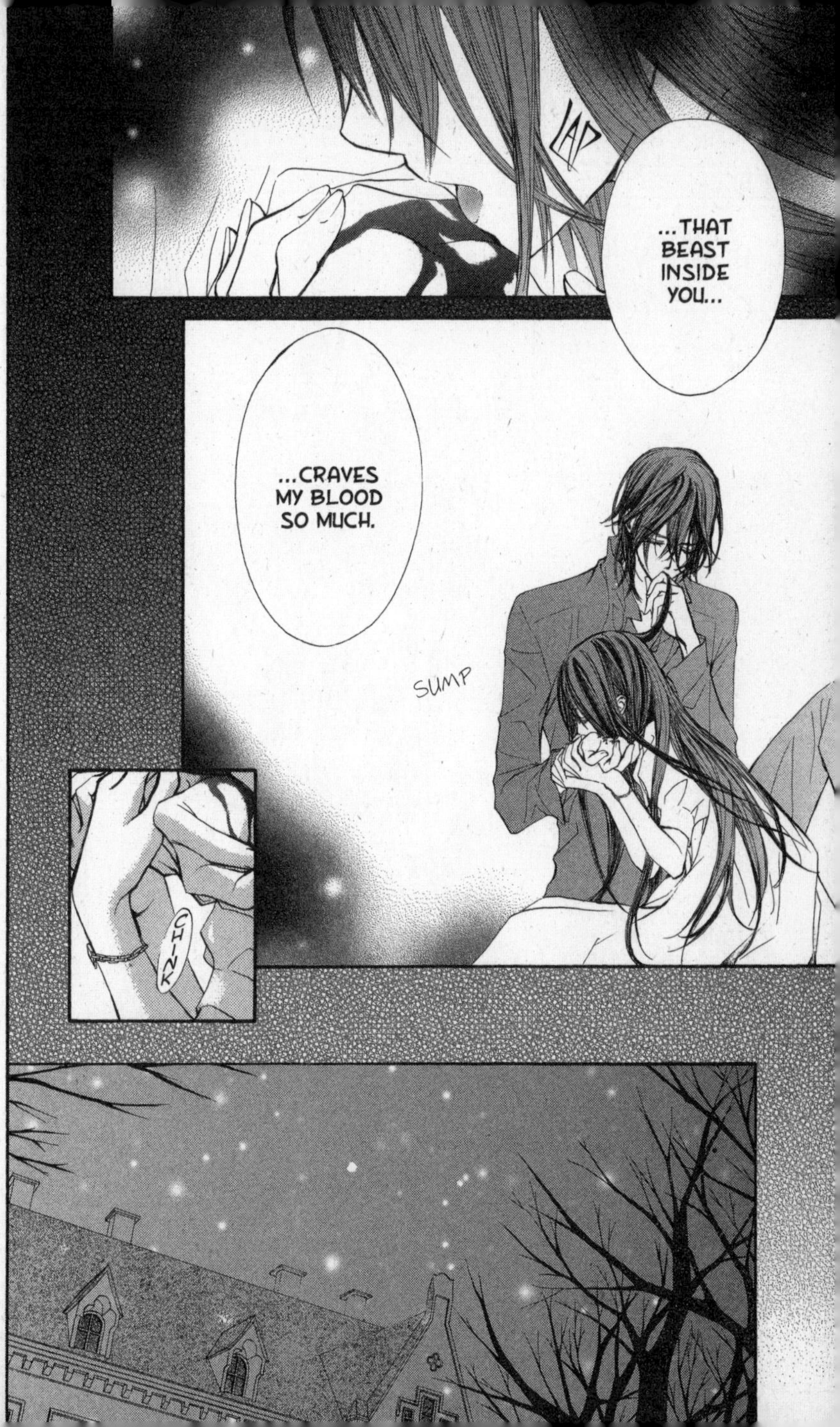
LAP
...THAT BEAST INSIDE YOU...
...CRAVES MY BLOOD SO MUCH.
SUMP
CHINK

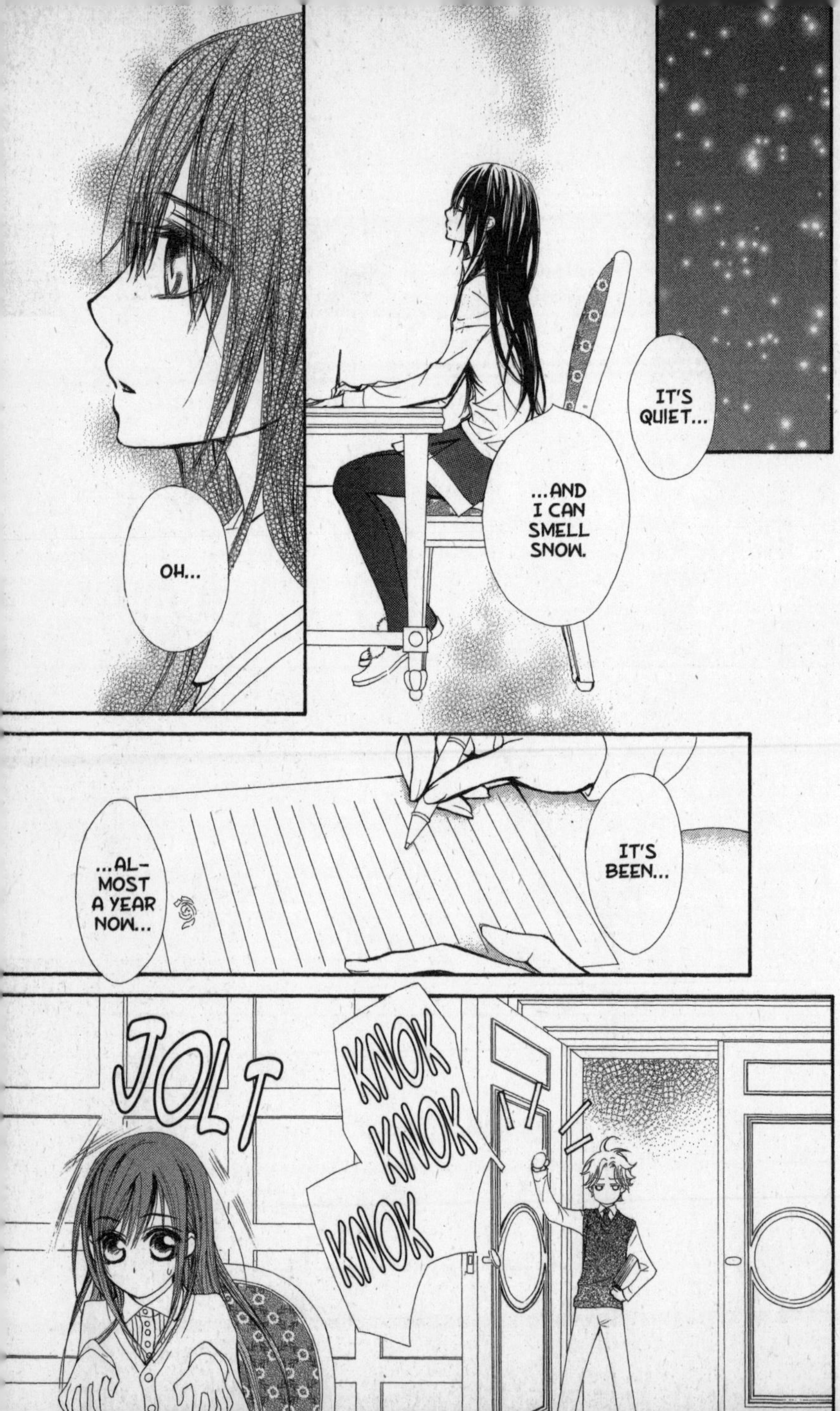
IT'S QUIET...
...AND I CAN SMELL SNOW.
OH...
IT'S BEEN...
...AL-MOST A YEAR NOW...
KNOK KNOK KNOK
JOLT

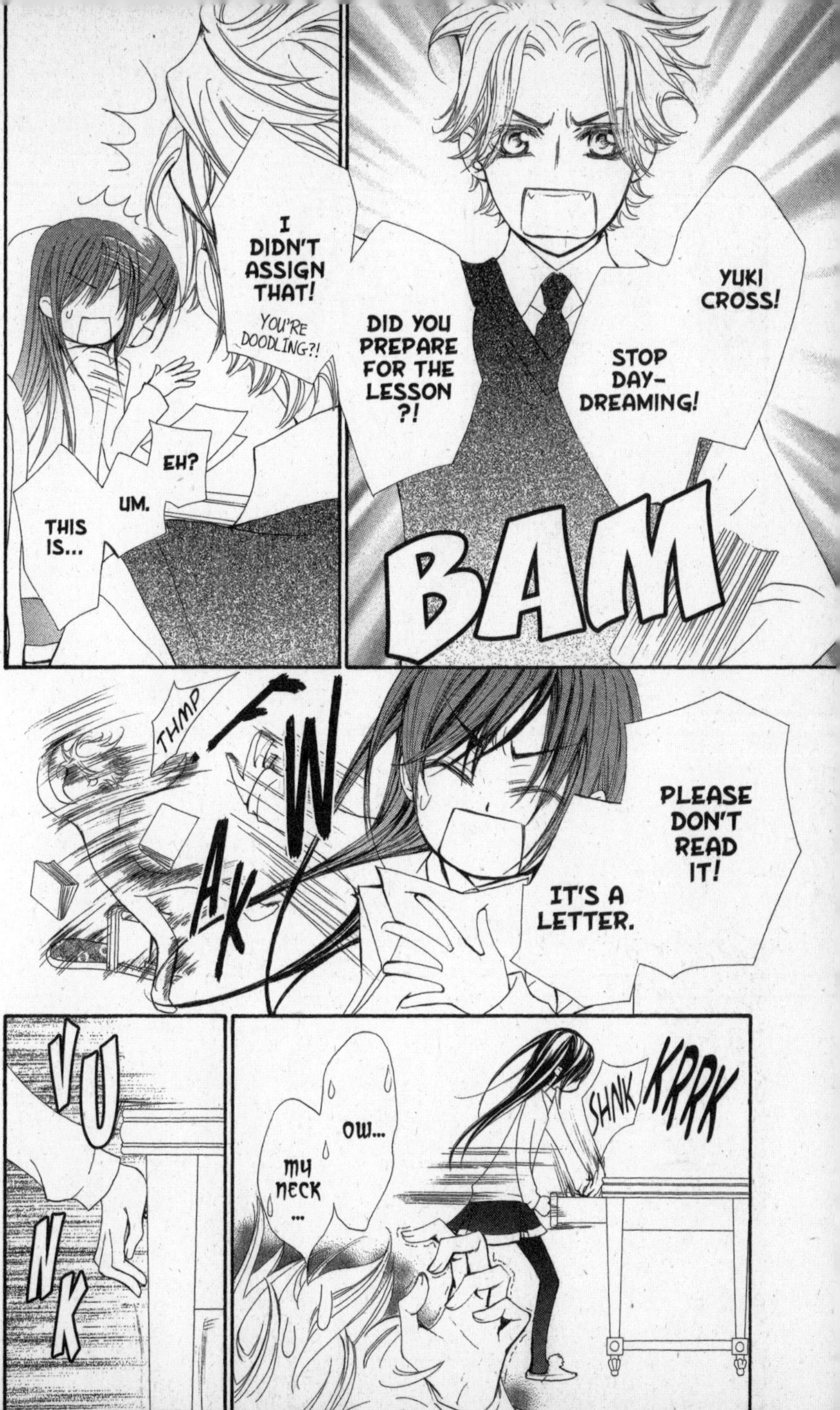
YUKI CROSS!
STOP DAY-DREAMING!
DID YOU PREPARE FOR THE LESSON?!
BAM
I DIDN'T ASSIGN THAT!
YOU'RE DOODLING?!
EH?
UM.
THIS IS...
PLEASE DON'T READ IT!
IT'S A LETTER.
FWAK
THMP
KRRK
SHNK
OW...
my neck...
VUNK

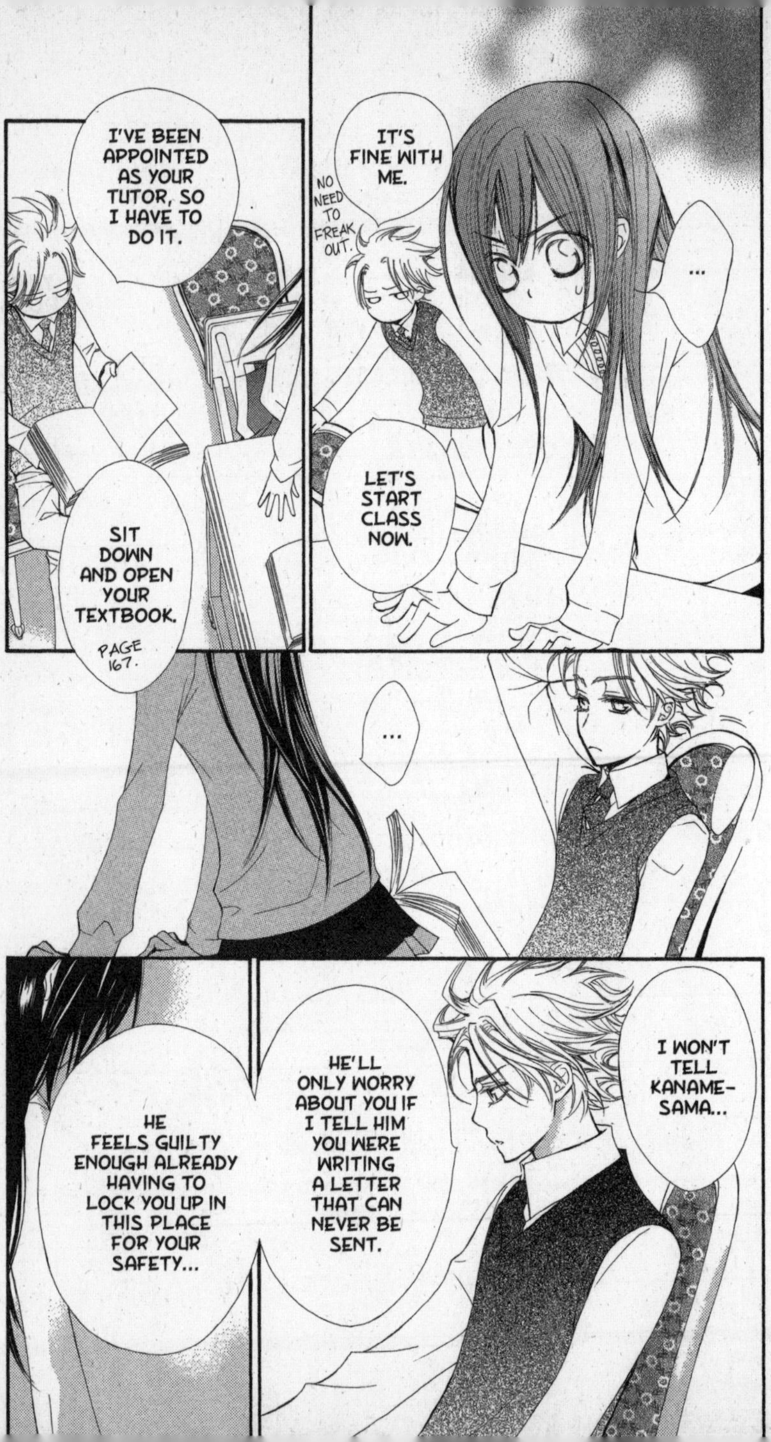
IT'S FINE WITH ME.
NO NEED TO FREAK OUT.
...
LET'S START CLASS NOW.
I'VE BEEN APPOINTED AS YOUR TUTOR, SO I HAVE TO DO IT.
SIT DOWN AND OPEN YOUR TEXTBOOK.
PAGE 167.
...
I WON'T TELL KANAME-SAMA...
HE'LL ONLY WORRY ABOUT YOU IF I TELL HIM YOU WERE WRITING A LETTER THAT CAN NEVER BE SENT.
HE FEELS GUILTY ENOUGH ALREADY HAVING TO LOCK YOU UP IN THIS PLACE FOR YOUR SAFETY...

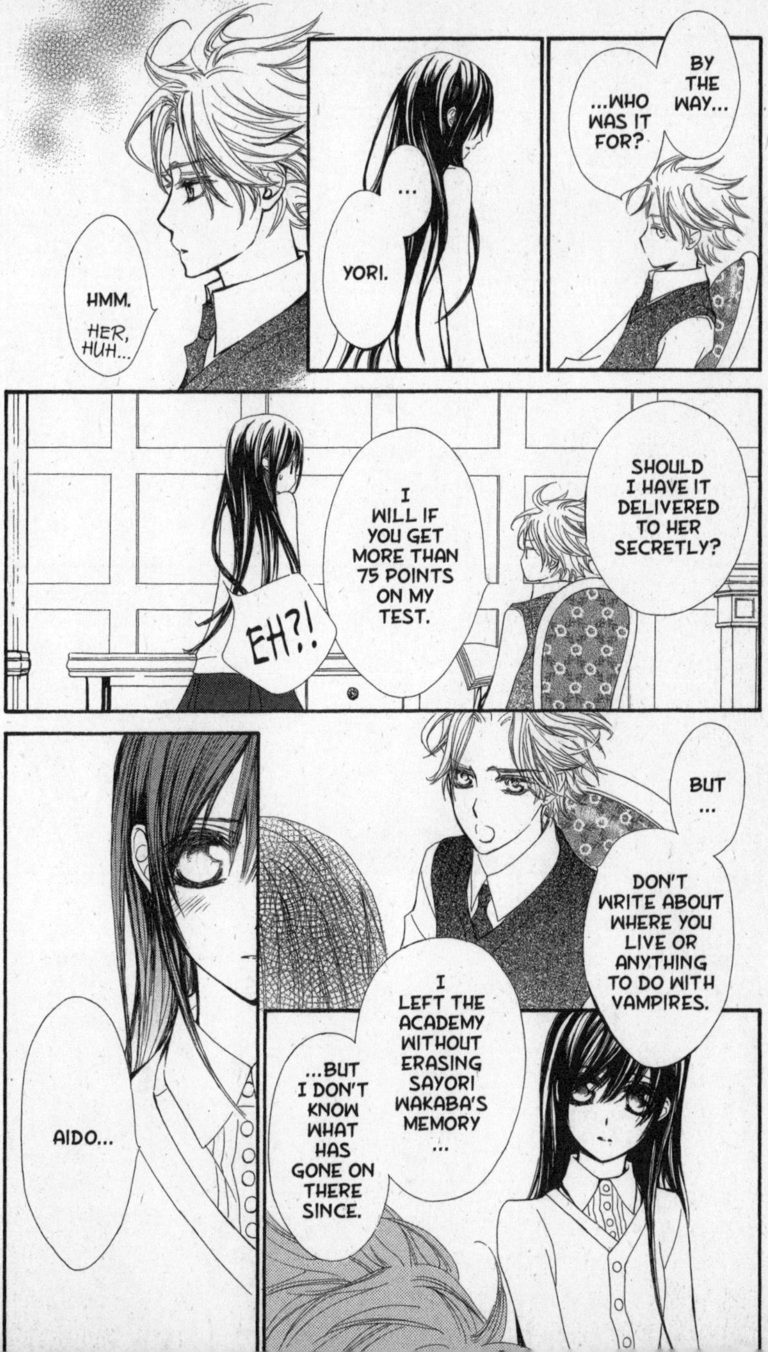
BY THE WAY...
...WHO WAS IT FOR?
...
YORI.
HMM.
HER, HUH...
SHOULD I HAVE IT DELIVERED TO HER SECRETLY?
I WILL IF YOU GET MORE THAN 75 POINTS ON MY TEST.
EH?!
BUT...
DON'T WRITE ABOUT WHERE YOU LIVE OR ANYTHING TO DO WITH VAMPIRES.
I LEFT THE ACADEMY WITHOUT ERASING SAYORI WAKABA'S MEMORY...
...BUT I DON'T KNOW WHAT HAS GONE ON THERE SINCE.
AIDO...

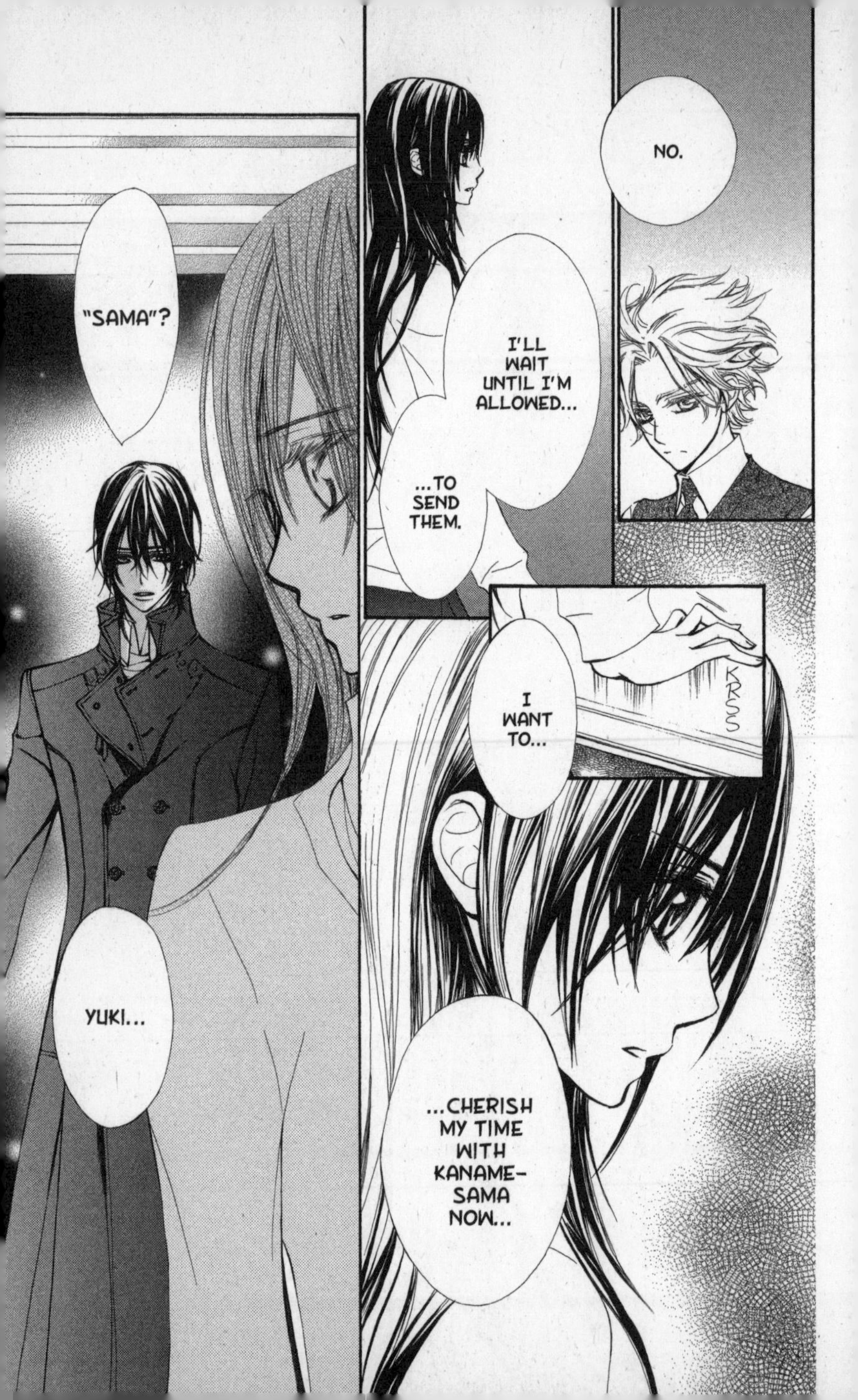
NO.
I'LL WAIT UNTIL I'M ALLOWED...
...TO SEND THEM.
KRSS
I WANT TO...
...CHERISH MY TIME WITH KANAME-SAMA NOW...
"SAMA"?
YUKI...

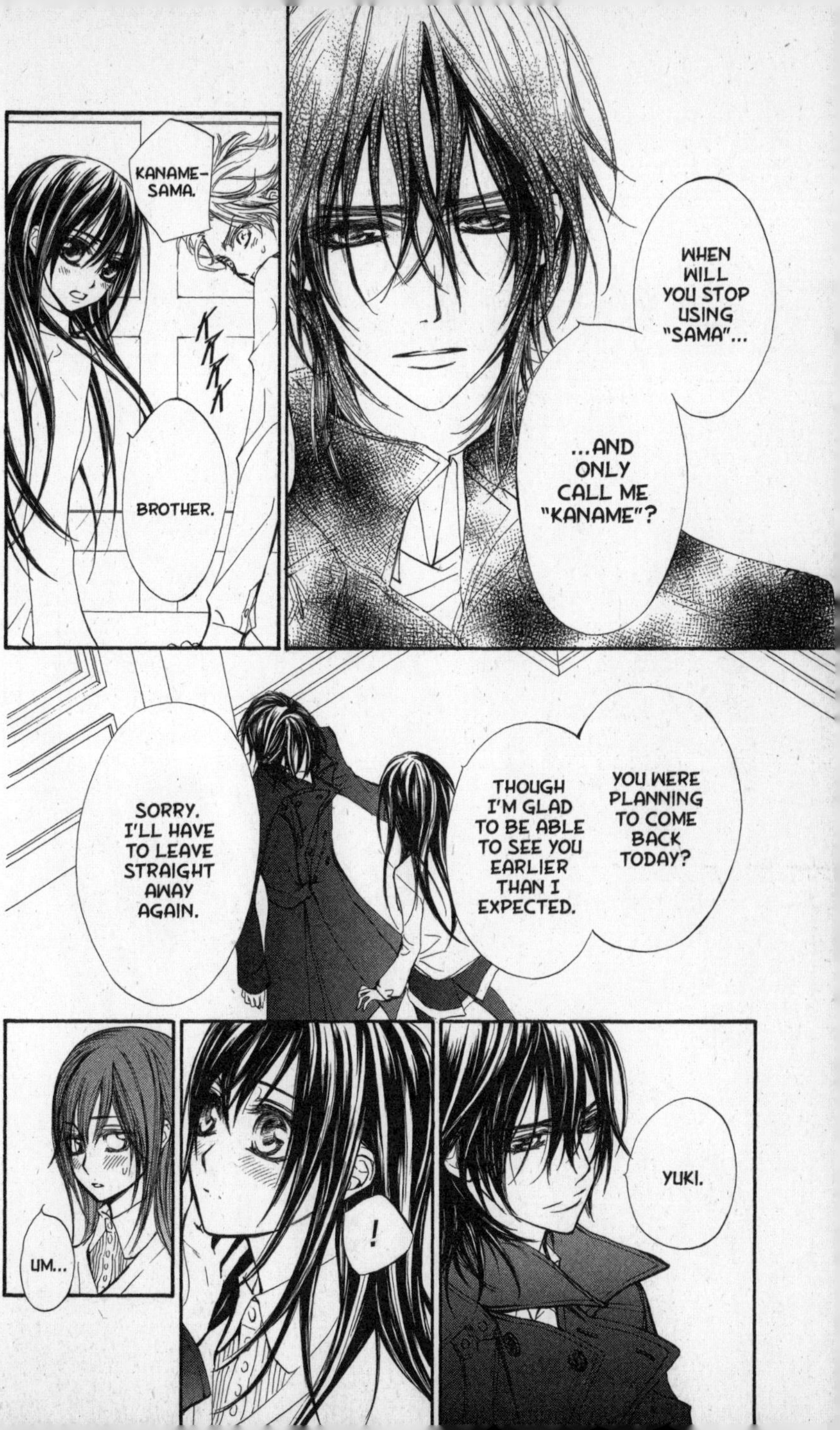
WHEN WILL YOU STOP USING "SAMA"...
...AND ONLY CALL ME "KANAME"?
KANAME-SAMA.
BROTHER.
YOU WERE PLANNING TO COME BACK TODAY?
THOUGH I'M GLAD TO BE ABLE TO SEE YOU EARLIER THAN I EXPECTED.
SORRY. I'LL HAVE TO LEAVE STRAIGHT AWAY AGAIN.
YUKI.
!
UM...

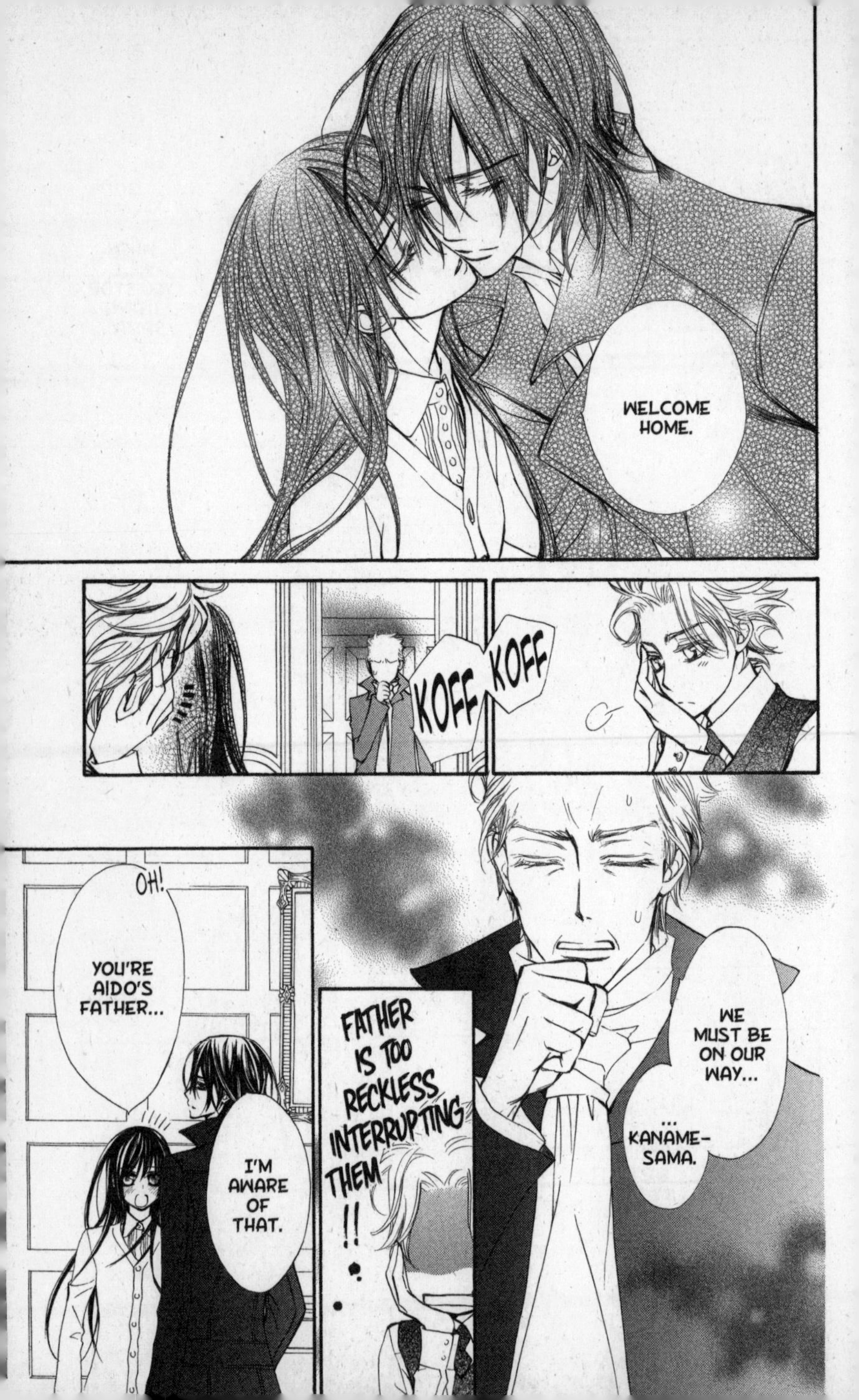
WELCOME HOME.
KOFF KOFF
OH!
YOU'RE AIDO'S FATHER...
WE MUST BE ON OUR WAY...
... KANAME-SAMA.
FATHER IS TOO RECKLESS INTERRUPTING THEM!!
I'M AWARE OF THAT.

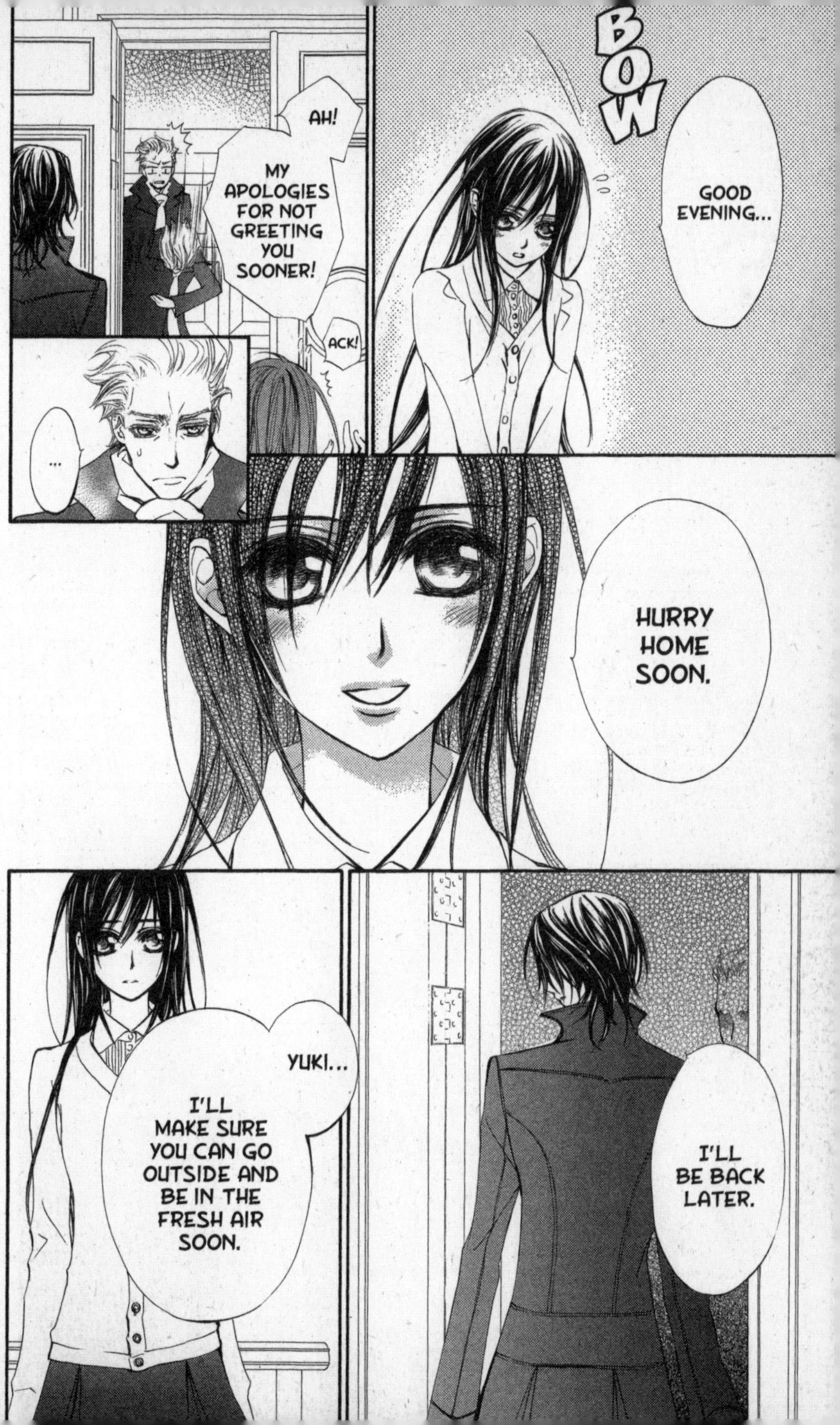
BOW
GOOD EVENING...
AH!
MY APOLOGIES FOR NOT GREETING YOU SOONER!
ACK!
...
HURRY HOME SOON.
I'LL BE BACK LATER.
YUKI...
I'LL MAKE SURE YOU CAN GO OUTSIDE AND BE IN THE FRESH AIR SOON.

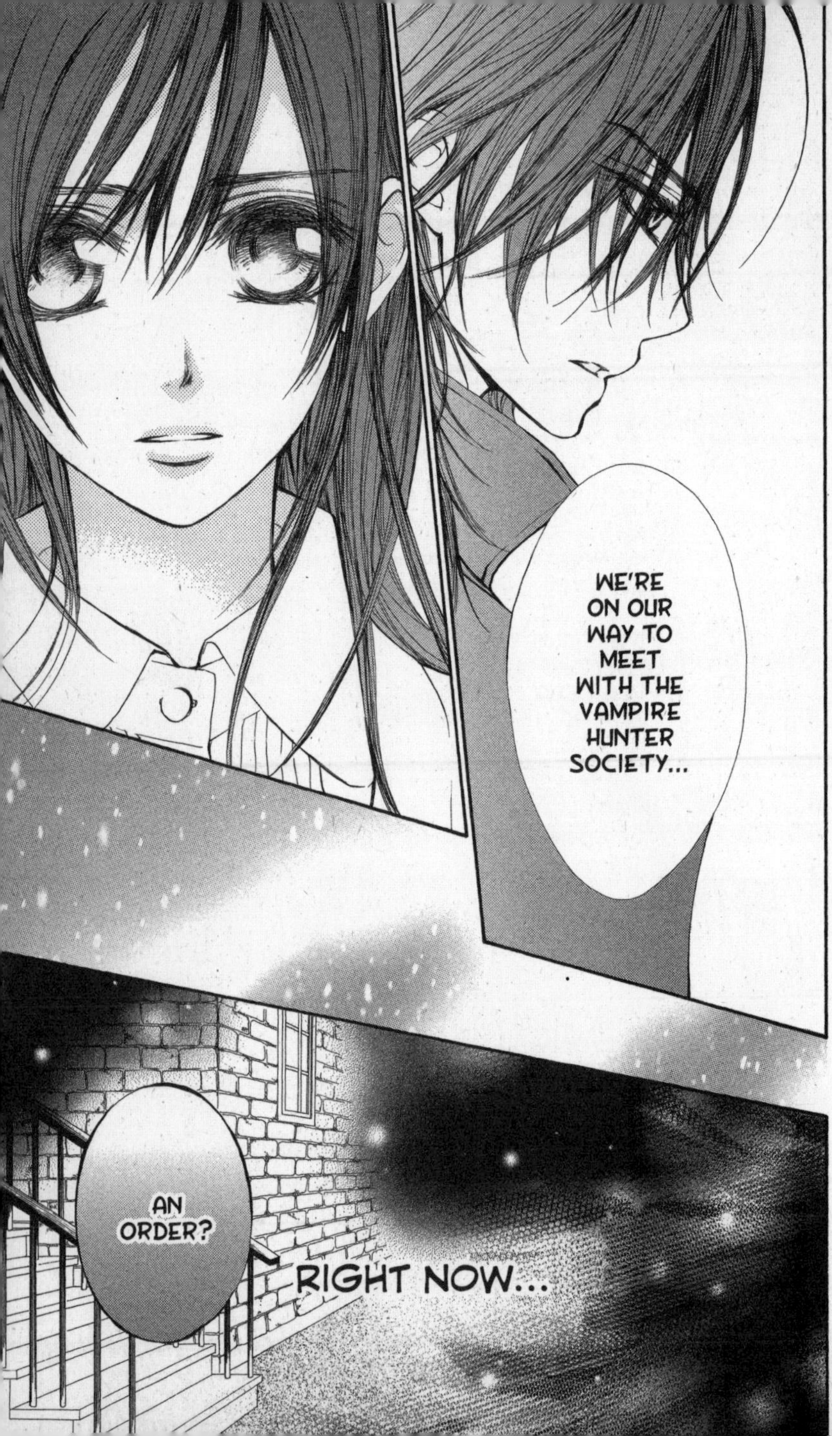
WE'RE ON OUR WAY TO MEET WITH THE VAMPIRE HUNTER SOCIETY...
RIGHT NOW...
AN ORDER?

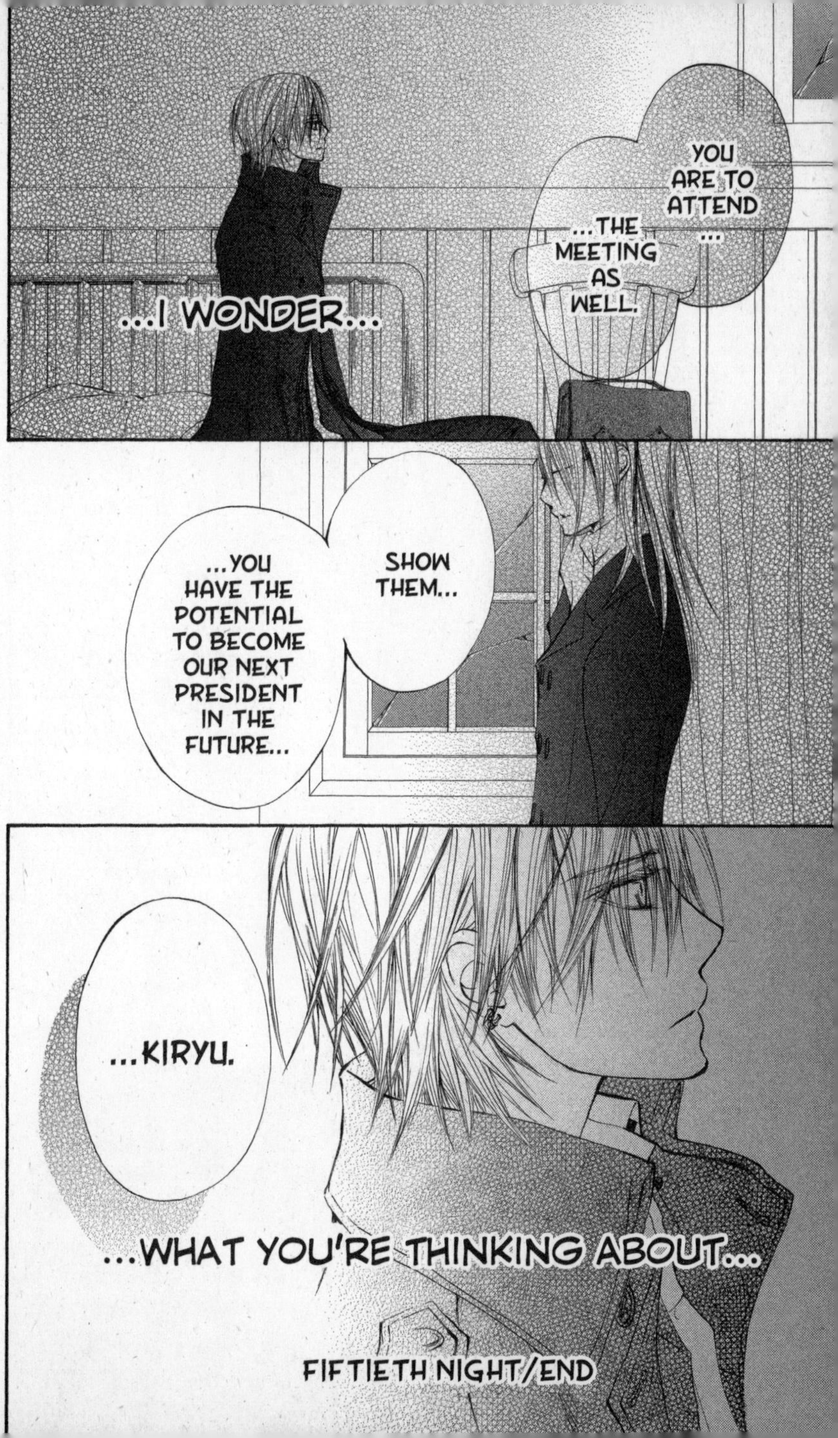
YOU ARE TO ATTEND...
...THE MEETING AS WELL.
...I WONDER...
SHOW THEM...
...YOU HAVE THE POTENTIAL TO BECOME OUR NEXT PRESIDENT IN THE FUTURE...
...KIRYU.
...WHAT YOU'RE THINKING ABOUT...
FIFTIETH NIGHT/END

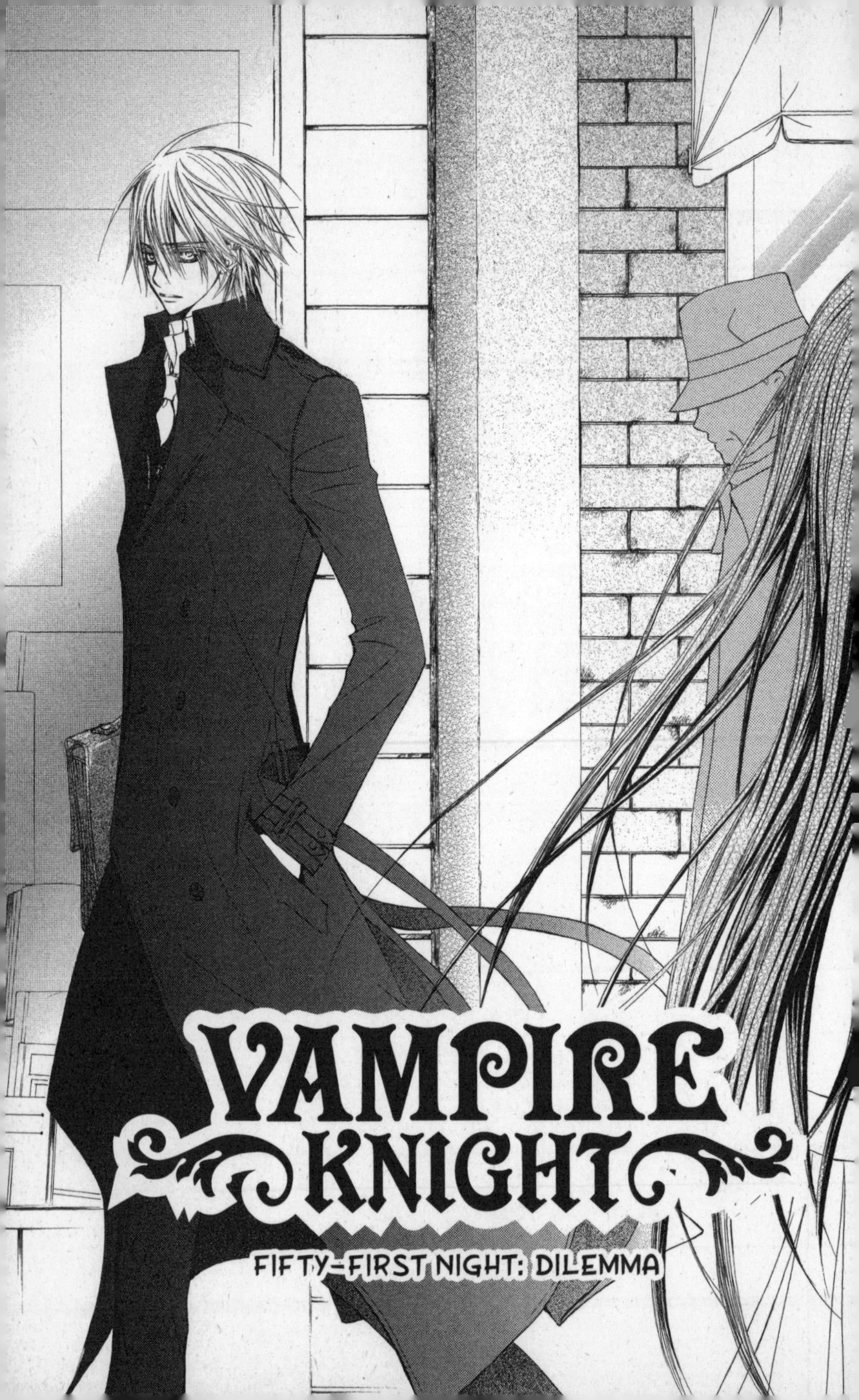
VAMPIRE KNIGHT
FIFTY-FIRST NIGHT: DILEMMA

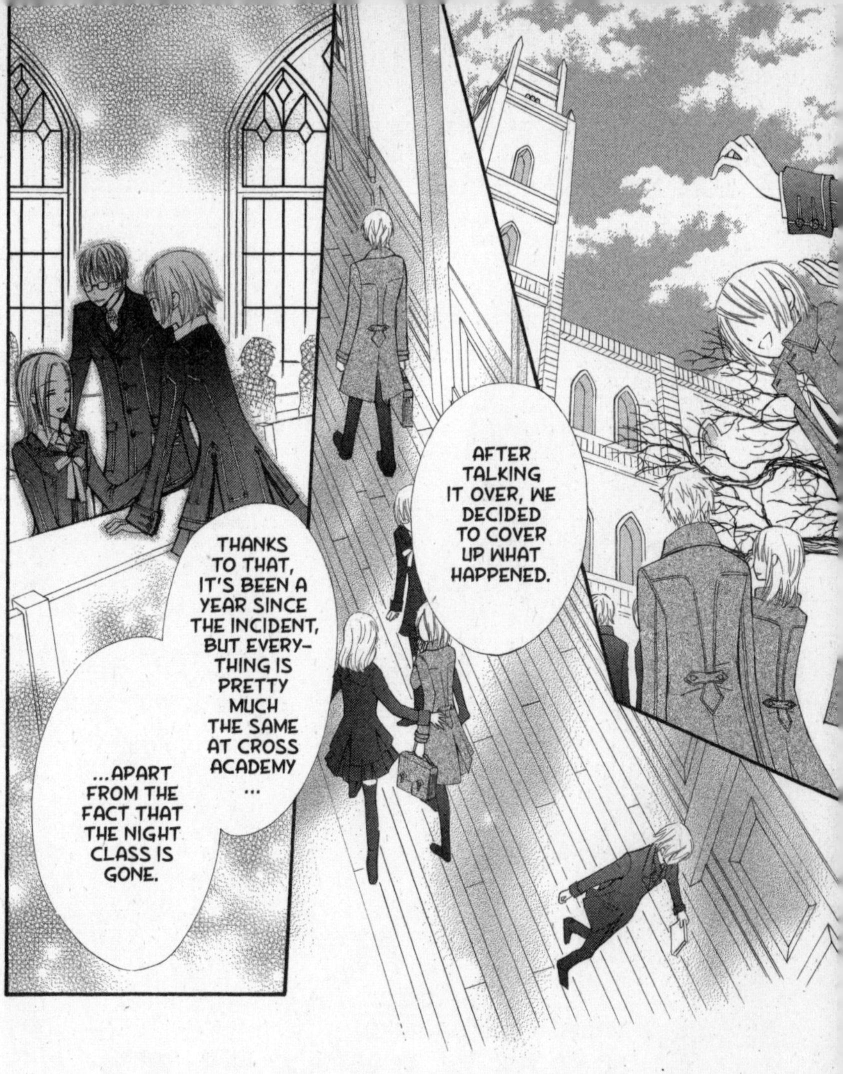
AFTER TALKING IT OVER, WE DECIDED TO COVER UP WHAT HAPPENED.
THANKS TO THAT, IT'S BEEN A YEAR SINCE THE INCIDENT, BUT EVERY-THING IS PRETTY MUCH THE SAME AT CROSS ACADEMY ...
...APART FROM THE FACT THAT THE NIGHT CLASS IS GONE.

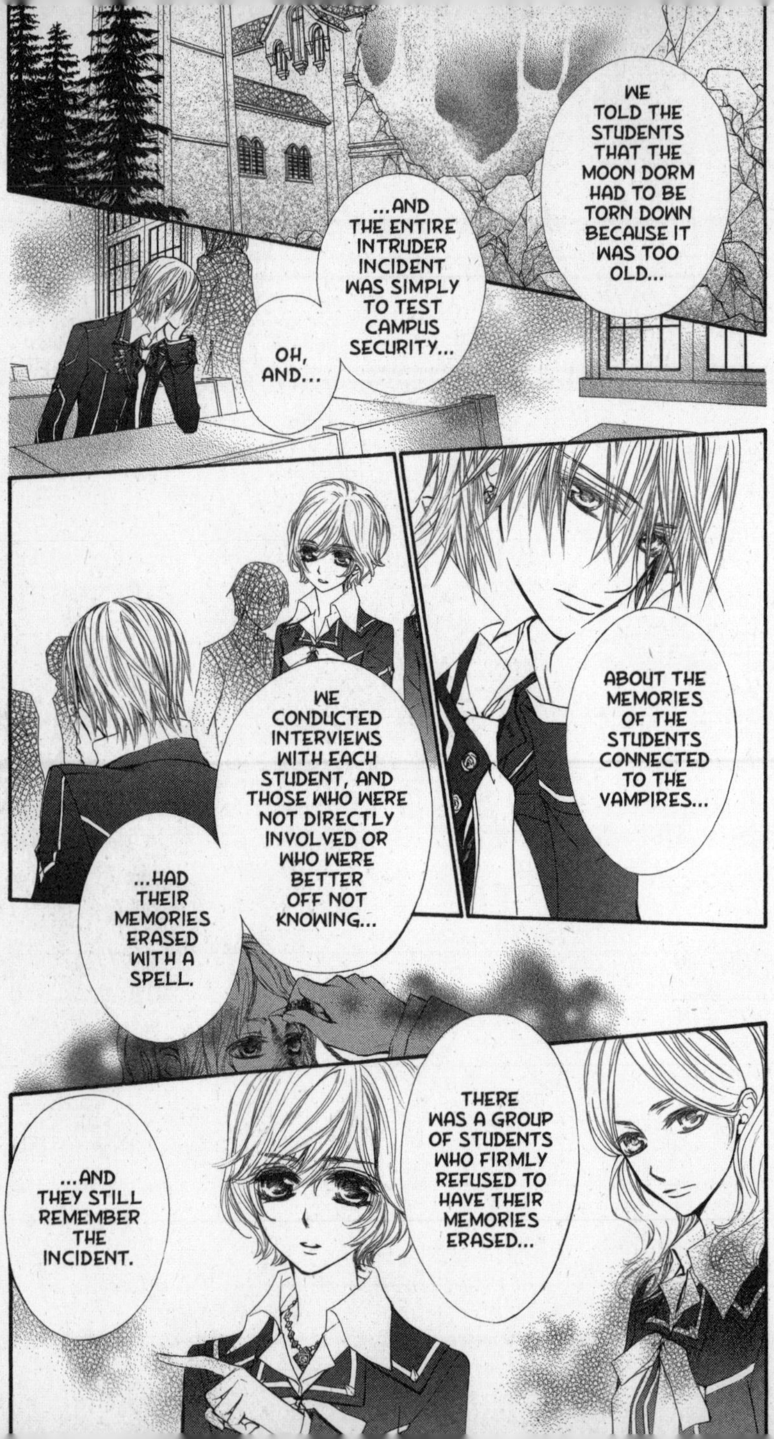
WE TOLD THE STUDENTS THAT THE MOON DORM HAD TO BE TORN DOWN BECAUSE IT WAS TOO OLD...
OH, AND...
...AND THE ENTIRE INTRUDER INCIDENT WAS SIMPLY TO TEST CAMPUS SECURITY...
ABOUT THE MEMORIES OF THE STUDENTS CONNECTED TO THE VAMPIRES...
WE CONDUCTED INTERVIEWS WITH EACH STUDENT, AND THOSE WHO WERE NOT DIRECTLY INVOLVED OR WHO WERE BETTER OFF NOT KNOWING...
...HAD THEIR MEMORIES ERASED WITH A SPELL.
THERE WAS A GROUP OF STUDENTS WHO FIRMLY REFUSED TO HAVE THEIR MEMORIES ERASED...
...AND THEY STILL REMEMBER THE INCIDENT.

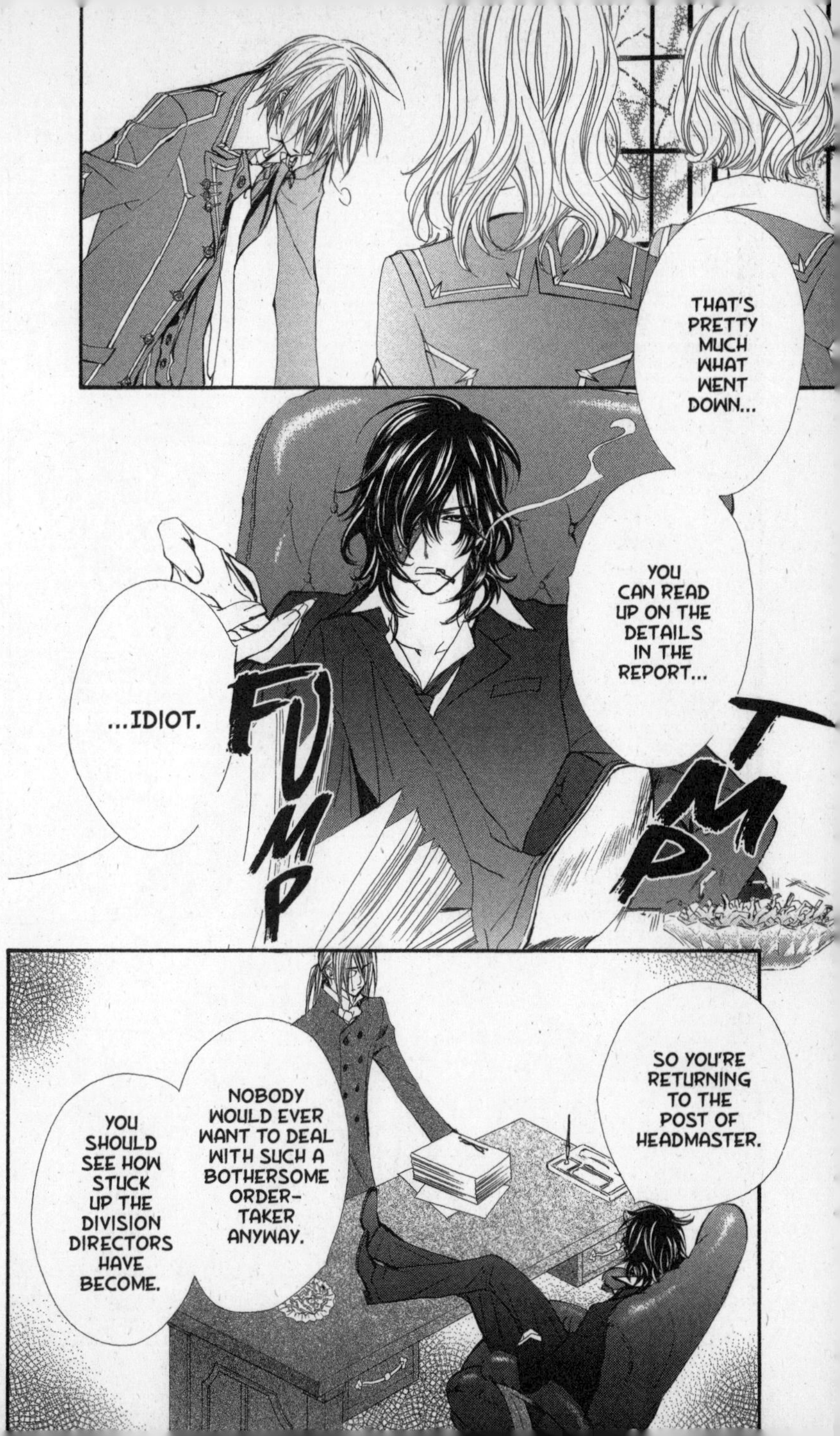
THAT'S PRETTY MUCH WHAT WENT DOWN...
YOU CAN READ UP ON THE DETAILS IN THE REPORT...
TMP
FUMP
...IDIOT.
SO YOU'RE RETURNING TO THE POST OF HEADMASTER.
NOBODY WOULD EVER WANT TO DEAL WITH SUCH A BOTHERSOME ORDER-TAKER ANYWAY.
YOU SHOULD SEE HOW STUCK UP THE DIVISION DIRECTORS HAVE BECOME.

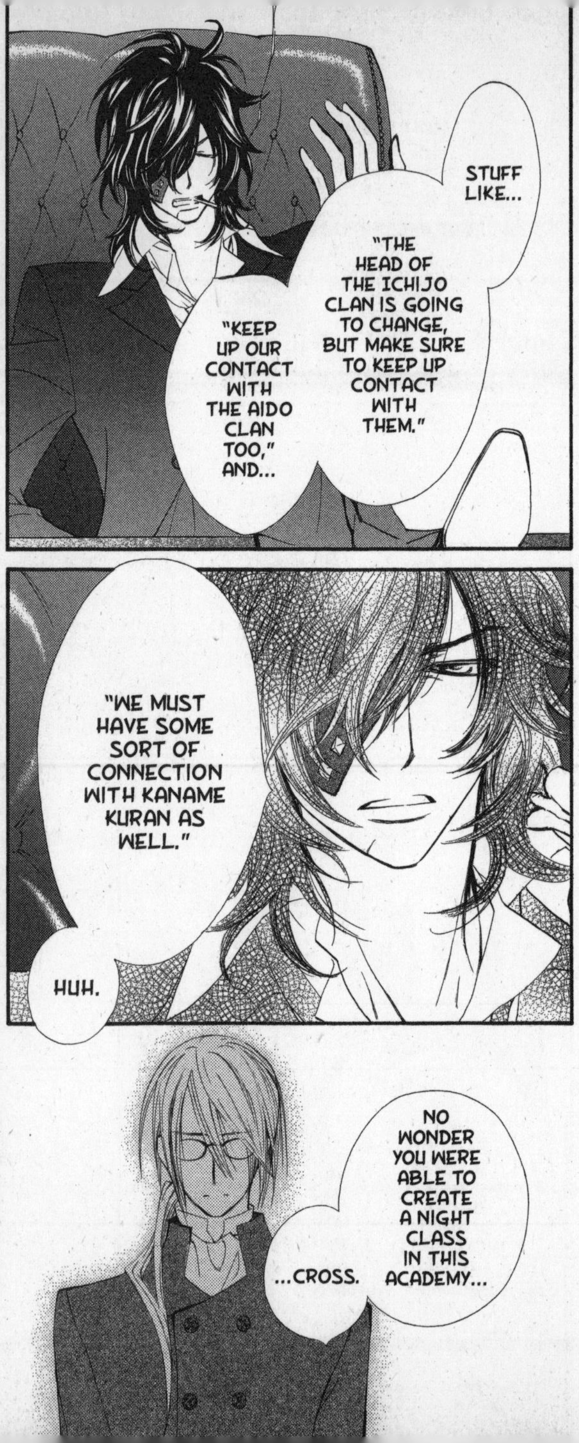
STUFF LIKE...
"THE HEAD OF THE ICHIJO CLAN IS GOING TO CHANGE, BUT MAKE SURE TO KEEP UP CONTACT WITH THEM."
"KEEP UP OUR CONTACT WITH THE AIDO CLAN TOO," AND...
"WE MUST HAVE SOME SORT OF CONNECTION WITH KANAME KURAN AS WELL."
HUH.
NO WONDER YOU WERE ABLE TO CREATE A NIGHT CLASS IN THIS ACADEMY...
...CROSS.

III

(→continued)

...lose my sense of being in a foreign country.♪ But one thing that really helped me was Kanon Wakeshima's album. I had my iPod and portable speakers in my room all the time. I listened to Wakeshima's "Shinshoku Dolce" endlessly. Interestingly, her song would naturally fade away into the atmosphere of Leipzig, helping me keep the fun image of "I'm in Germany right now!" while I tried to do something about my swollen eyes.♡ Carlsen Comics, the German publisher, gave me a very warm surprise welcome with flowers and a small cake with chocolates that had the faces of my characters printed on them. It made me feel happy every time I saw it!!

I held an autograph session (and other things too) on a large stage set inside the huge book fair at Leipzig. It was like a festival from start to finish, and I cannot explain in words how fun it was. Thank you very much!! Also, I...

(→ continues)

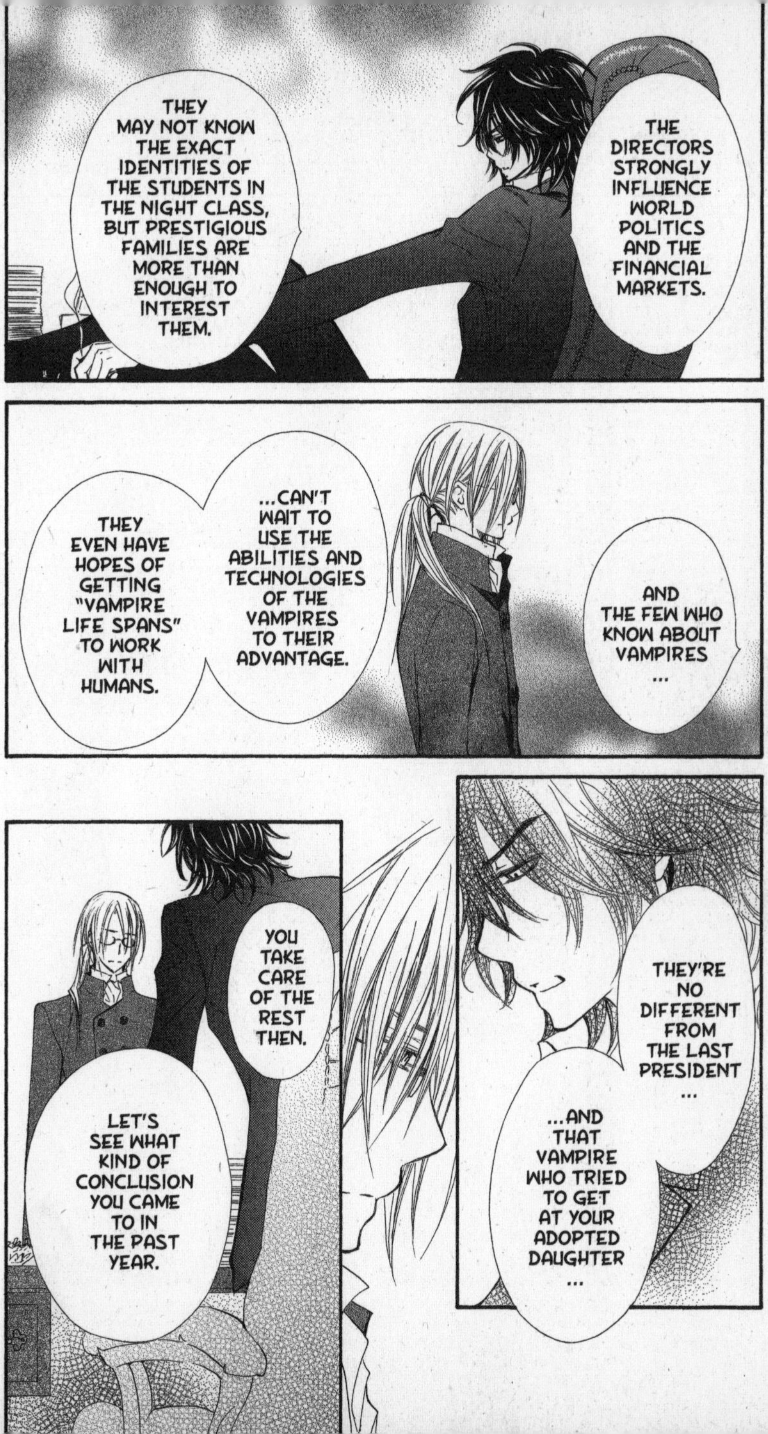
THE DIRECTORS STRONGLY INFLUENCE WORLD POLITICS AND THE FINANCIAL MARKETS.
THEY MAY NOT KNOW THE EXACT IDENTITIES OF THE STUDENTS IN THE NIGHT CLASS, BUT PRESTIGIOUS FAMILIES ARE MORE THAN ENOUGH TO INTEREST THEM.
AND THE FEW WHO KNOW ABOUT VAMPIRES ...
...CAN'T WAIT TO USE THE ABILITIES AND TECHNOLOGIES OF THE VAMPIRES TO THEIR ADVANTAGE.
THEY EVEN HAVE HOPES OF GETTING "VAMPIRE LIFE SPANS" TO WORK WITH HUMANS.
THEY'RE NO DIFFERENT FROM THE LAST PRESIDENT ...
...AND THAT VAMPIRE WHO TRIED TO GET AT YOUR ADOPTED DAUGHTER ...
YOU TAKE CARE OF THE REST THEN.
LET'S SEE WHAT KIND OF CONCLUSION YOU CAME TO IN THE PAST YEAR.

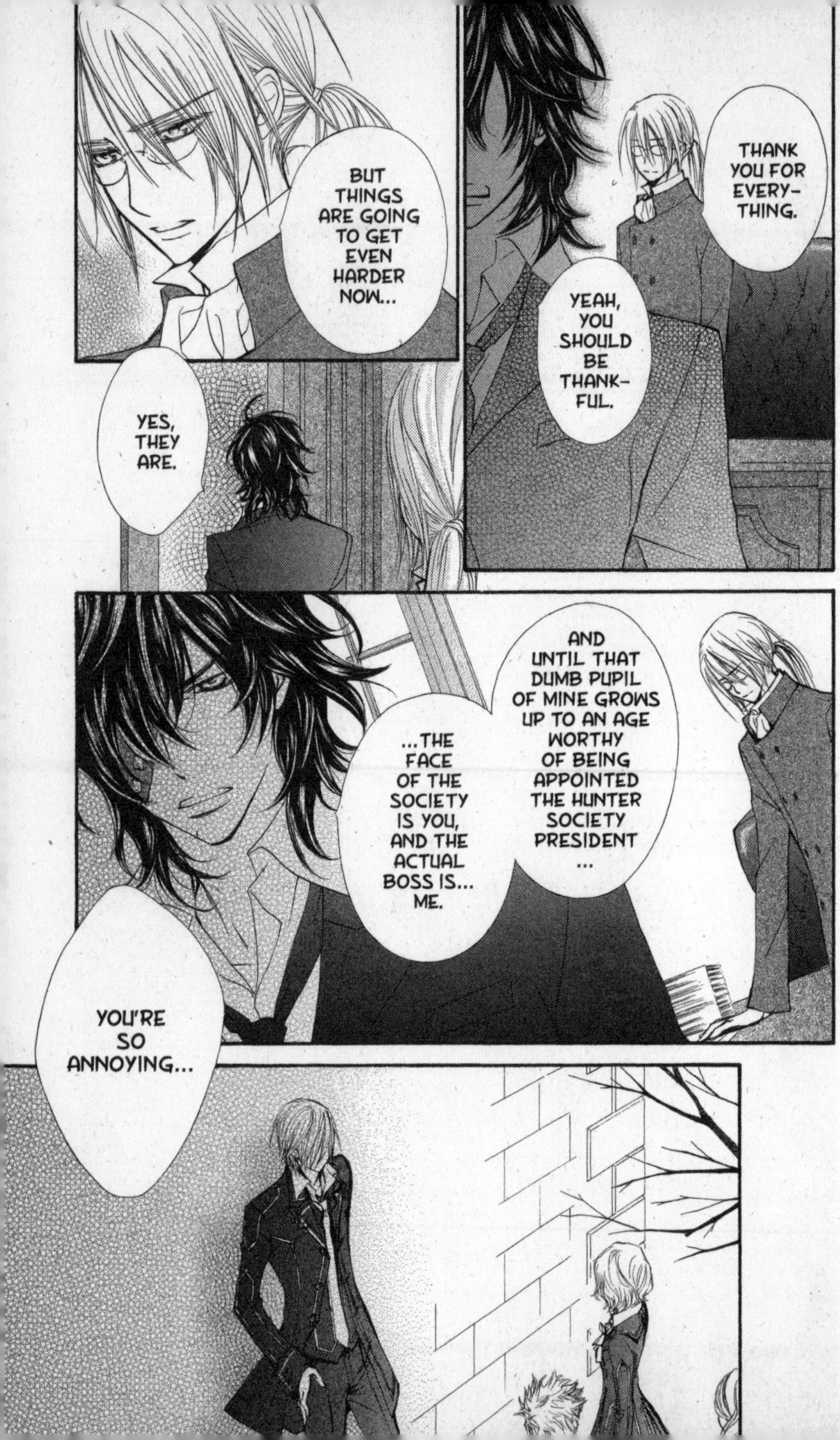
THANK YOU FOR EVERY-THING.
YEAH, YOU SHOULD BE THANK-FUL.
BUT THINGS ARE GOING TO GET EVEN HARDER NOW...
YES, THEY ARE.
AND UNTIL THAT DUMB PUPIL OF MINE GROWS UP TO AN AGE WORTHY OF BEING APPOINTED THE HUNTER SOCIETY PRESIDENT ...
...THE FACE OF THE SOCIETY IS YOU, AND THE ACTUAL BOSS IS... ME.
YOU'RE SO ANNOYING...

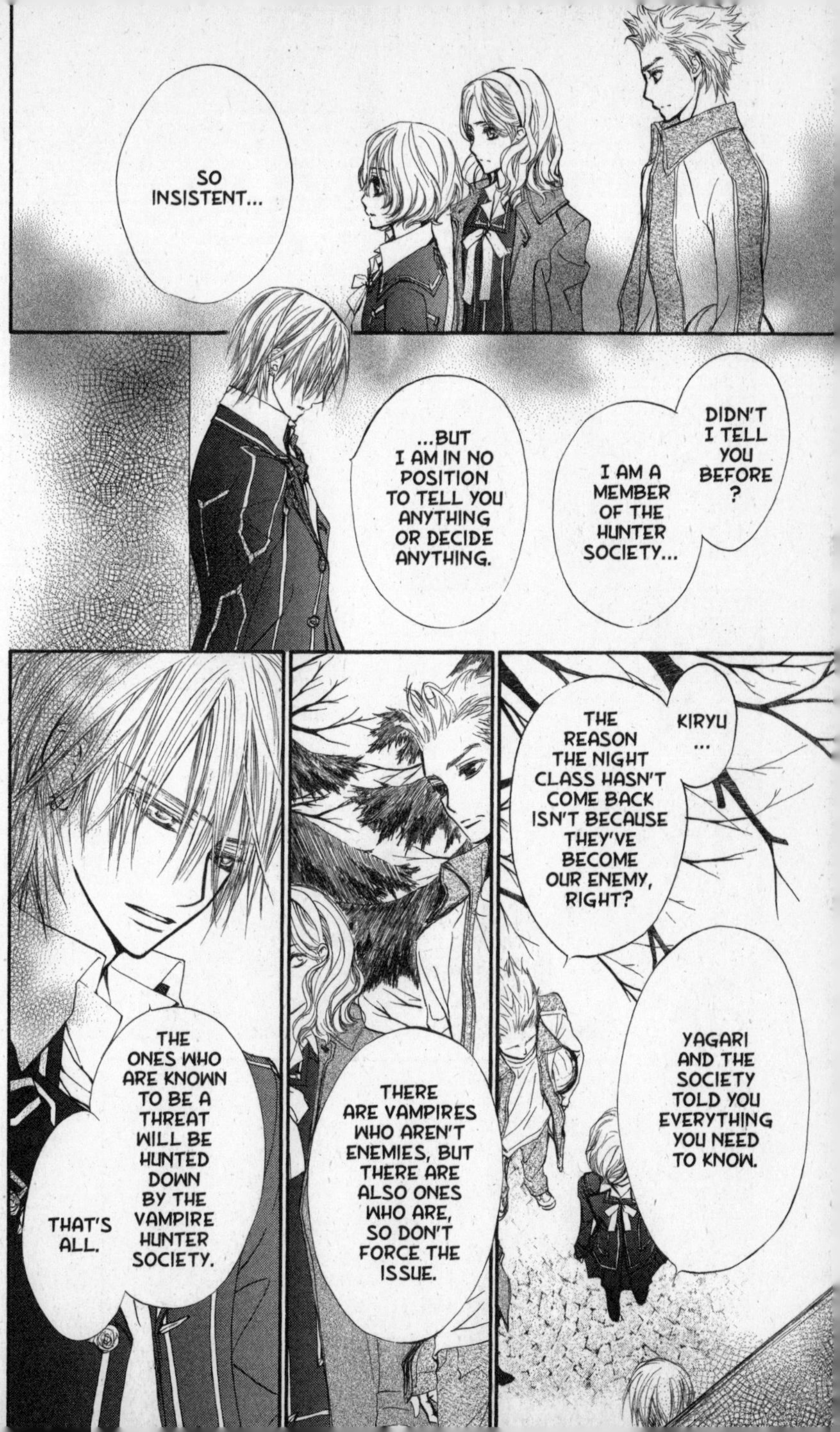
SO INSISTENT...
DIDN'T I TELL YOU BEFORE?
I AM A MEMBER OF THE HUNTER SOCIETY...
...BUT I AM IN NO POSITION TO TELL YOU ANYTHING OR DECIDE ANYTHING.
KIRYU...
THE REASON THE NIGHT CLASS HASN'T COME BACK ISN'T BECAUSE THEY'VE BECOME OUR ENEMY, RIGHT?
YAGARI AND THE SOCIETY TOLD YOU EVERYTHING YOU NEED TO KNOW.
THERE ARE VAMPIRES WHO AREN'T ENEMIES, BUT THERE ARE ALSO ONES WHO ARE, SO DON'T FORCE THE ISSUE.
THE ONES WHO ARE KNOWN TO BE A THREAT WILL BE HUNTED DOWN BY THE VAMPIRE HUNTER SOCIETY.
THAT'S ALL.

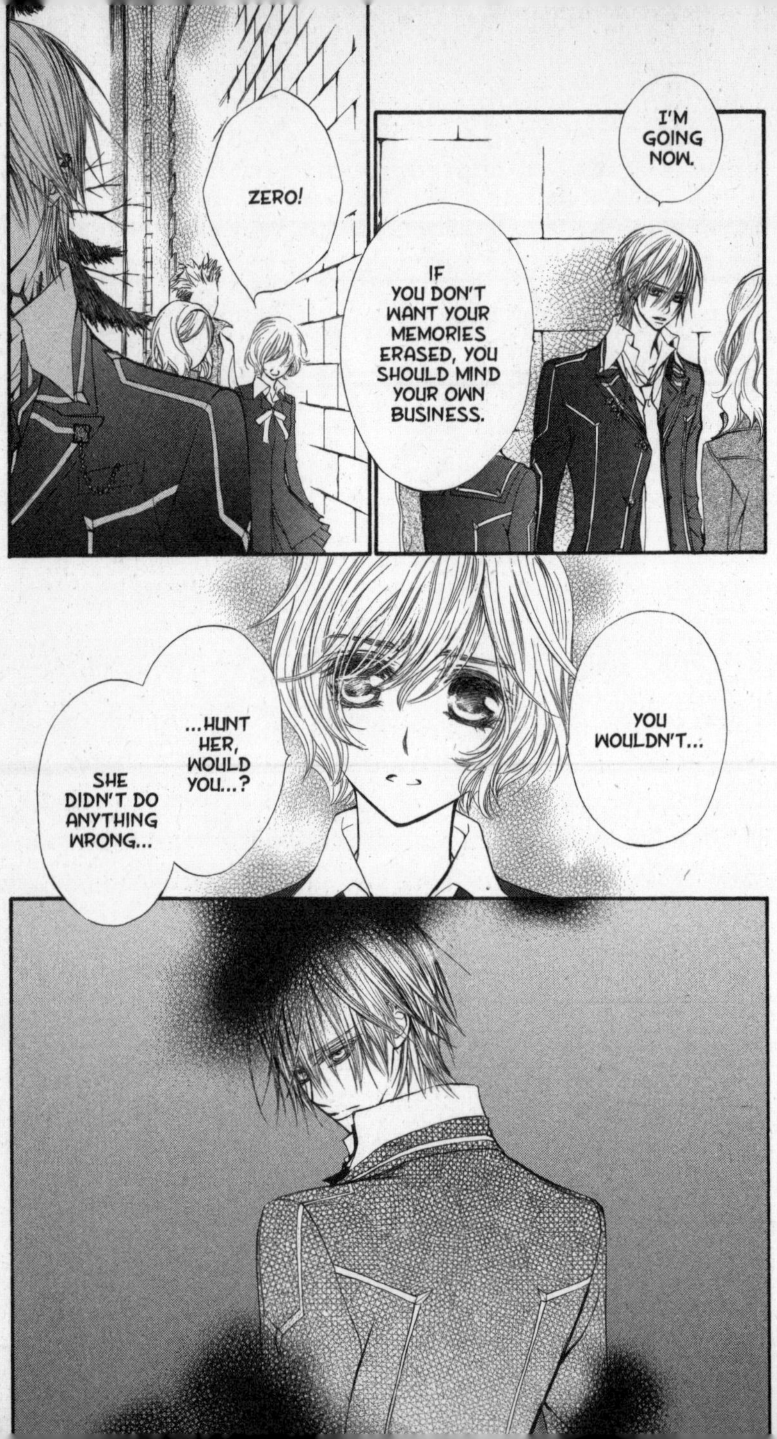
I'M GOING NOW.
IF YOU DON'T WANT YOUR MEMORIES ERASED, YOU SHOULD MIND YOUR OWN BUSINESS.
ZERO!
YOU WOULDN'T...
...HUNT HER, WOULD YOU...?
SHE DIDN'T DO ANYTHING WRONG...

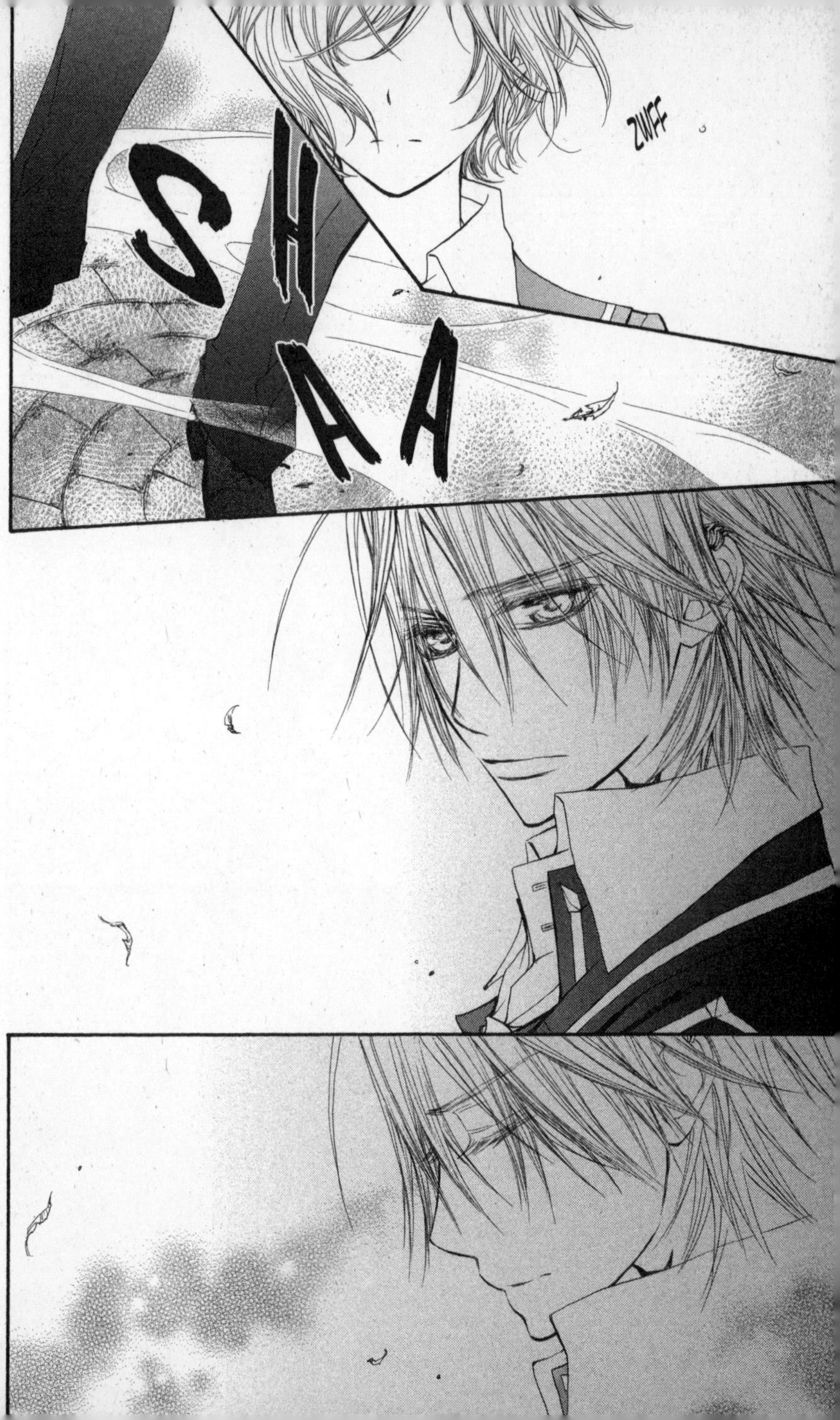
ZWFF
SHAA

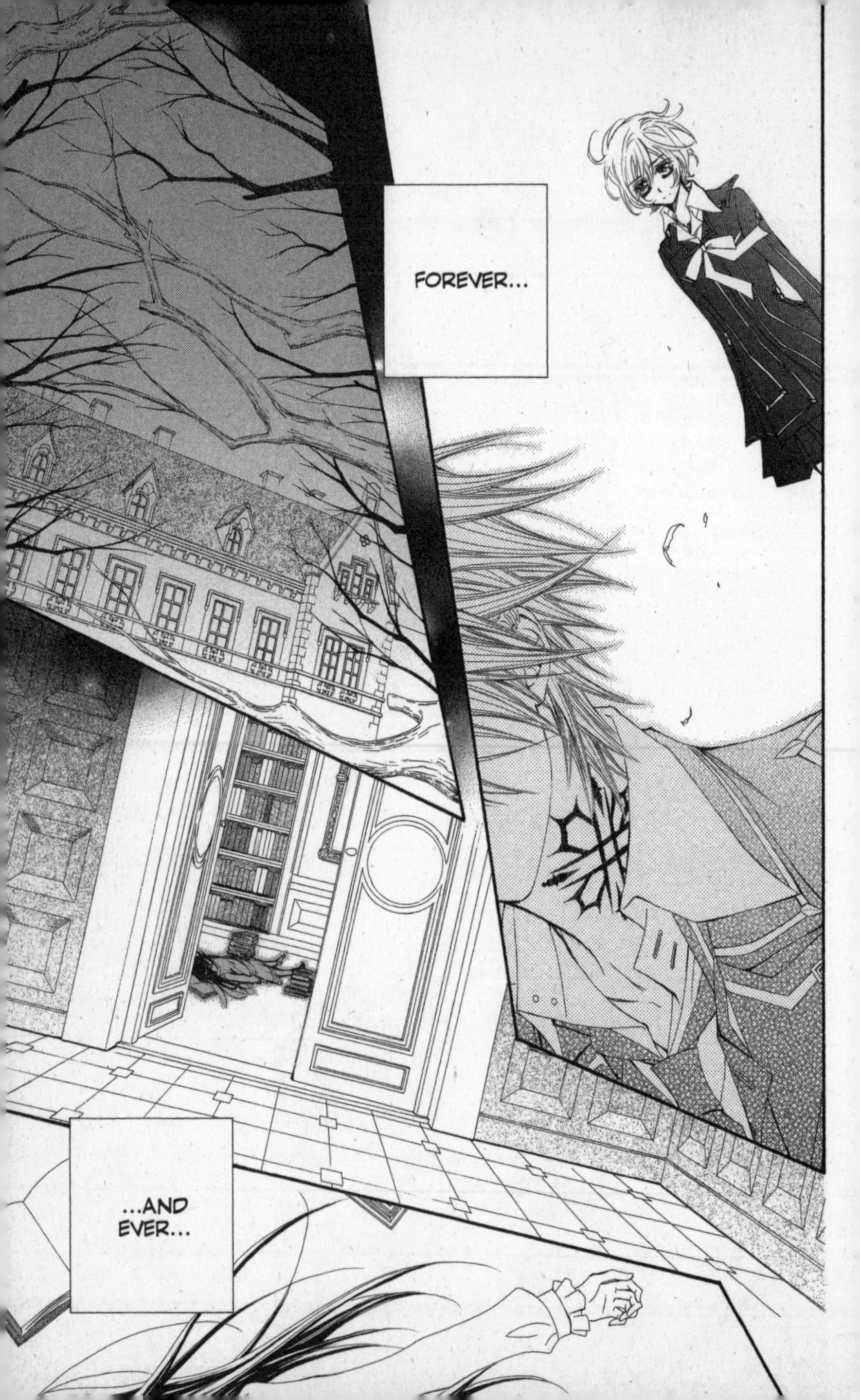
FOREVER...
...AND EVER...

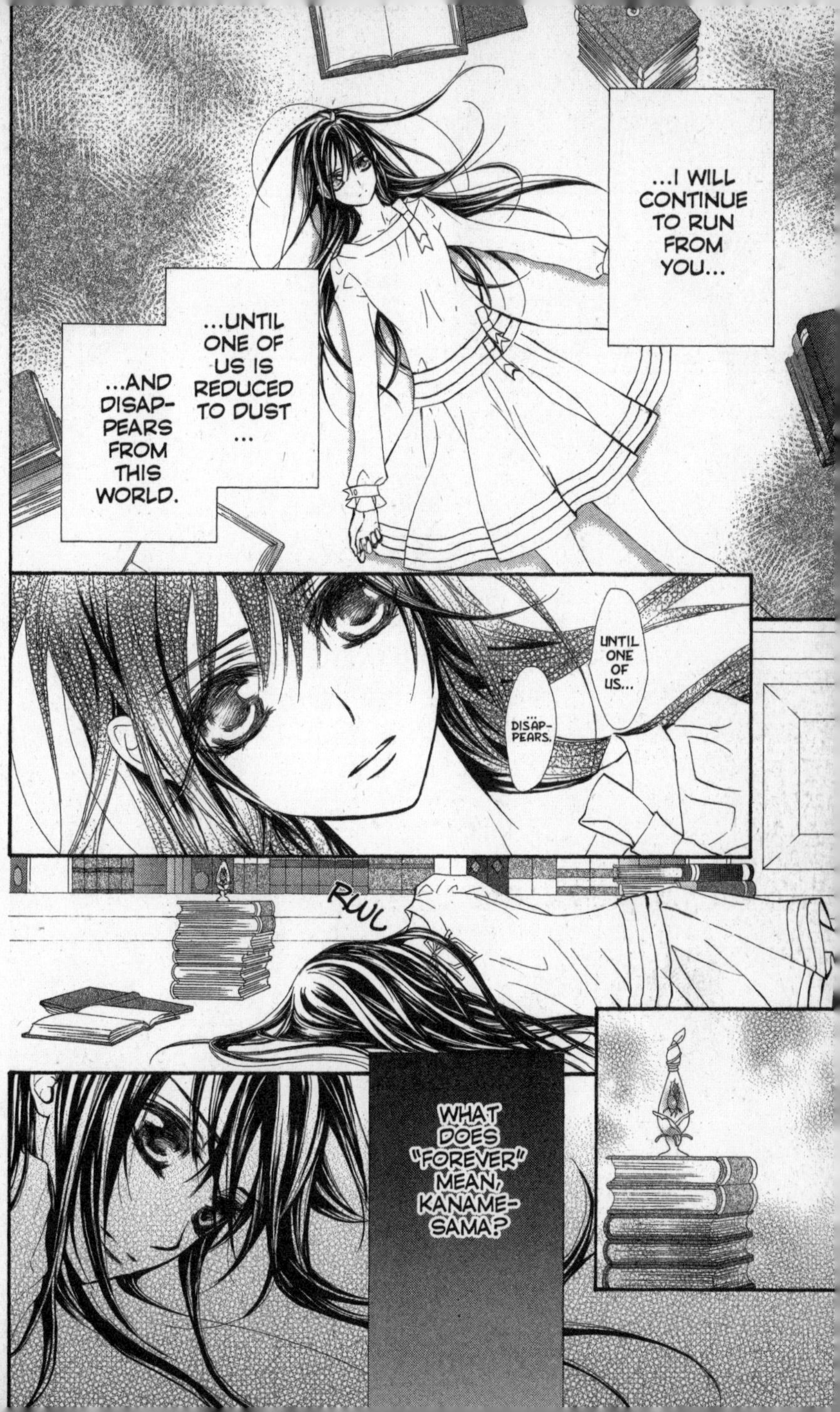
...I WILL CONTINUE TO RUN FROM YOU...
...UNTIL ONE OF US IS REDUCED TO DUST...
...AND DISAPPEARS FROM THIS WORLD.
UNTIL ONE OF US...
...DISAPPEARS.
RUUL
WHAT DOES "FOREVER" MEAN, KANAME-SAMA?

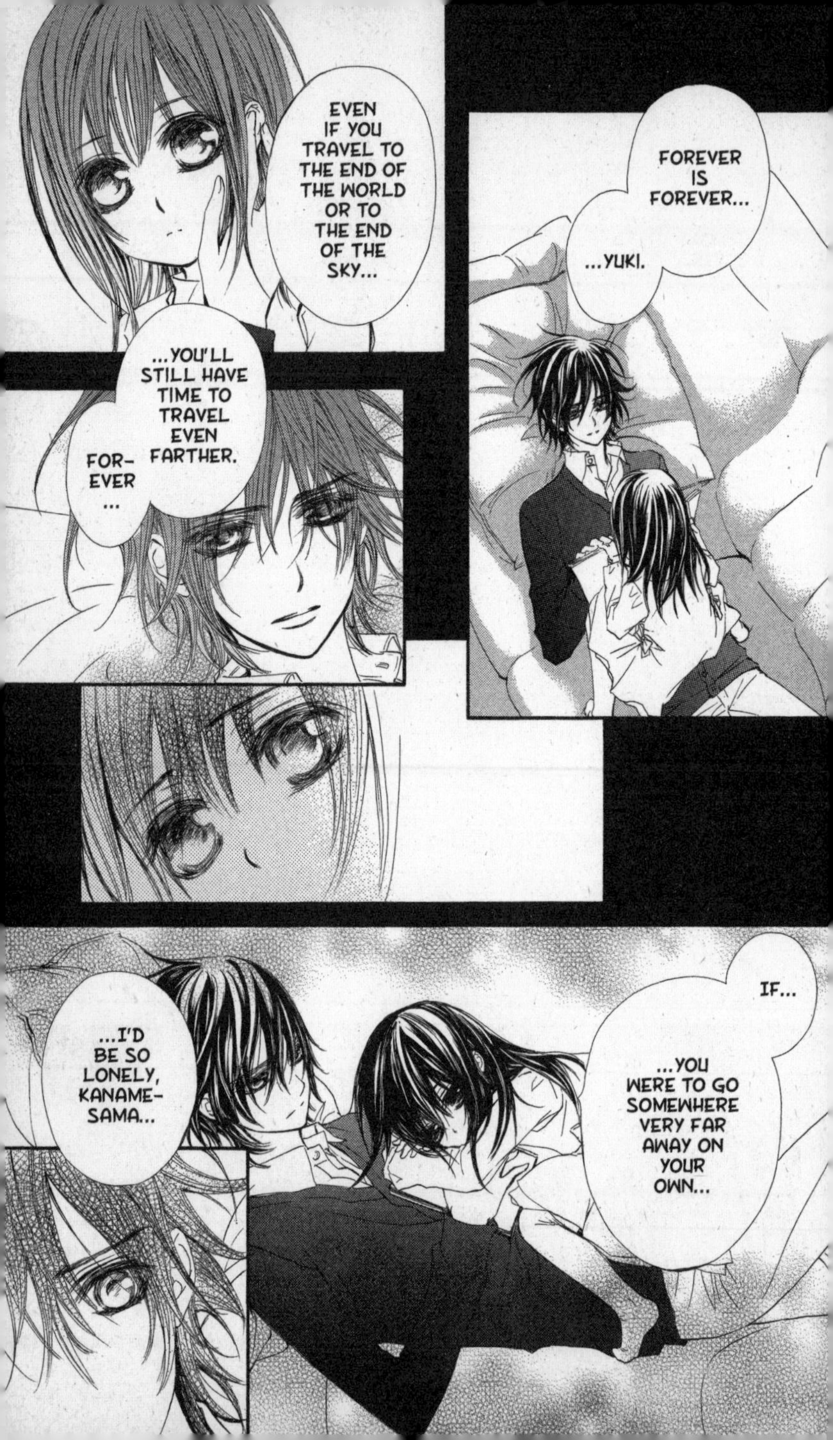
FOREVER IS FOREVER...
...YUKI.
EVEN IF YOU TRAVEL TO THE END OF THE WORLD OR TO THE END OF THE SKY...
...YOU'LL STILL HAVE TIME TO TRAVEL EVEN FARTHER.
FOR-EVER ...
IF...
...YOU WERE TO GO SOMEWHERE VERY FAR AWAY ON YOUR OWN...
...I'D BE SO LONELY, KANAME-SAMA...

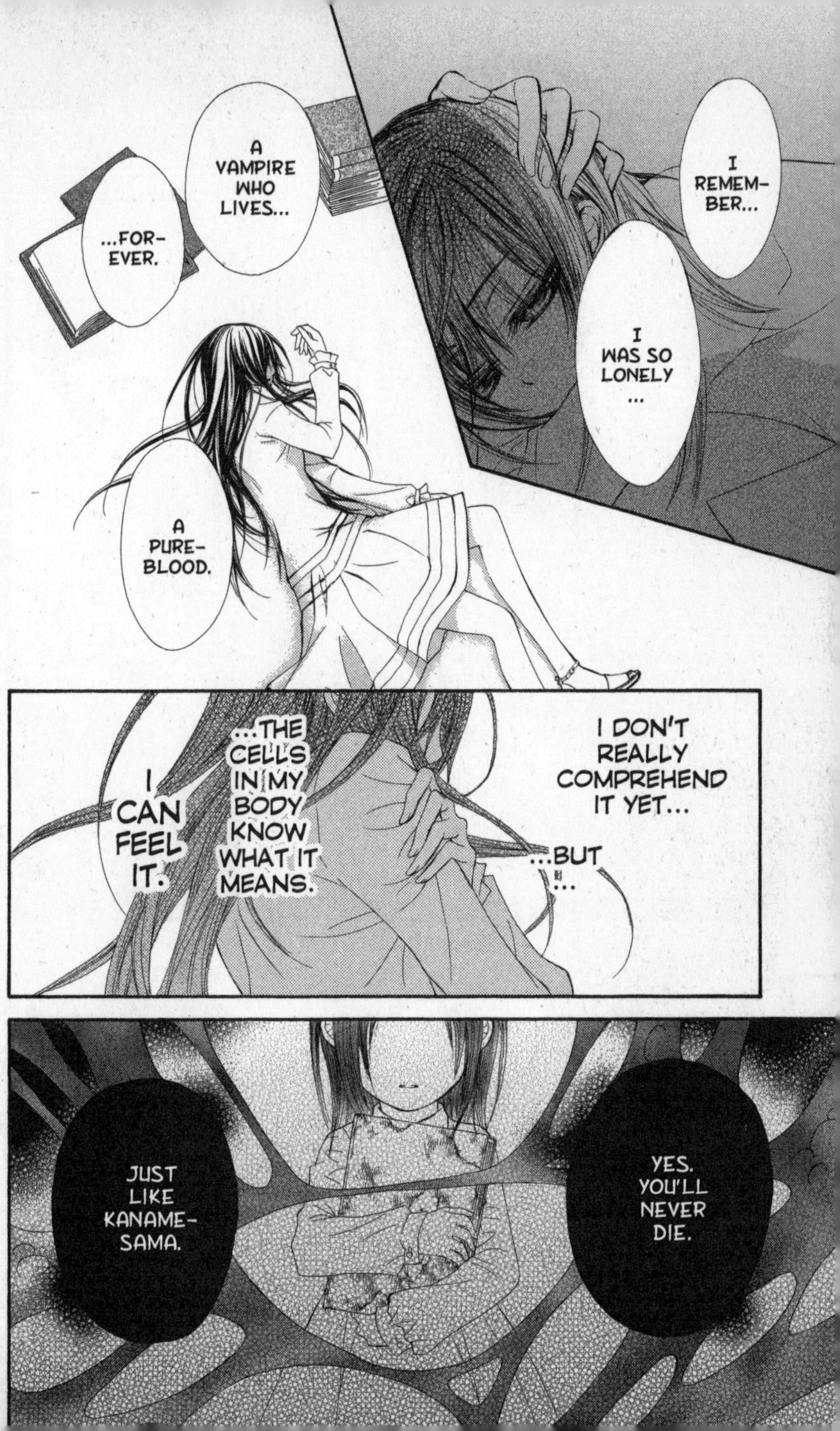
I REMEMBER...
I WAS SO LONELY...
A VAMPIRE WHO LIVES...
...FOREVER.
A PUREBLOOD.
I DON'T REALLY COMPREHEND IT YET...
...BUT...
...THE CELLS IN MY BODY KNOW WHAT IT MEANS.
I CAN FEEL IT.
YES. YOU'LL NEVER DIE.
JUST LIKE KANAME-SAMA.

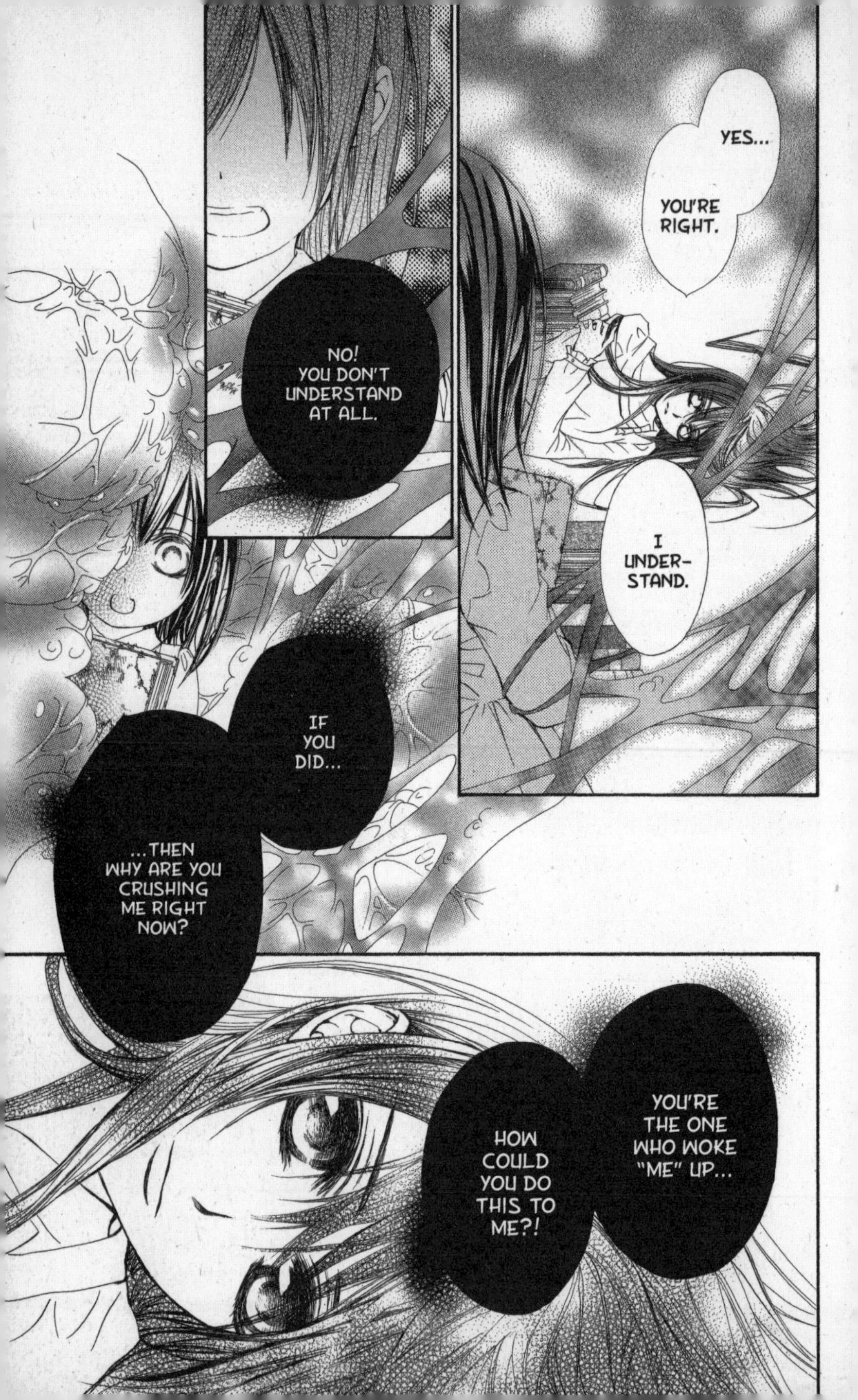
YES...
YOU'RE RIGHT.
I UNDERSTAND.
NO! YOU DON'T UNDERSTAND AT ALL.
IF YOU DID...
...THEN WHY ARE YOU CRUSHING ME RIGHT NOW?
YOU'RE THE ONE WHO WOKE "ME" UP...
HOW COULD YOU DO THIS TO ME?!

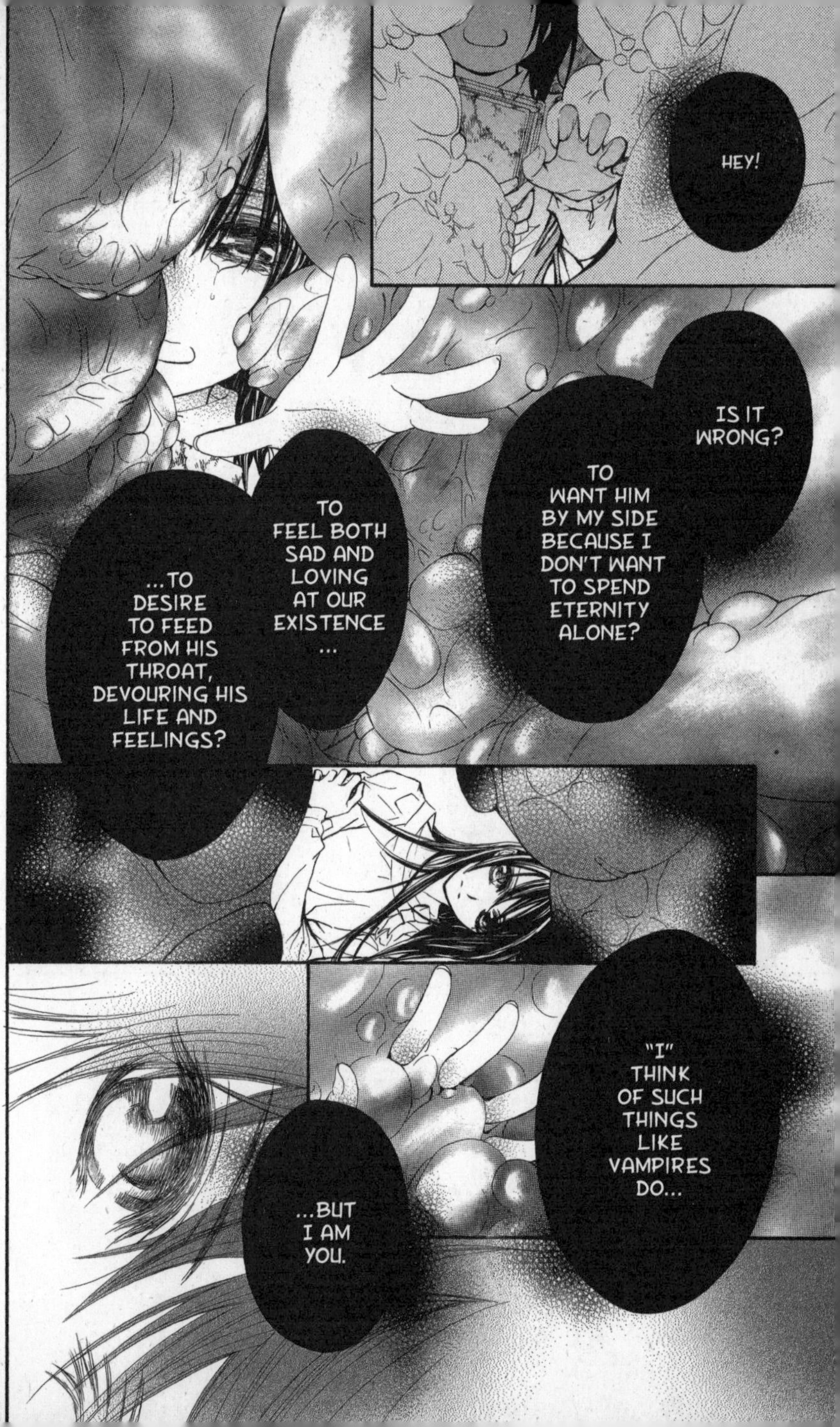
HEY!
IS IT WRONG?
TO WANT HIM BY MY SIDE BECAUSE I DON'T WANT TO SPEND ETERNITY ALONE?
TO FEEL BOTH SAD AND LOVING AT OUR EXISTENCE...
...TO DESIRE TO FEED FROM HIS THROAT, DEVOURING HIS LIFE AND FEELINGS?
"I" THINK OF SUCH THINGS LIKE VAMPIRES DO...
...BUT I AM YOU.

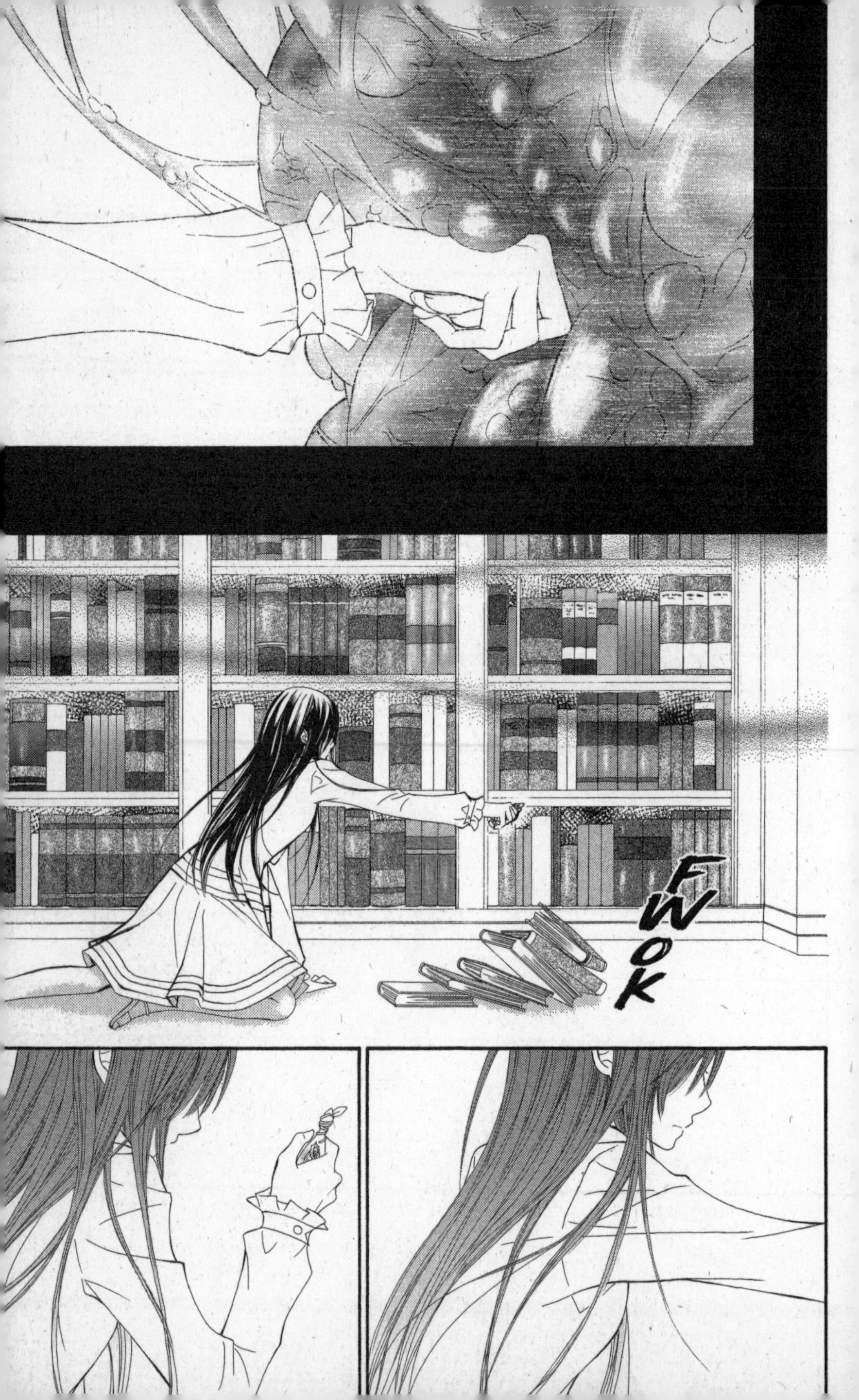
FWOK

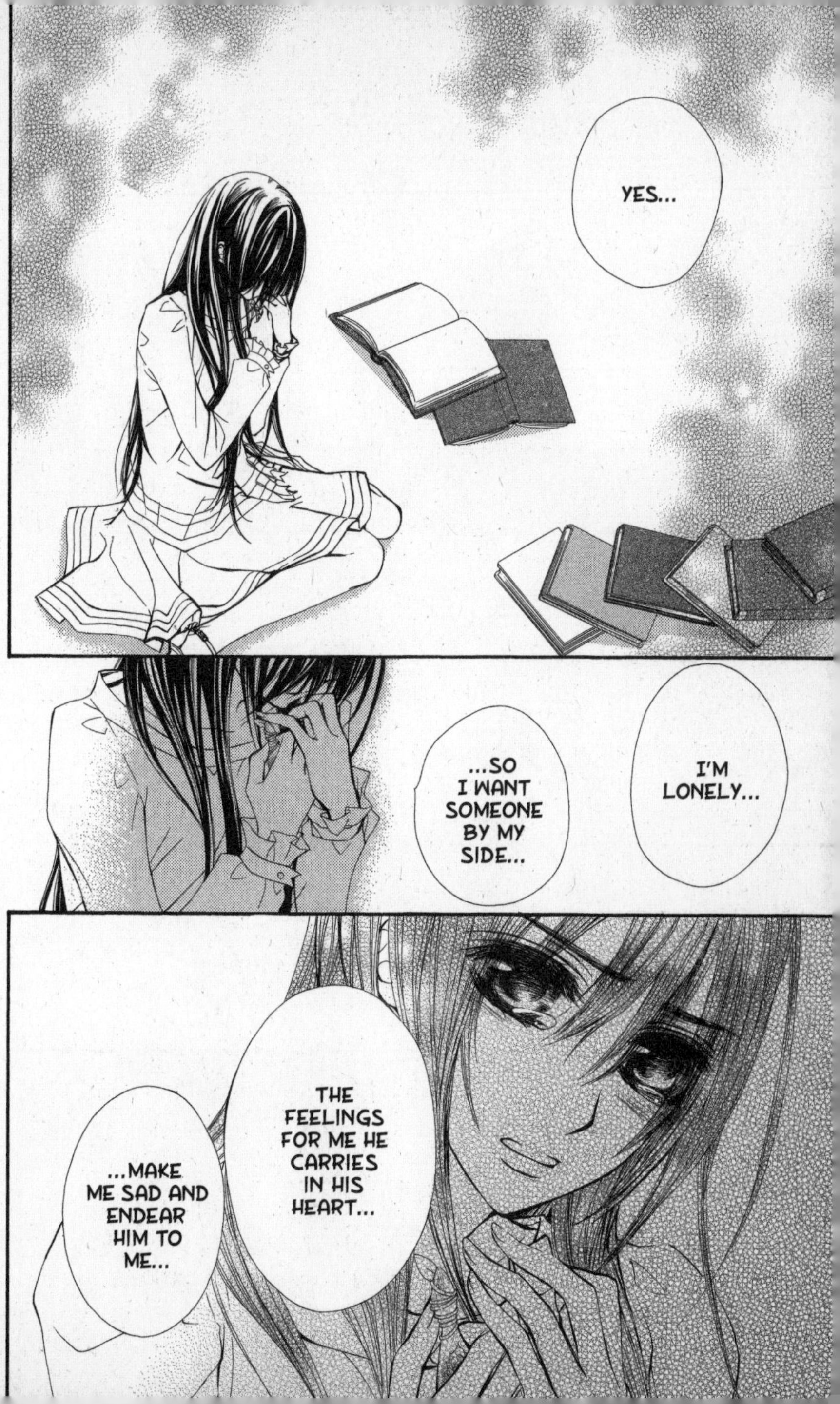
YES...
I'M LONELY...
...SO I WANT SOMEONE BY MY SIDE...
THE FEELINGS FOR ME HE CARRIES IN HIS HEART...
...MAKE ME SAD AND ENDEAR HIM TO ME...

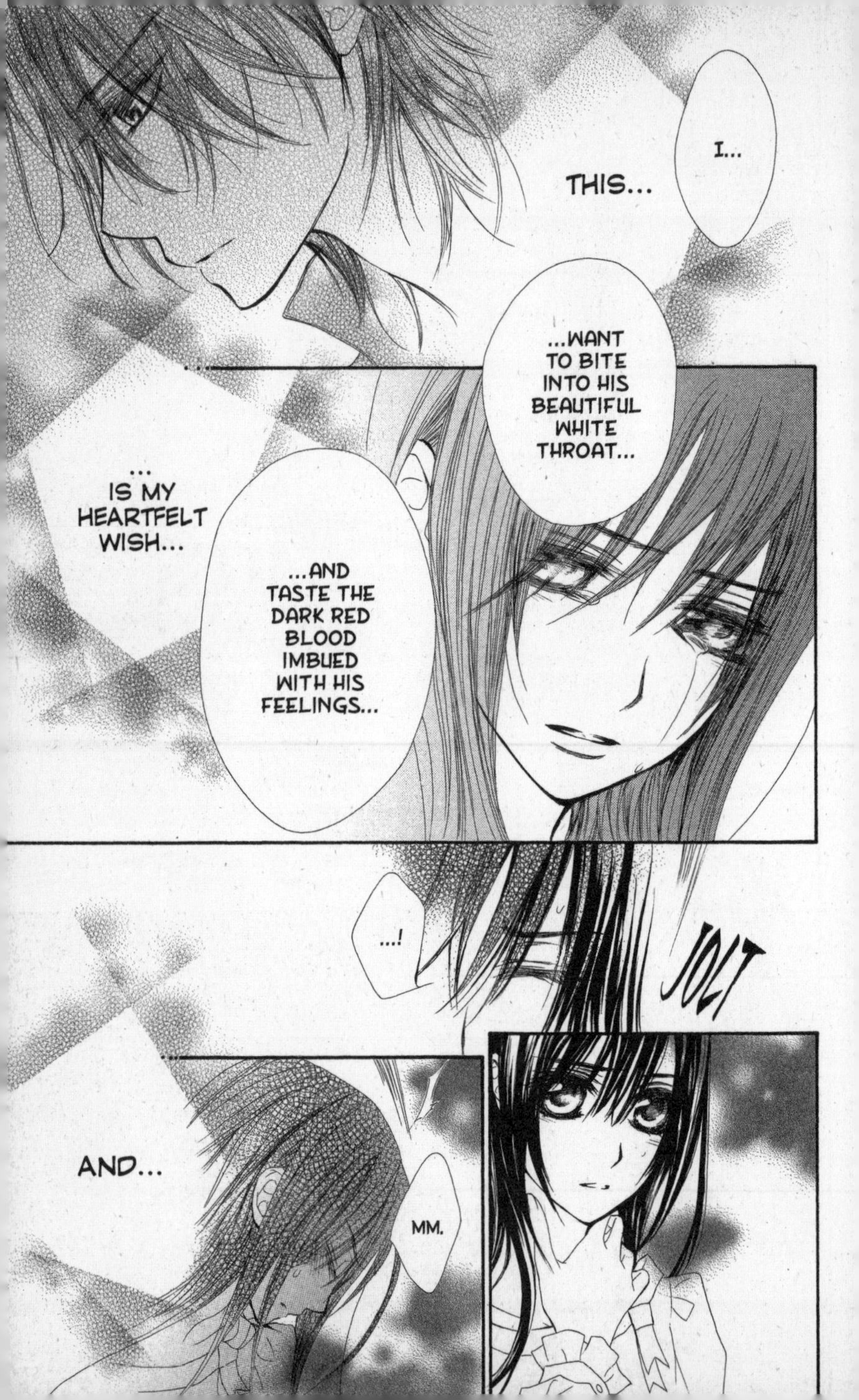
I...
...WANT TO BITE INTO HIS BEAUTIFUL WHITE THROAT...
...AND TASTE THE DARK RED BLOOD IMBUED WITH HIS FEELINGS...
THIS...
... IS MY HEARTFELT WISH...
JOLT
...!
MM.
AND...

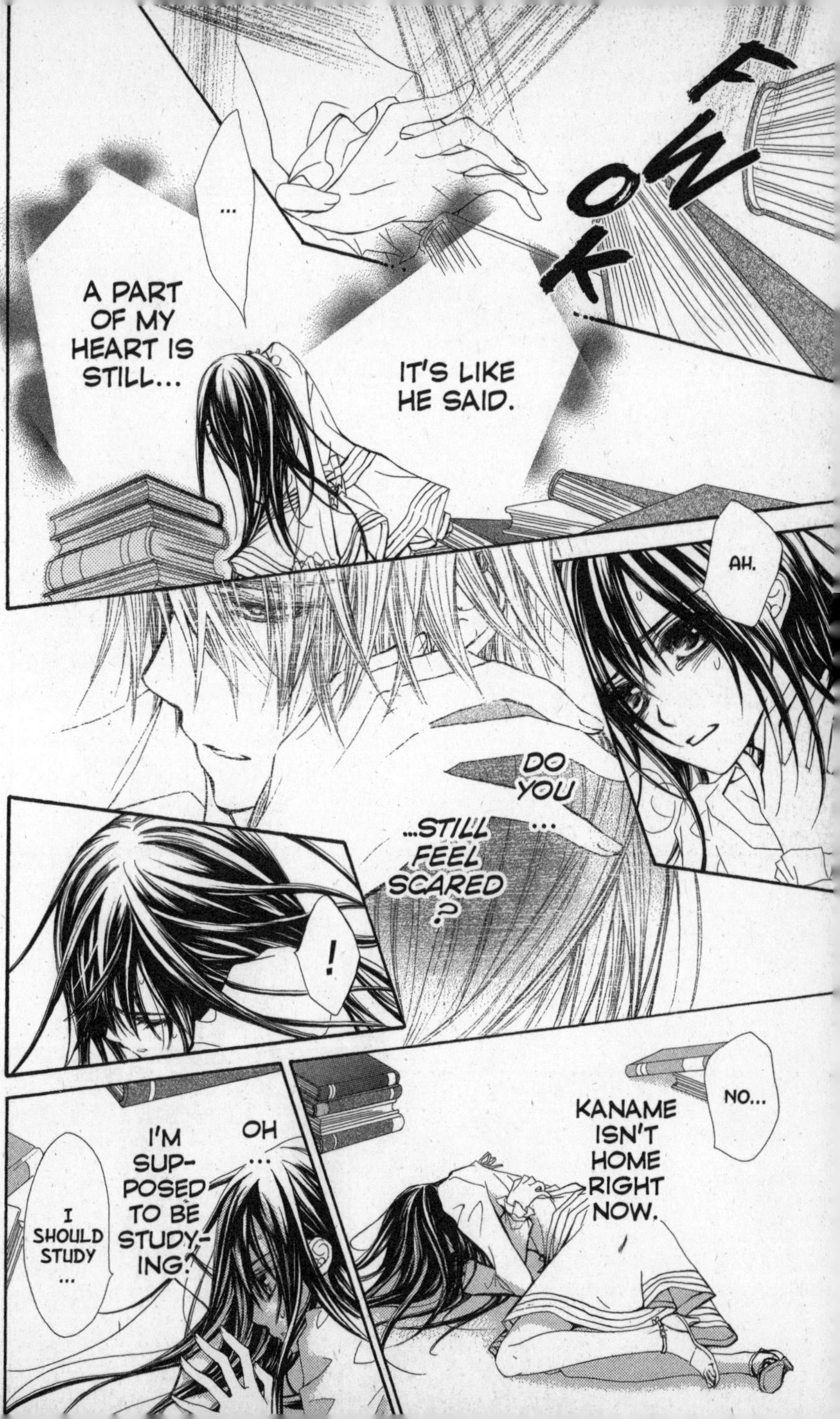
FWOK
...
IT'S LIKE HE SAID.
A PART OF MY HEART IS STILL...
AH.
DO YOU...
...STILL FEEL SCARED?
!
NO...
KANAME ISN'T HOME RIGHT NOW.
OH...
I'M SUP-POSED TO BE STUDY-ING.
I SHOULD STUDY...

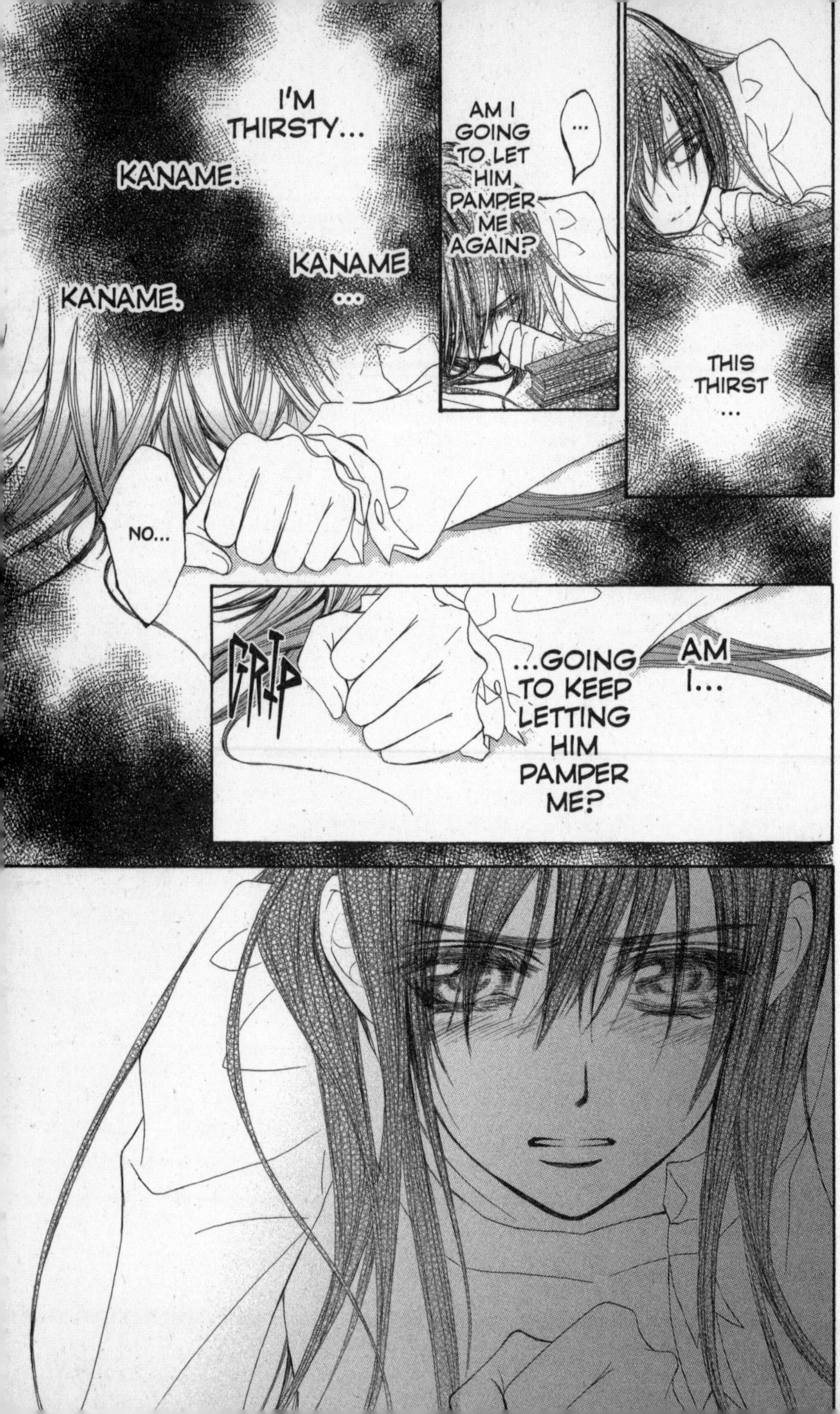

...
THIS THIRST ...
AM I GOING TO LET HIM PAMPER ME AGAIN?
I'M THIRSTY...
KANAME.
KANAME ...
KANAME.
NO...
AM I...
...GOING TO KEEP LETTING HIM PAMPER ME?
GRIP

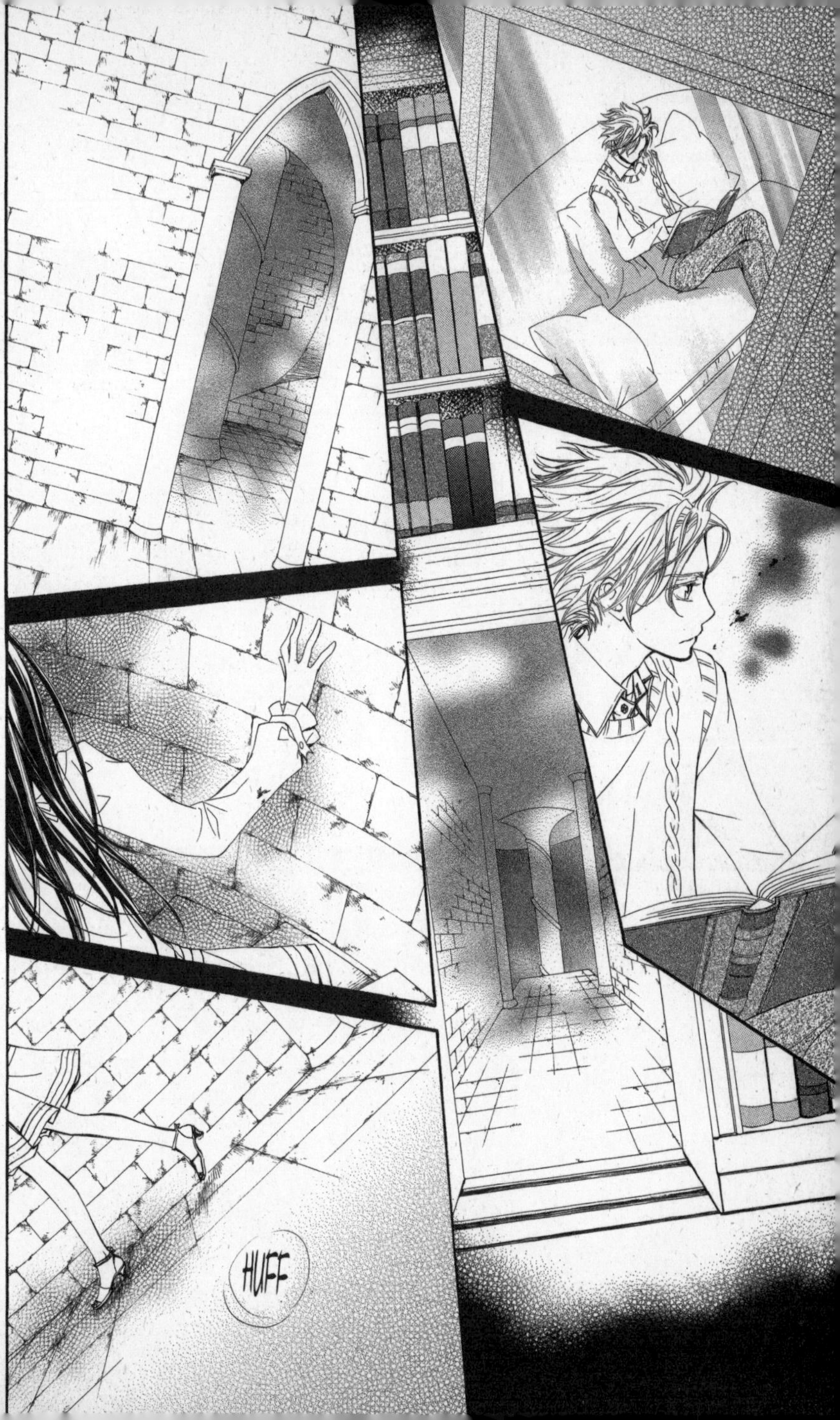
HUFF

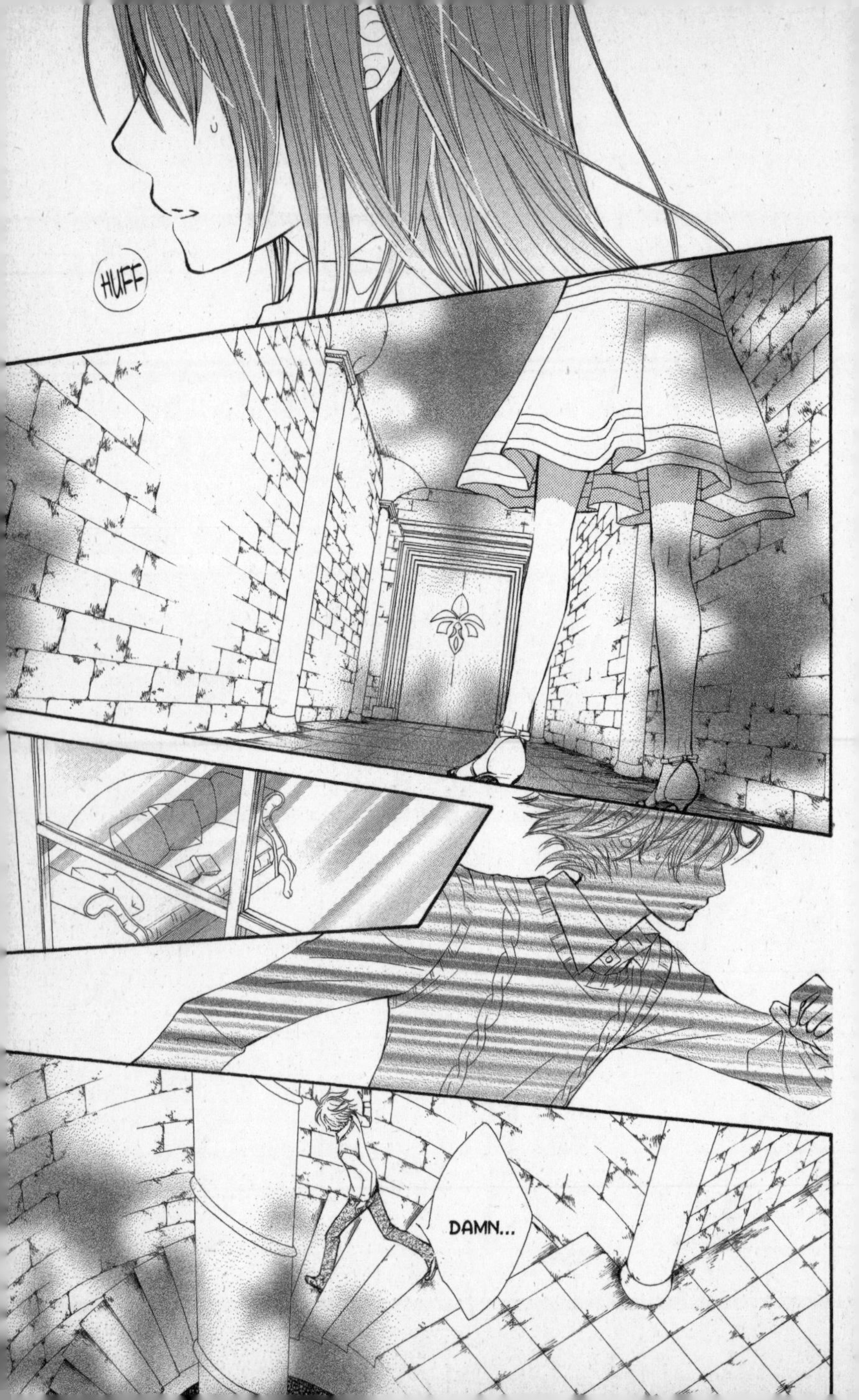
HUFF
DAMN...

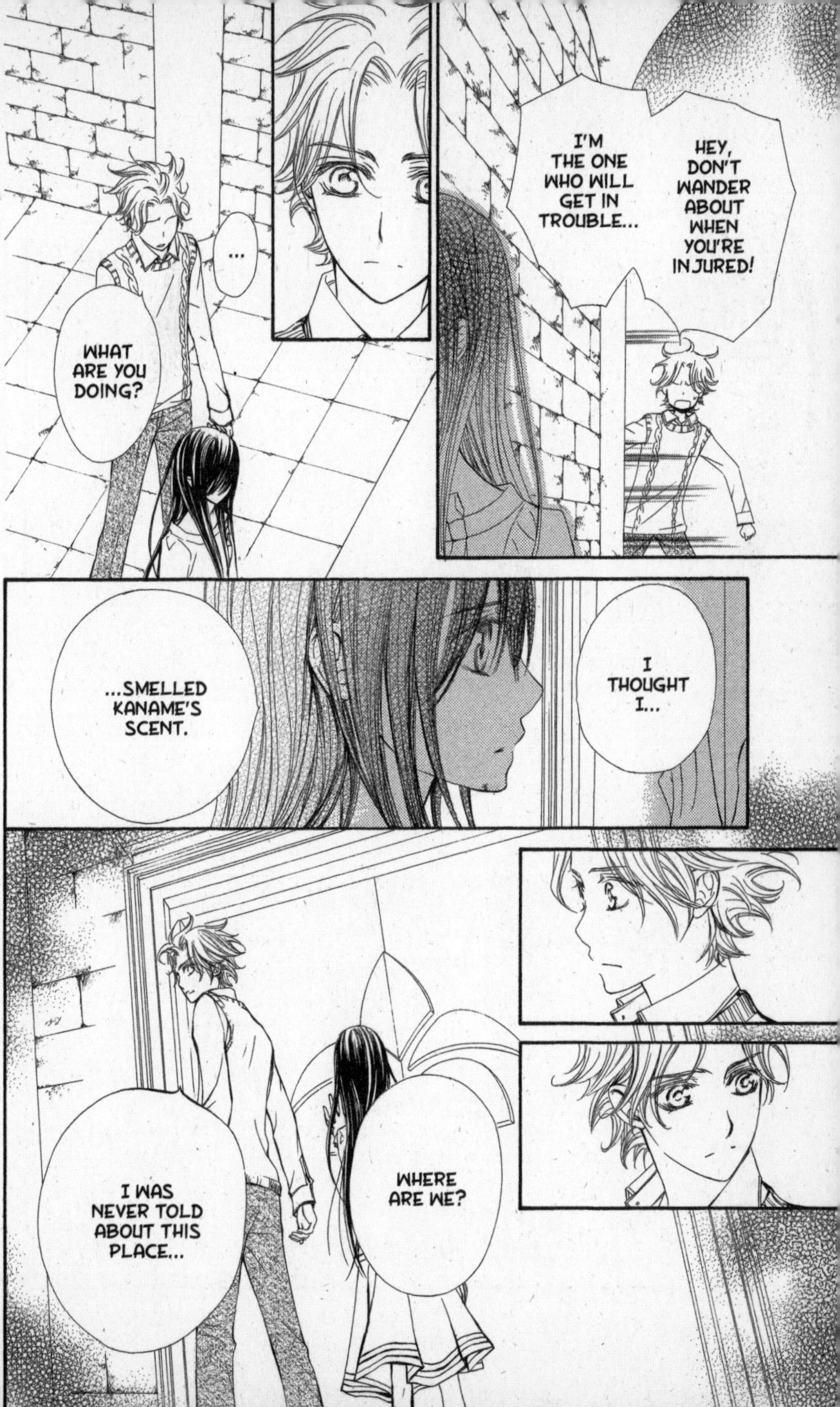
HEY, DON'T WANDER ABOUT WHEN YOU'RE INJURED!
I'M THE ONE WHO WILL GET IN TROUBLE...
...
WHAT ARE YOU DOING?
I THOUGHT I...
...SMELLED KANAME'S SCENT.
WHERE ARE WE?
I WAS NEVER TOLD ABOUT THIS PLACE...

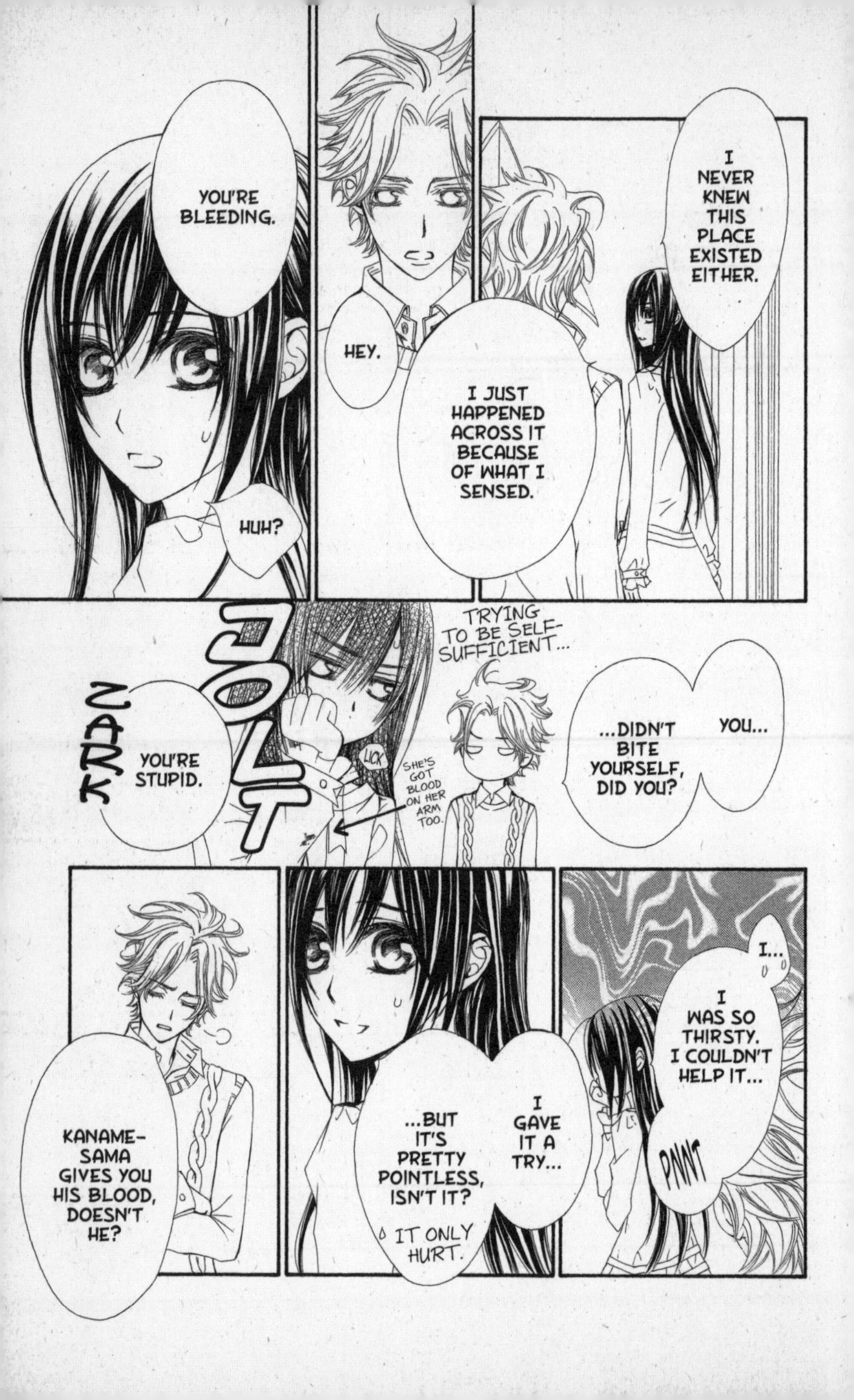

I NEVER KNEW THIS PLACE EXISTED EITHER.
I JUST HAPPENED ACROSS IT BECAUSE OF WHAT I SENSED.
HEY.
YOU'RE BLEEDING.
HUH?
YOU... ...DIDN'T BITE YOURSELF, DID YOU?
TRYING TO BE SELF-SUFFICIENT...
SHE'S GOT BLOOD ON HER ARM TOO.
LICK
JOLT
ZARK
YOU'RE STUPID.
I...
I WAS SO THIRSTY. I COULDN'T HELP IT...
PNNT
I GAVE IT A TRY... ...BUT IT'S PRETTY POINTLESS, ISN'T IT?
IT ONLY HURT.
KANAME-SAMA GIVES YOU HIS BLOOD, DOESN'T HE?

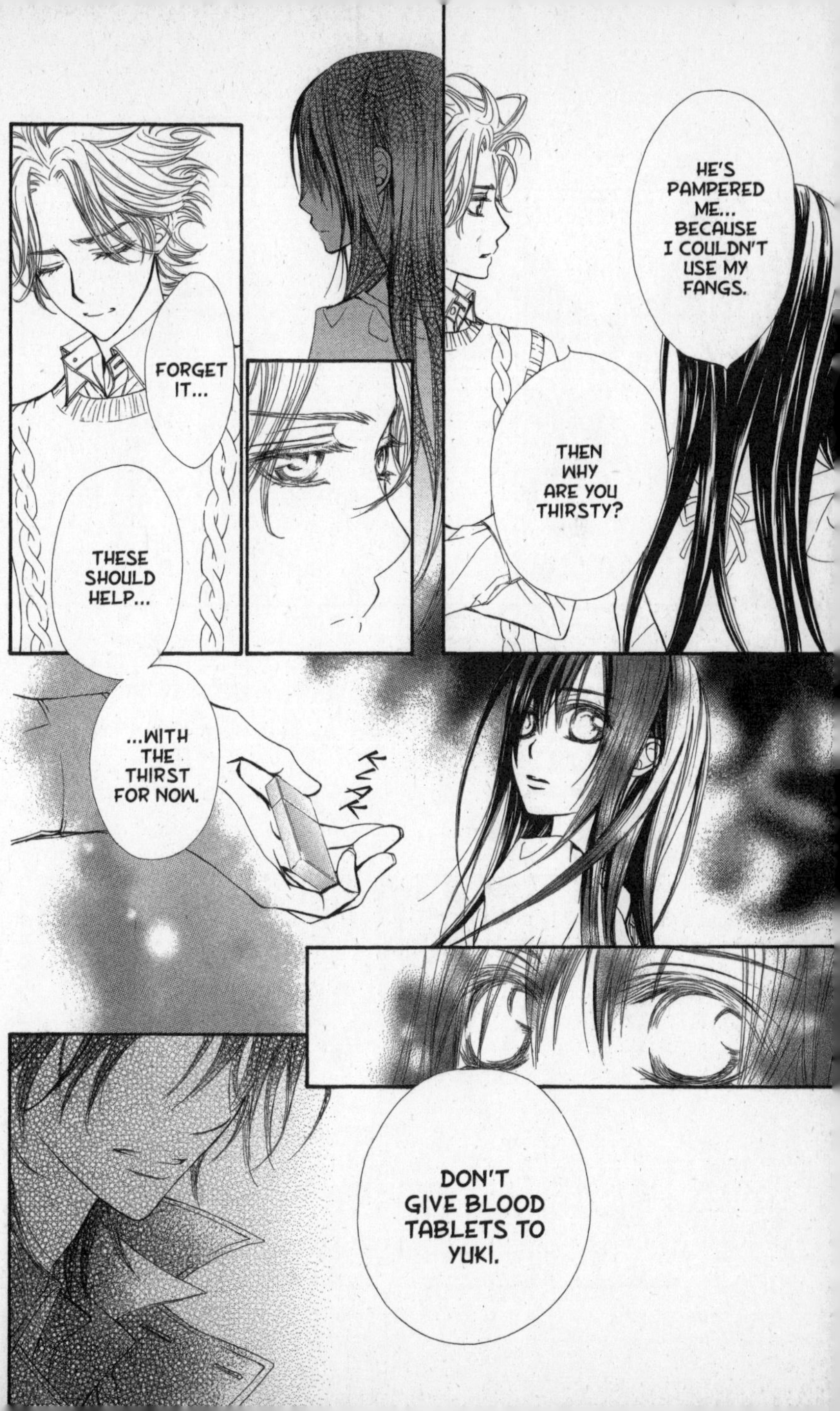
HE'S PAMPERED ME... BECAUSE I COULDN'T USE MY FANGS.
THEN WHY ARE YOU THIRSTY?
FORGET IT...
THESE SHOULD HELP...
...WITH THE THIRST FOR NOW.
KVAK
DON'T GIVE BLOOD TABLETS TO YUKI.

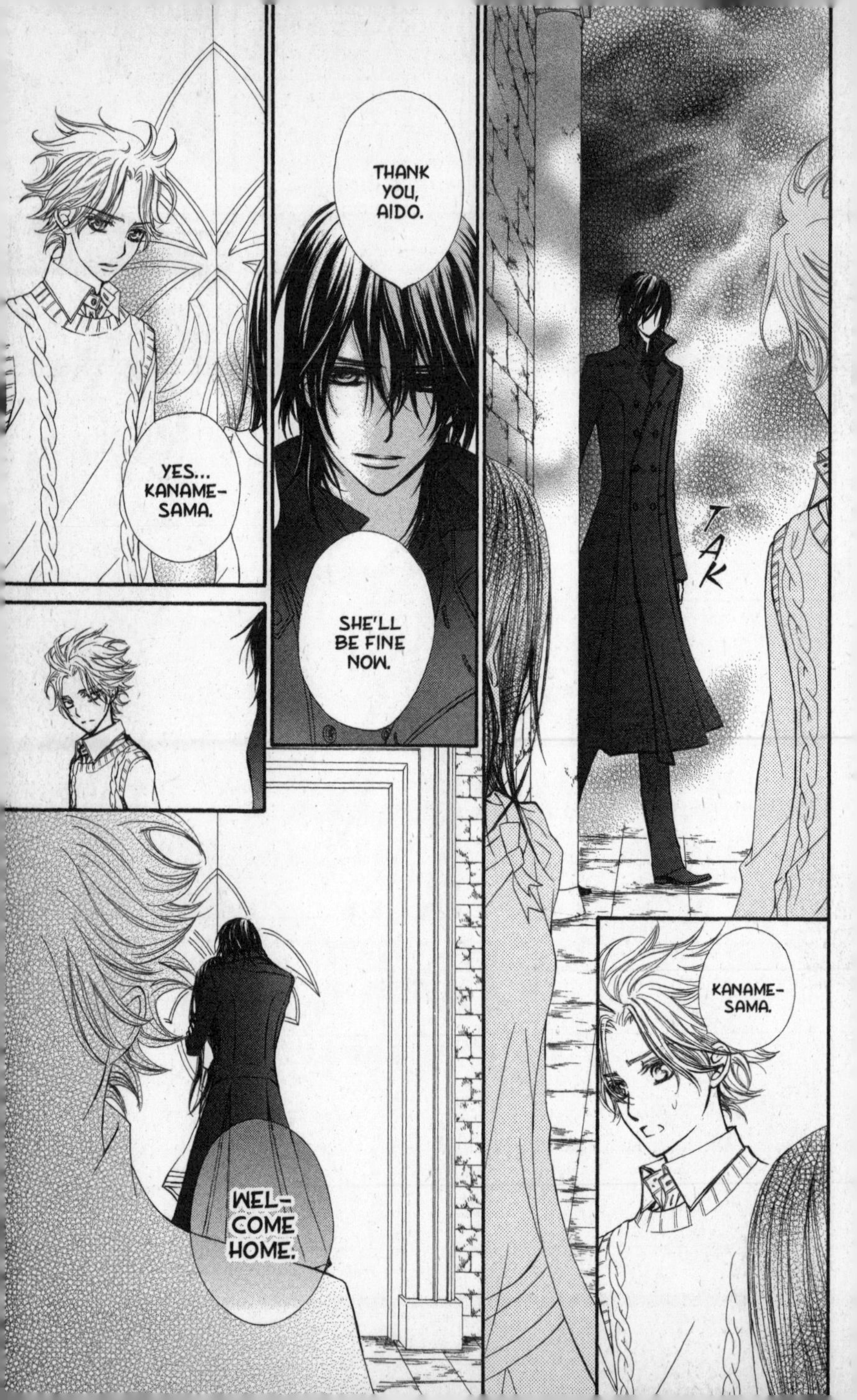
TAK
KANAME-SAMA.
THANK YOU, AIDO.
SHE'LL BE FINE NOW.
YES... KANAME-SAMA.
WEL-COME HOME.

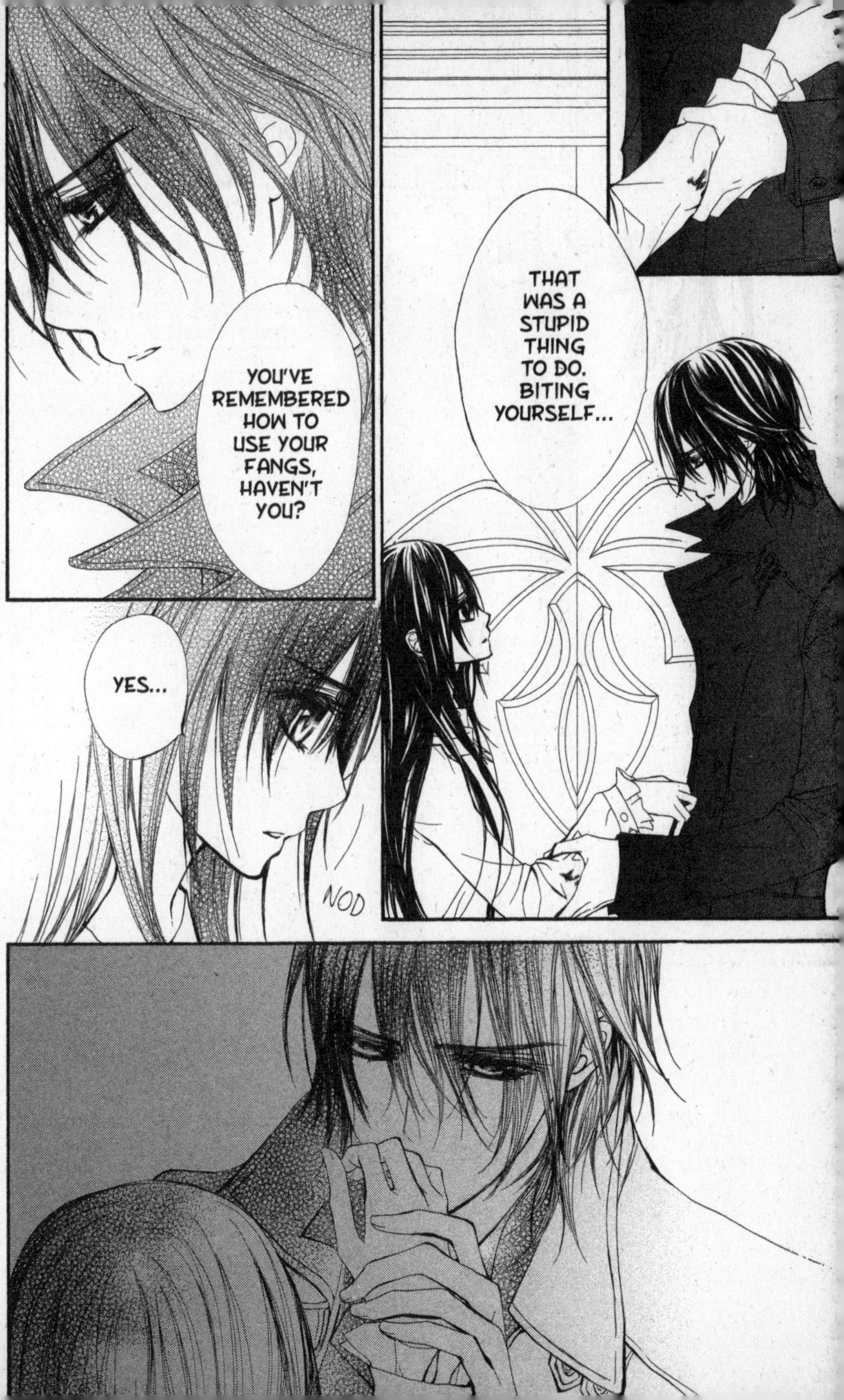
THAT WAS A STUPID THING TO DO. BITING YOURSELF...
YOU'VE REMEMBERED HOW TO USE YOUR FANGS, HAVEN'T YOU?
YES...
NOD

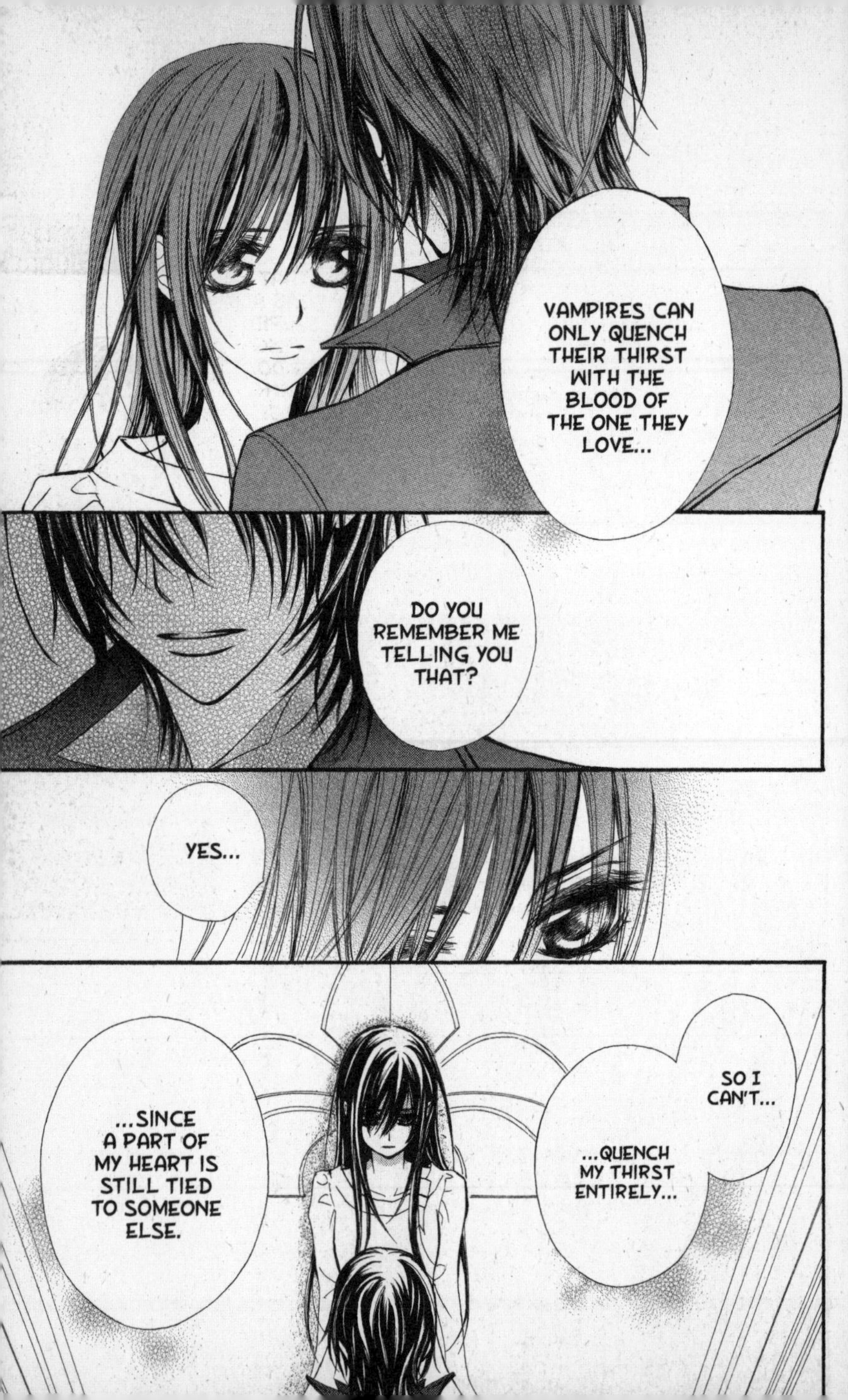
VAMPIRES CAN ONLY QUENCH THEIR THIRST WITH THE BLOOD OF THE ONE THEY LOVE...
DO YOU REMEMBER ME TELLING YOU THAT?
YES...
SO I CAN'T...
...QUENCH MY THIRST ENTIRELY...
...SINCE A PART OF MY HEART IS STILL TIED TO SOMEONE ELSE.

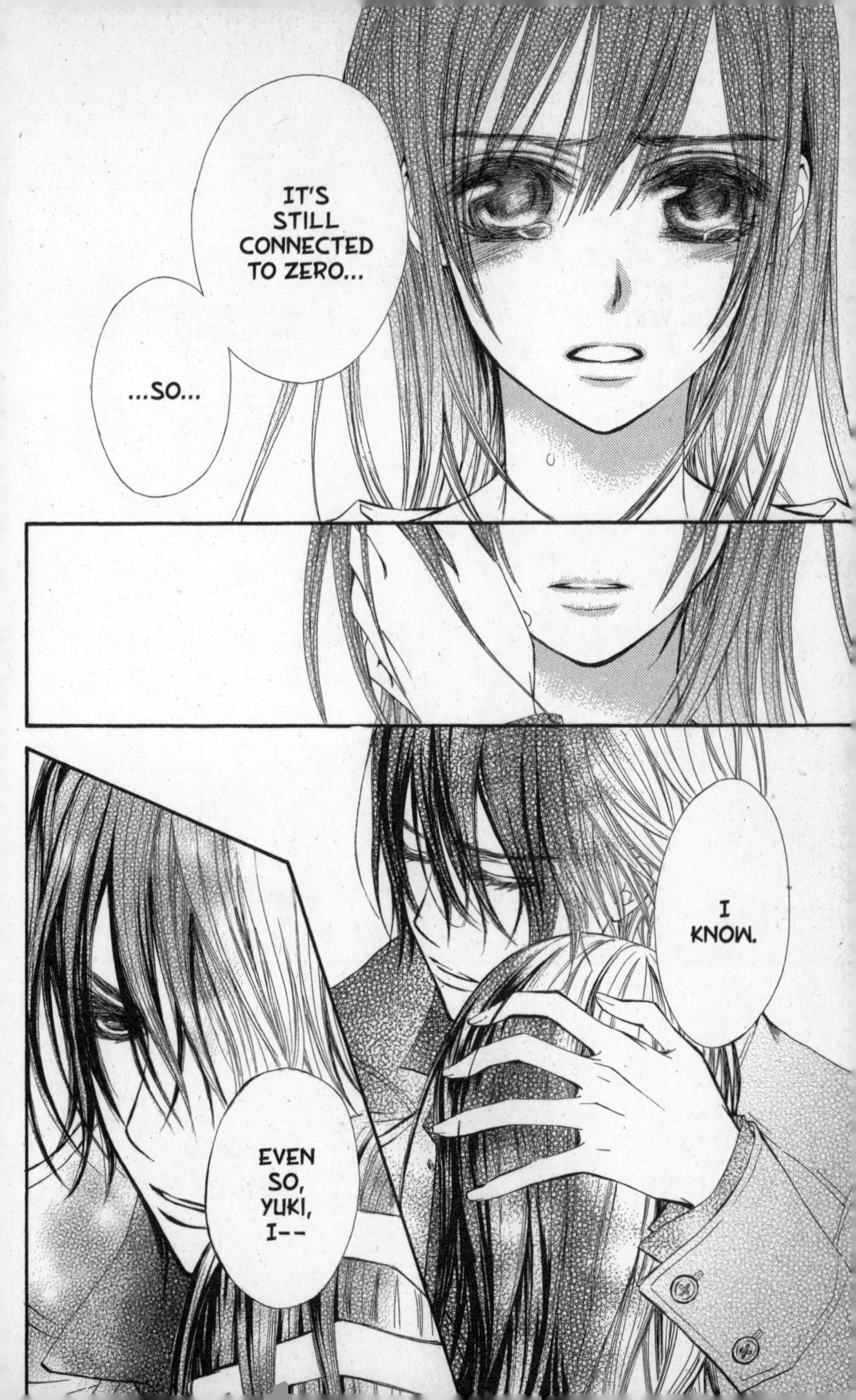
IT'S STILL CONNECTED TO ZERO...
...SO...
I KNOW.
EVEN SO, YUKI, I--

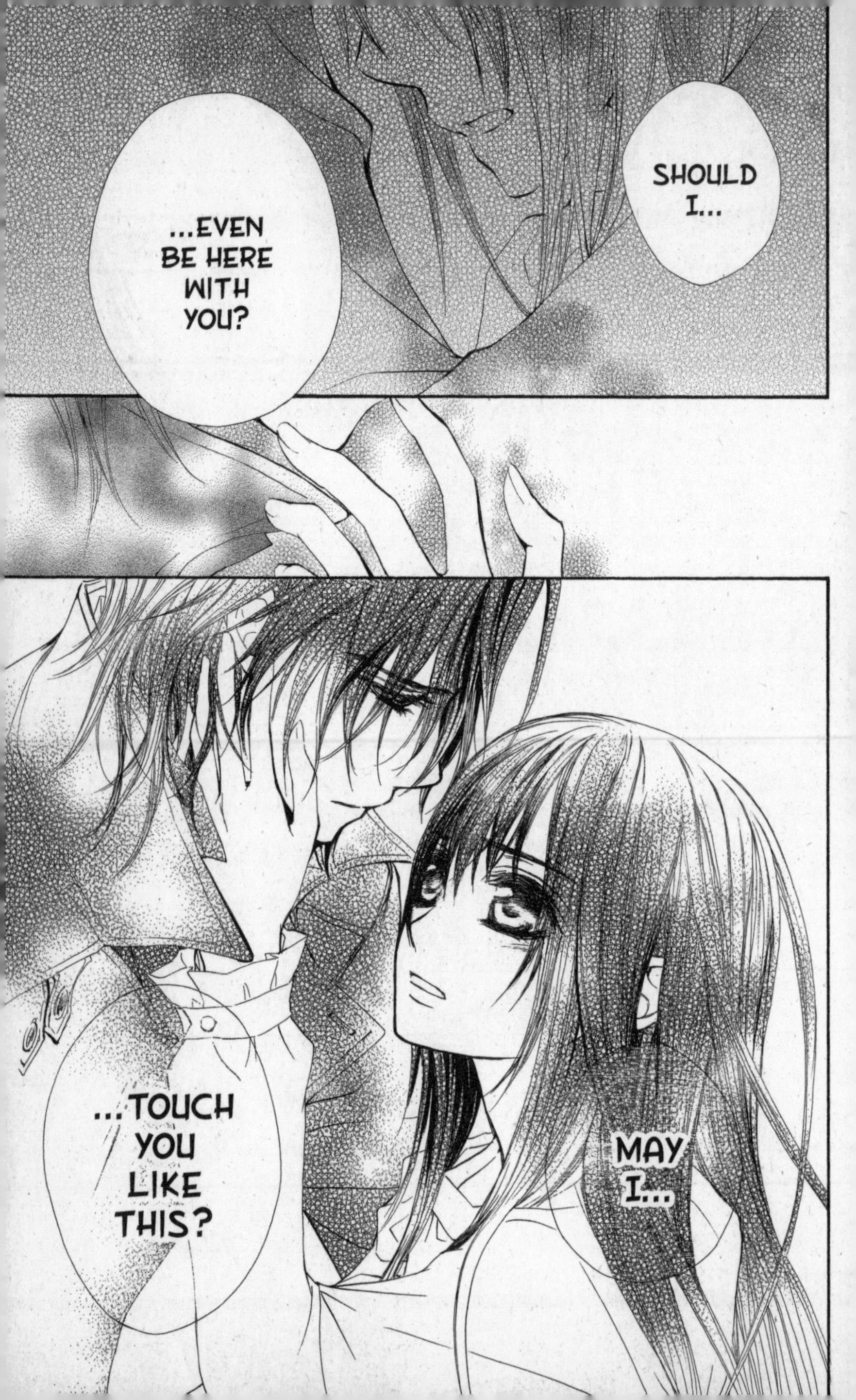
SHOULD I...
...EVEN BE HERE WITH YOU?
MAY I...
...TOUCH YOU LIKE THIS?

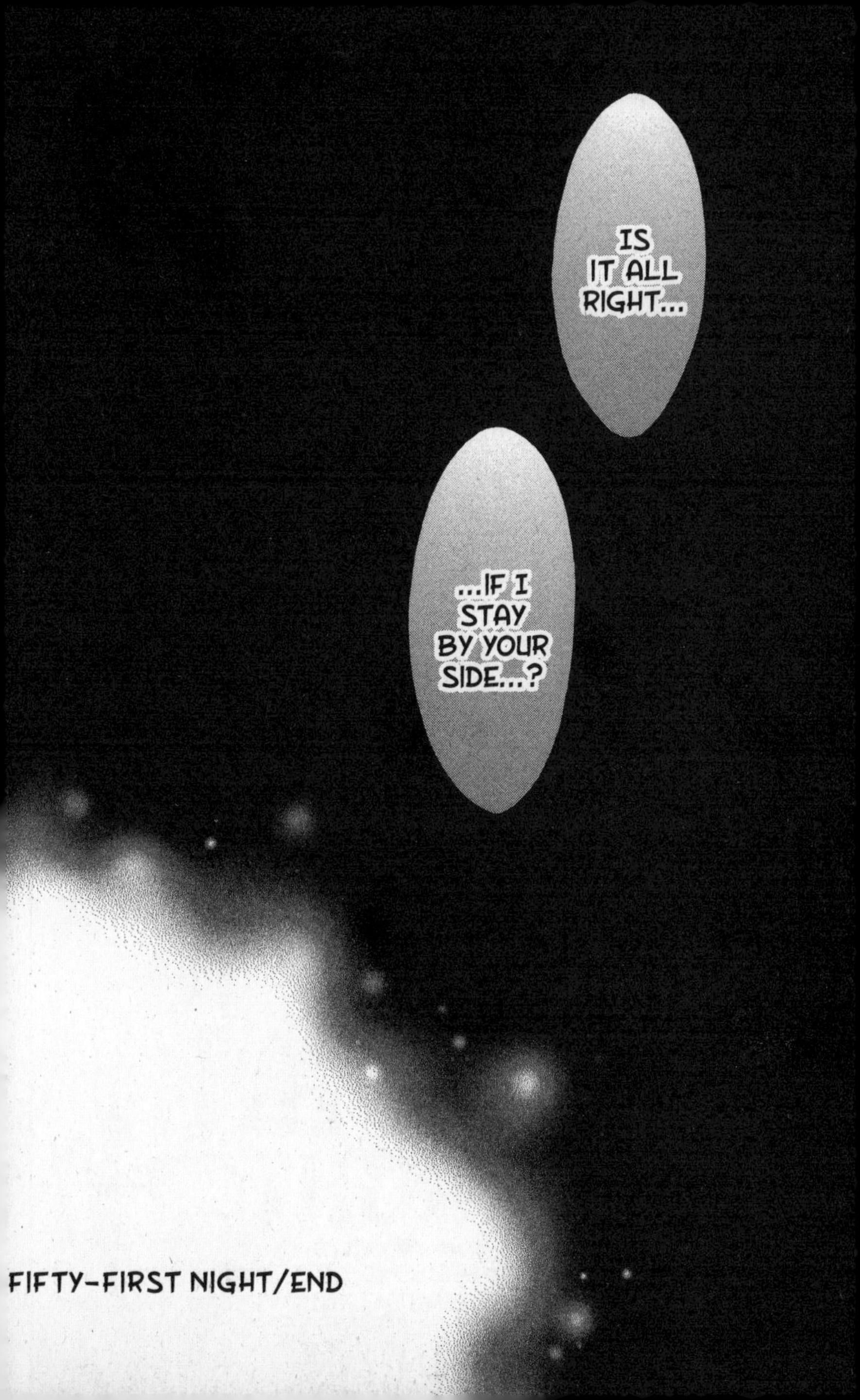
IS IT ALL RIGHT...
...IF I STAY BY YOUR SIDE...?
FIFTY-FIRST NIGHT/END

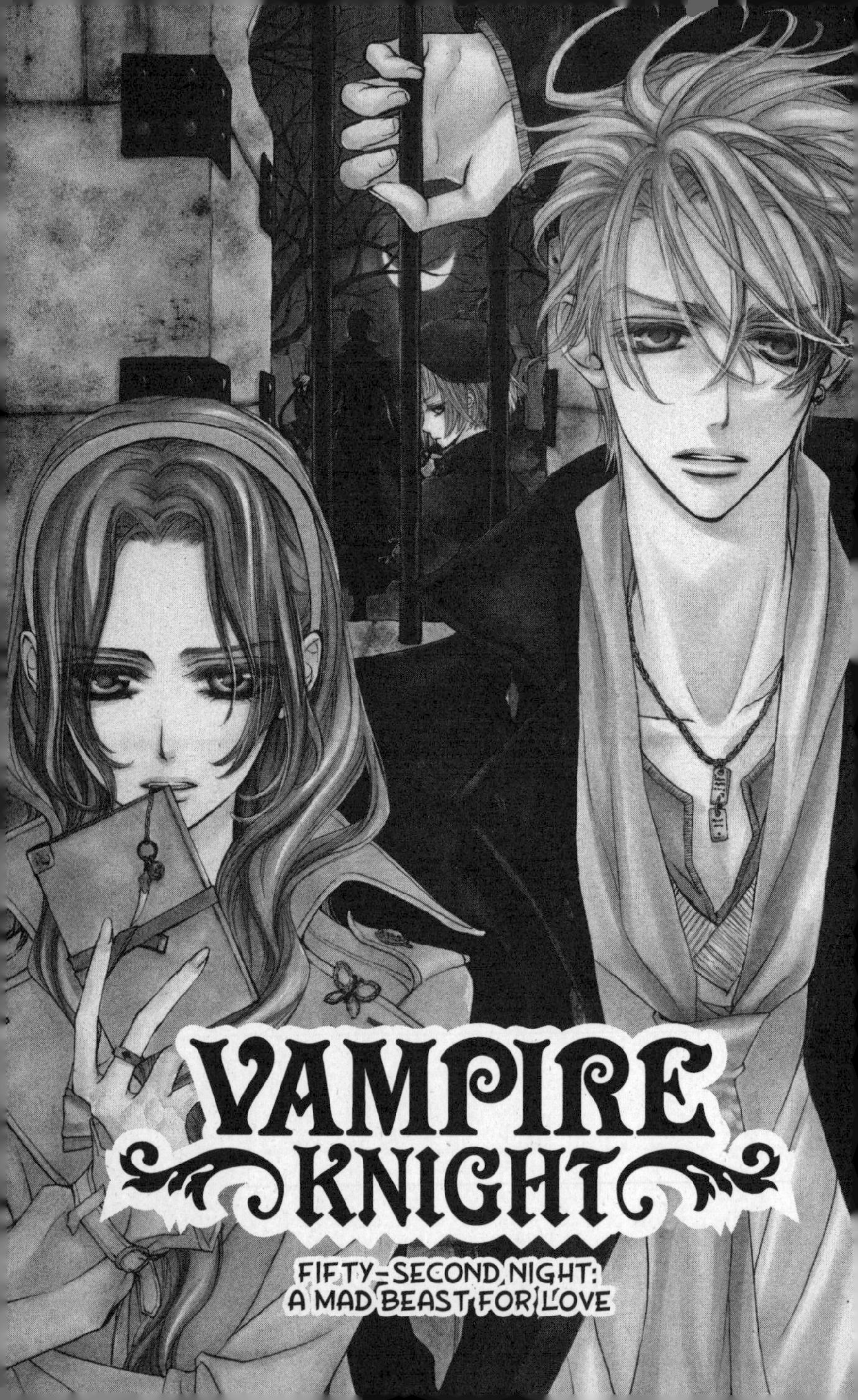
VAMPIRE KNIGHT
FIFTY-SECOND NIGHT:
A MAD BEAST FOR LOVE

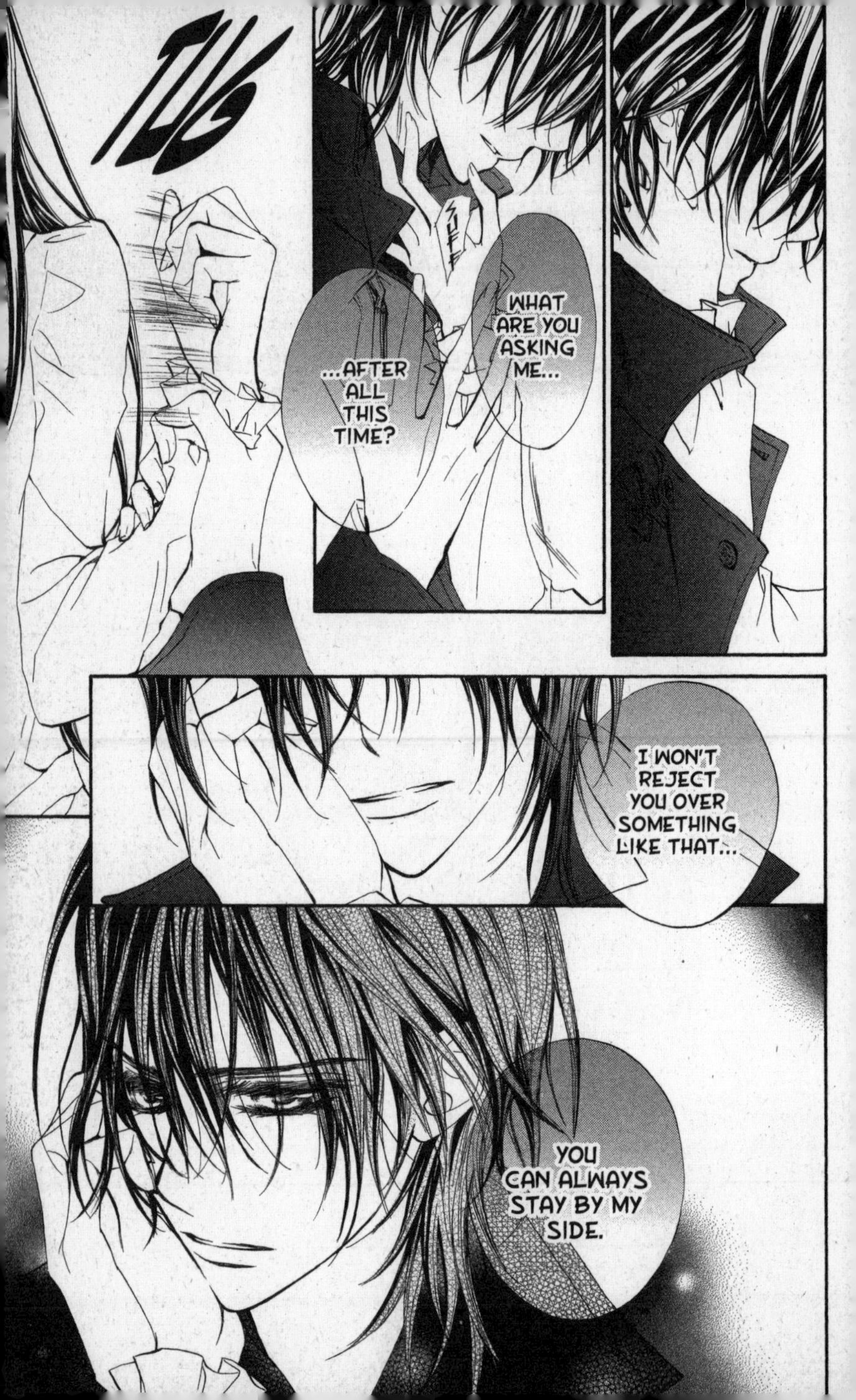
WHAT ARE YOU ASKING ME...
...AFTER ALL THIS TIME?
I WON'T REJECT YOU OVER SOMETHING LIKE THAT...
YOU CAN ALWAYS STAY BY MY SIDE.

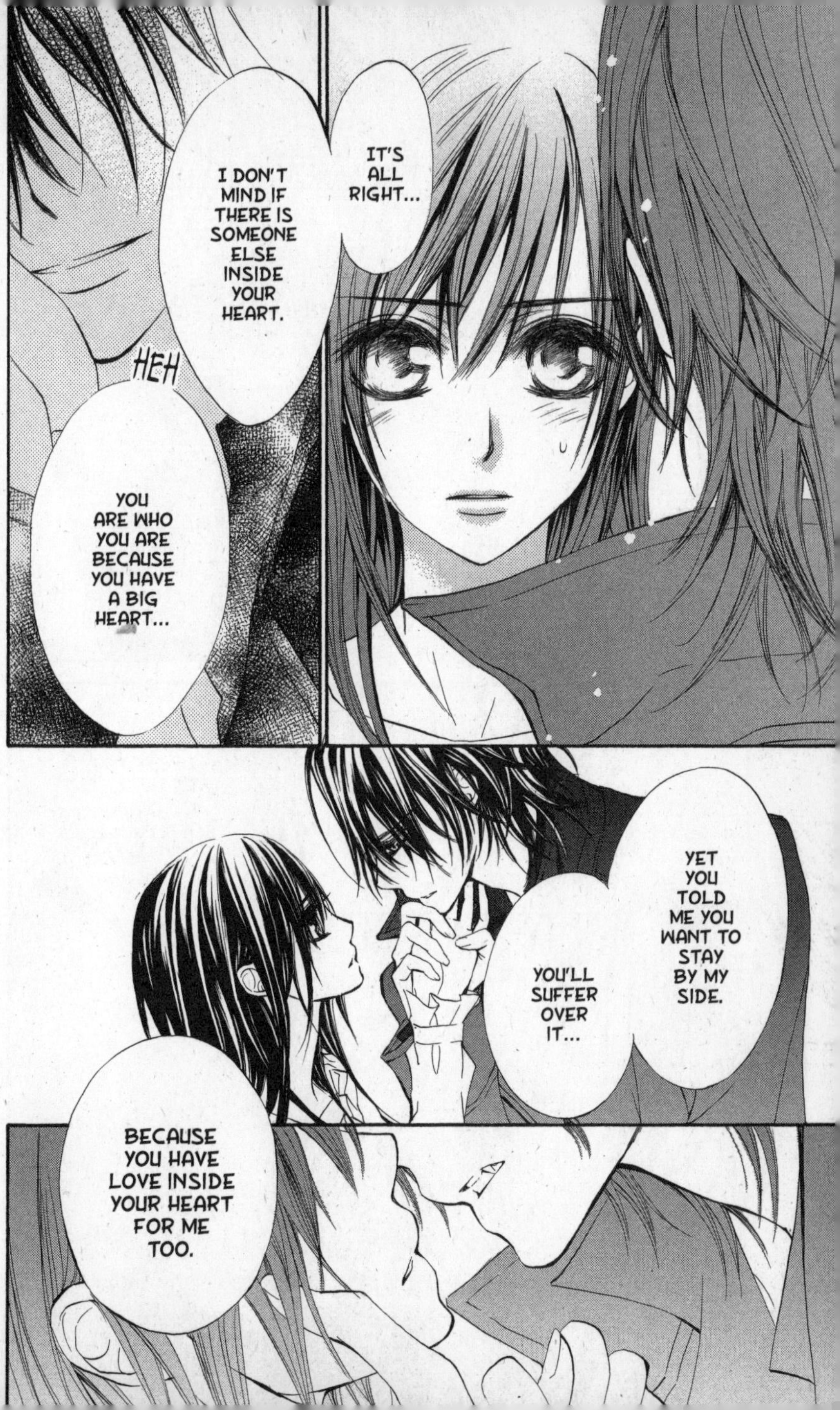
IT'S ALL RIGHT...
I DON'T MIND IF THERE IS SOMEONE ELSE INSIDE YOUR HEART.
HEH
YOU ARE WHO YOU ARE BECAUSE YOU HAVE A BIG HEART...
YET YOU TOLD ME YOU WANT TO STAY BY MY SIDE.
YOU'LL SUFFER OVER IT...
BECAUSE YOU HAVE LOVE INSIDE YOUR HEART FOR ME TOO.

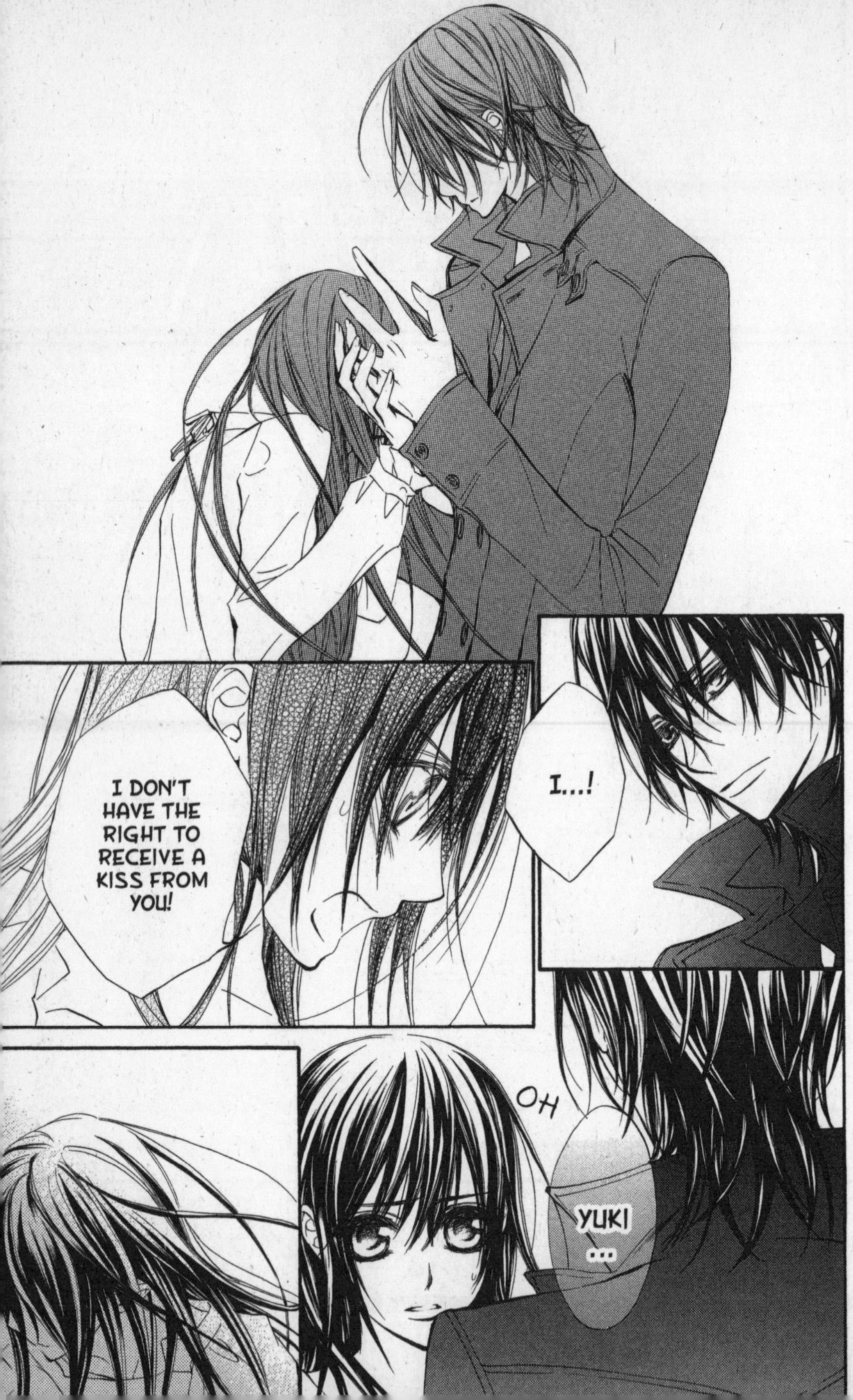
I...!
I DON'T HAVE THE RIGHT TO RECEIVE A KISS FROM YOU!
OH
YUKI ...

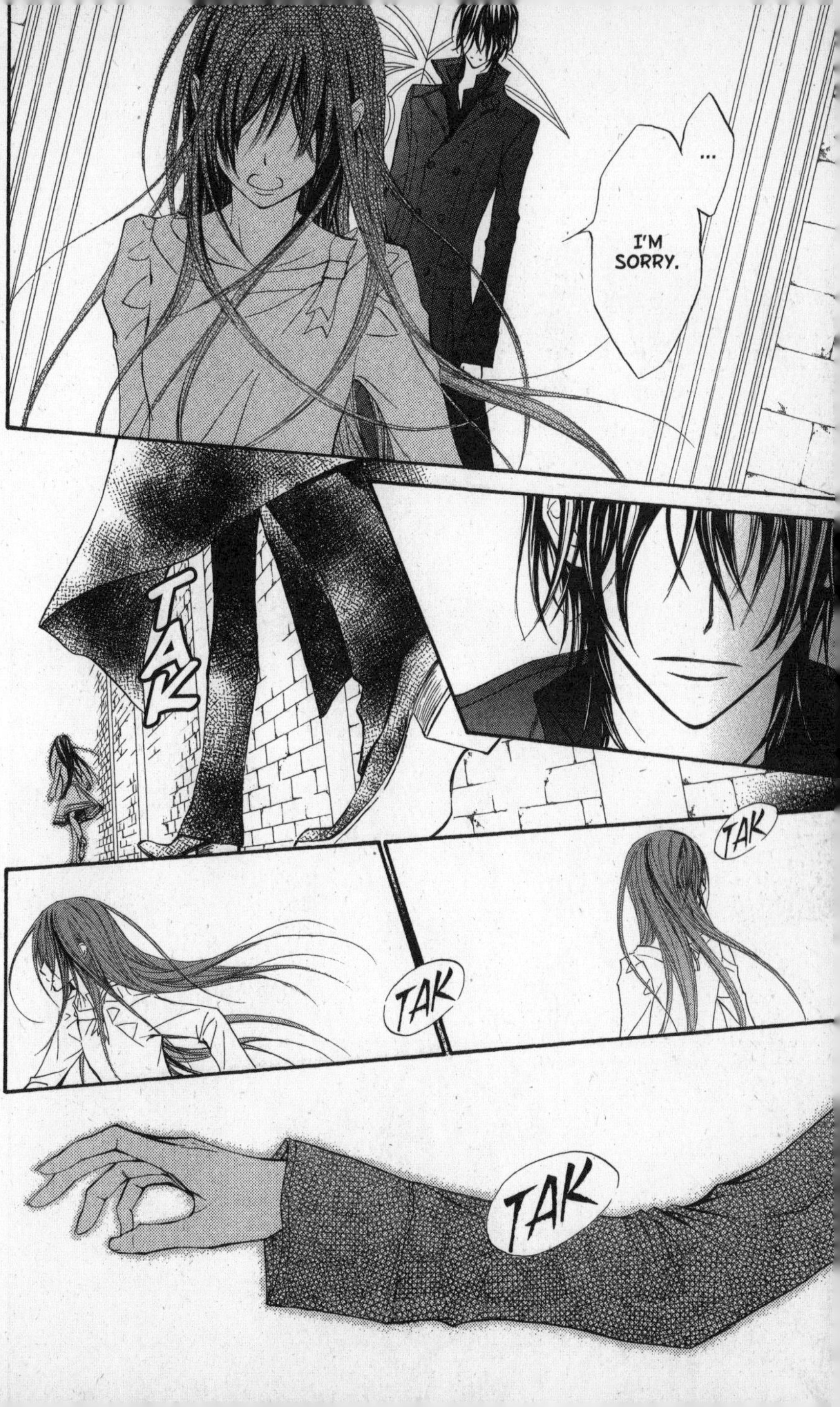
...
I'M SORRY.
TAK
TAK
TAK
TAK

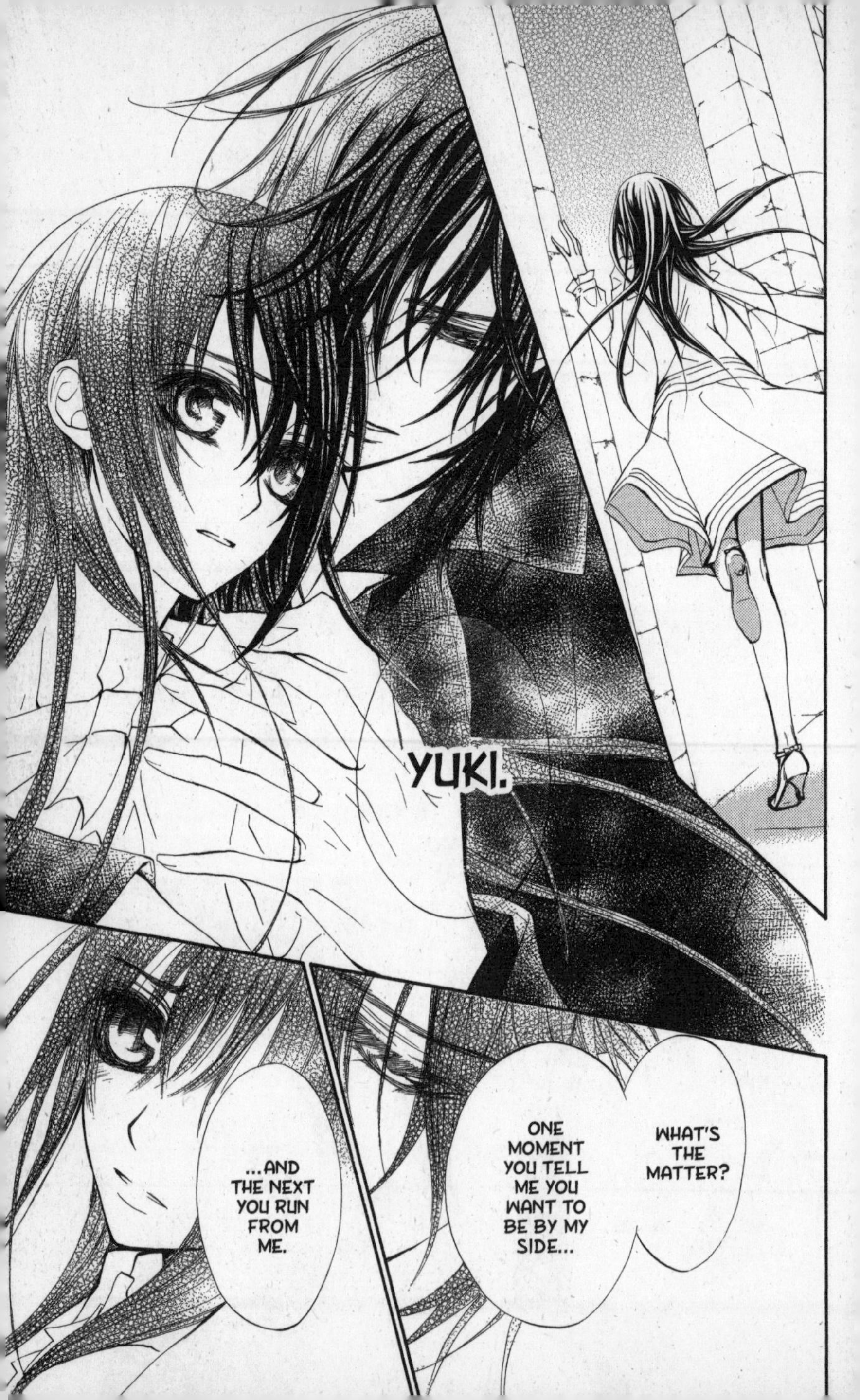
YUKI.
WHAT'S THE MATTER?
ONE MOMENT YOU TELL ME YOU WANT TO BE BY MY SIDE...
...AND THE NEXT YOU RUN FROM ME.

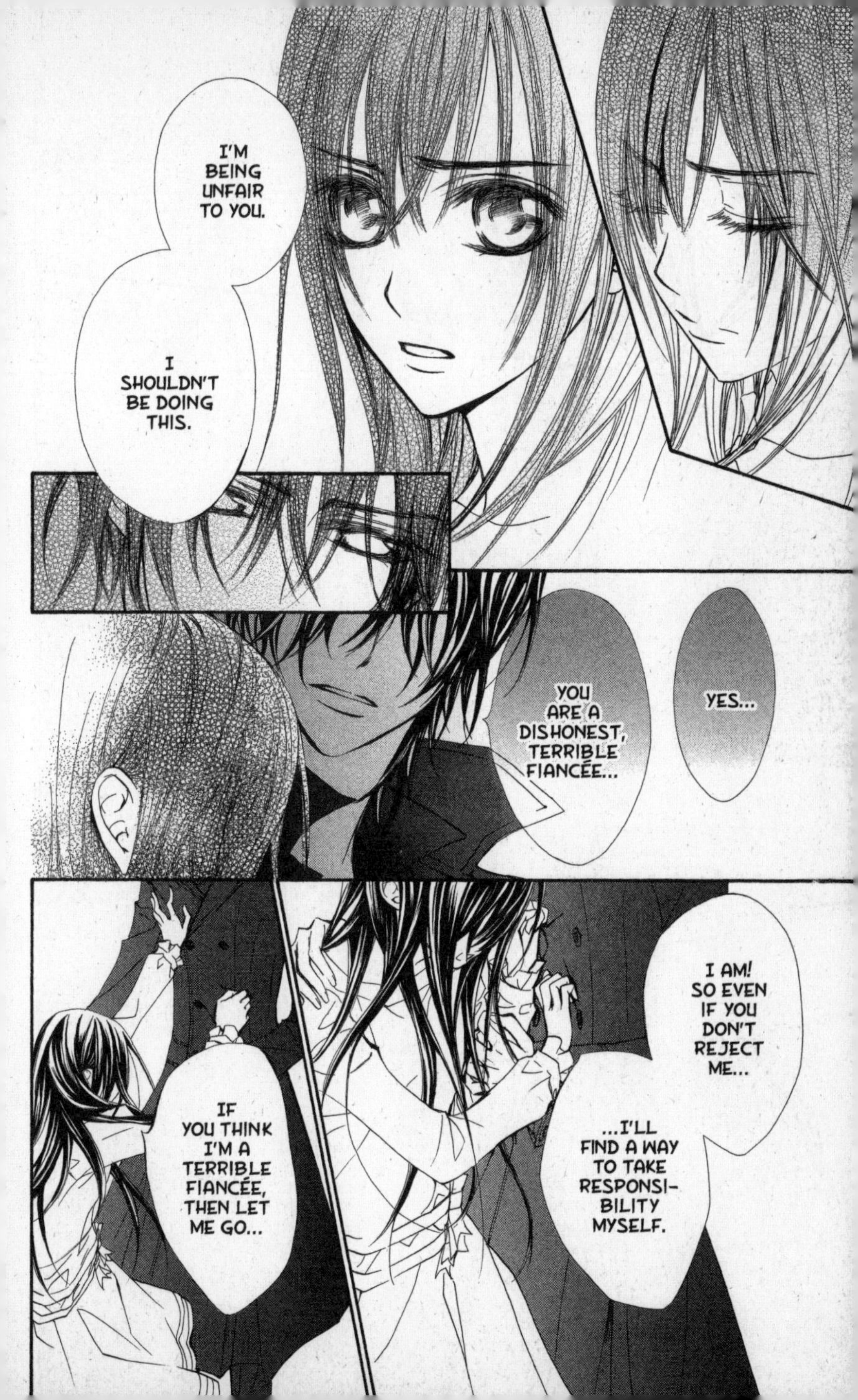
I'M BEING UNFAIR TO YOU.
I SHOULDN'T BE DOING THIS.
YES...
YOU ARE A DISHONEST, TERRIBLE FIANCÉE...
I AM! SO EVEN IF YOU DON'T REJECT ME...
...I'LL FIND A WAY TO TAKE RESPONSI-BILITY MYSELF.
IF YOU THINK I'M A TERRIBLE FIANCÉE, THEN LET ME GO...

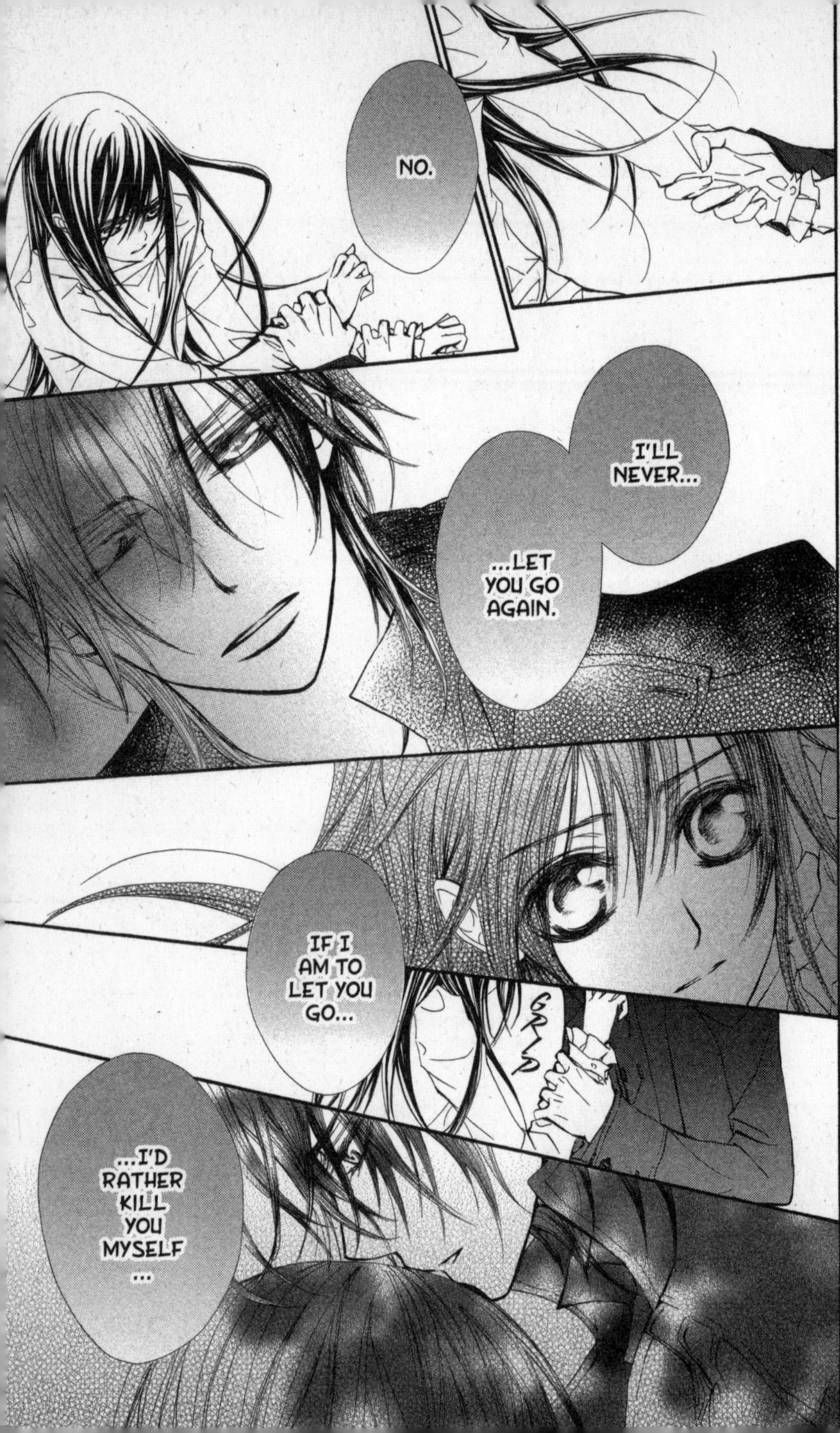
NO.
I'LL NEVER...
...LET YOU GO AGAIN.
IF I AM TO LET YOU GO...
GRIP
...I'D RATHER KILL YOU MYSELF...

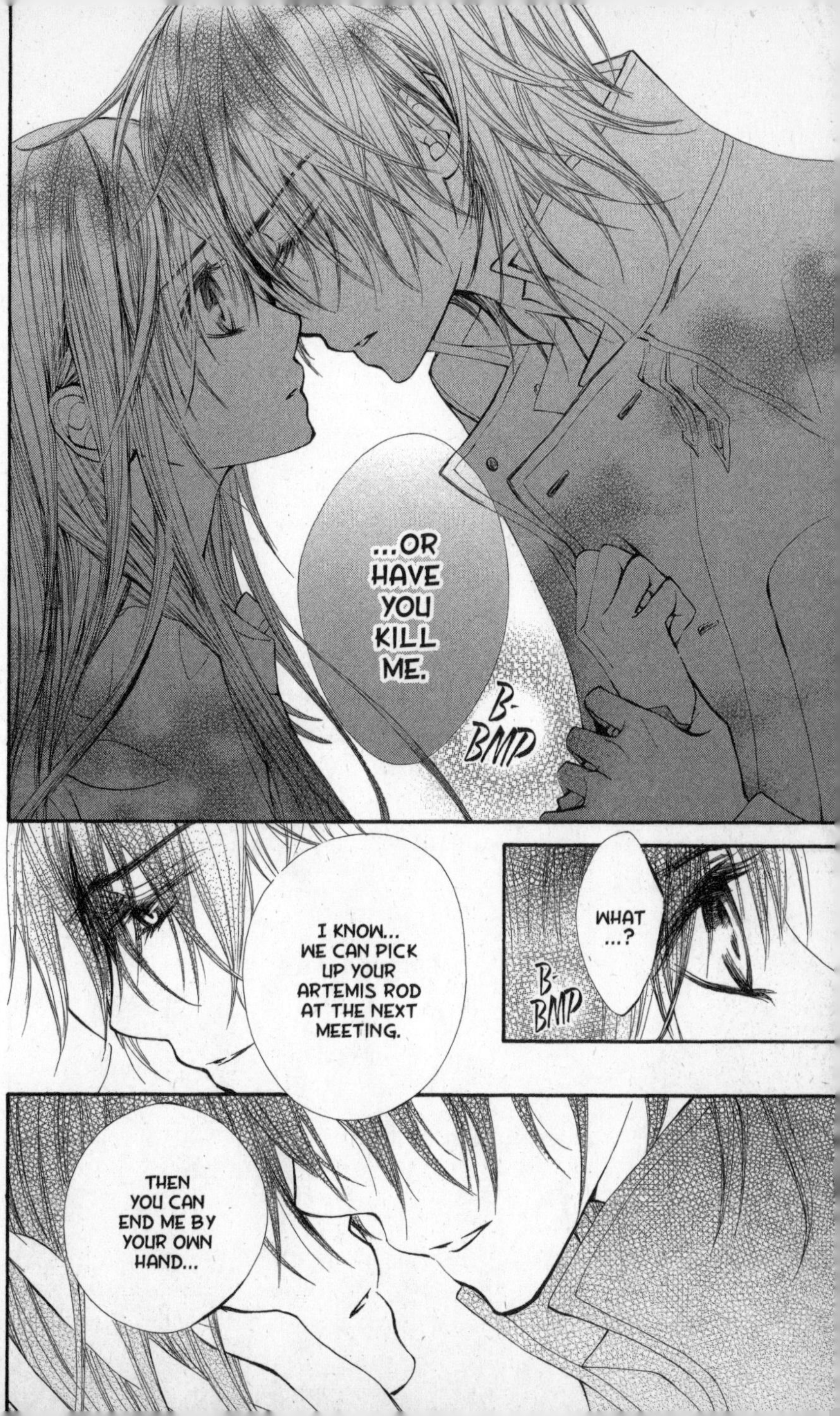
...OR HAVE YOU KILL ME.
B-BMP
WHAT ...?
B-BMP
I KNOW... WE CAN PICK UP YOUR ARTEMIS ROD AT THE NEXT MEETING.
THEN YOU CAN END ME BY YOUR OWN HAND...

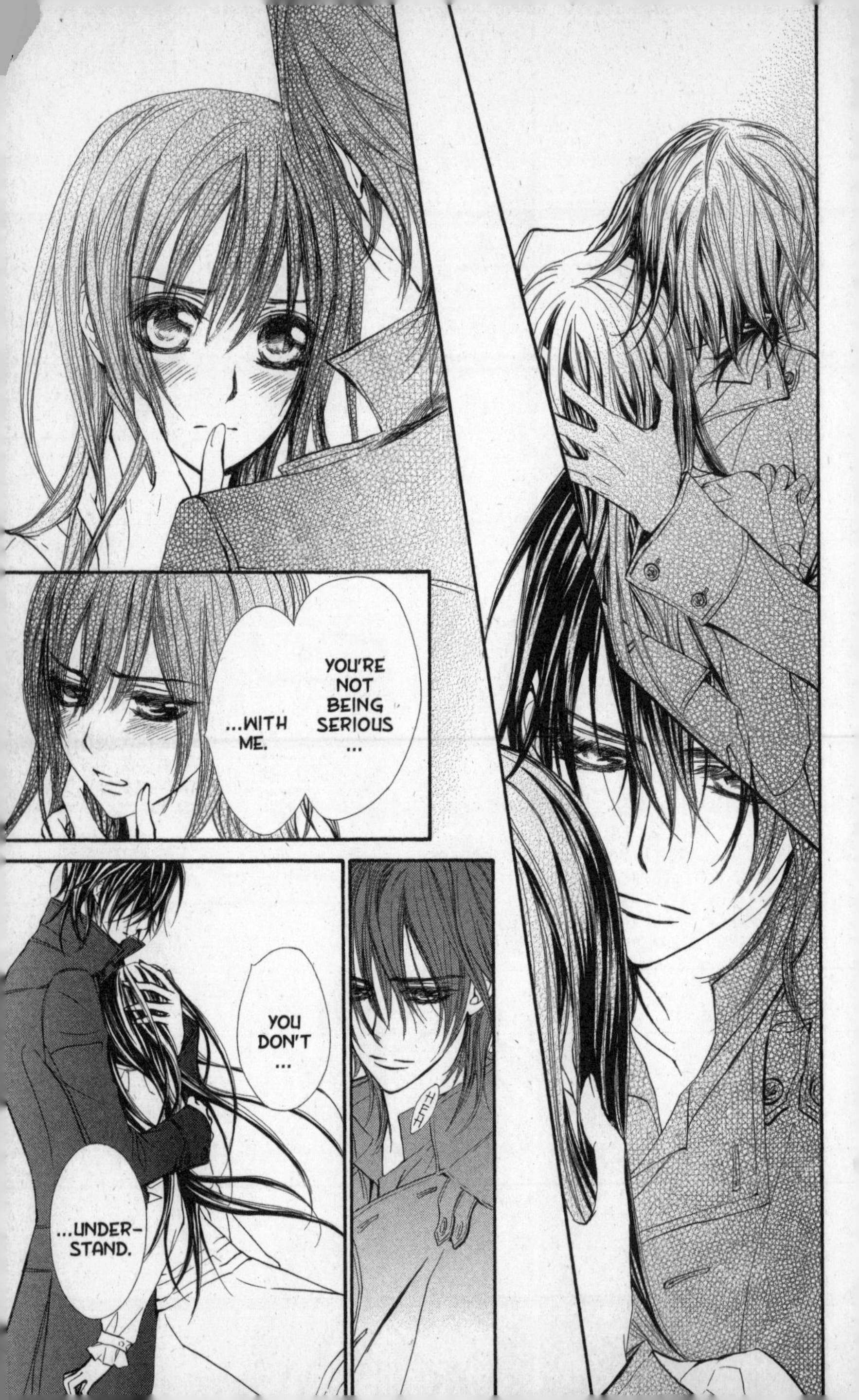
YOU'RE NOT BEING SERIOUS...
...WITH ME.
YOU DON'T...
...UNDER-STAND.

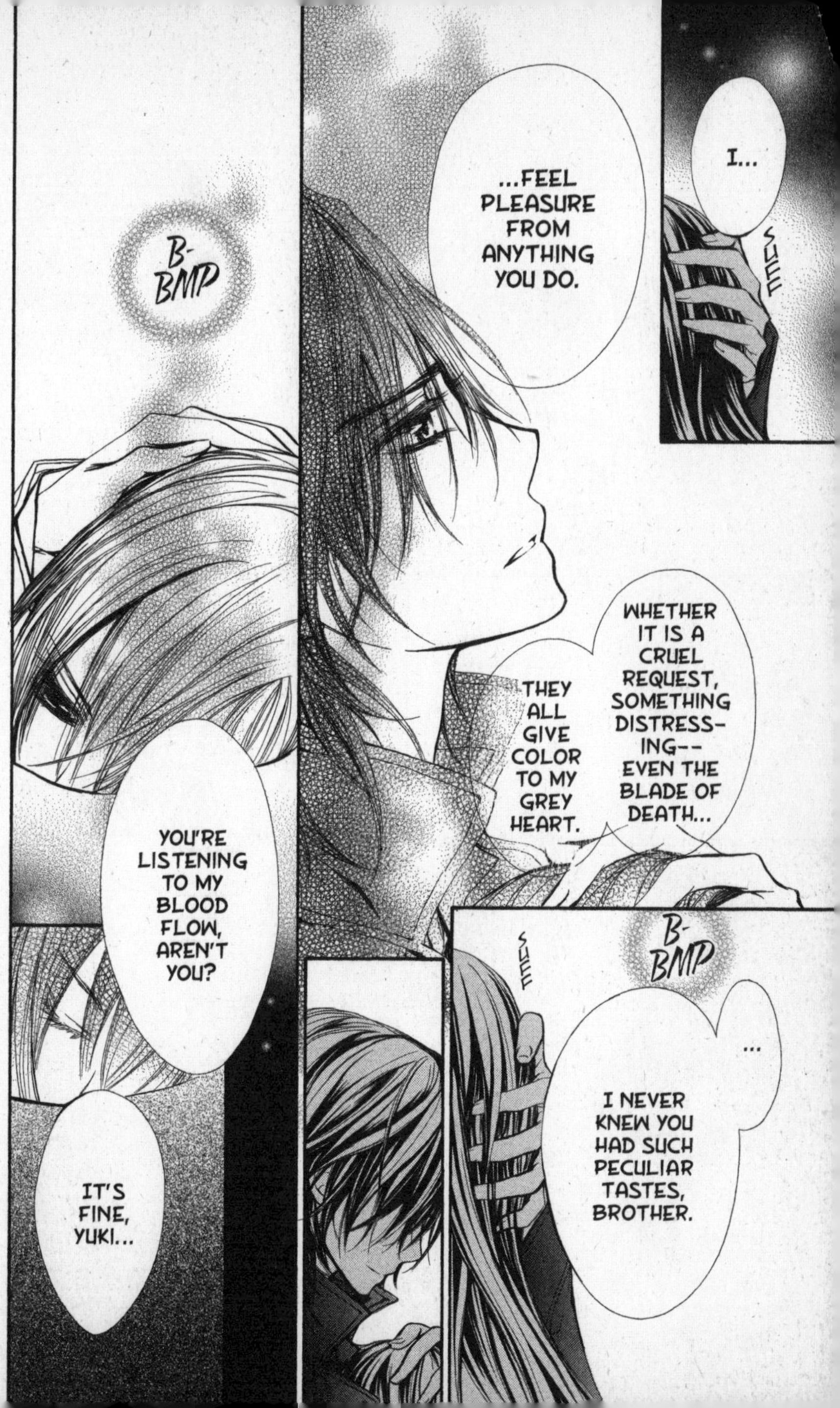
I...
SUFF
...FEEL PLEASURE FROM ANYTHING YOU DO.
WHETHER IT IS A CRUEL REQUEST, SOMETHING DISTRESS-ING-- EVEN THE BLADE OF DEATH...
THEY ALL GIVE COLOR TO MY GREY HEART.
SUFF
B-BMP
...
I NEVER KNEW YOU HAD SUCH PECULIAR TASTES, BROTHER.
B-BMP
YOU'RE LISTENING TO MY BLOOD FLOW, AREN'T YOU?
IT'S FINE, YUKI...

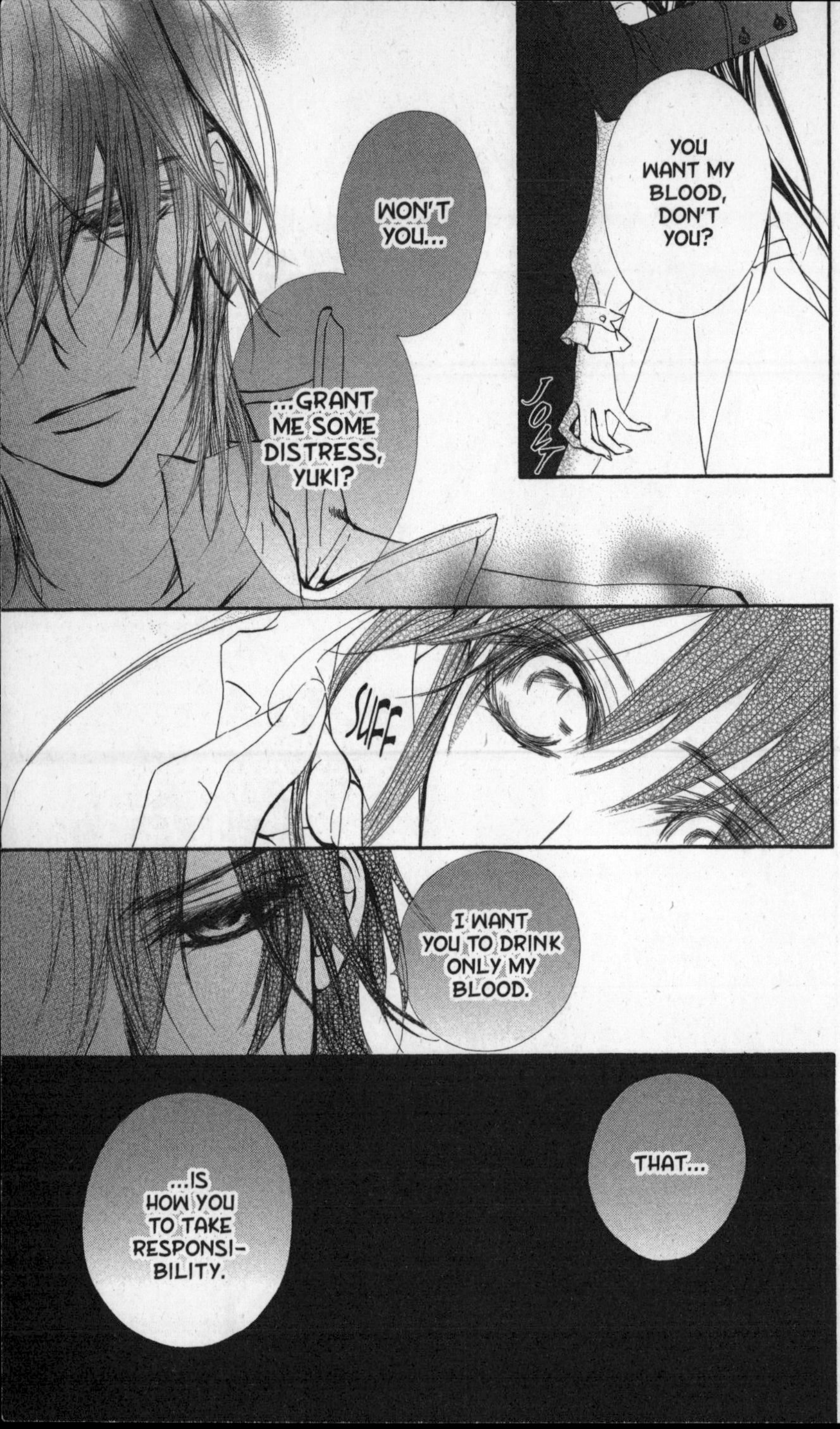
YOU WANT MY BLOOD, DON'T YOU?
JOLT
WON'T YOU...
...GRANT ME SOME DISTRESS, YUKI?
SUFF
I WANT YOU TO DRINK ONLY MY BLOOD.
THAT...
...IS HOW YOU TO TAKE RESPONSI-BILITY.

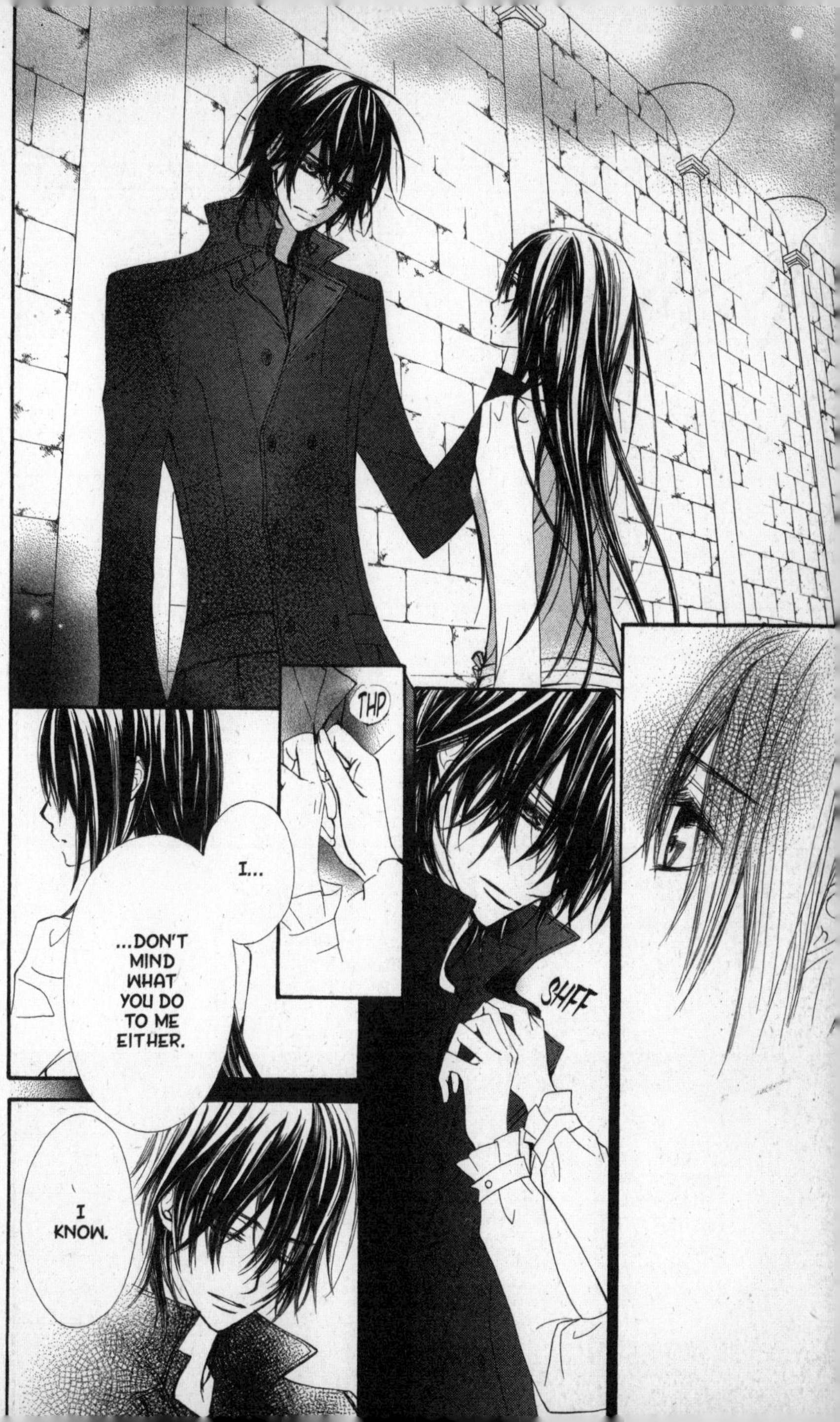
THP
SHFF
I...
...DON'T MIND WHAT YOU DO TO ME EITHER.
I KNOW.

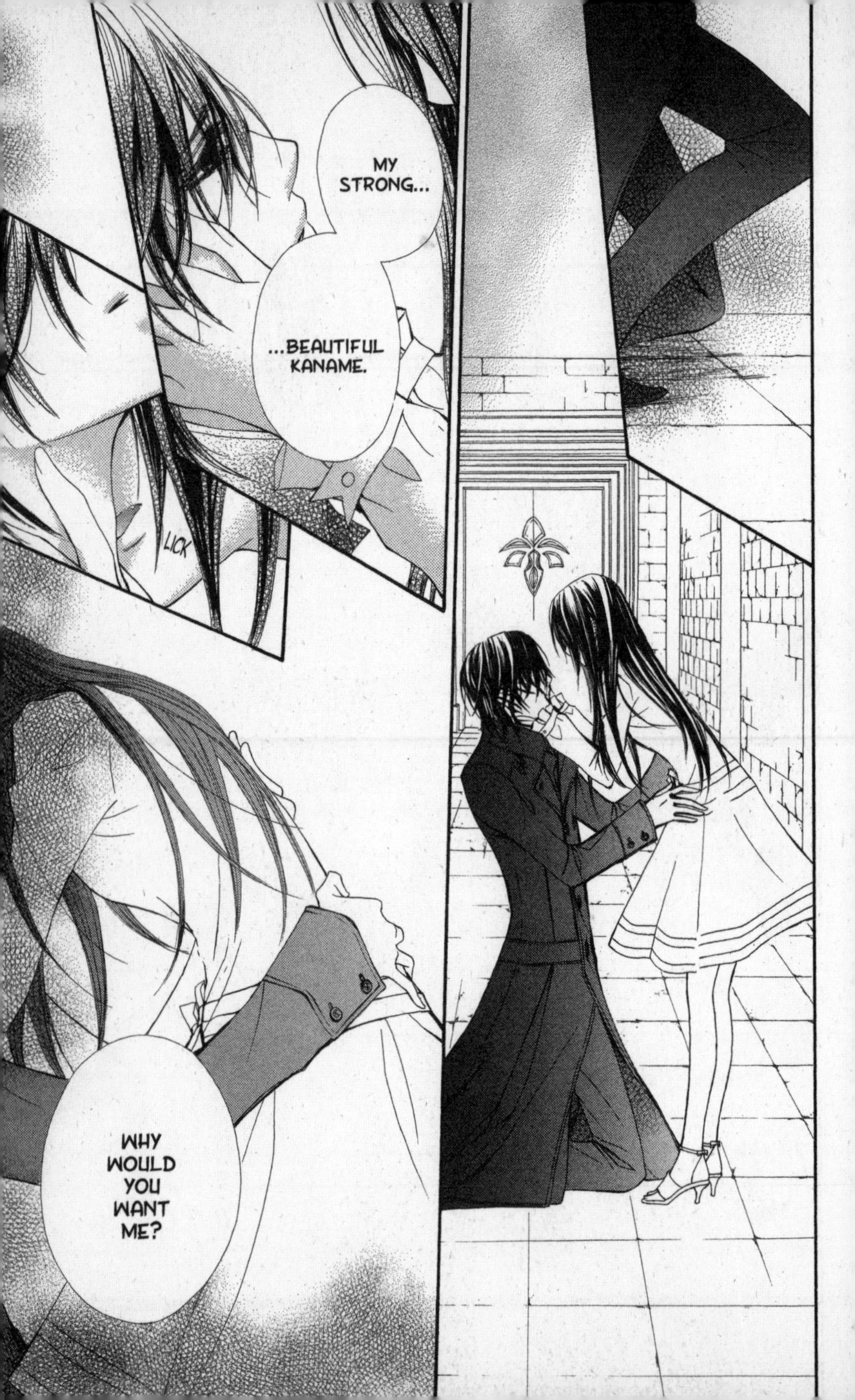
MY STRONG...
...BEAUTIFUL KANAME.
LICK
WHY WOULD YOU WANT ME?

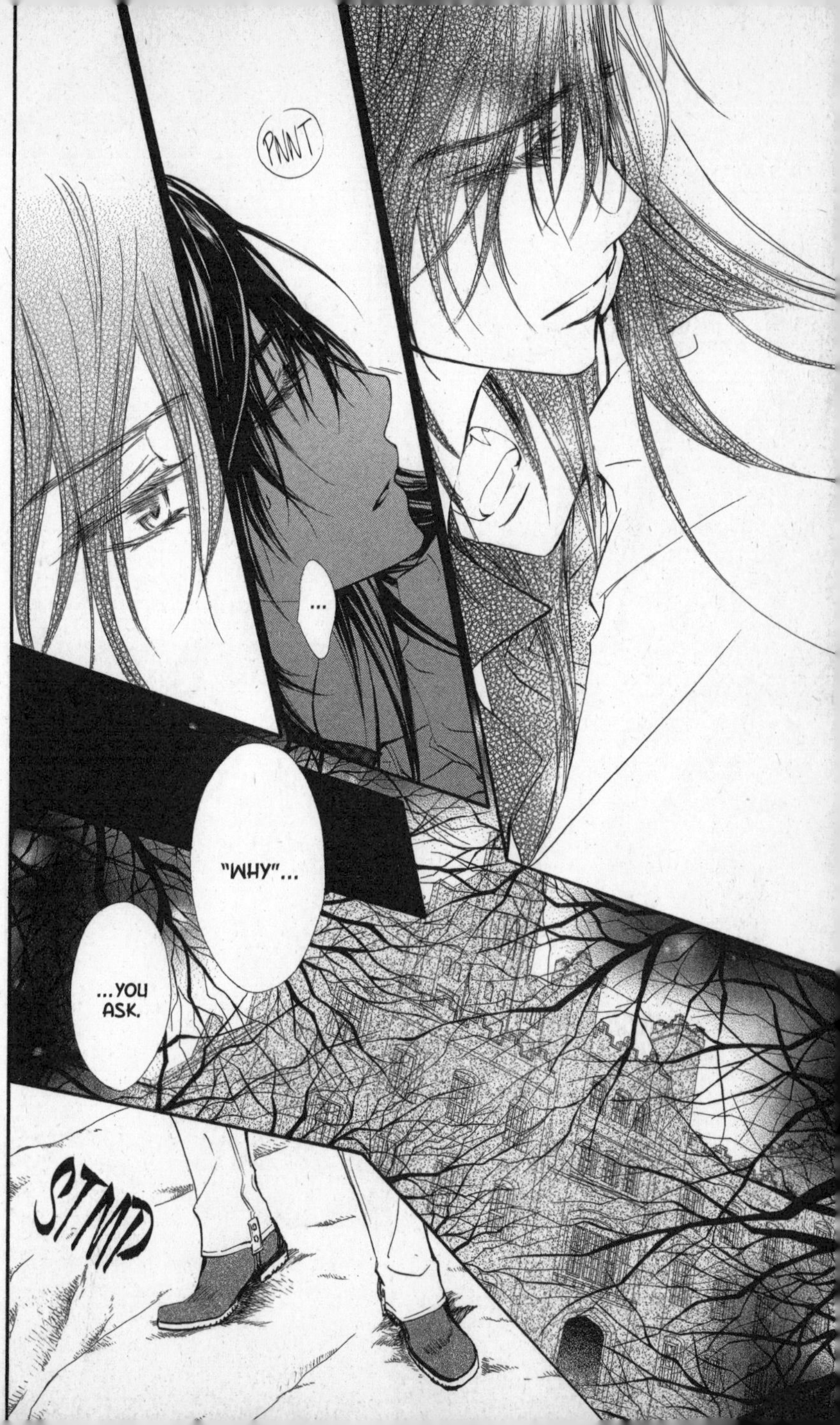
PNNT
...
"WHY"...
...YOU ASK.
STMP

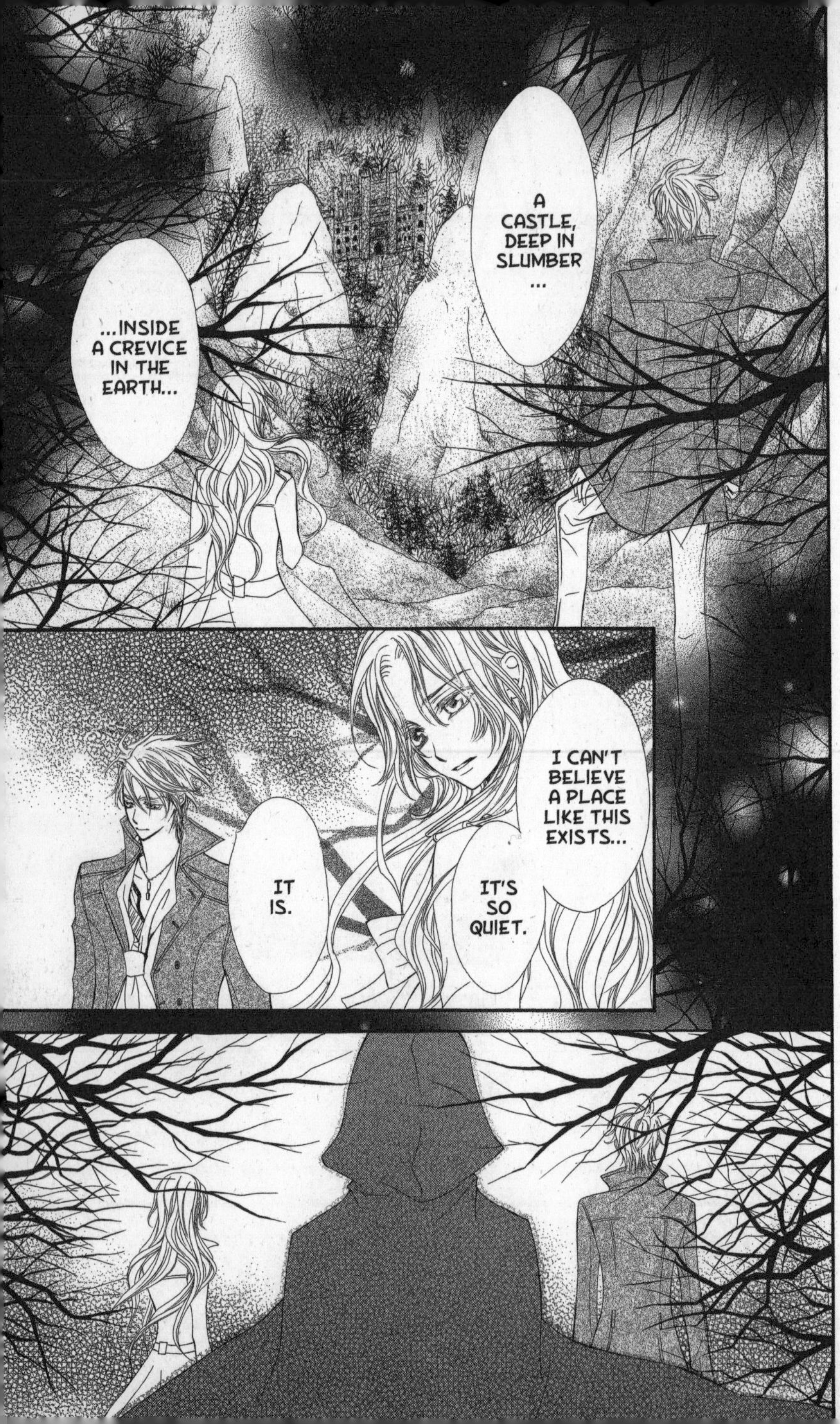
A CASTLE, DEEP IN SLUMBER...
...INSIDE A CREVICE IN THE EARTH...
I CAN'T BELIEVE A PLACE LIKE THIS EXISTS...
IT'S SO QUIET.
IT IS.

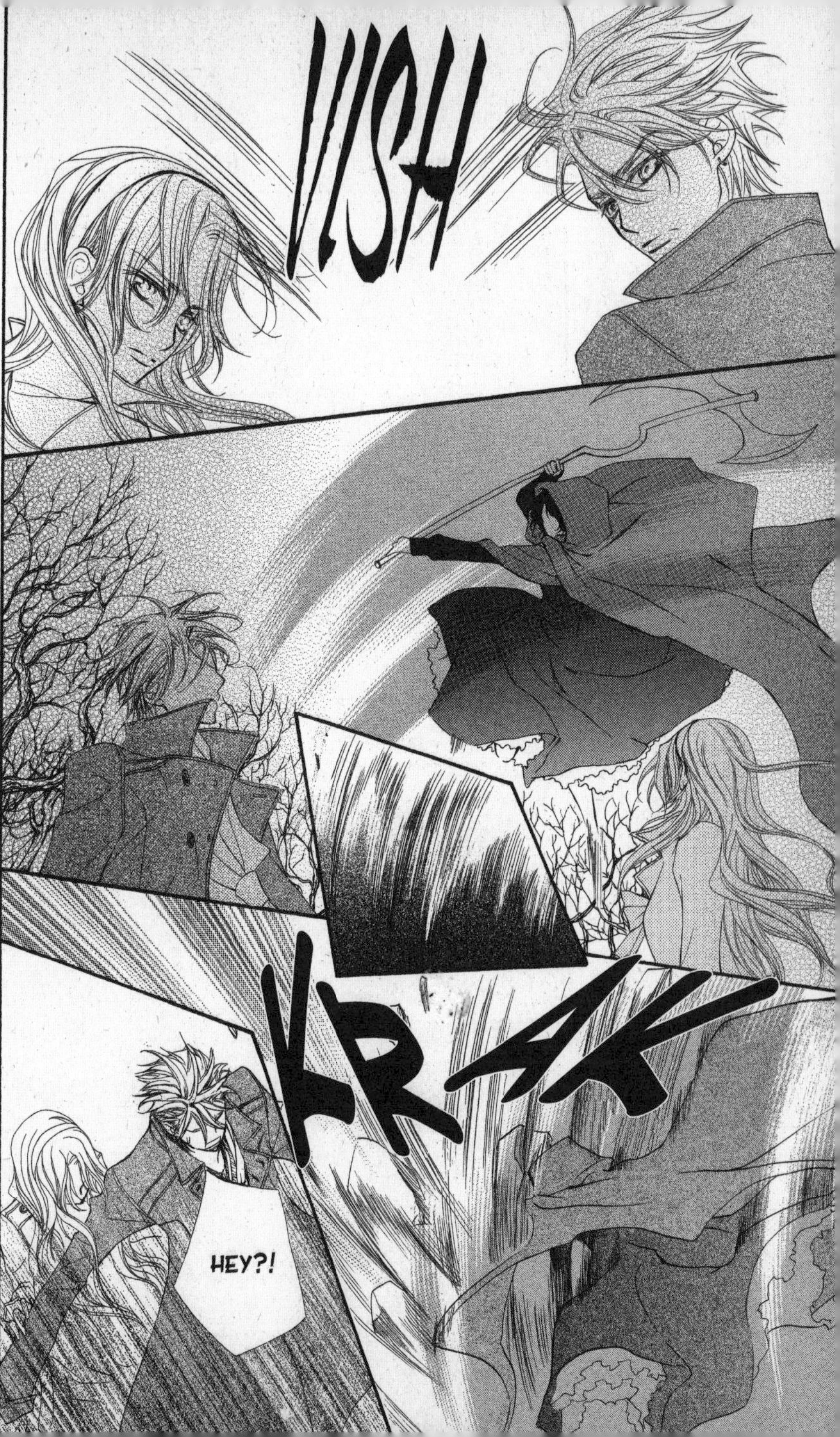
VISH
KRAK
HEY?!

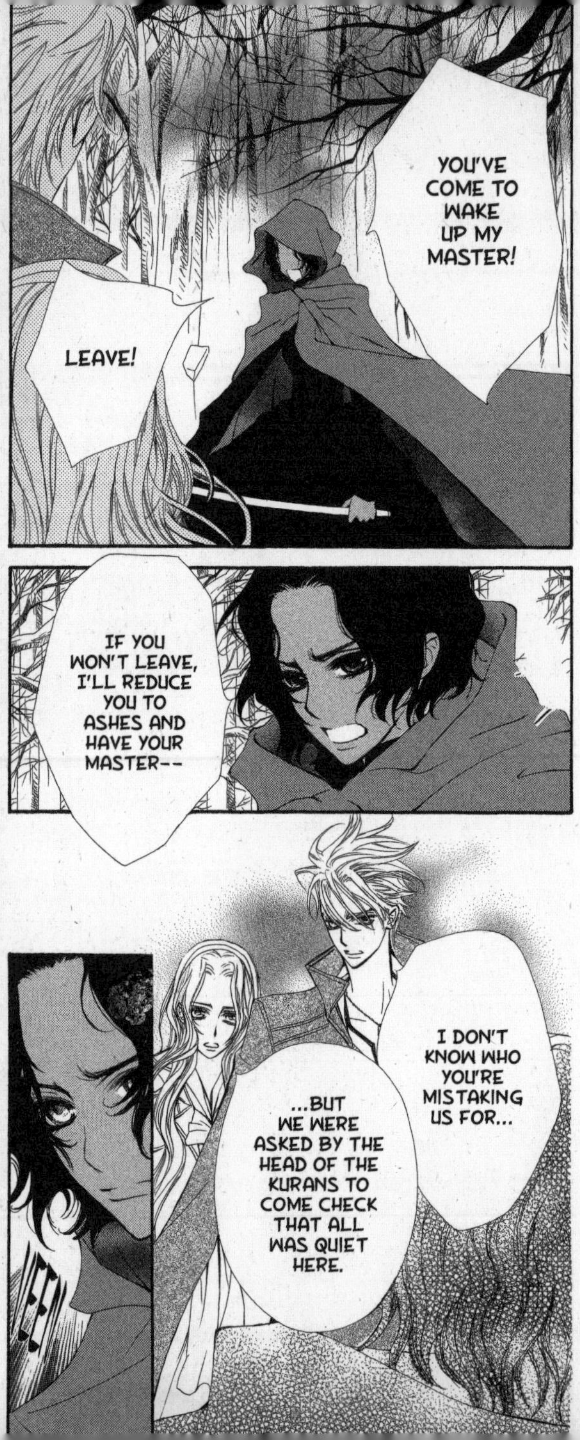
YOU'VE COME TO WAKE UP MY MASTER!
LEAVE!
IF YOU WON'T LEAVE, I'LL REDUCE YOU TO ASHES AND HAVE YOUR MASTER--
I DON'T KNOW WHO YOU'RE MISTAKING US FOR...
...BUT WE WERE ASKED BY THE HEAD OF THE KURANS TO COME CHECK THAT ALL WAS QUIET HERE.

IV

(→continued)
...was able to meet many wonderful people, but I'm unable to write about it all here! (I'm ashamed by my lack of skills as a writer.)
Here's a summary of the things I had never experienced before in my life.↓

- For the first time in my life, I had two bodyguards give me iron-clad protection for two days. (It could be because I asked them to prohibit video and photographs, so apart from the time I was onstage, I was always hidden from the participants...) I...I'm sorry...)
- I rode in a BMW for the first time. The expressways in Germany have no speed limit, so the car would go 99 miles per hour, but it was such a cozy ride that I fell asleep!
- Two or three hundred staff members of the book fair would gather at a bar that was like a cave, and we'd party every night. It was an all-you-can-drink place with a live rock band in the back. It was a very ethereal experience, like I was attending a mysterious underground gathering. I could tell that it was going to be a passionate book fair.♪
- Being interviewed onstage! I was only able to get past that thanks to Horie, my interpreter.♪

The book fair ended and... (continues)

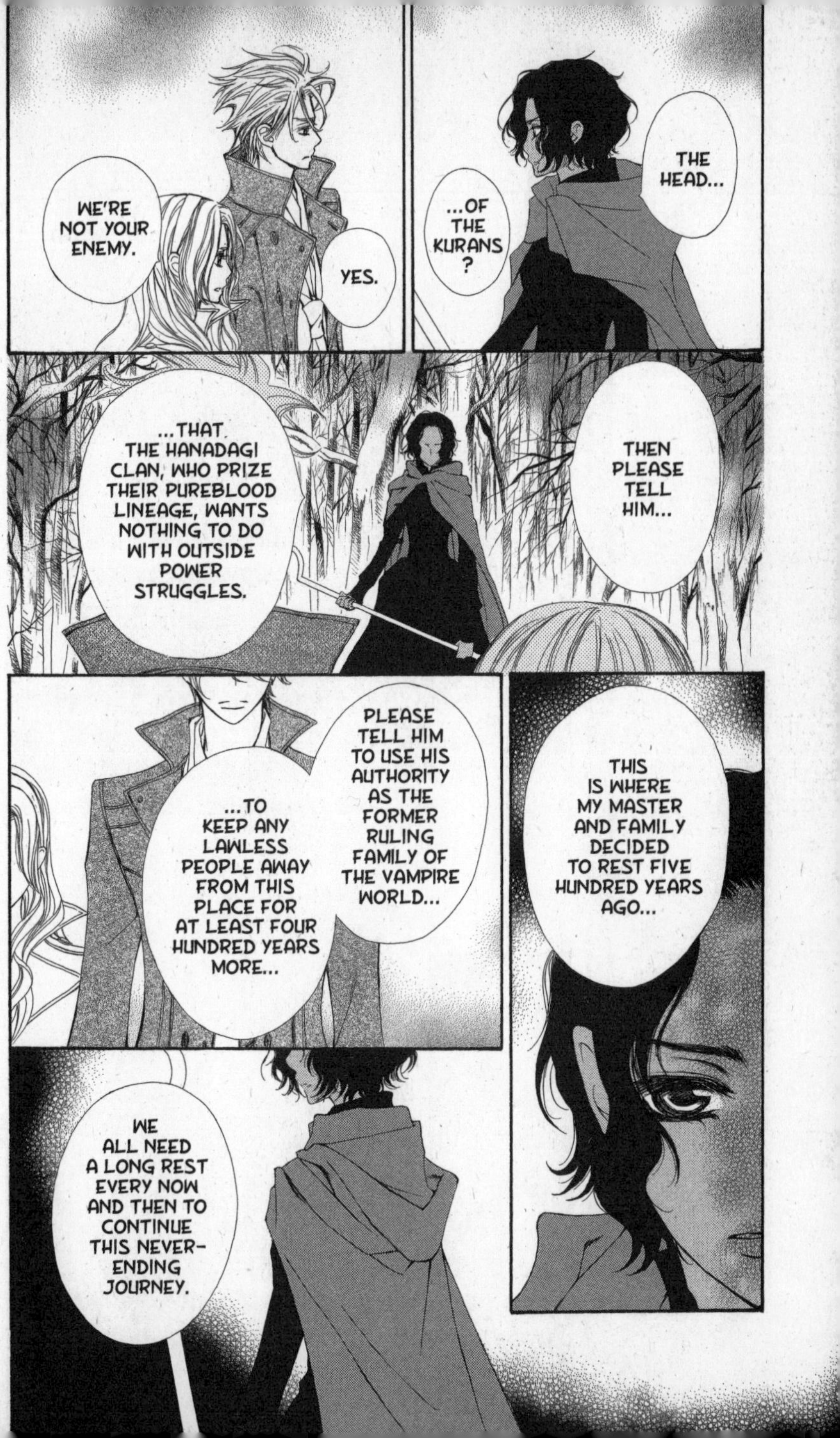
THE HEAD...
...OF THE KURANS?
YES.
WE'RE NOT YOUR ENEMY.
THEN PLEASE TELL HIM...
...THAT THE HANADAGI CLAN, WHO PRIZE THEIR PUREBLOOD LINEAGE, WANTS NOTHING TO DO WITH OUTSIDE POWER STRUGGLES.
THIS IS WHERE MY MASTER AND FAMILY DECIDED TO REST FIVE HUNDRED YEARS AGO...
PLEASE TELL HIM TO USE HIS AUTHORITY AS THE FORMER RULING FAMILY OF THE VAMPIRE WORLD...
...TO KEEP ANY LAWLESS PEOPLE AWAY FROM THIS PLACE FOR AT LEAST FOUR HUNDRED YEARS MORE...
WE ALL NEED A LONG REST EVERY NOW AND THEN TO CONTINUE THIS NEVER-ENDING JOURNEY.

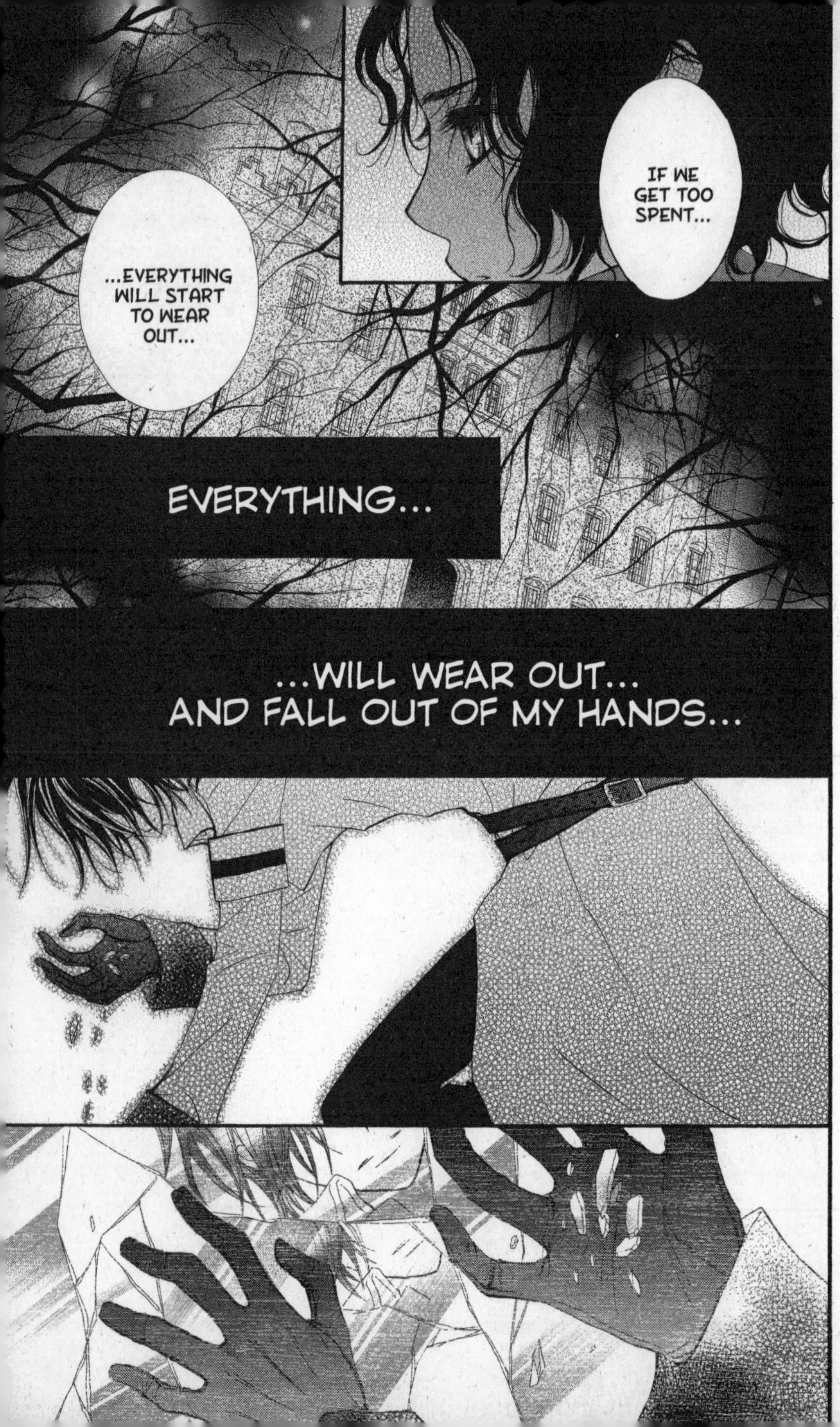
IF WE GET TOO SPENT...
...EVERYTHING WILL START TO WEAR OUT...
EVERYTHING...
...WILL WEAR OUT... AND FALL OUT OF MY HANDS...

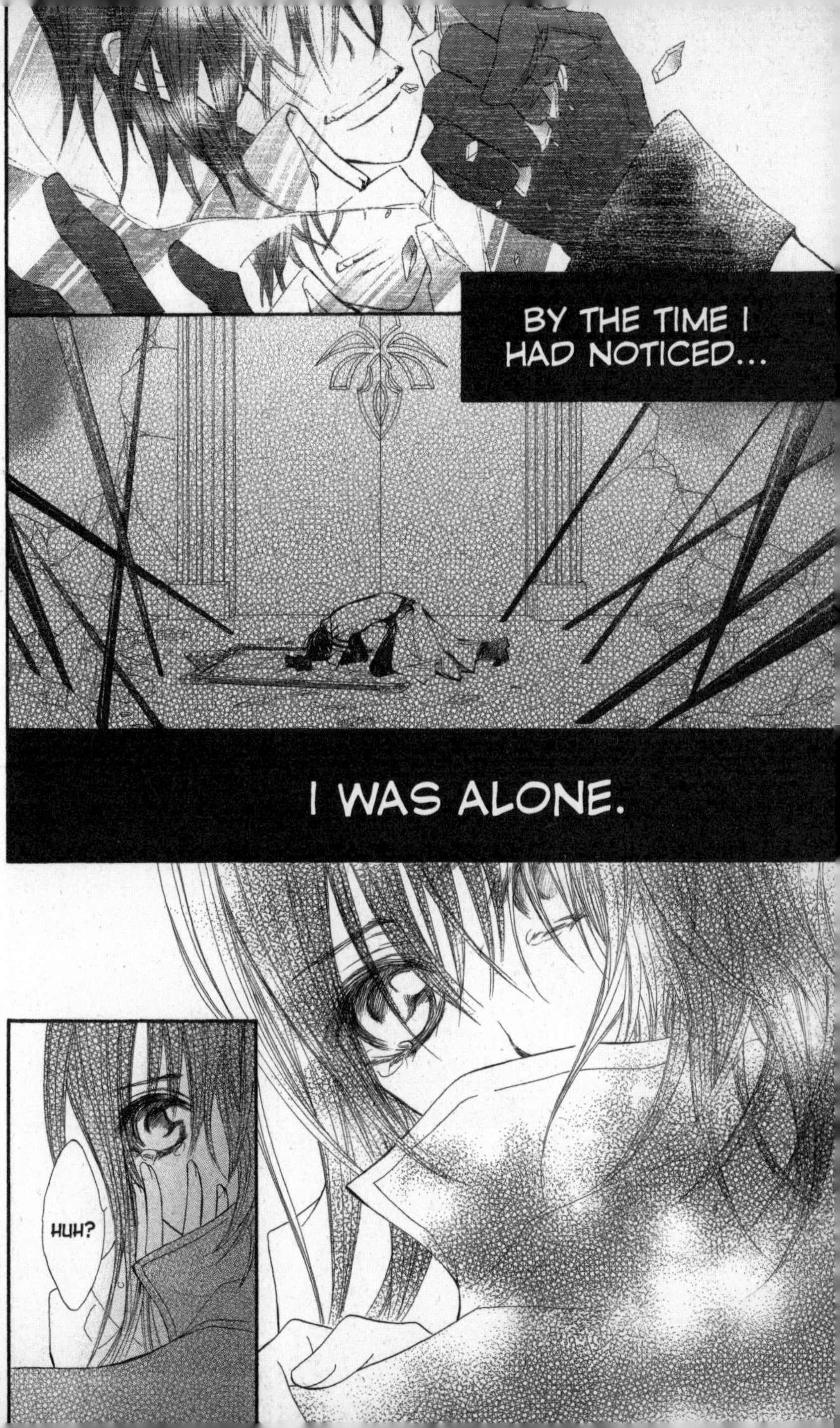
BY THE TIME I HAD NOTICED...
I WAS ALONE.
HUH?

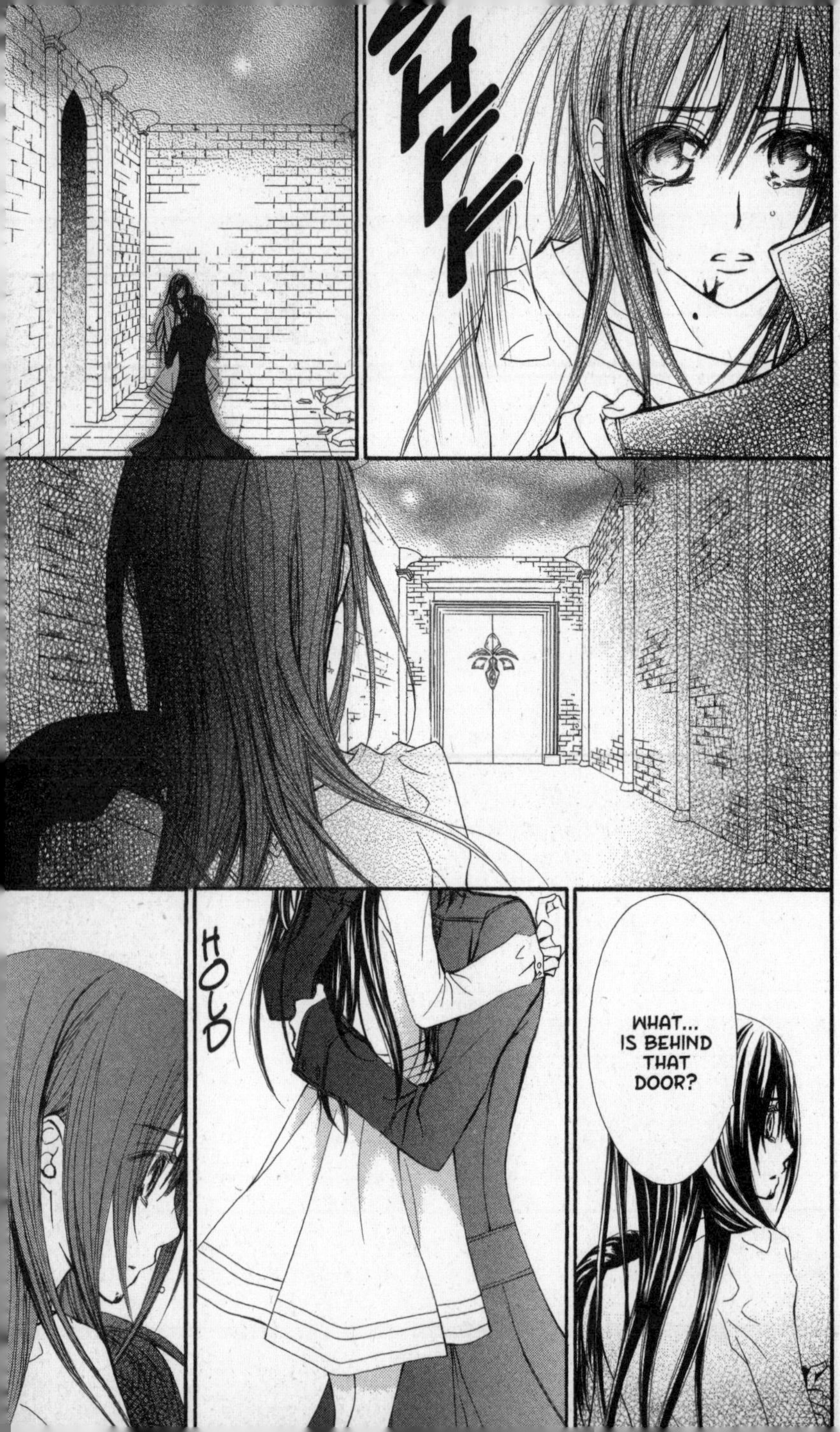
SHFFF
WHAT... IS BEHIND THAT DOOR?
HOLD

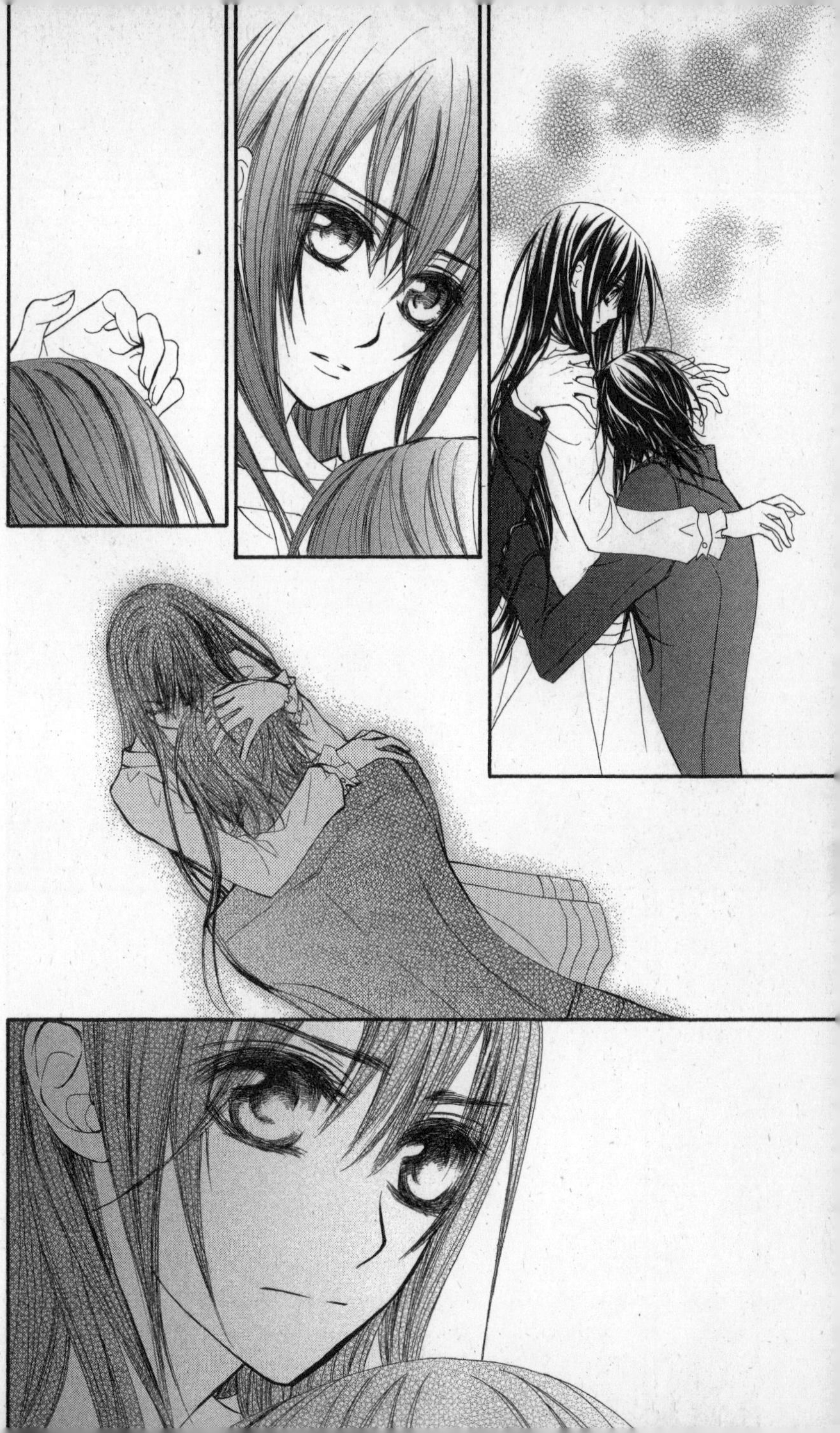

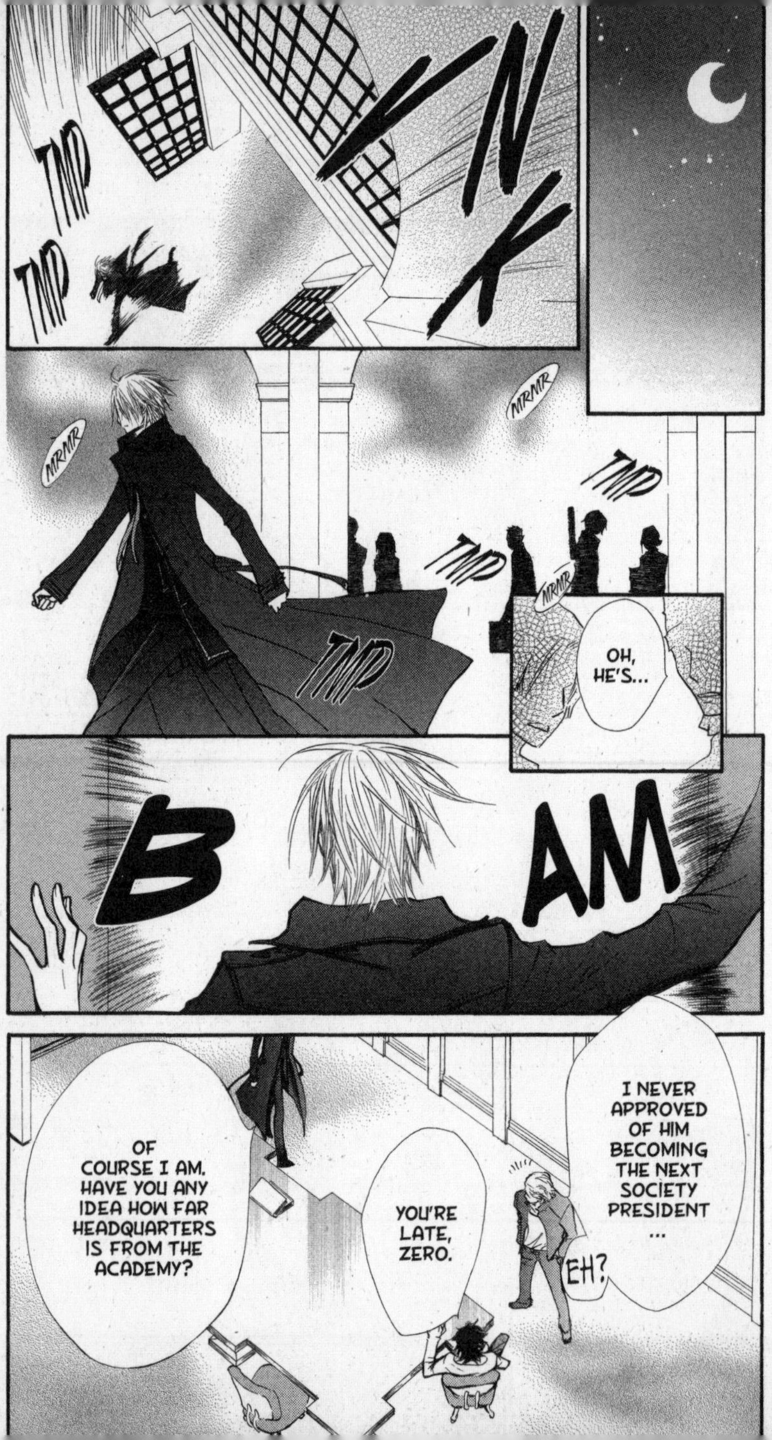
KNK
TMP
TMP
TMP
TMP
MRMR
OH, HE'S...
MRMR
MRMR
TMP
BAM
I NEVER APPROVED OF HIM BECOMING THE NEXT SOCIETY PRESIDENT ...
EH?
YOU'RE LATE, ZERO.
OF COURSE I AM. HAVE YOU ANY IDEA HOW FAR HEADQUARTERS IS FROM THE ACADEMY?

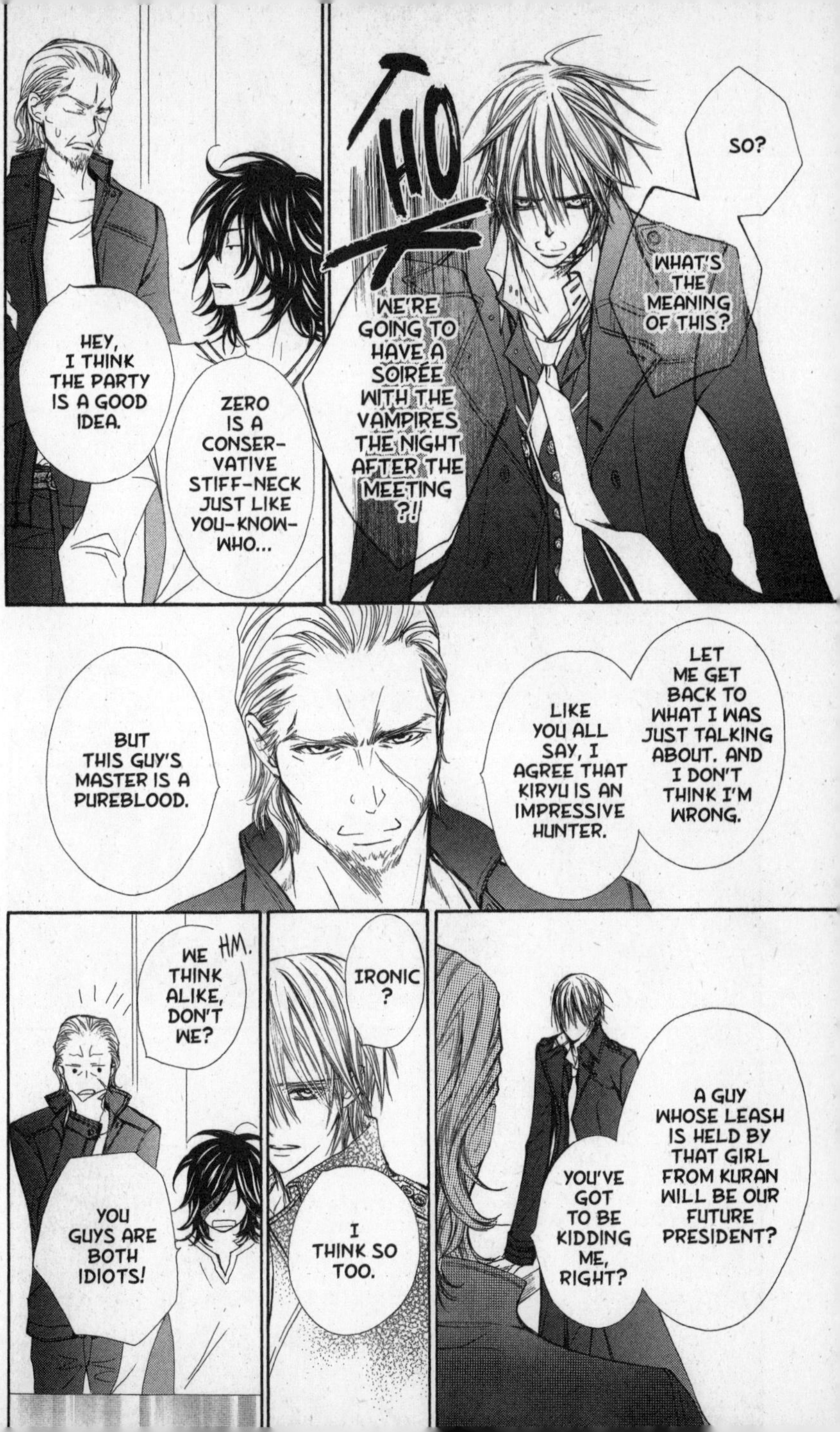
SO?
WHAT'S THE MEANING OF THIS?
WE'RE GOING TO HAVE A SOIRÉE WITH THE VAMPIRES THE NIGHT AFTER THE MEETING ?!
ZERO IS A CONSERVATIVE STIFF-NECK JUST LIKE YOU-KNOW-WHO...
HEY, I THINK THE PARTY IS A GOOD IDEA.
LET ME GET BACK TO WHAT I WAS JUST TALKING ABOUT. AND I DON'T THINK I'M WRONG.
LIKE YOU ALL SAY, I AGREE THAT KIRYU IS AN IMPRESSIVE HUNTER.
BUT THIS GUY'S MASTER IS A PUREBLOOD.
A GUY WHOSE LEASH IS HELD BY THAT GIRL FROM KURAN WILL BE OUR FUTURE PRESIDENT?
YOU'VE GOT TO BE KIDDING ME, RIGHT?
IRONIC?
I THINK SO TOO.
HM.
WE THINK ALIKE, DON'T WE?
YOU GUYS ARE BOTH IDIOTS!

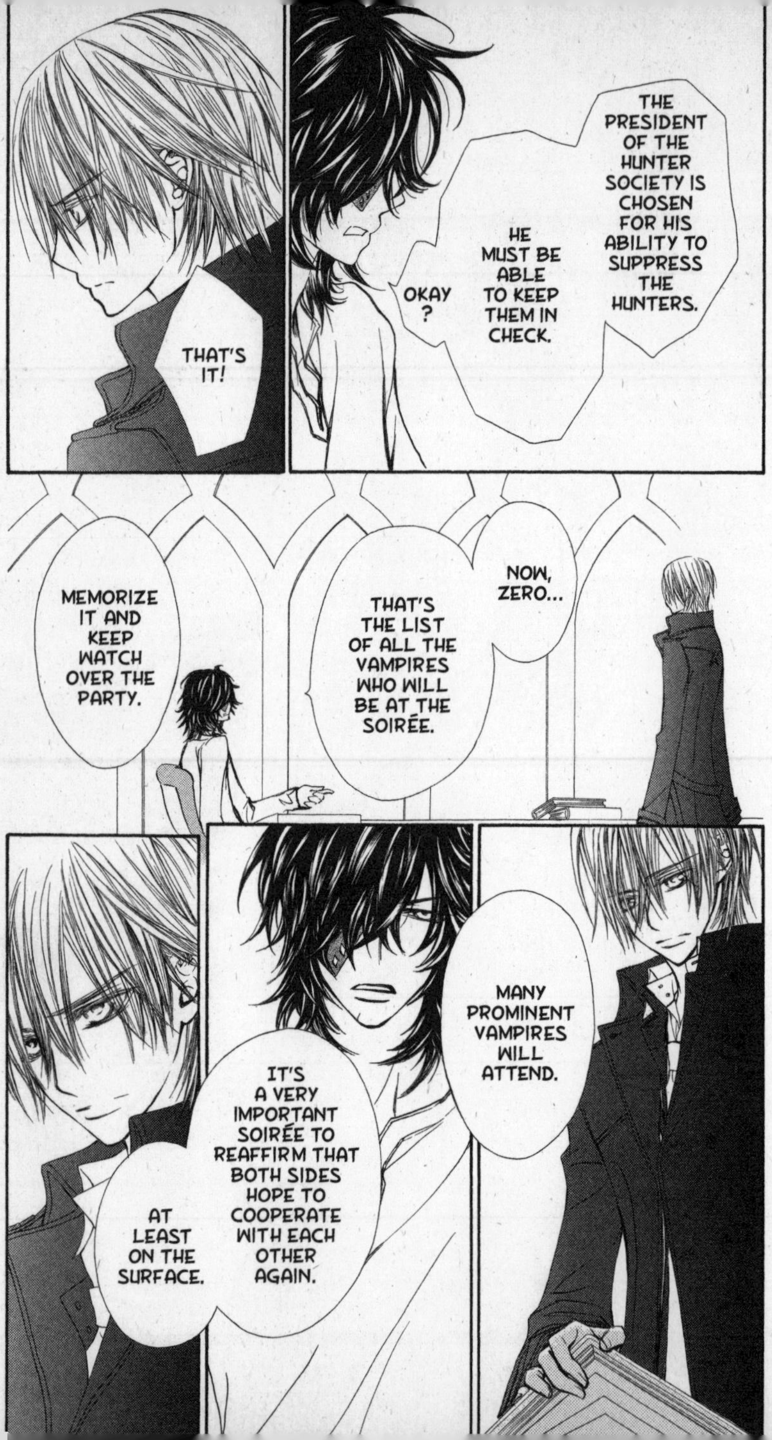
THE PRESIDENT OF THE HUNTER SOCIETY IS CHOSEN FOR HIS ABILITY TO SUPPRESS THE HUNTERS.
HE MUST BE ABLE TO KEEP THEM IN CHECK.
OKAY?
THAT'S IT!
NOW, ZERO...
THAT'S THE LIST OF ALL THE VAMPIRES WHO WILL BE AT THE SOIRÉE.
MEMORIZE IT AND KEEP WATCH OVER THE PARTY.
MANY PROMINENT VAMPIRES WILL ATTEND.
IT'S A VERY IMPORTANT SOIRÉE TO REAFFIRM THAT BOTH SIDES HOPE TO COOPERATE WITH EACH OTHER AGAIN.
AT LEAST ON THE SURFACE.

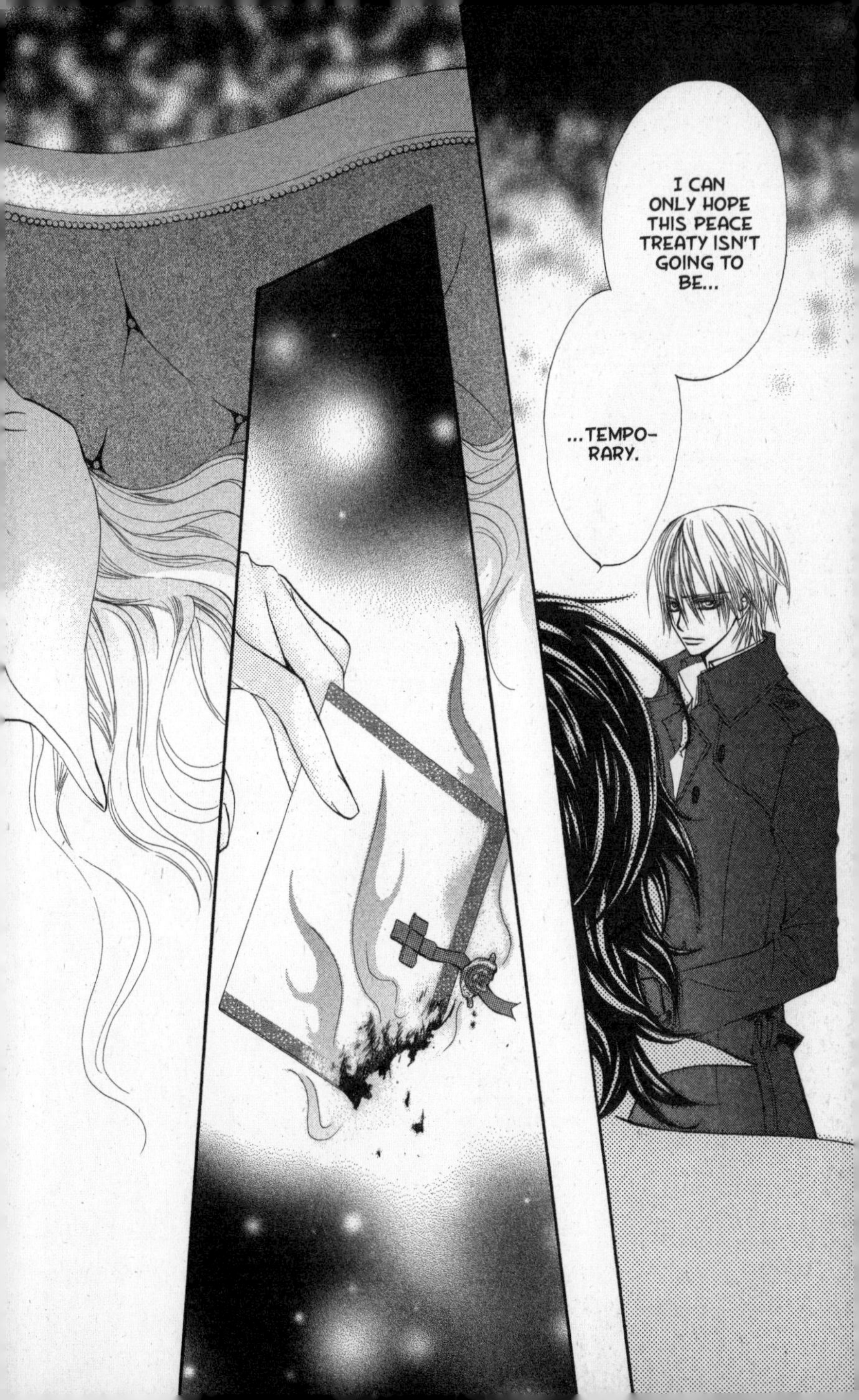
I CAN ONLY HOPE THIS PEACE TREATY ISN'T GOING TO BE...
...TEMPO-RARY.

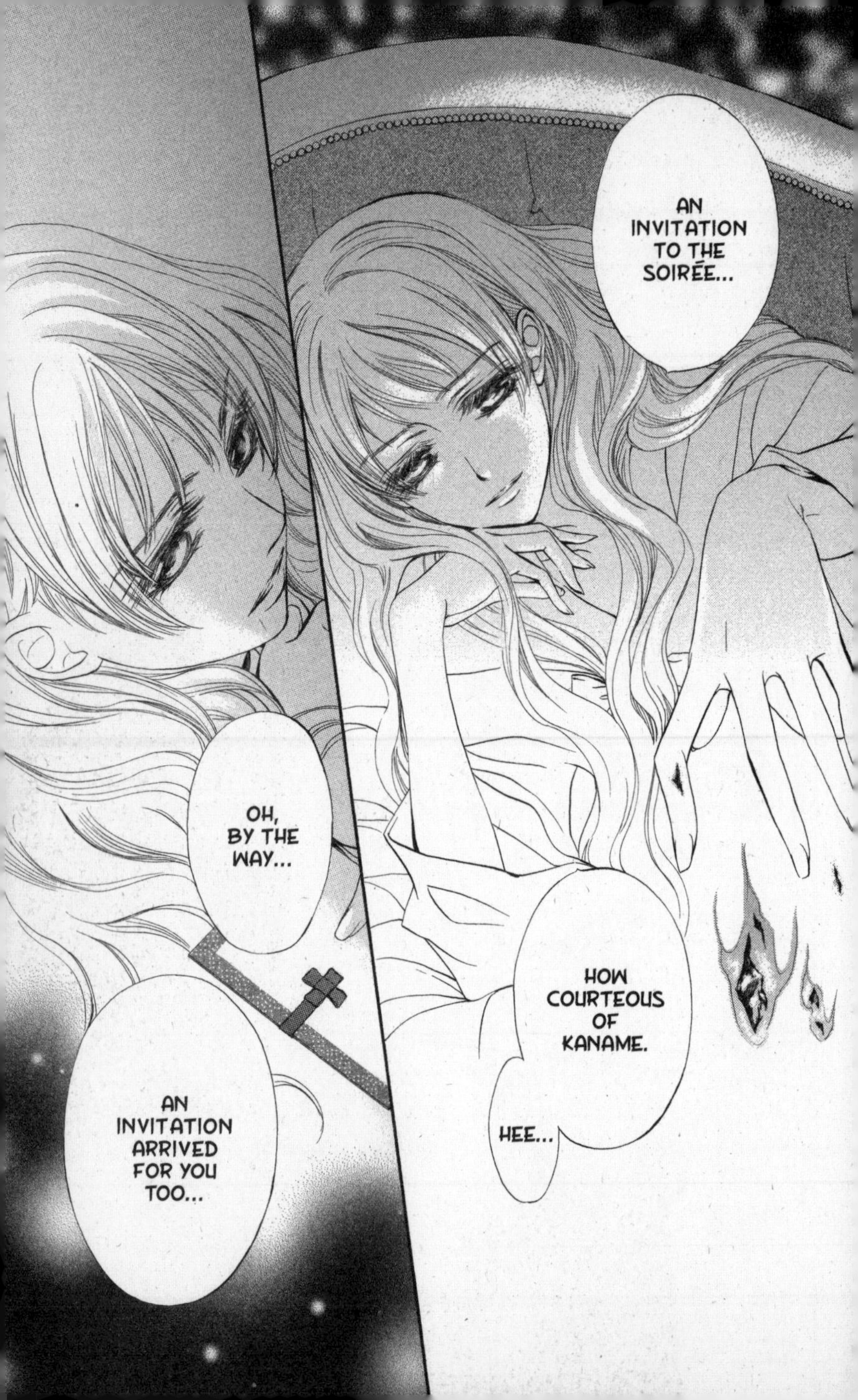
AN INVITATION TO THE SOIRÉE...
HOW COURTEOUS OF KANAME.
HEE...
OH, BY THE WAY...
AN INVITATION ARRIVED FOR YOU TOO...

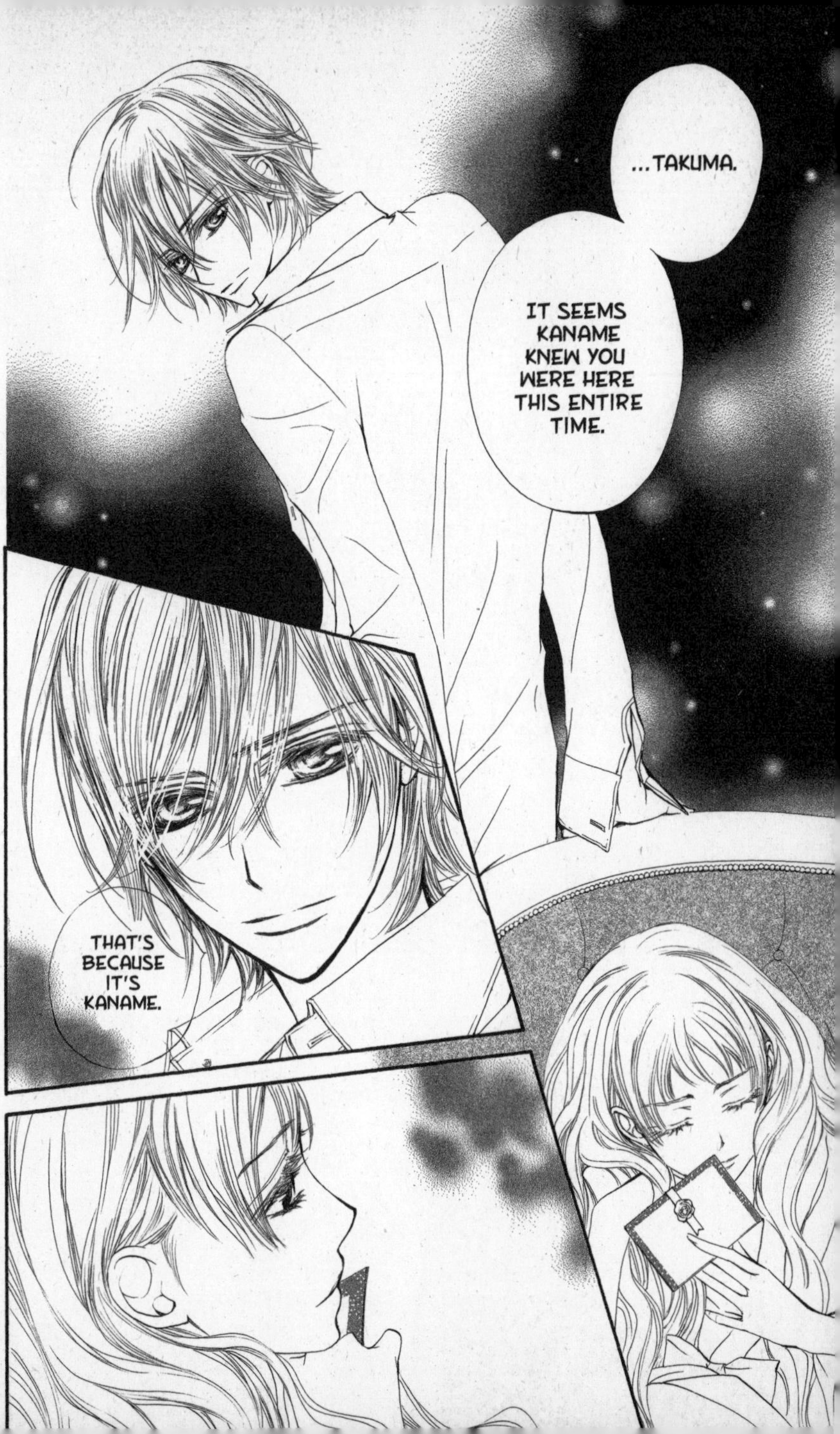
...TAKUMA.
IT SEEMS KANAME KNEW YOU WERE HERE THIS ENTIRE TIME.
THAT'S BECAUSE IT'S KANAME.

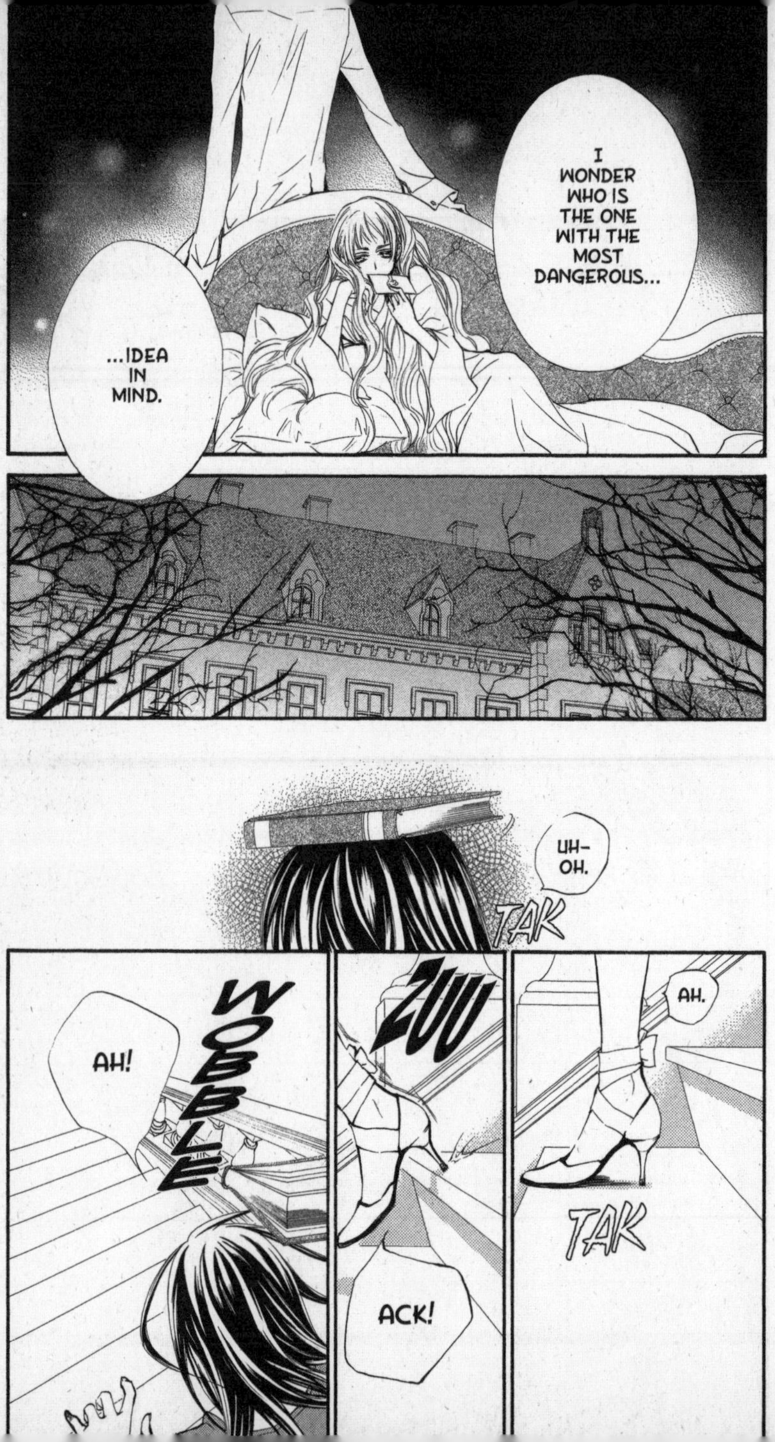
I WONDER WHO IS THE ONE WITH THE MOST DANGEROUS...
...IDEA IN MIND.
UH-OH.
TAK
AH.
TAK
ZUU
ACK!
WOBBLE
AH!

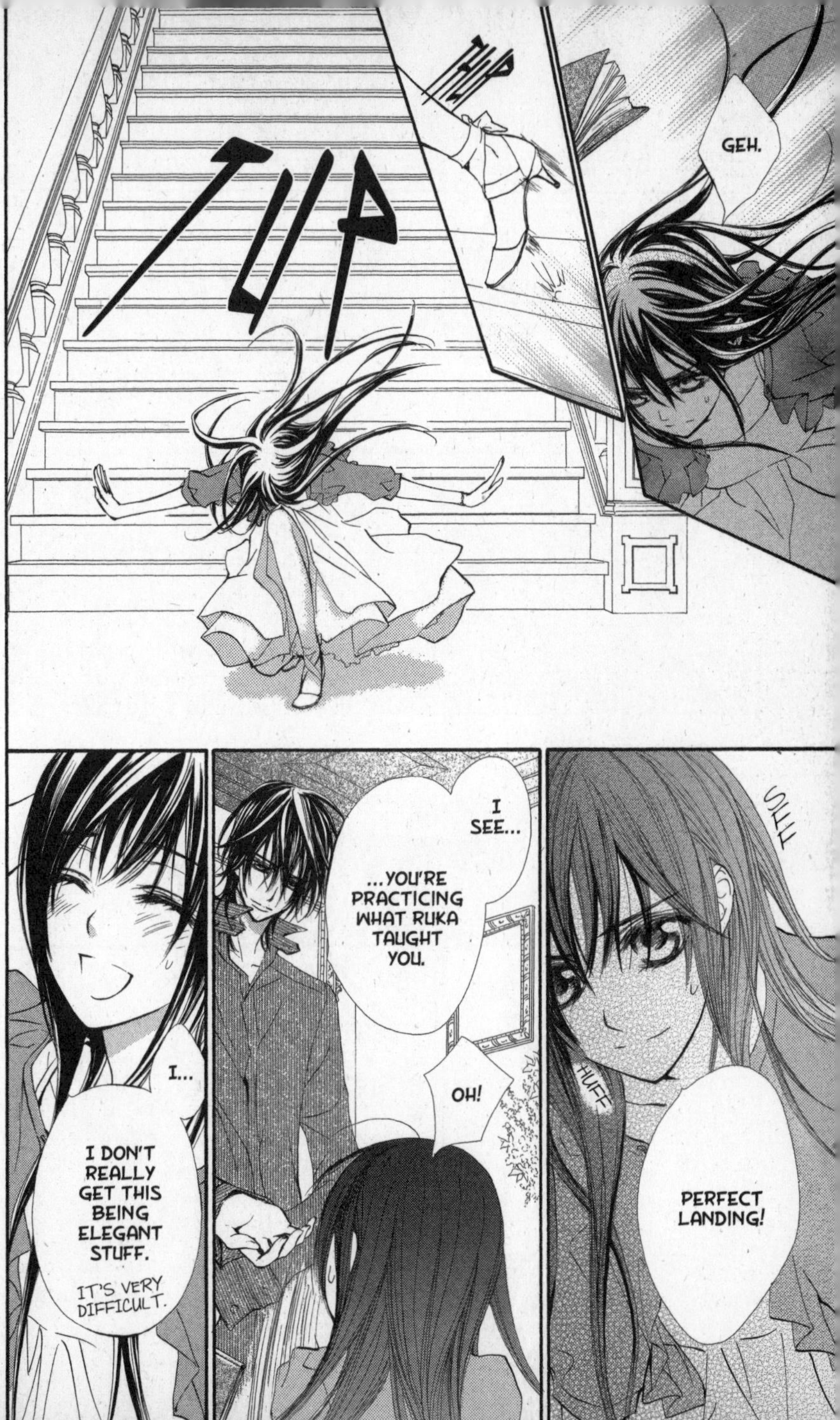
THP
GEH.
TUP
PERFECT LANDING!
HUFF
I SEE...
...YOU'RE PRACTICING WHAT RUKA TAUGHT YOU.
OH!
I...
I DON'T REALLY GET THIS BEING ELEGANT STUFF.
IT'S VERY DIFFICULT.

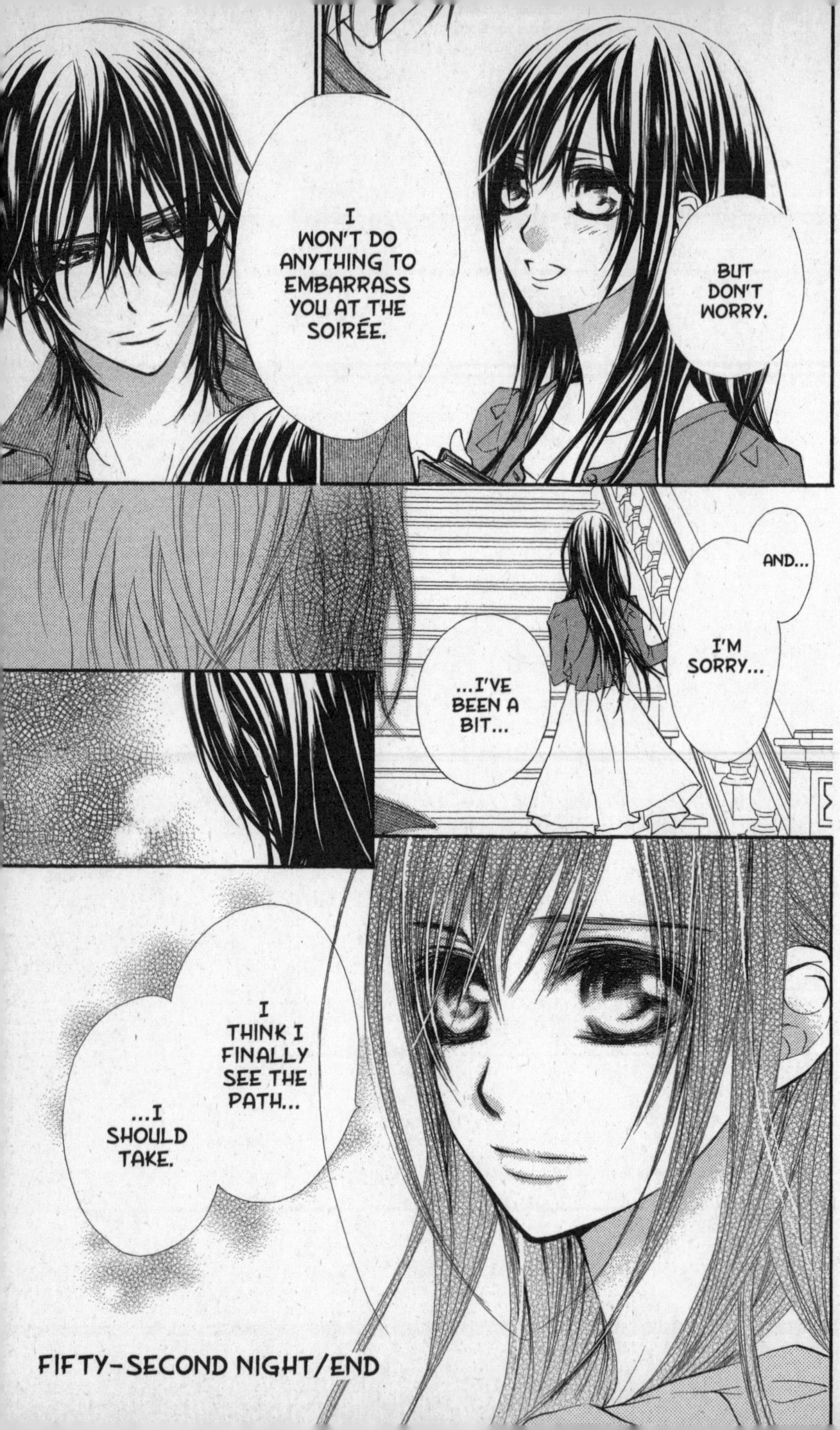
BUT DON'T WORRY.
I WON'T DO ANYTHING TO EMBARRASS YOU AT THE SOIRÉE.
AND...
I'M SORRY...
...I'VE BEEN A BIT...
I THINK I FINALLY SEE THE PATH...
...I SHOULD TAKE.
FIFTY-SECOND NIGHT/END

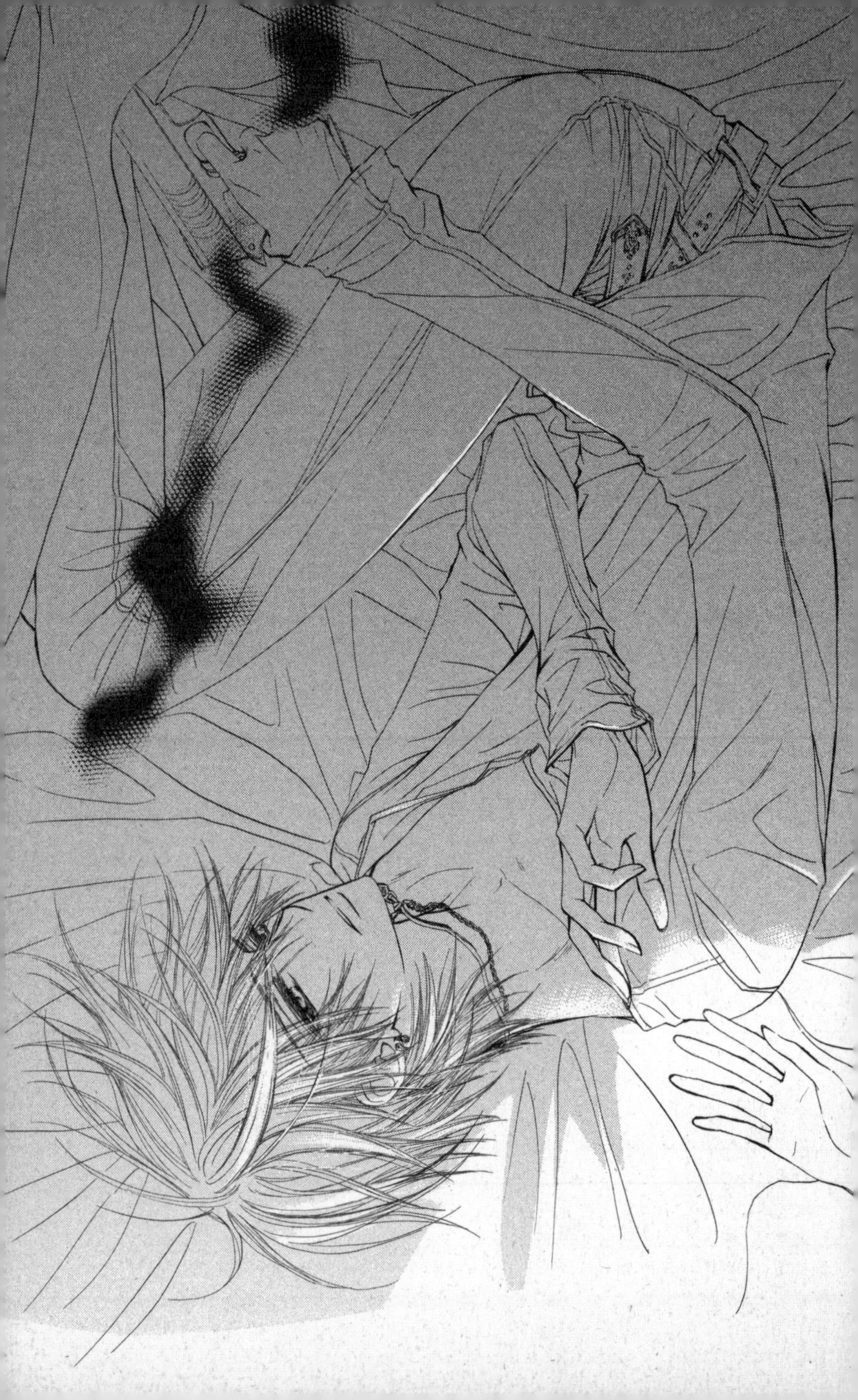

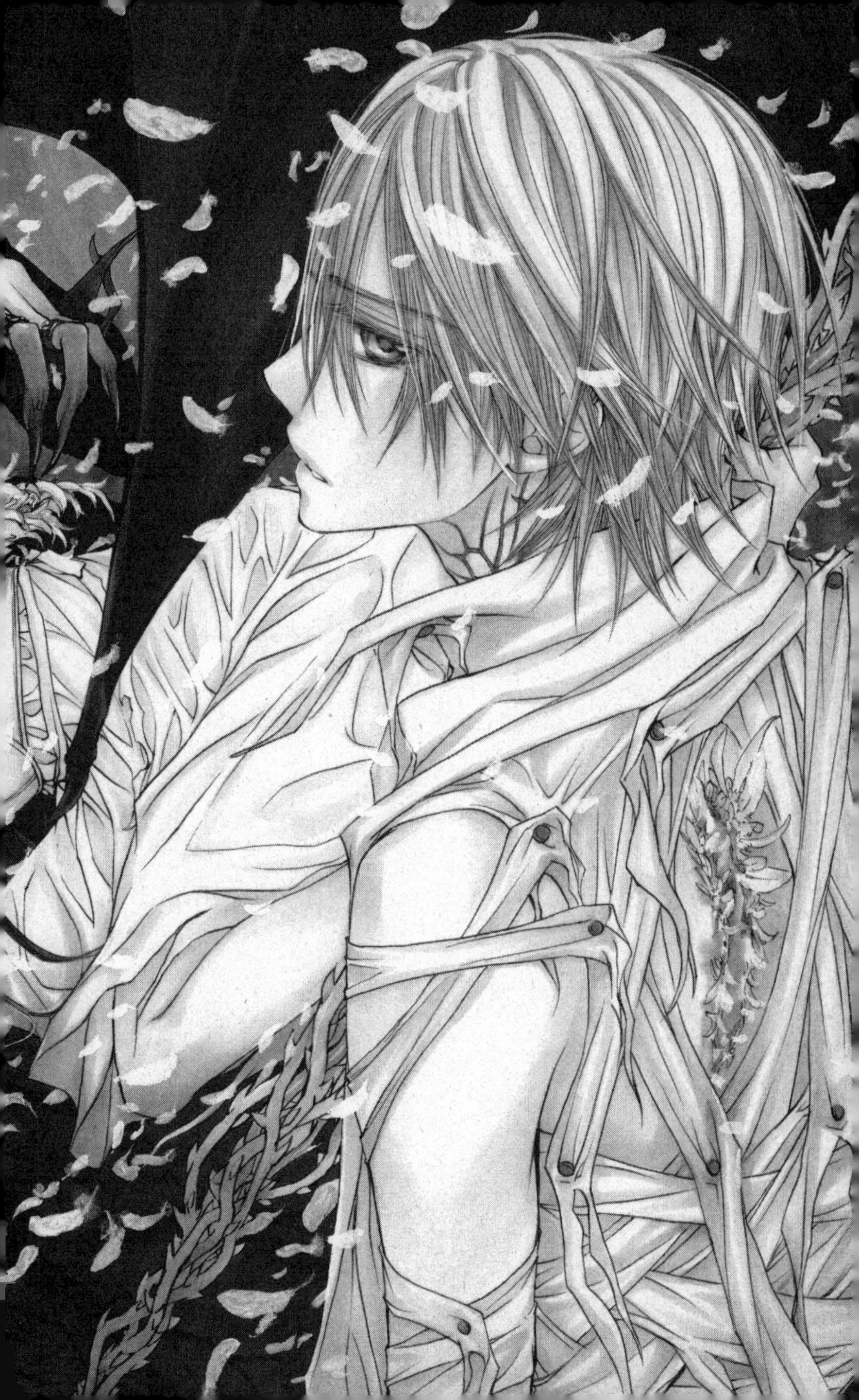

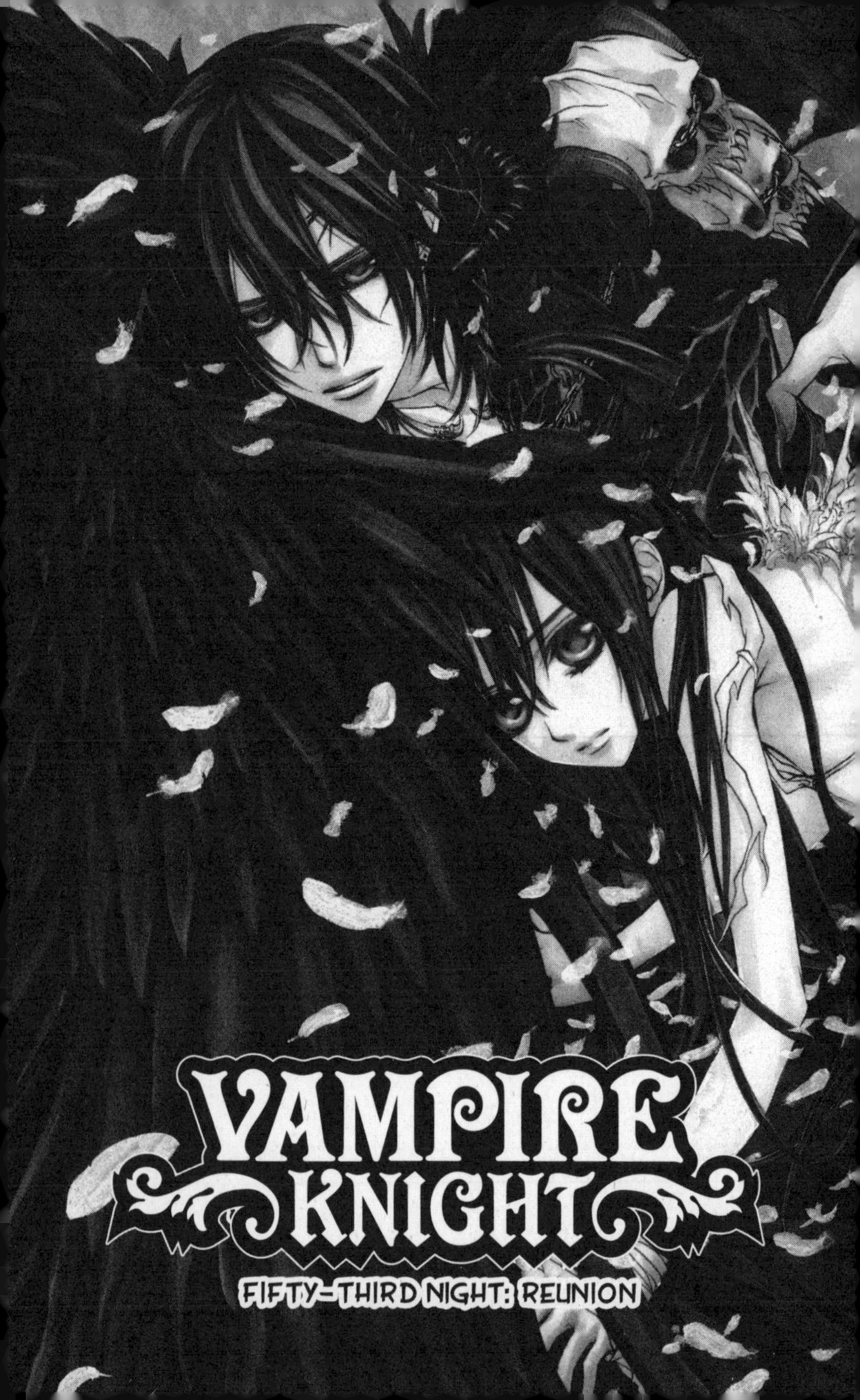
VAMPIRE KNIGHT
FIFTY-THIRD NIGHT: REUNION

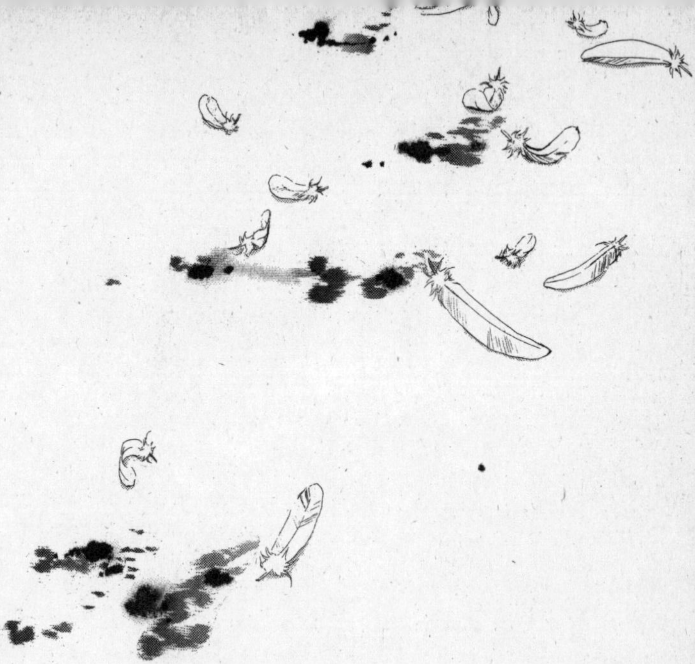

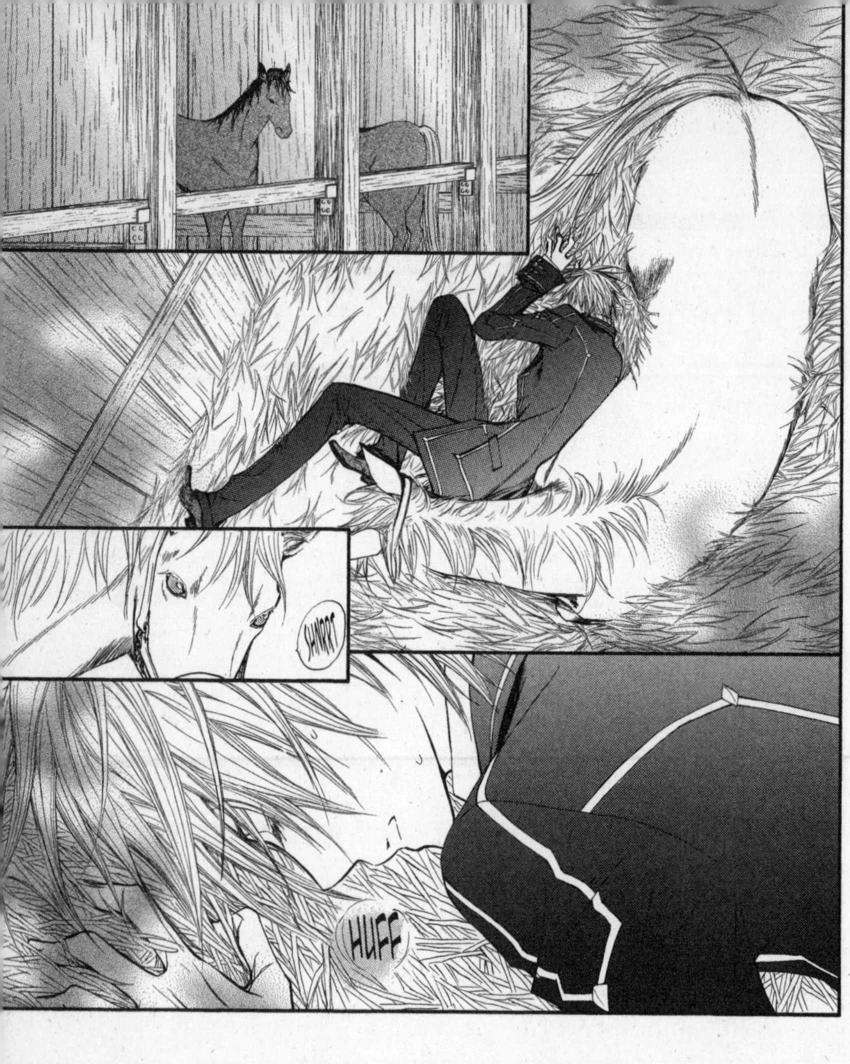
SHNRRT
HUFF

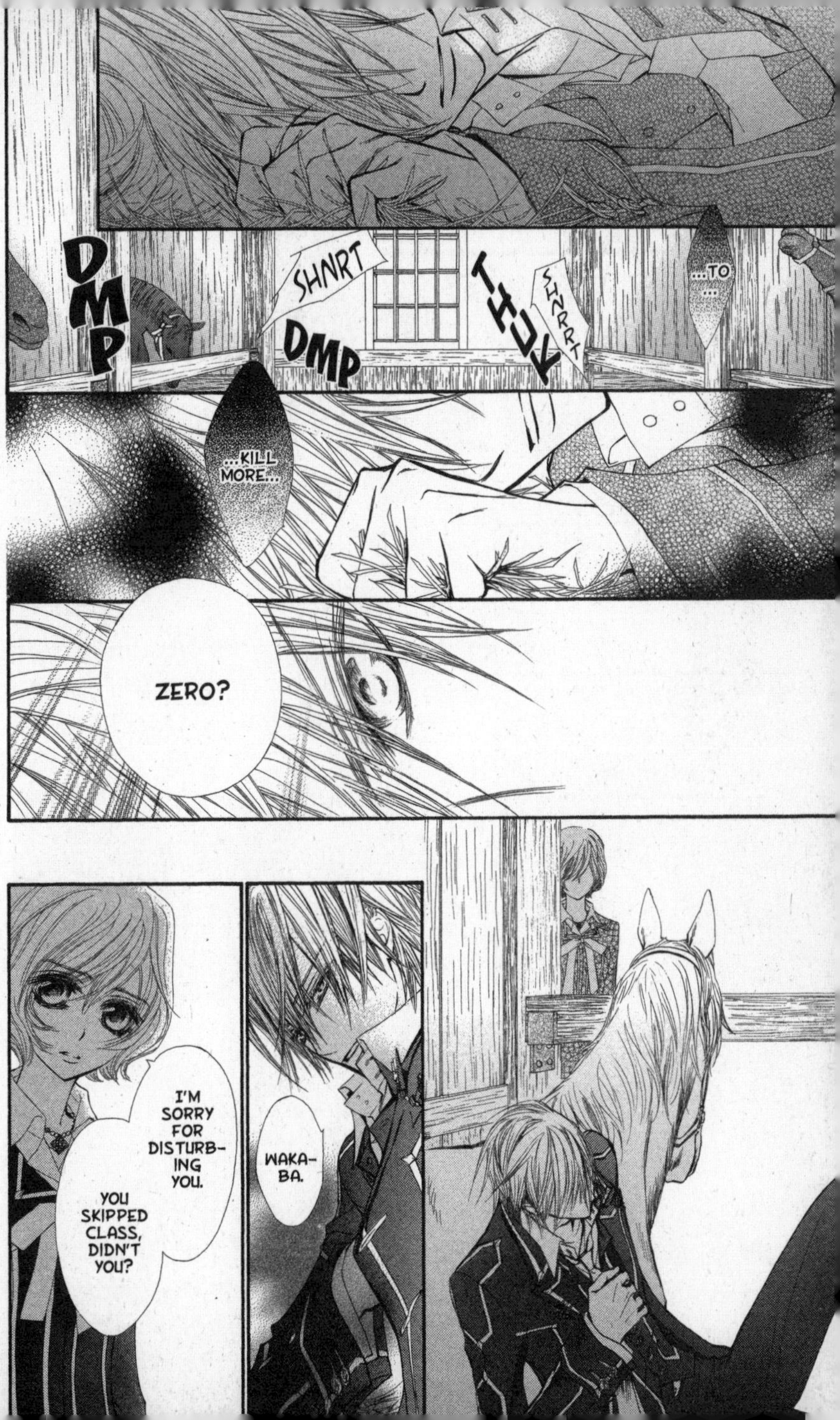
...TO ...
SHNRRT
THUD
DMP
SHNRT
DMP
...KILL MORE...
ZERO?
WAKA-BA.
I'M SORRY FOR DISTURB-ING YOU.
YOU SKIPPED CLASS, DIDN'T YOU?

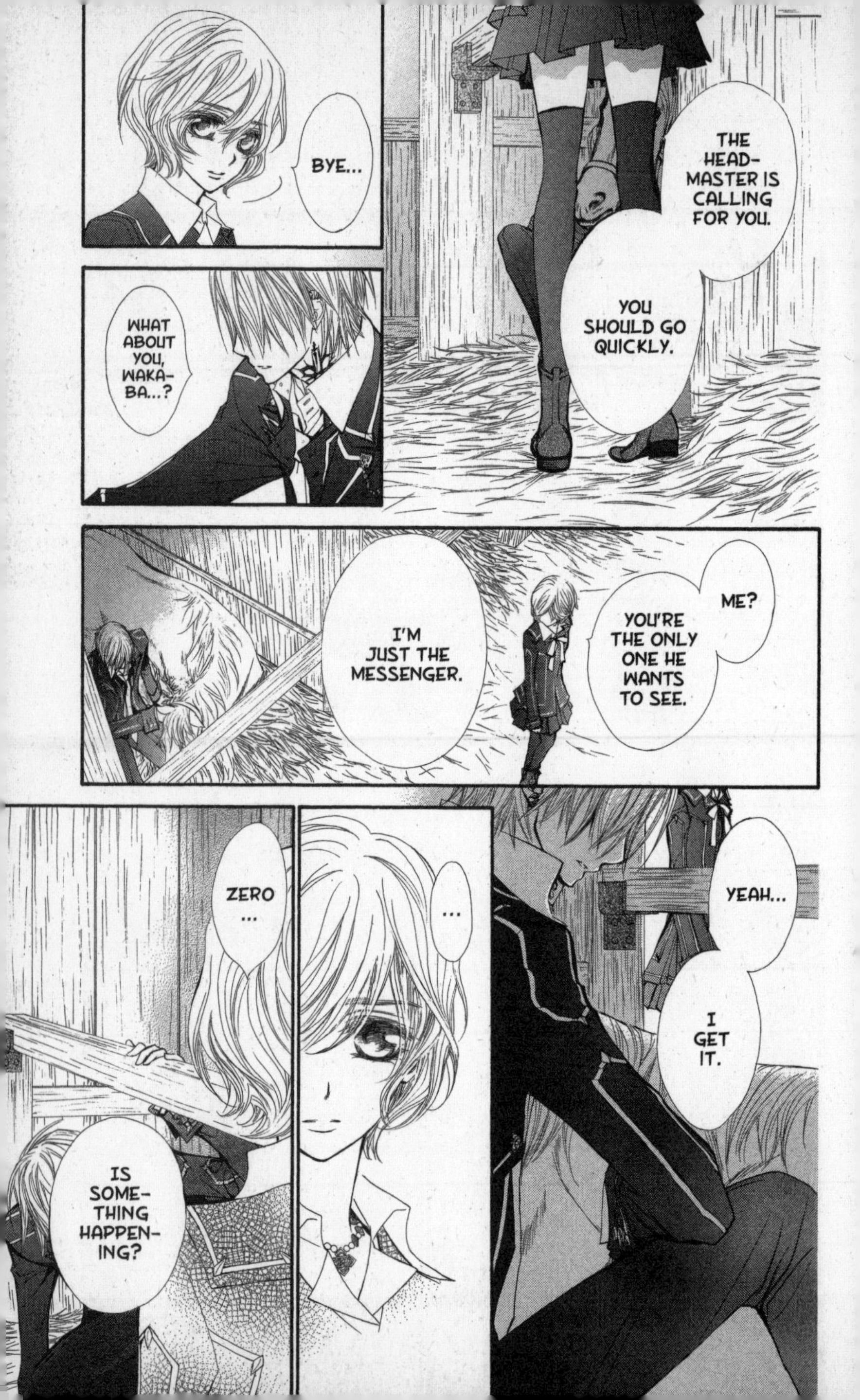
THE HEAD-MASTER IS CALLING FOR YOU.
YOU SHOULD GO QUICKLY.
BYE...
WHAT ABOUT YOU, WAKA-BA...?
ME?
YOU'RE THE ONLY ONE HE WANTS TO SEE.
I'M JUST THE MESSENGER.
YEAH...
I GET IT.
...
ZERO ...
IS SOME-THING HAPPEN-ING?

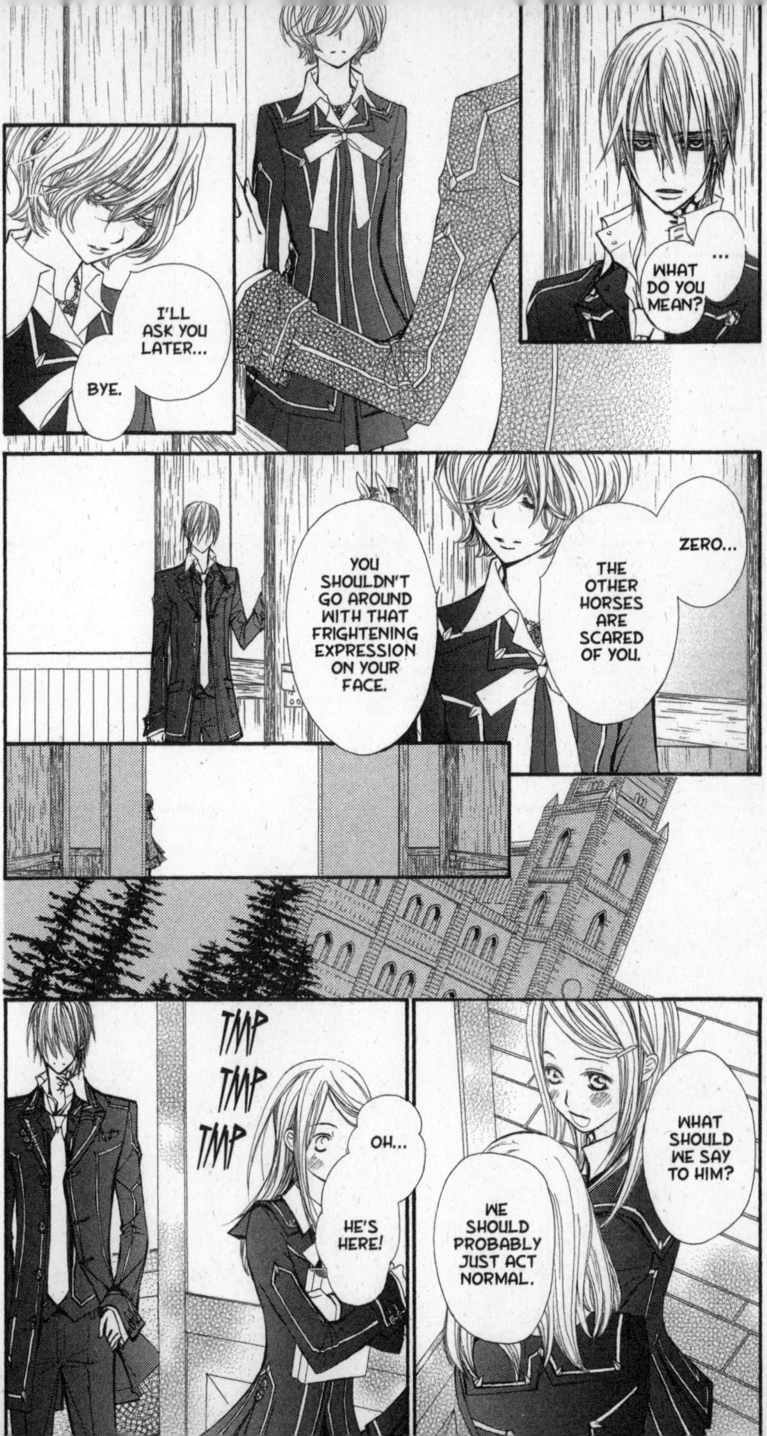
... WHAT DO YOU MEAN?
I'LL ASK YOU LATER...
BYE.
ZERO... THE OTHER HORSES ARE SCARED OF YOU.
YOU SHOULDN'T GO AROUND WITH THAT FRIGHTENING EXPRESSION ON YOUR FACE.
WHAT SHOULD WE SAY TO HIM?
WE SHOULD PROBABLY JUST ACT NORMAL.
OH...
HE'S HERE!
TMP TMP TMP

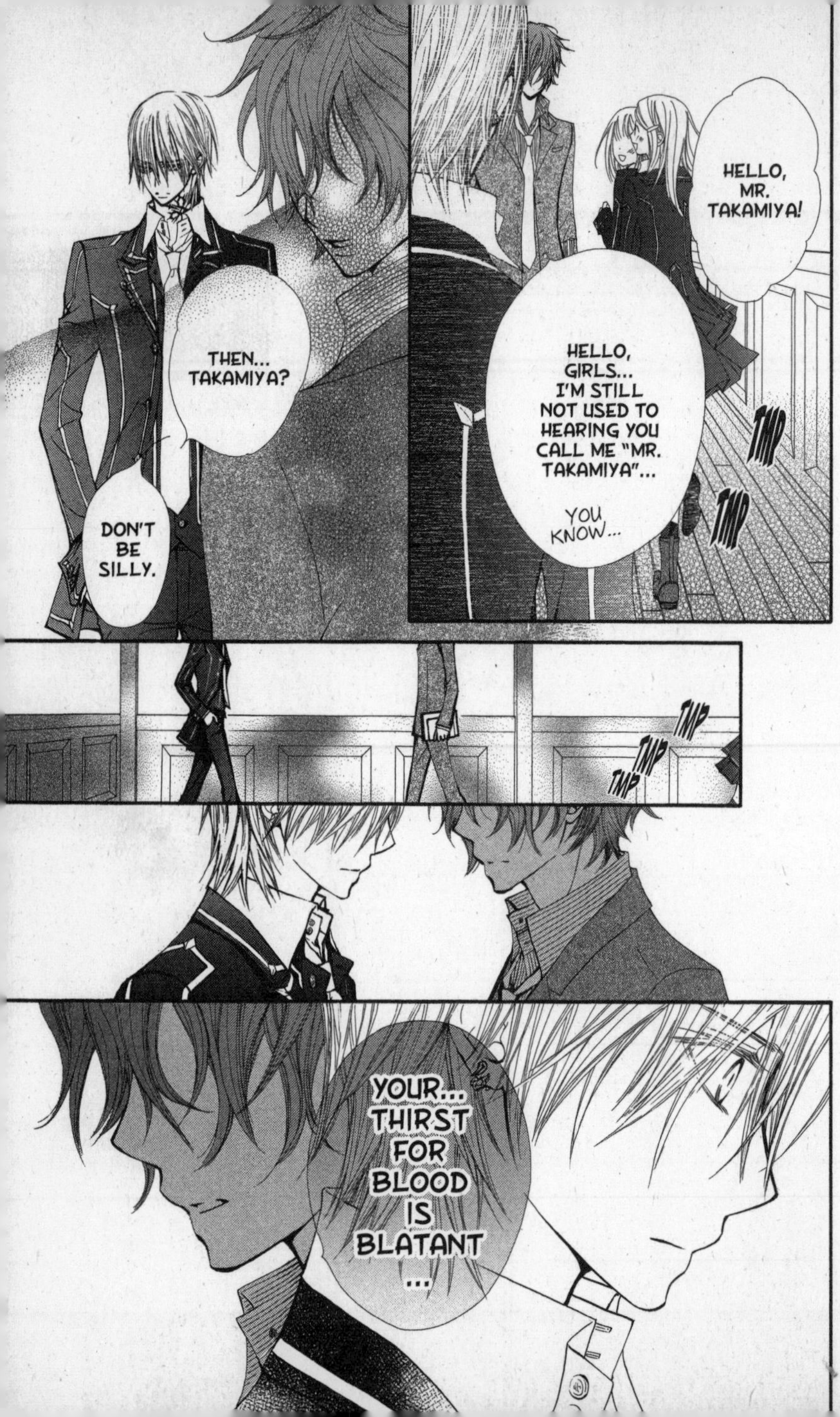
HELLO, MR. TAKAMIYA!
HELLO, GIRLS... I'M STILL NOT USED TO HEARING YOU CALL ME "MR. TAKAMIYA"...
YOU KNOW...
TMP
TMP
THEN... TAKAMIYA?
DON'T BE SILLY.
TMP
TMP
TMP
YOUR... THIRST FOR BLOOD IS BLATANT...

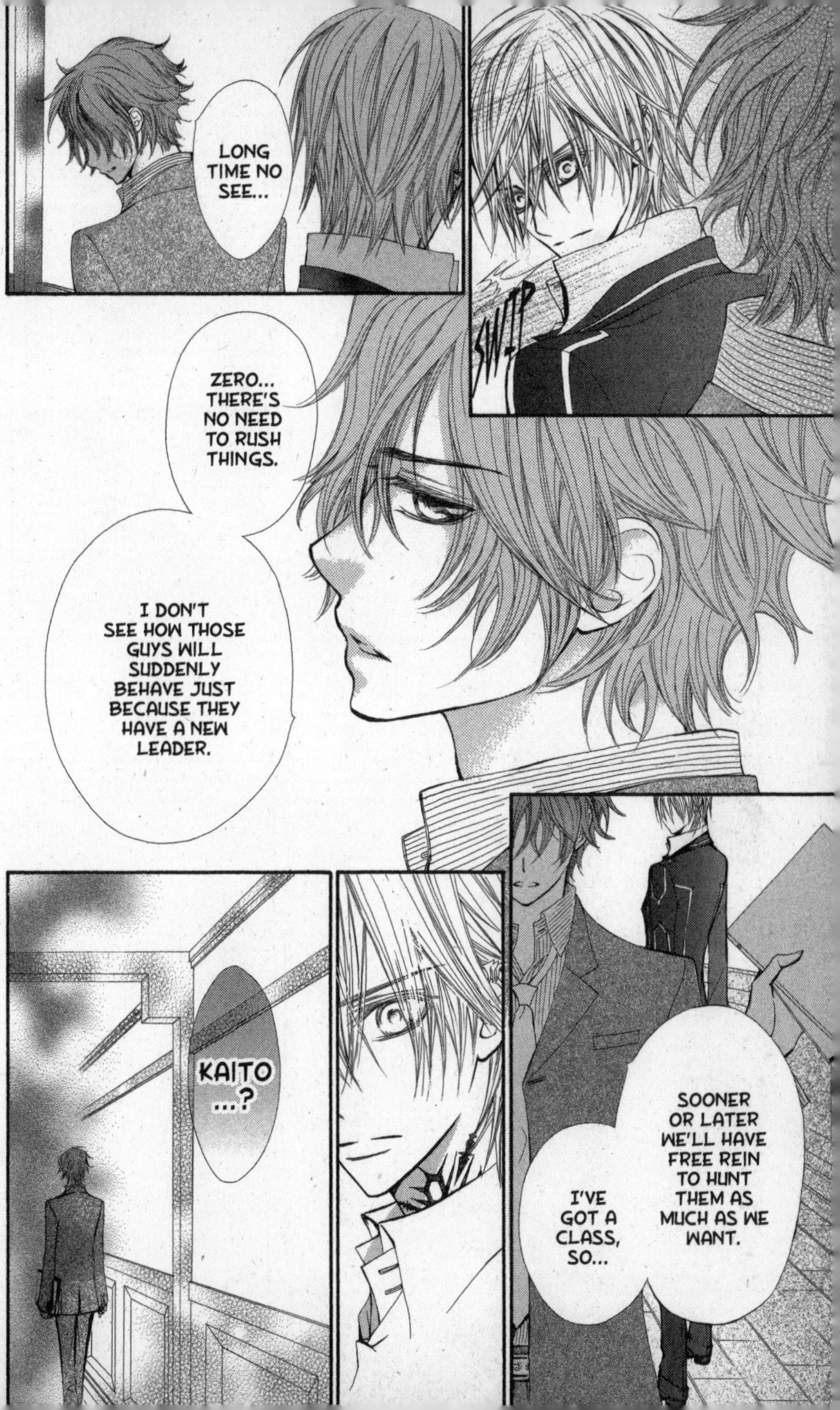
SWIP
LONG TIME NO SEE...
ZERO... THERE'S NO NEED TO RUSH THINGS.
I DON'T SEE HOW THOSE GUYS WILL SUDDENLY BEHAVE JUST BECAUSE THEY HAVE A NEW LEADER.
SOONER OR LATER WE'LL HAVE FREE REIN TO HUNT THEM AS MUCH AS WE WANT.
I'VE GOT A CLASS, SO...
KAITO ...?

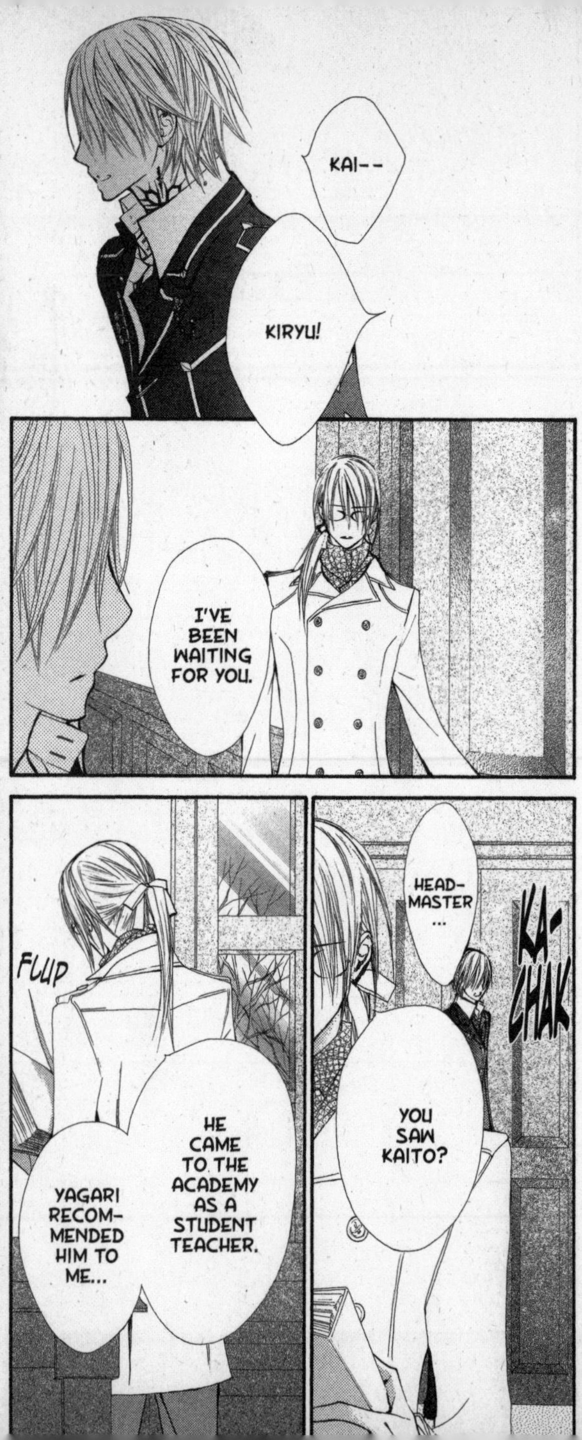
KAI--
KIRYU!
I'VE BEEN WAITING FOR YOU.
HEAD-MASTER...
KA-CHAK
YOU SAW KAITO?
FLIP
HE CAME TO THE ACADEMY AS A STUDENT TEACHER.
YAGARI RECOMMENDED HIM TO ME...

V

Germany. On the last day, I went for a walk in the forest at Kassel with my editor and spoke about the final chapter. I'm glad I was able to talk about it quietly in a forest in a faraway country rather than sitting in front of my desk. The food there was great, and the German people were very kind and cheerful, so I really fell in love with that country before I returned to Japan. I'm sorry this was filled with all sorts of personal stories which would never help as a guide to Germany. ;;
I hope to answer the questions (the ones I can answer) from the letters I received in the next volume. I'll do my best. ^^
Thank you very much for picking this book up! See you all in volume 12. ♡
Matsuri Hino
People I'd like to thank:
Anne, Mr. Horie (In Germany)
Editorial Department and staff.
O. Mio-sama, K. Midori-sama
I. Asami-sama, A.M-sama
W.Y-sama, and to my mother, friends, and all the readers!

I started my own blog. "http://hitoyasumi-hinomatsuri.under.jp/" "Hitoyasumi ☆ Hinomachuri"
I'll place entries and announcements every now and then on it.

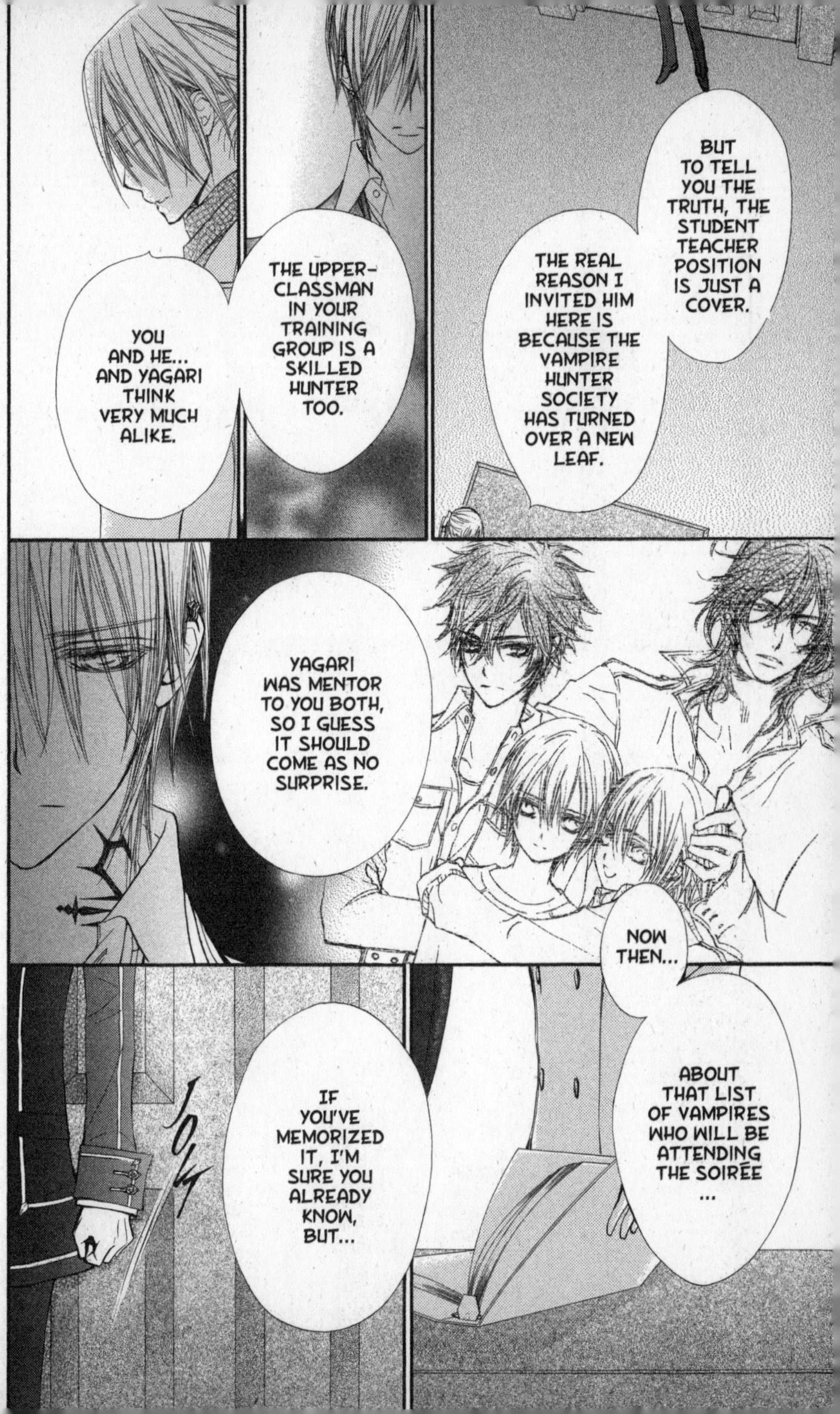
BUT TO TELL YOU THE TRUTH, THE STUDENT TEACHER POSITION IS JUST A COVER.
THE REAL REASON I INVITED HIM HERE IS BECAUSE THE VAMPIRE HUNTER SOCIETY HAS TURNED OVER A NEW LEAF.
THE UPPER-CLASSMAN IN YOUR TRAINING GROUP IS A SKILLED HUNTER TOO.
YOU AND HE... AND YAGARI THINK VERY MUCH ALIKE.
YAGARI WAS MENTOR TO YOU BOTH, SO I GUESS IT SHOULD COME AS NO SURPRISE.
NOW THEN...
ABOUT THAT LIST OF VAMPIRES WHO WILL BE ATTENDING THE SOIRÉE ...
IF YOU'VE MEMORIZED IT, I'M SURE YOU ALREADY KNOW, BUT...
JOW

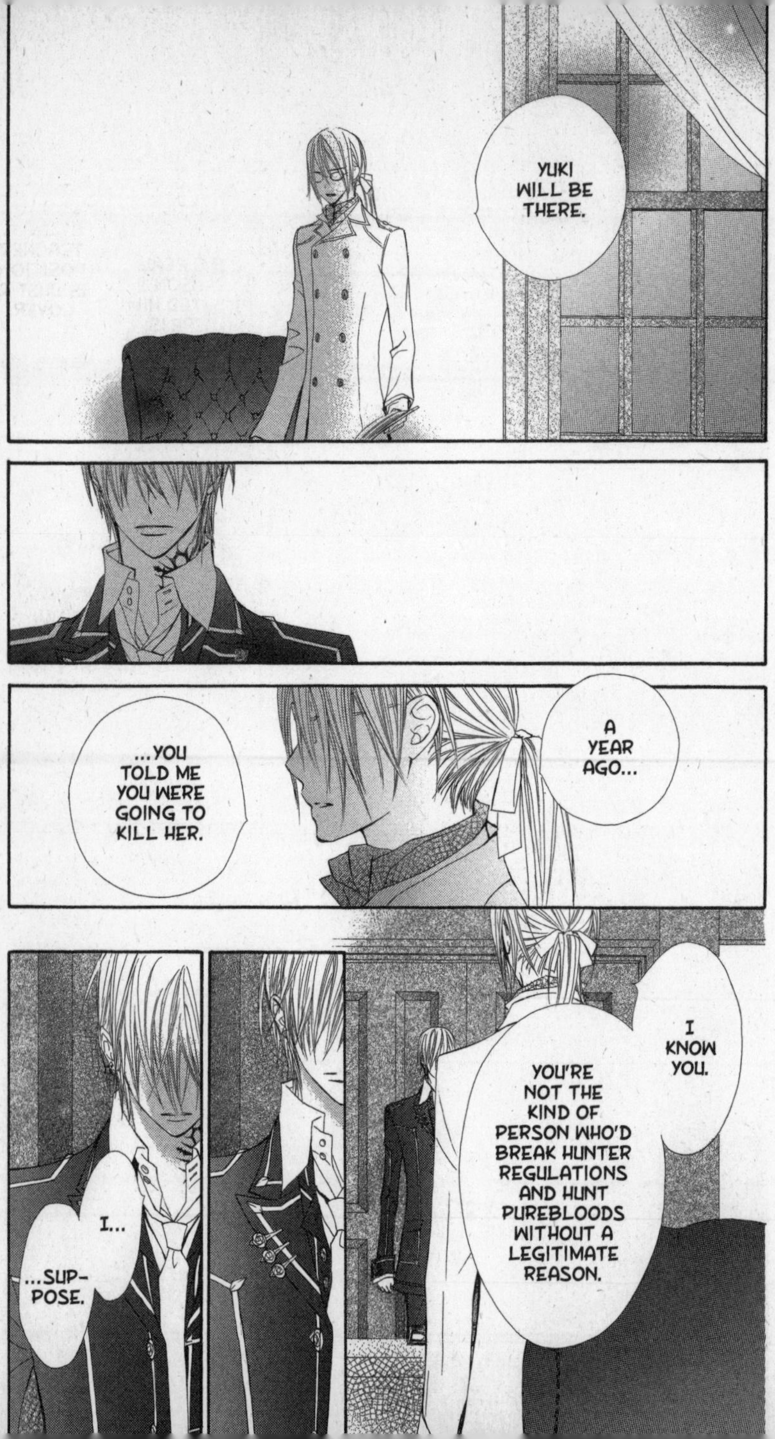
YUKI WILL BE THERE.
A YEAR AGO...
...YOU TOLD ME YOU WERE GOING TO KILL HER.
I KNOW YOU.
YOU'RE NOT THE KIND OF PERSON WHO'D BREAK HUNTER REGULATIONS AND HUNT PUREBLOODS WITHOUT A LEGITIMATE REASON.
I...
...SUP-POSE.

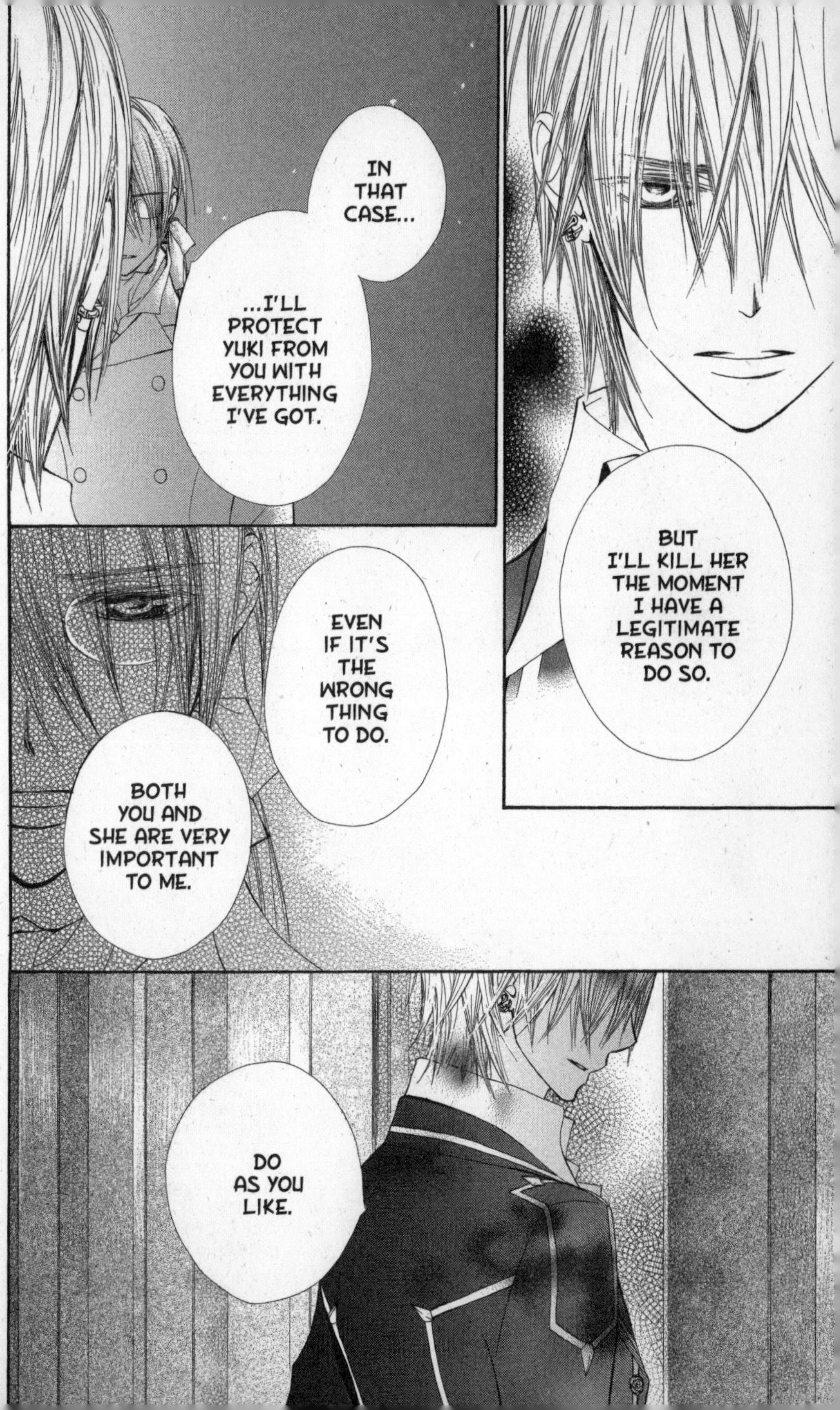
BUT I'LL KILL HER THE MOMENT I HAVE A LEGITIMATE REASON TO DO SO.
IN THAT CASE...
...I'LL PROTECT YUKI FROM YOU WITH EVERYTHING I'VE GOT.
EVEN IF IT'S THE WRONG THING TO DO.
BOTH YOU AND SHE ARE VERY IMPORTANT TO ME.
DO AS YOU LIKE.

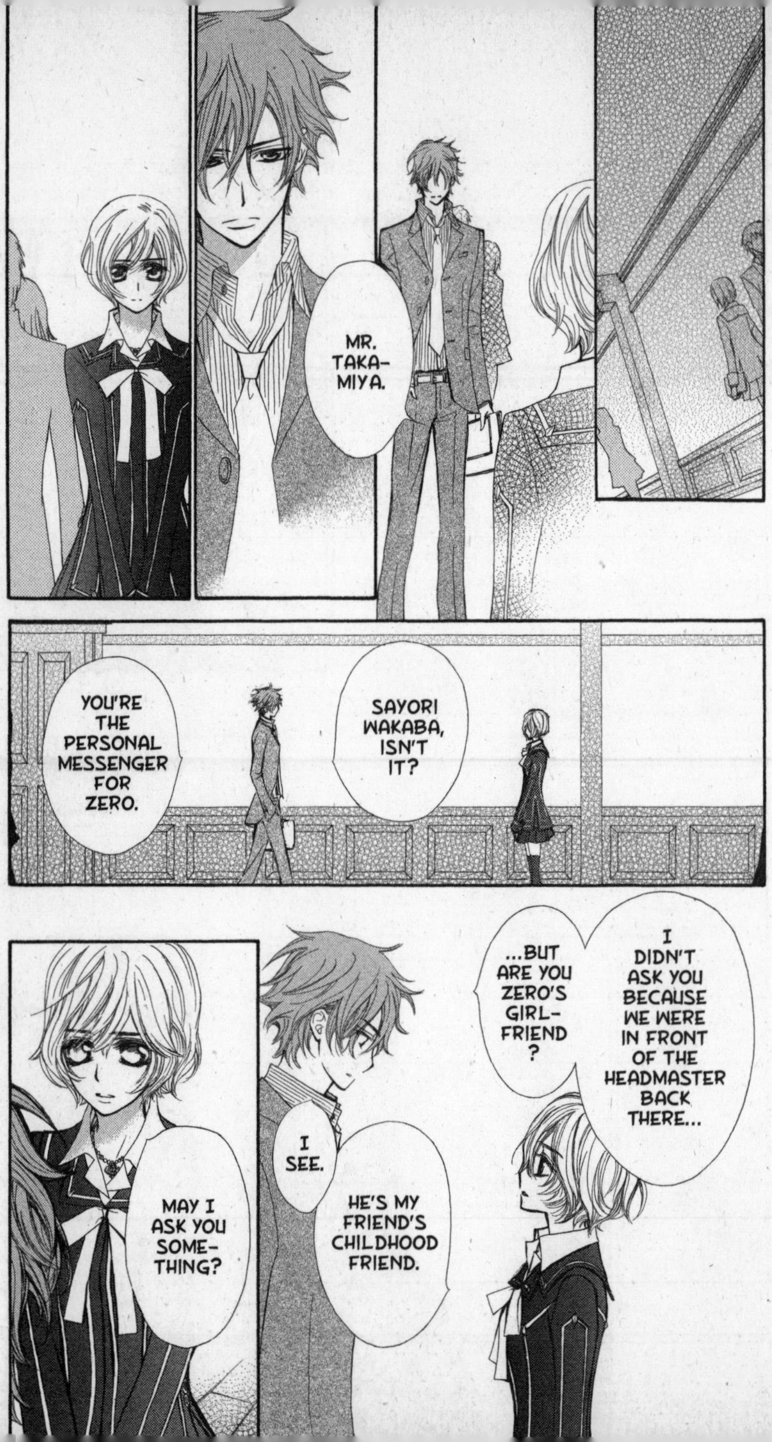
MR. TAKA-MIYA.
SAYORI WAKABA, ISN'T IT?
YOU'RE THE PERSONAL MESSENGER FOR ZERO.
I DIDN'T ASK YOU BECAUSE WE WERE IN FRONT OF THE HEADMASTER BACK THERE...
...BUT ARE YOU ZERO'S GIRL-FRIEND?
HE'S MY FRIEND'S CHILDHOOD FRIEND.
I SEE.
MAY I ASK YOU SOMETHING?

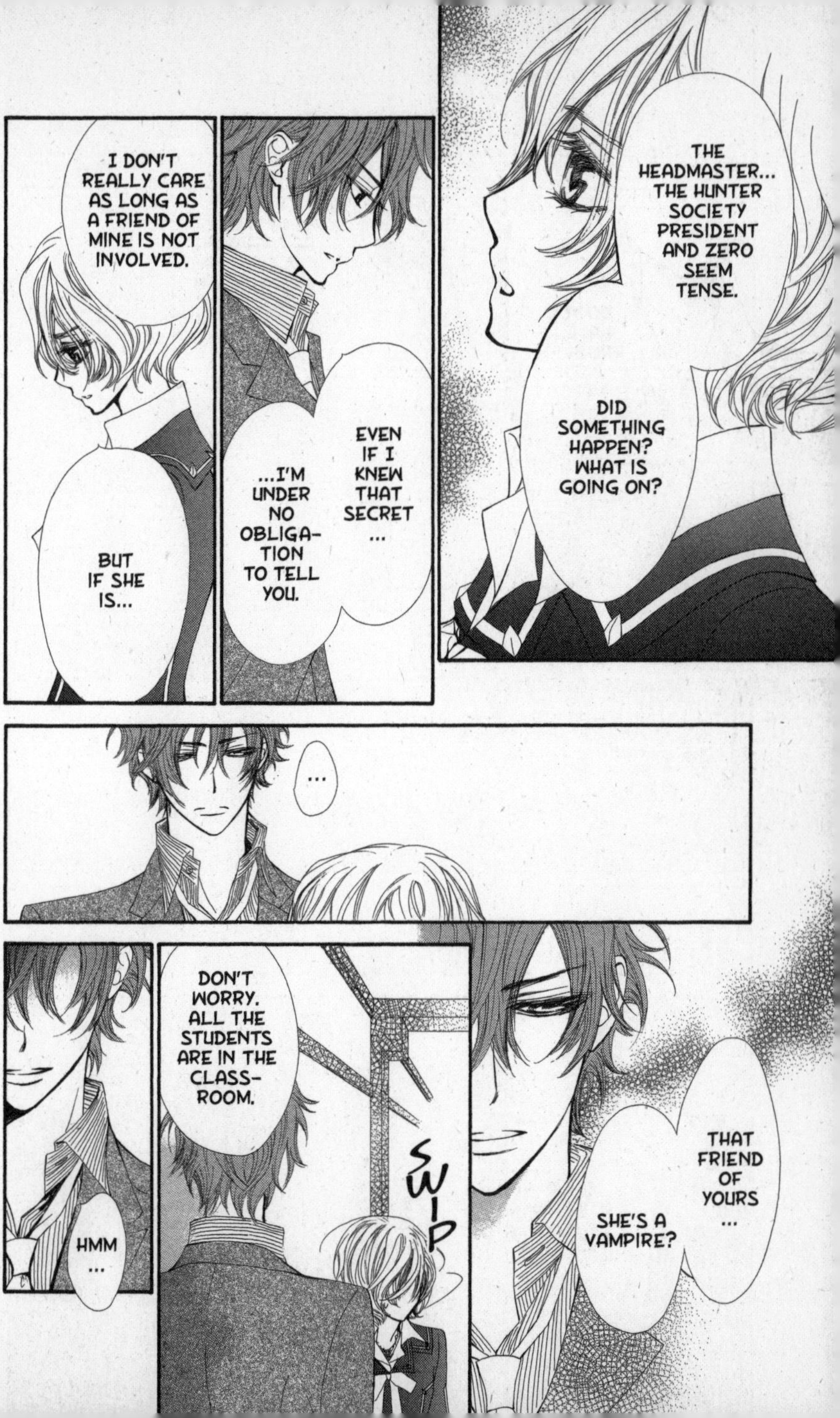
THE HEADMASTER... THE HUNTER SOCIETY PRESIDENT AND ZERO SEEM TENSE.
DID SOMETHING HAPPEN? WHAT IS GOING ON?
EVEN IF I KNEW THAT SECRET...
...I'M UNDER NO OBLIGA-TION TO TELL YOU.
I DON'T REALLY CARE AS LONG AS A FRIEND OF MINE IS NOT INVOLVED.
BUT IF SHE IS...
...
THAT FRIEND OF YOURS...
SHE'S A VAMPIRE?
DON'T WORRY. ALL THE STUDENTS ARE IN THE CLASS-ROOM.
SWIP
HMM...

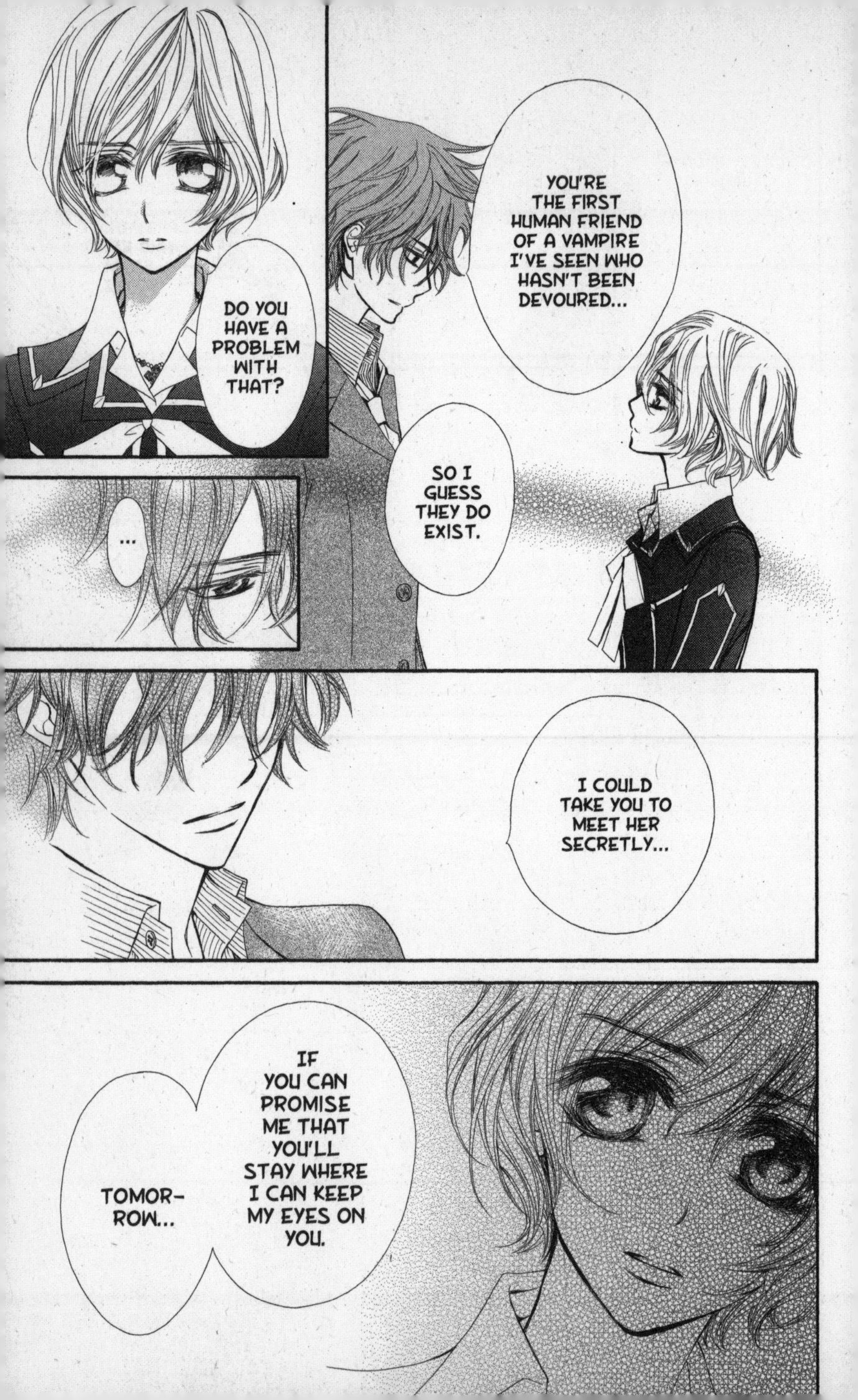
YOU'RE THE FIRST HUMAN FRIEND OF A VAMPIRE I'VE SEEN WHO HASN'T BEEN DEVOURED...
SO I GUESS THEY DO EXIST.
DO YOU HAVE A PROBLEM WITH THAT?
...
I COULD TAKE YOU TO MEET HER SECRETLY...
IF YOU CAN PROMISE ME THAT YOU'LL STAY WHERE I CAN KEEP MY EYES ON YOU.
TOMOR-ROW...

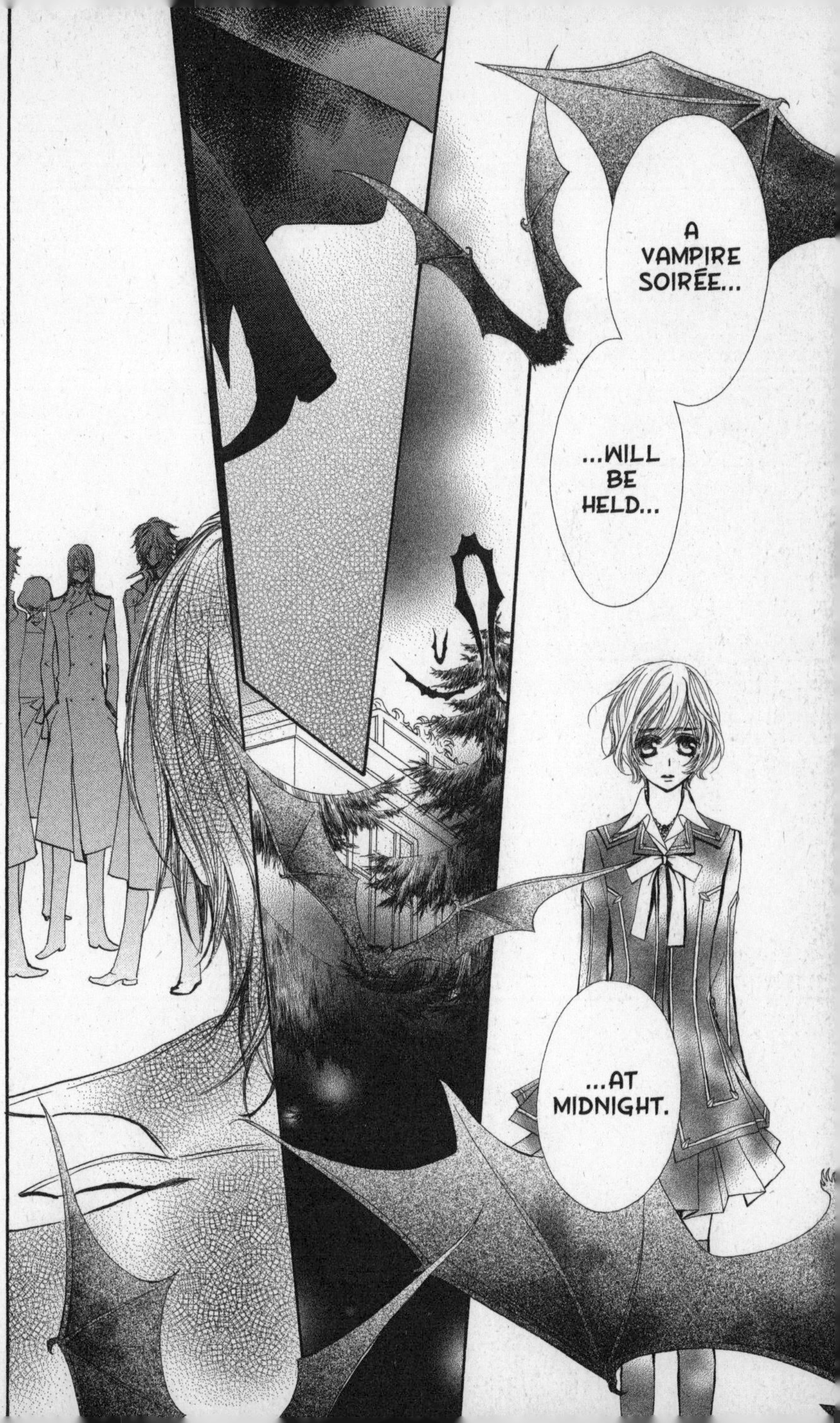
A VAMPIRE SOIRÉE...
...WILL BE HELD...
...AT MIDNIGHT.

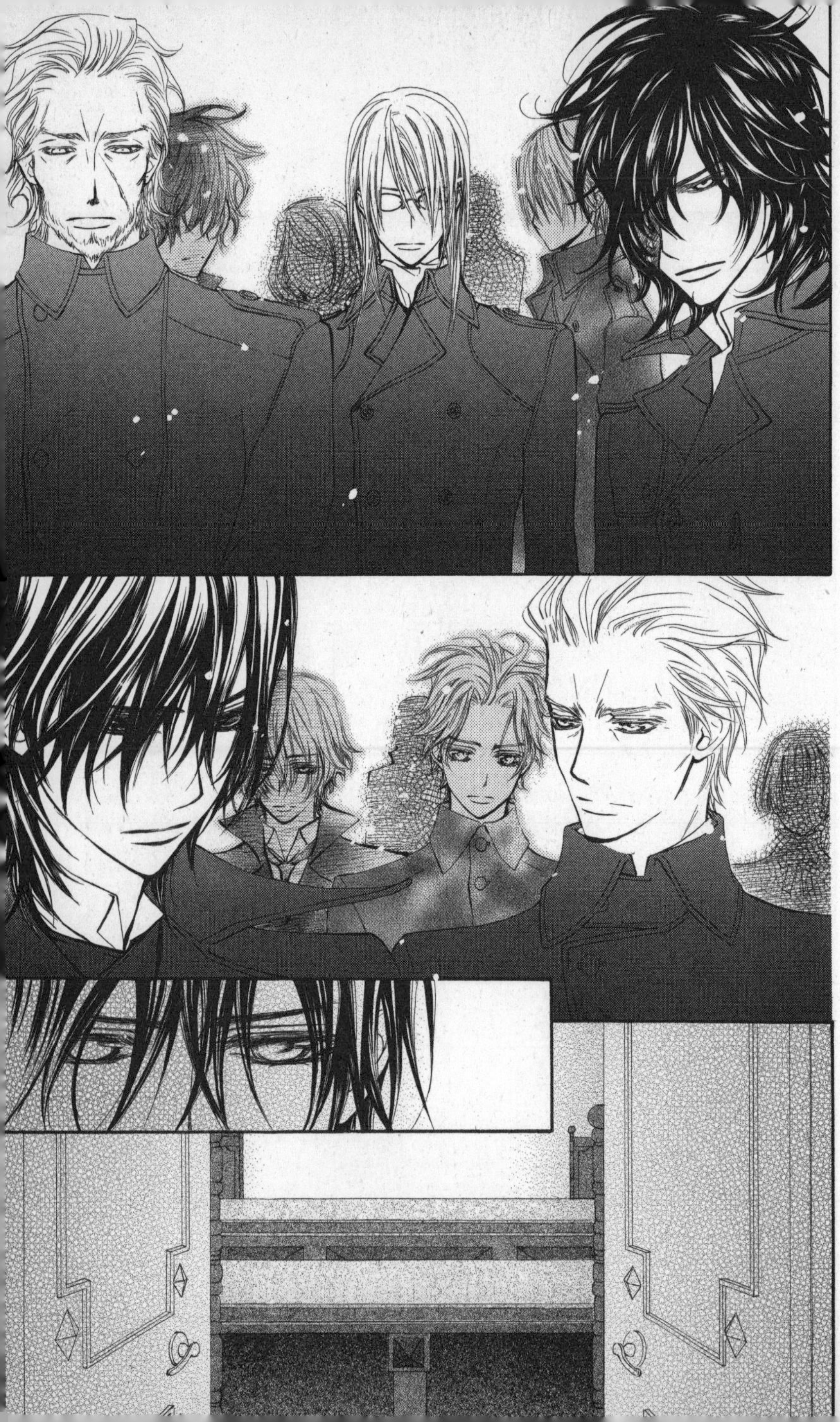

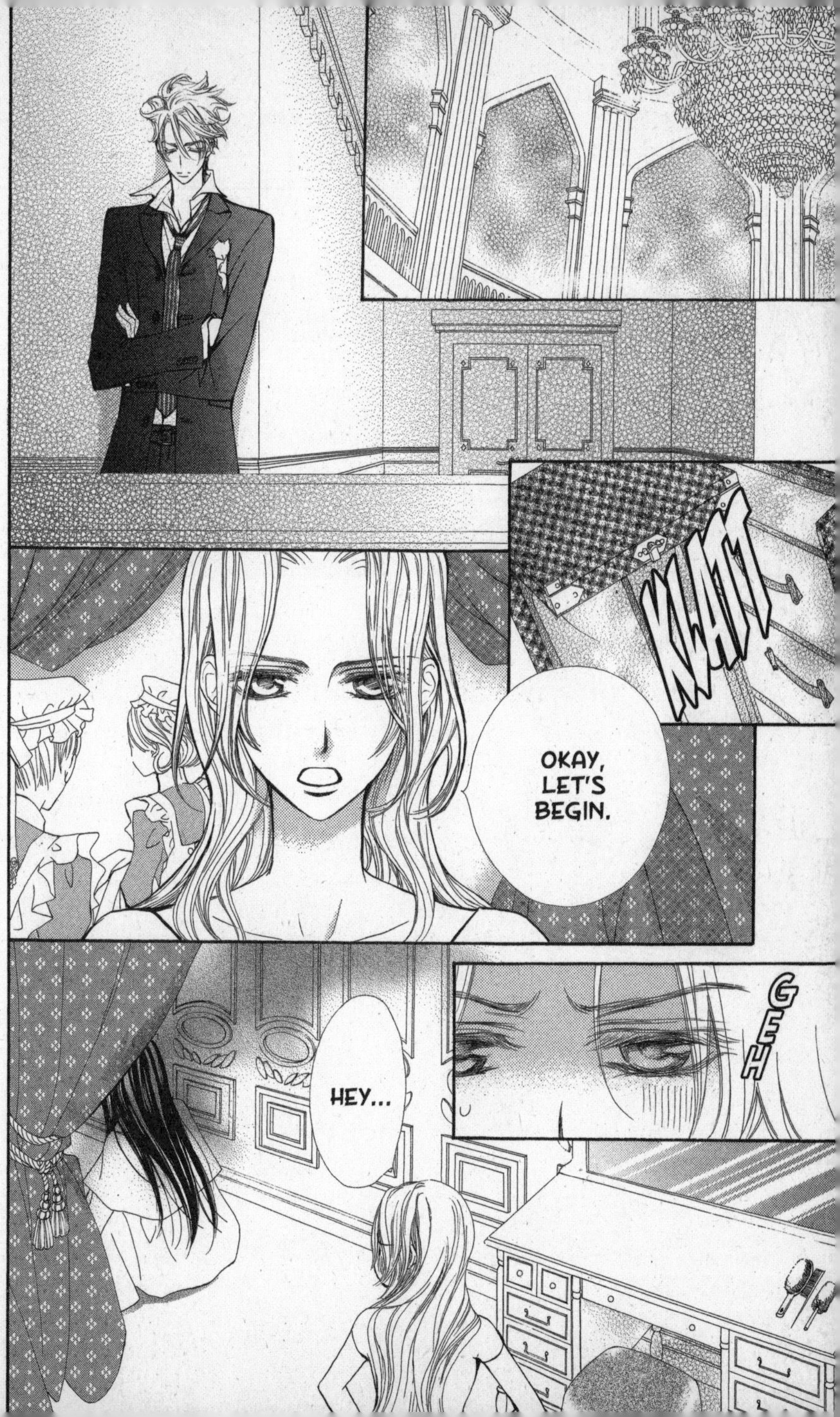
KLATT
OKAY, LET'S BEGIN.
GEH
HEY...

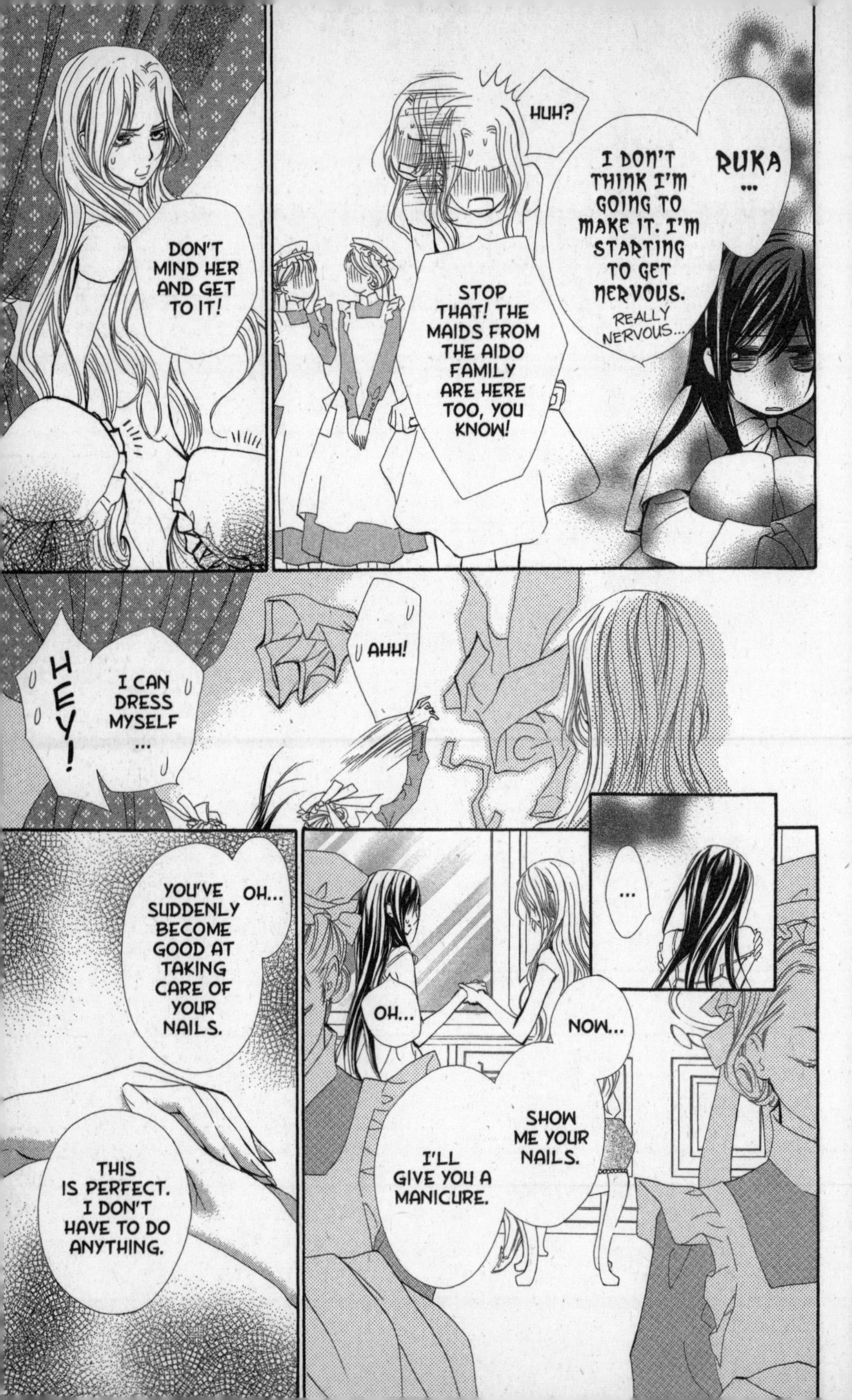
RUKA ...
I DON'T THINK I'M GOING TO MAKE IT. I'M STARTING TO GET NERVOUS.
REALLY NERVOUS...
HUH?
STOP THAT! THE MAIDS FROM THE AIDO FAMILY ARE HERE TOO, YOU KNOW!
DON'T MIND HER AND GET TO IT!
AHH!
HEY!
I CAN DRESS MYSELF ...
...
NOW...
OH...
SHOW ME YOUR NAILS.
I'LL GIVE YOU A MANICURE.
OH...
YOU'VE SUDDENLY BECOME GOOD AT TAKING CARE OF YOUR NAILS.
THIS IS PERFECT. I DON'T HAVE TO DO ANYTHING.

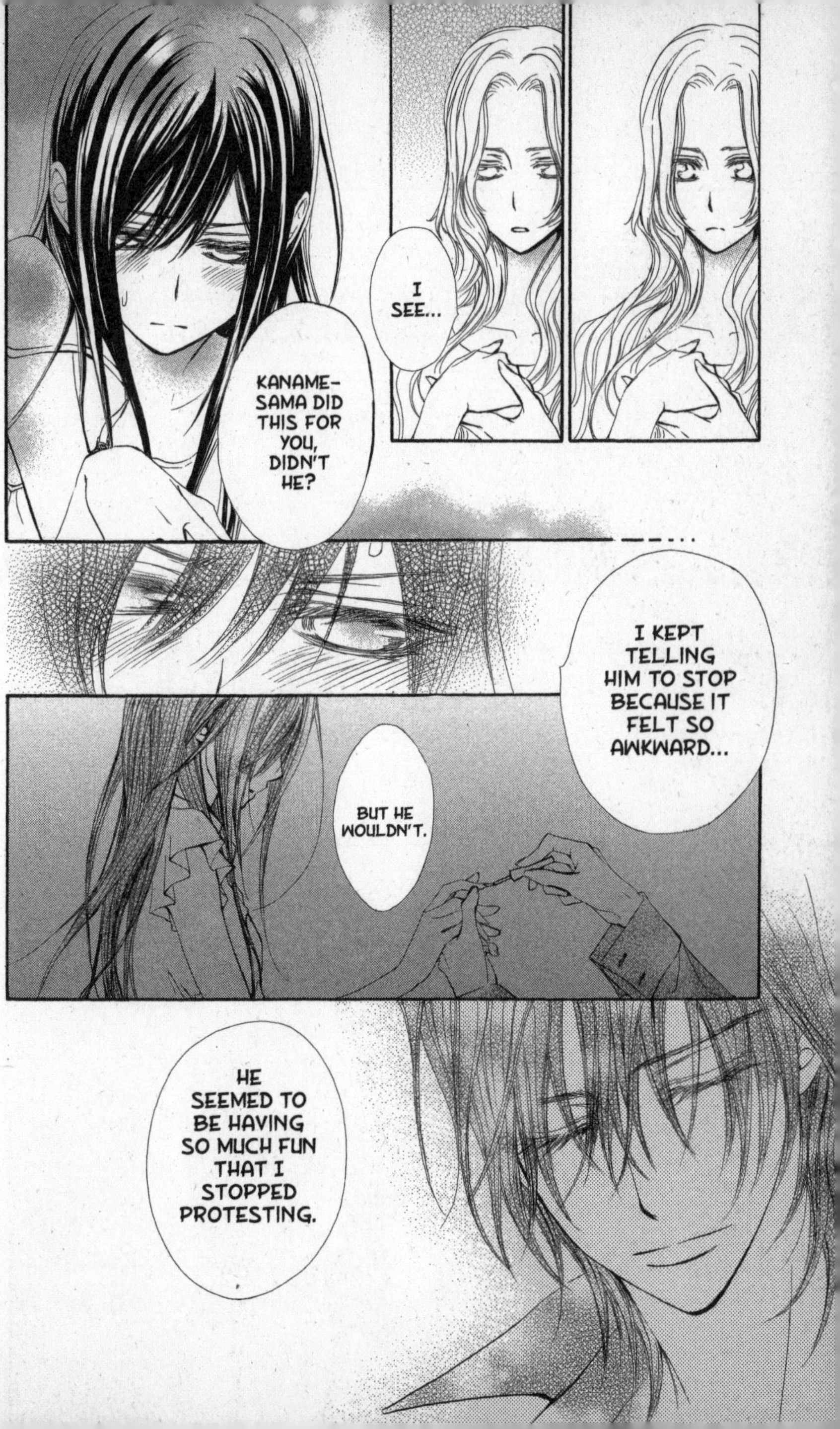
I SEE...
KANAME-SAMA DID THIS FOR YOU, DIDN'T HE?
——...
I KEPT TELLING HIM TO STOP BECAUSE IT FELT SO AWKWARD...
BUT HE WOULDN'T.
HE SEEMED TO BE HAVING SO MUCH FUN THAT I STOPPED PROTESTING.

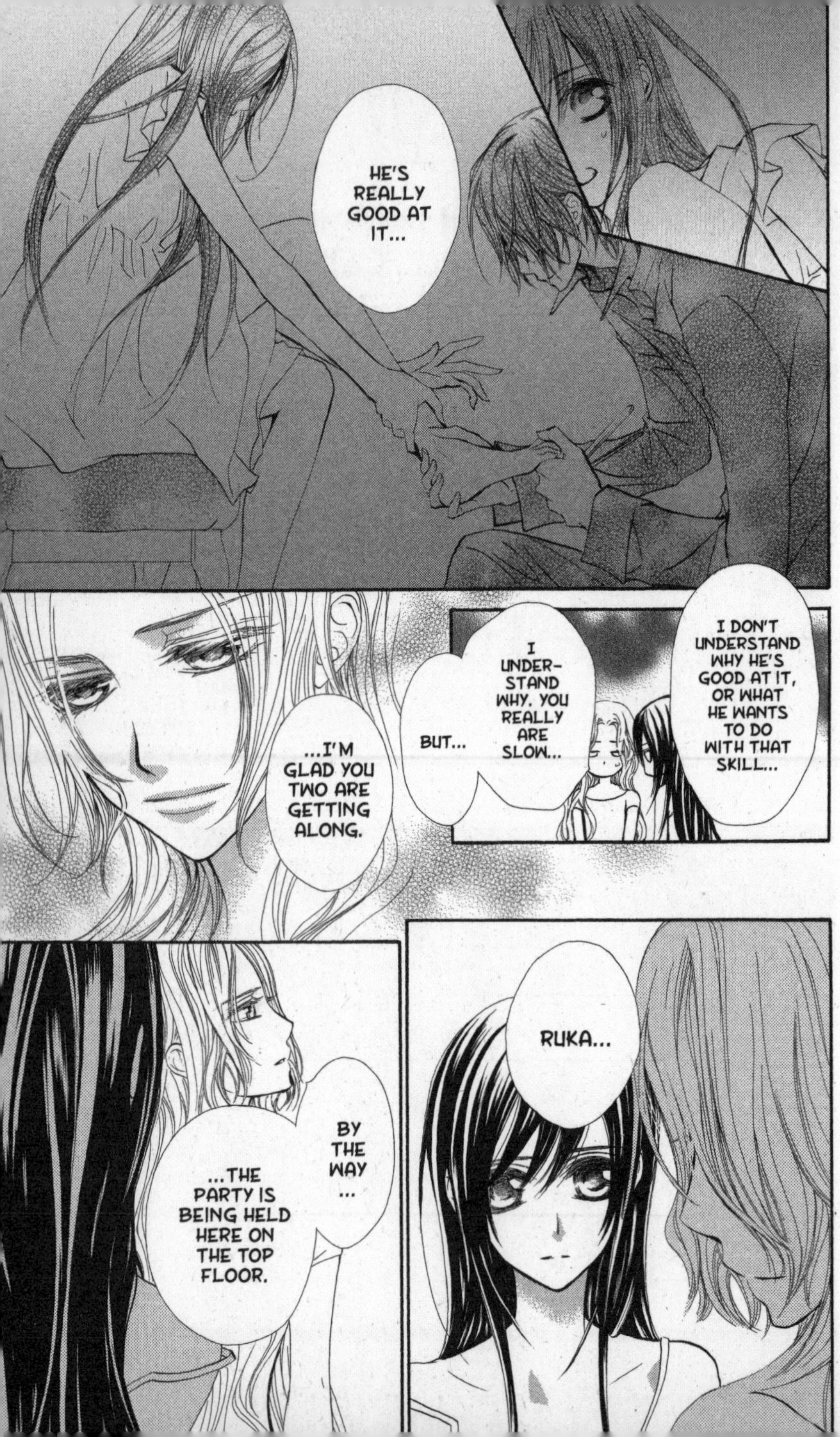
HE'S REALLY GOOD AT IT...
I DON'T UNDERSTAND WHY HE'S GOOD AT IT, OR WHAT HE WANTS TO DO WITH THAT SKILL...
I UNDER-STAND WHY. YOU REALLY ARE SLOW...
BUT...
...I'M GLAD YOU TWO ARE GETTING ALONG.
RUKA...
BY THE WAY...
...THE PARTY IS BEING HELD HERE ON THE TOP FLOOR.

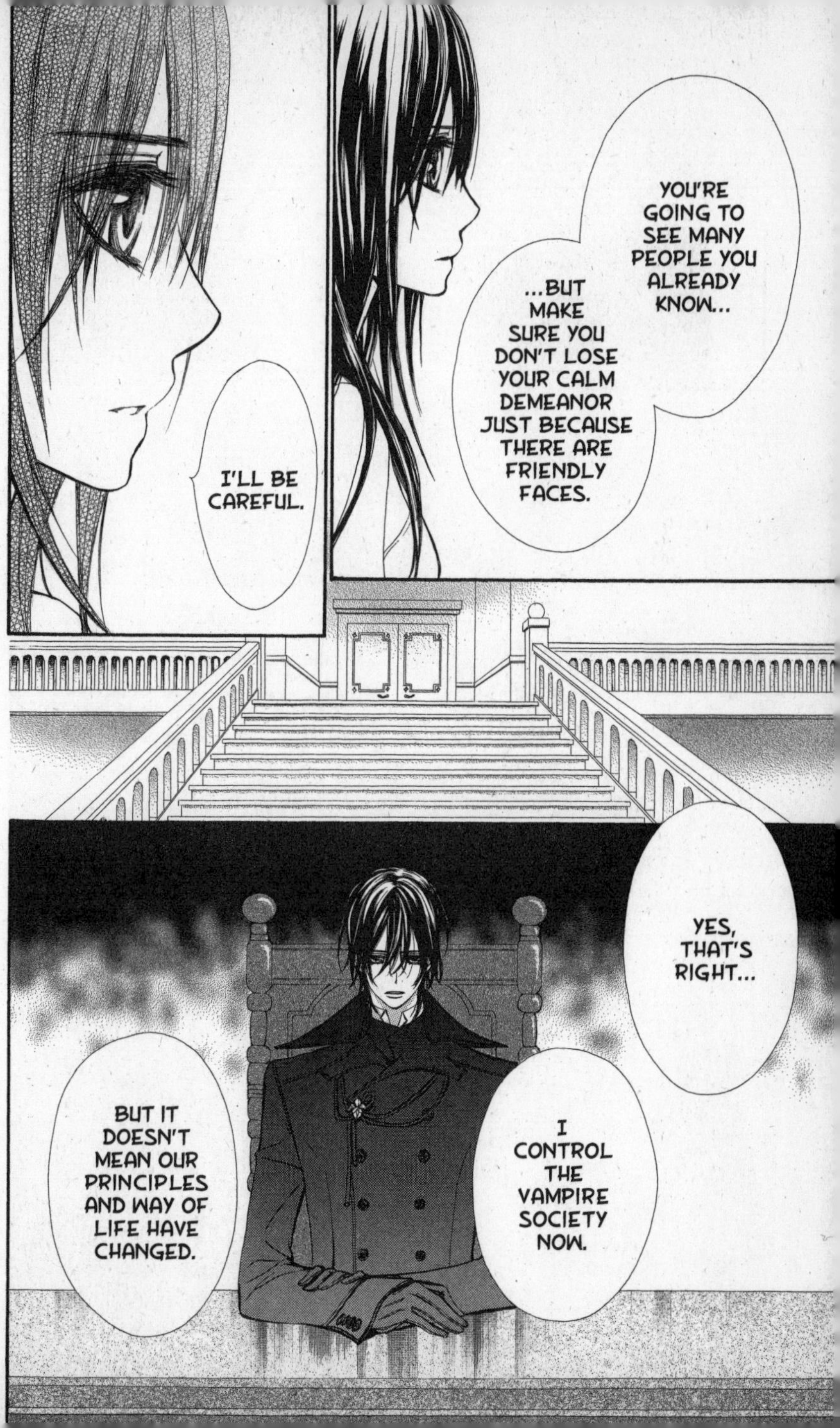
YOU'RE GOING TO SEE MANY PEOPLE YOU ALREADY KNOW...
...BUT MAKE SURE YOU DON'T LOSE YOUR CALM DEMEANOR JUST BECAUSE THERE ARE FRIENDLY FACES.
I'LL BE CAREFUL.
YES, THAT'S RIGHT...
I CONTROL THE VAMPIRE SOCIETY NOW.
BUT IT DOESN'T MEAN OUR PRINCIPLES AND WAY OF LIFE HAVE CHANGED.

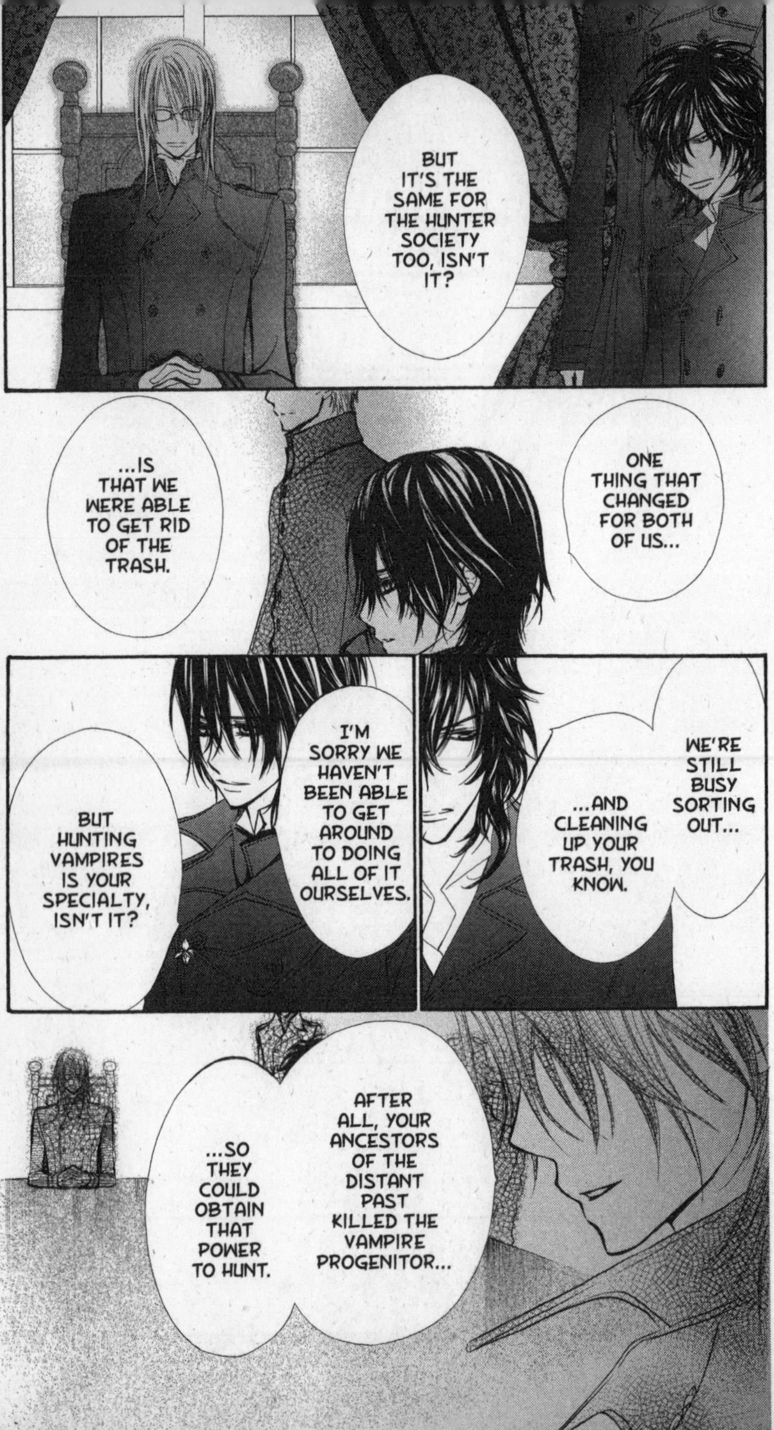
BUT IT'S THE SAME FOR THE HUNTER SOCIETY TOO, ISN'T IT?
ONE THING THAT CHANGED FOR BOTH OF US...
...IS THAT WE WERE ABLE TO GET RID OF THE TRASH.
WE'RE STILL BUSY SORTING OUT...
...AND CLEANING UP YOUR TRASH, YOU KNOW.
I'M SORRY WE HAVEN'T BEEN ABLE TO GET AROUND TO DOING ALL OF IT OURSELVES.
BUT HUNTING VAMPIRES IS YOUR SPECIALTY, ISN'T IT?
AFTER ALL, YOUR ANCESTORS OF THE DISTANT PAST KILLED THE VAMPIRE PROGENITOR...
...SO THEY COULD OBTAIN THAT POWER TO HUNT.

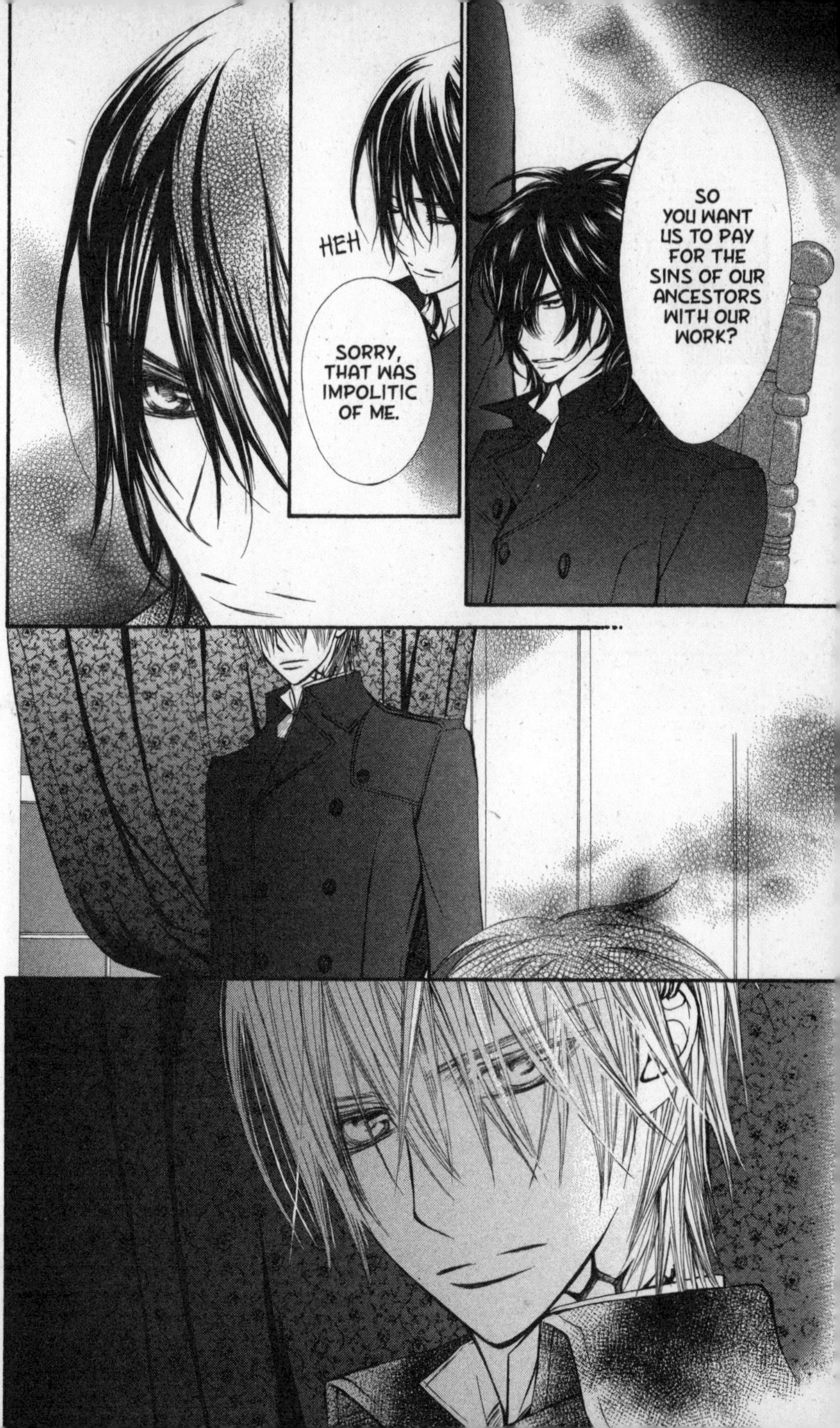
SO YOU WANT US TO PAY FOR THE SINS OF OUR ANCESTORS WITH OUR WORK?
HEH
SORRY, THAT WAS IMPOLITIC OF ME.

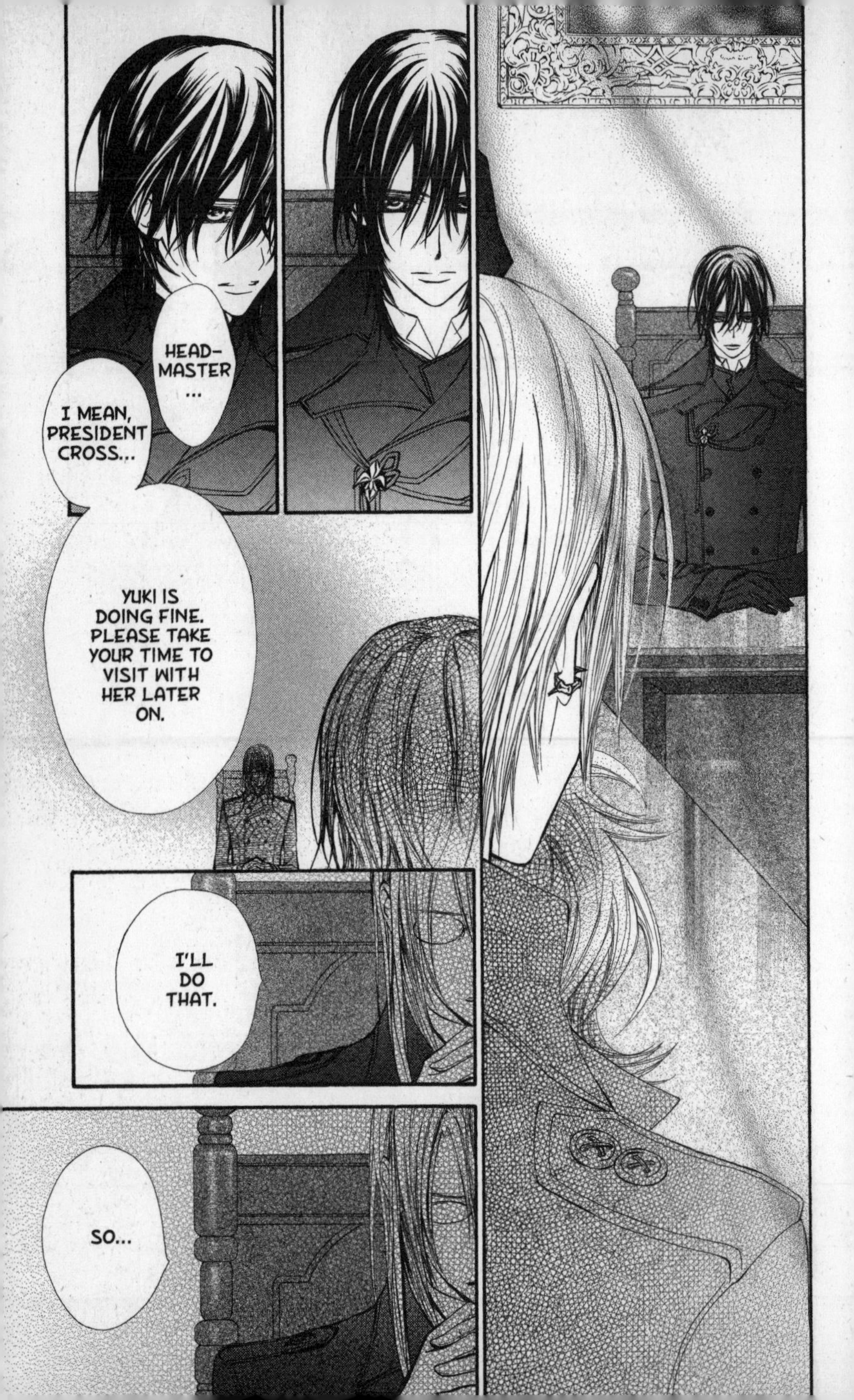
HEAD-MASTER ...
I MEAN, PRESIDENT CROSS...
YUKI IS DOING FINE. PLEASE TAKE YOUR TIME TO VISIT WITH HER LATER ON.
I'LL DO THAT.
SO...

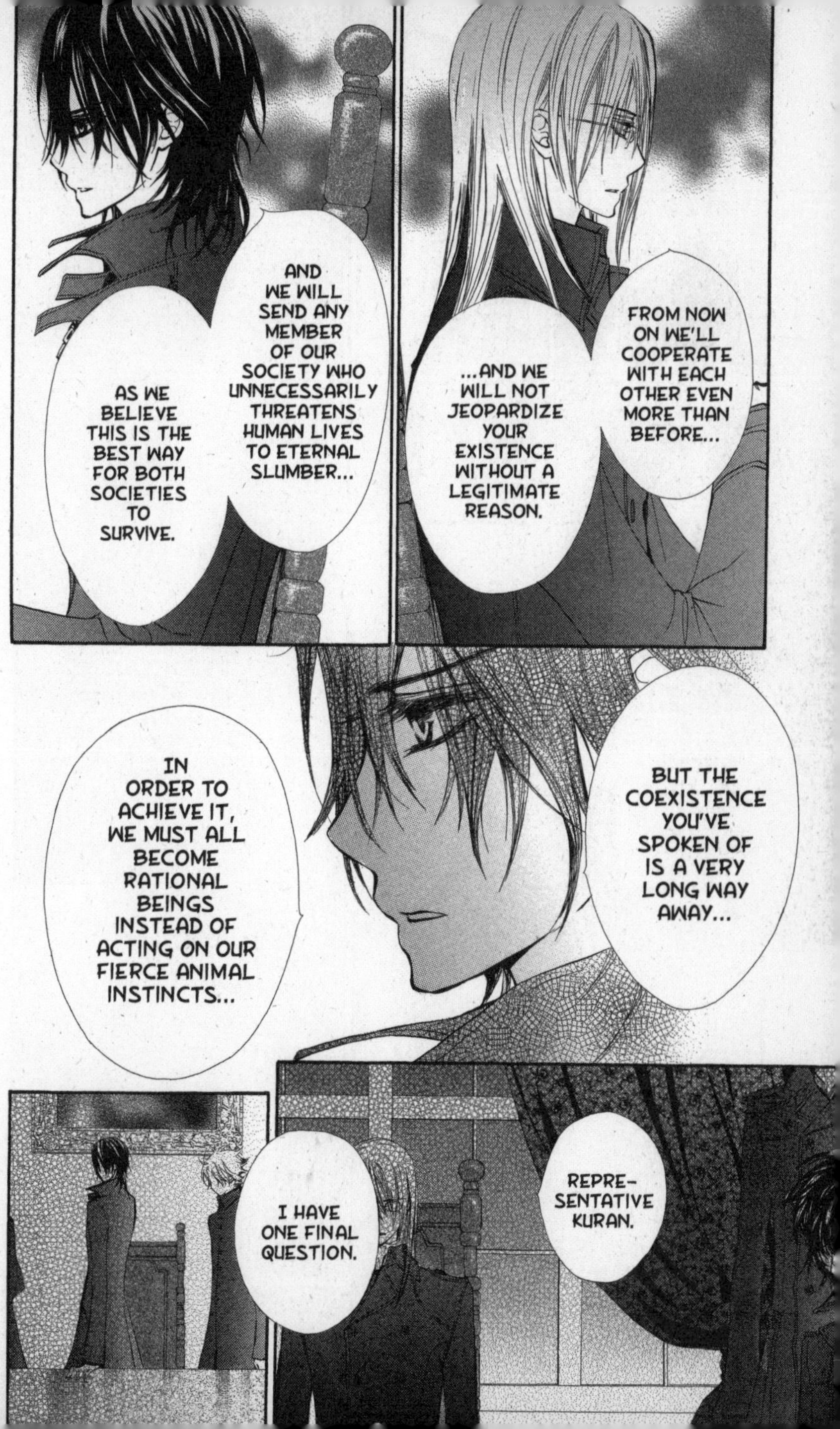
FROM NOW ON WE'LL COOPERATE WITH EACH OTHER EVEN MORE THAN BEFORE...
...AND WE WILL NOT JEOPARDIZE YOUR EXISTENCE WITHOUT A LEGITIMATE REASON.
AND WE WILL SEND ANY MEMBER OF OUR SOCIETY WHO UNNECESSARILY THREATENS HUMAN LIVES TO ETERNAL SLUMBER...
AS WE BELIEVE THIS IS THE BEST WAY FOR BOTH SOCIETIES TO SURVIVE.
BUT THE COEXISTENCE YOU'VE SPOKEN OF IS A VERY LONG WAY AWAY...
IN ORDER TO ACHIEVE IT, WE MUST ALL BECOME RATIONAL BEINGS INSTEAD OF ACTING ON OUR FIERCE ANIMAL INSTINCTS...
REPRE-SENTATIVE KURAN.
I HAVE ONE FINAL QUESTION.

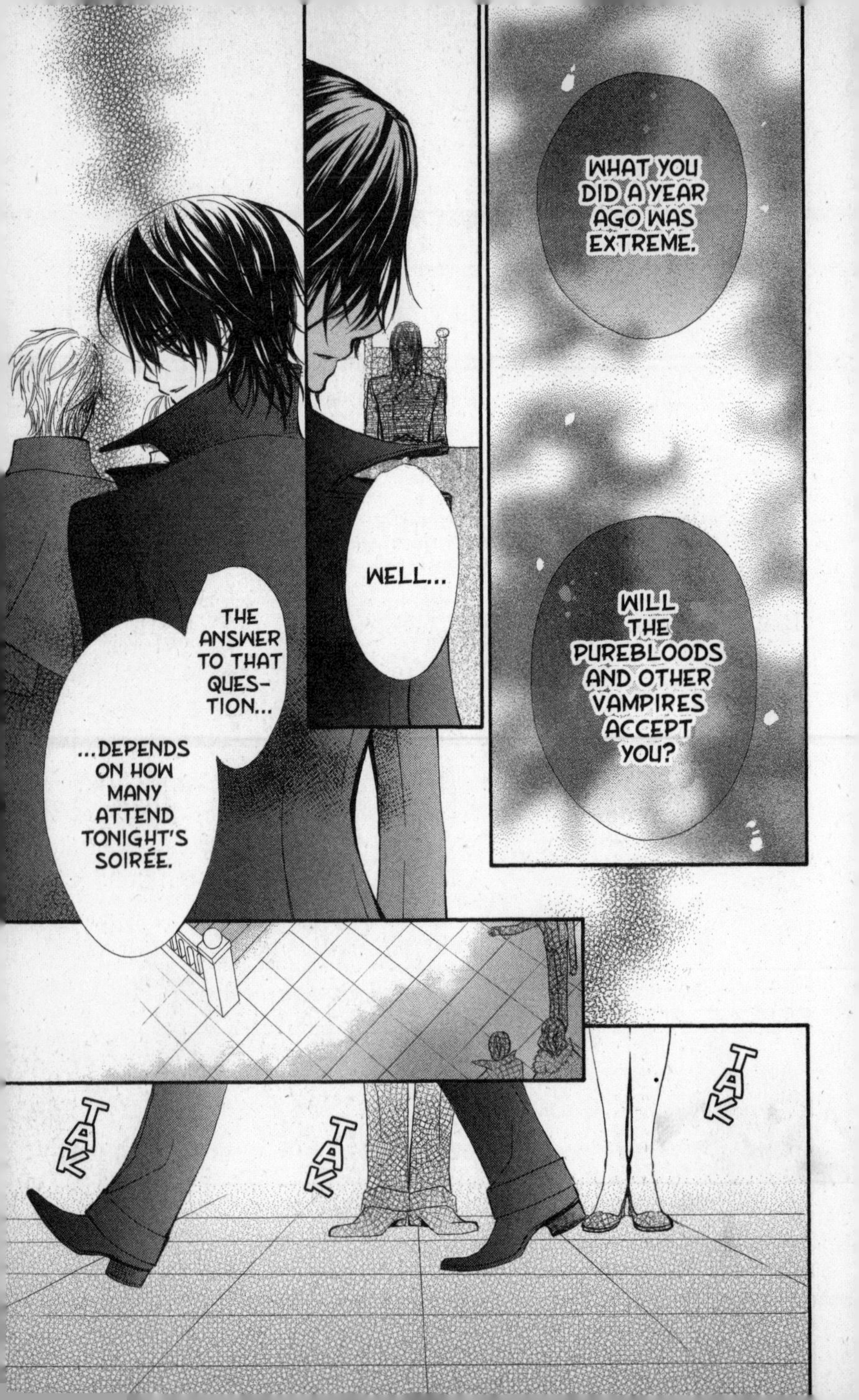
WHAT YOU DID A YEAR AGO WAS EXTREME.
WILL THE PUREBLOODS AND OTHER VAMPIRES ACCEPT YOU?
WELL...
THE ANSWER TO THAT QUES-TION...
...DEPENDS ON HOW MANY ATTEND TONIGHT'S SOIRÉE.
TAK
TAK
TAK

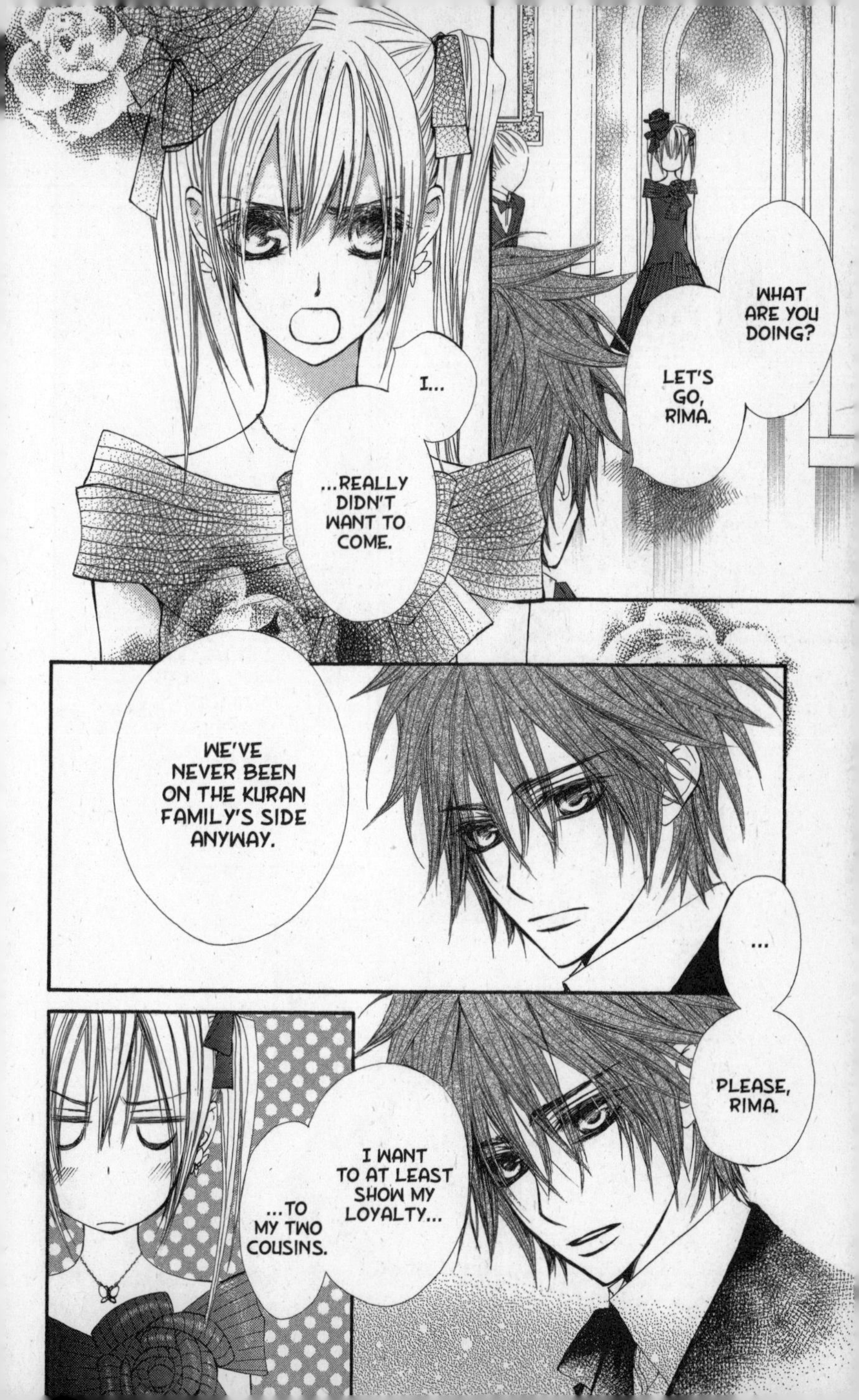
WHAT ARE YOU DOING?
LET'S GO, RIMA.
I...
...REALLY DIDN'T WANT TO COME.
WE'VE NEVER BEEN ON THE KURAN FAMILY'S SIDE ANYWAY.
...
PLEASE, RIMA.
I WANT TO AT LEAST SHOW MY LOYALTY...
...TO MY TWO COUSINS.

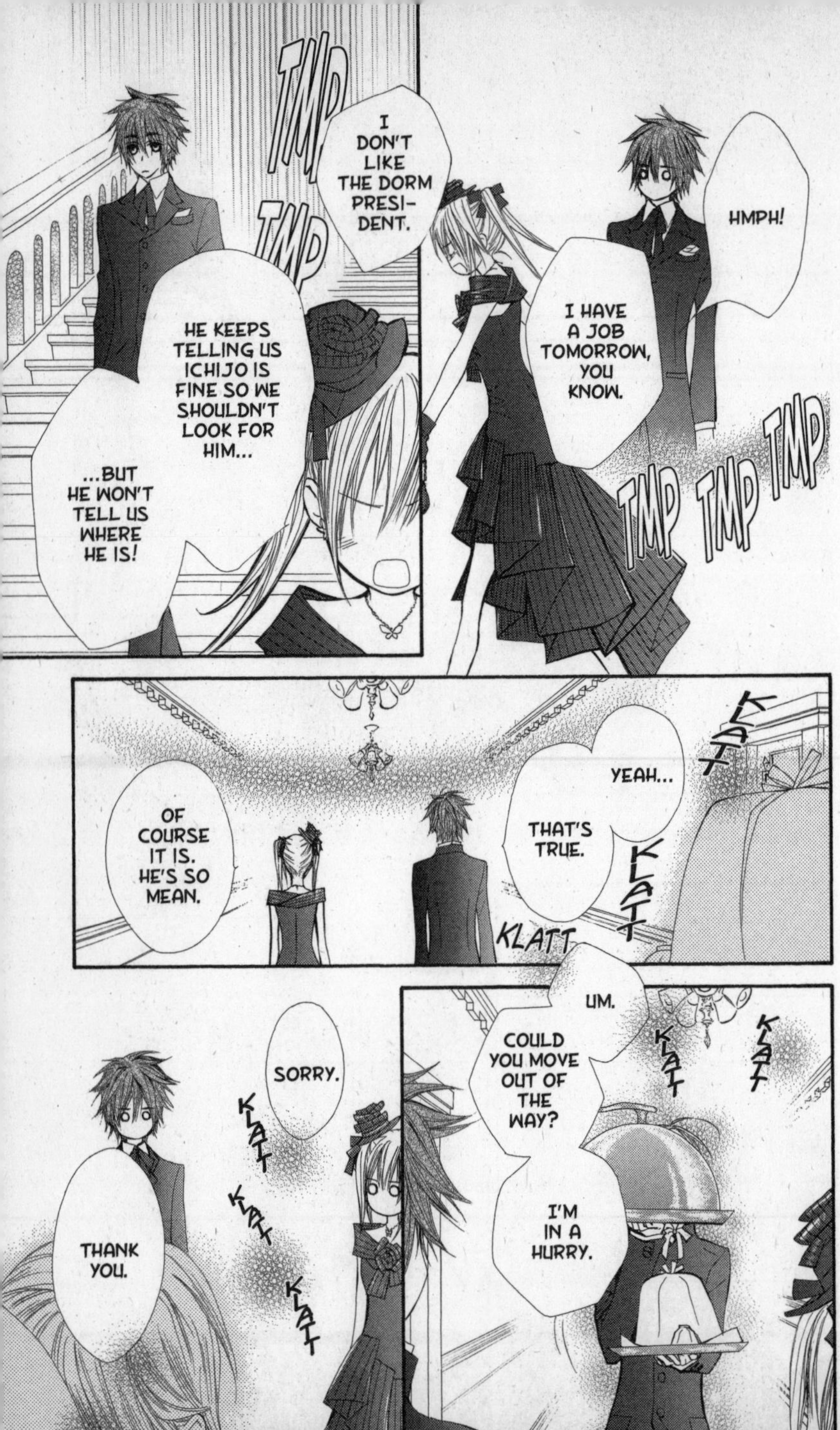
HMPH!
I HAVE A JOB TOMORROW, YOU KNOW.
TMP TMP TMP
TMP TMP
I DON'T LIKE THE DORM PRESI-DENT.
HE KEEPS TELLING US ICHIJO IS FINE SO WE SHOULDN'T LOOK FOR HIM...
...BUT HE WON'T TELL US WHERE HE IS!
KLATT
YEAH...
THAT'S TRUE.
KLATT
KLATT
OF COURSE IT IS. HE'S SO MEAN.
UM.
KLATT
KLATT
COULD YOU MOVE OUT OF THE WAY?
I'M IN A HURRY.
SORRY.
KLATT
KLATT
KLATT
THANK YOU.

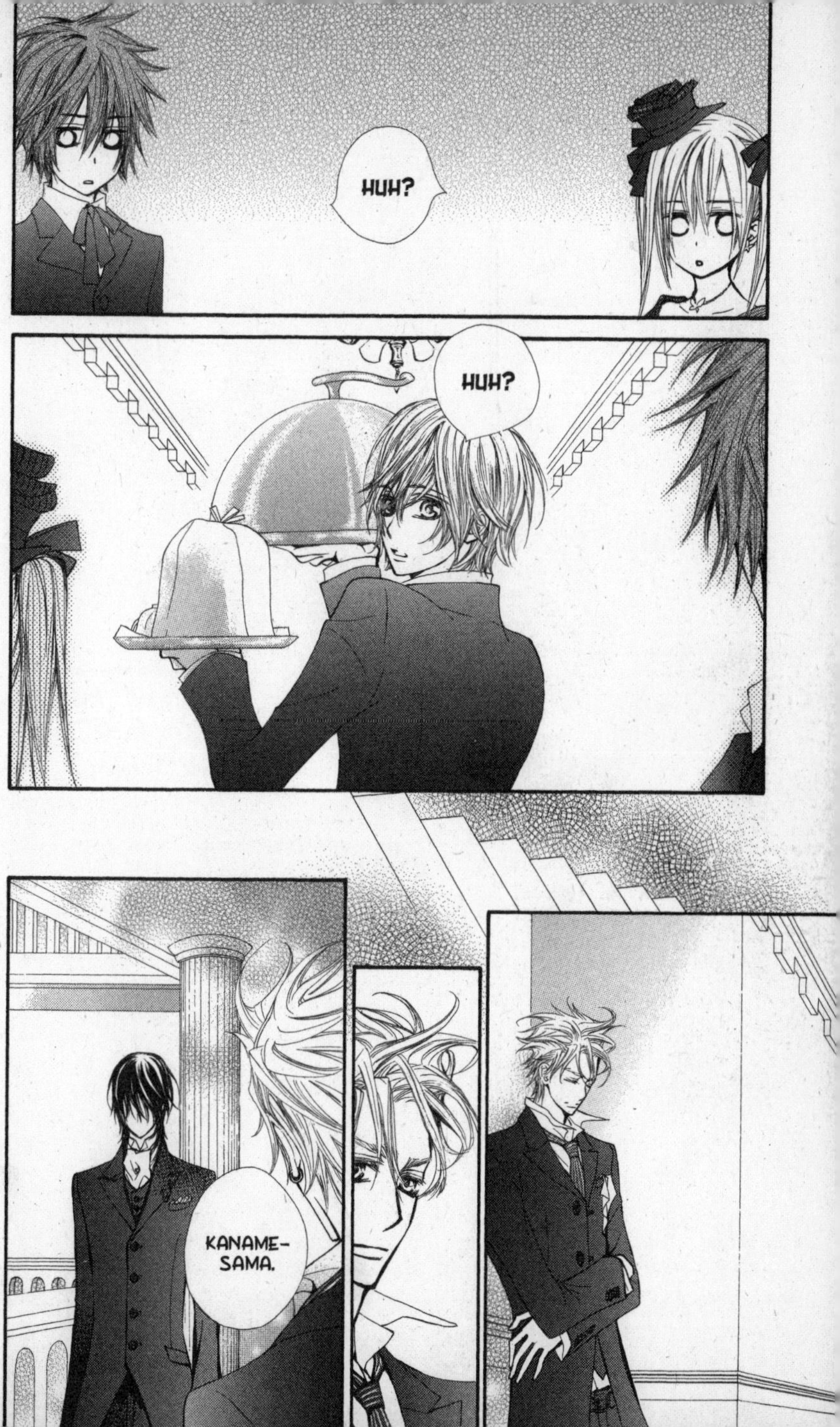
HUH?
HUH?
KANAME-SAMA.

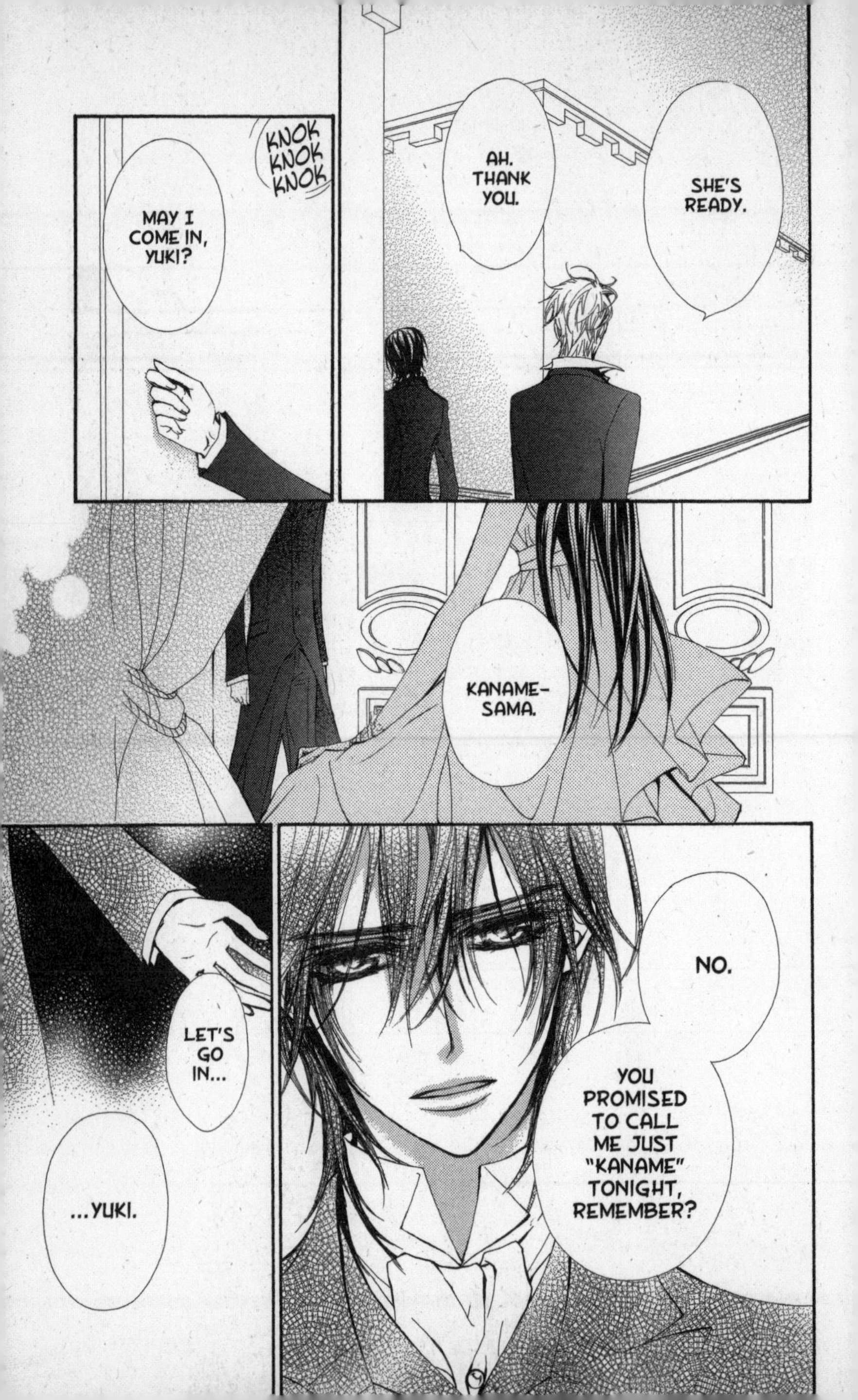
SHE'S READY.
AH. THANK YOU.
KNOK KNOK KNOK
MAY I COME IN, YUKI?
KANAME-SAMA.
NO.
YOU PROMISED TO CALL ME JUST "KANAME" TONIGHT, REMEMBER?
LET'S GO IN...
...YUKI.

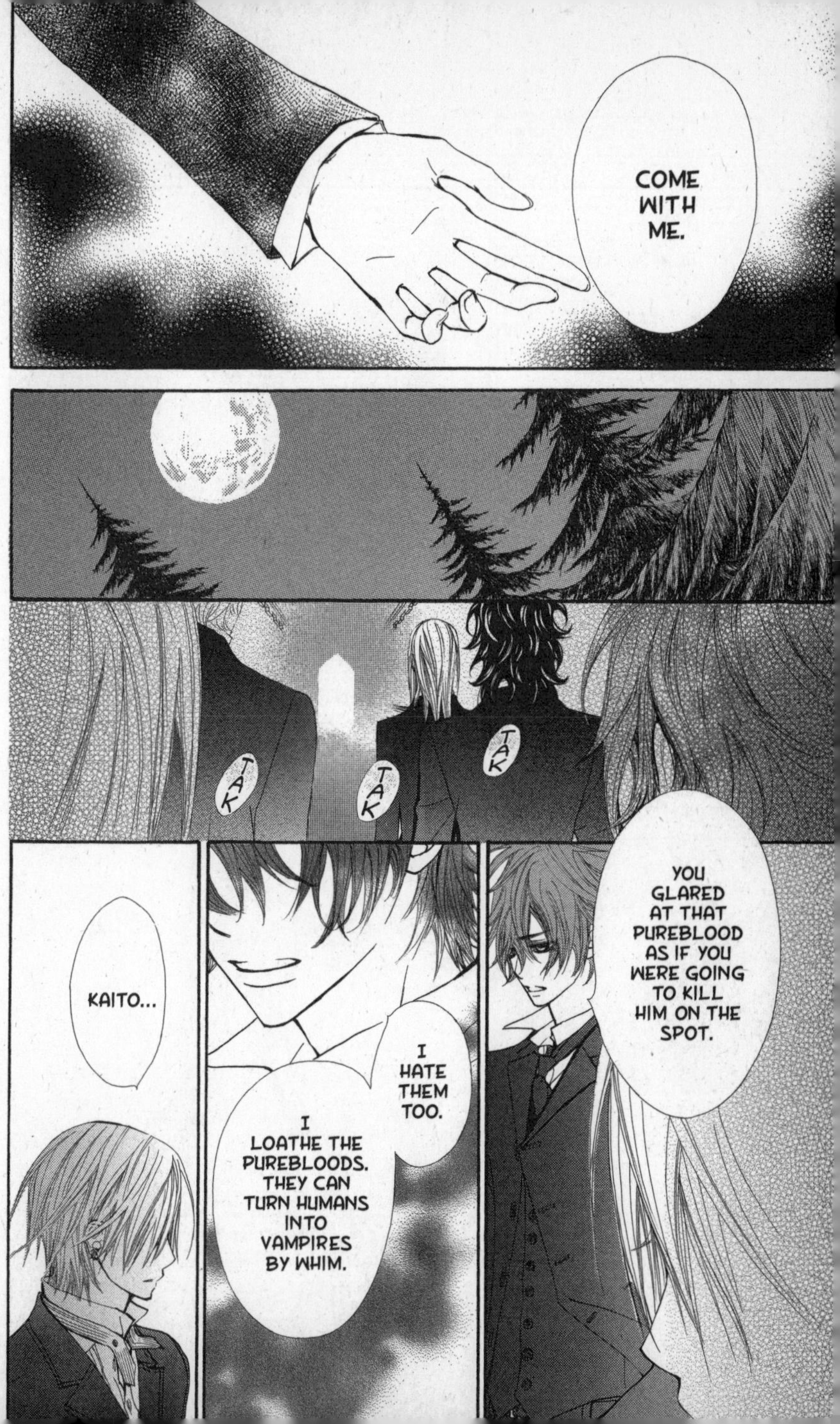
COME WITH ME.
TAK
TAK
TAK
YOU GLARED AT THAT PUREBLOOD AS IF YOU WERE GOING TO KILL HIM ON THE SPOT.
I HATE THEM TOO.
I LOATHE THE PUREBLOODS. THEY CAN TURN HUMANS INTO VAMPIRES BY WHIM.
KAITO...

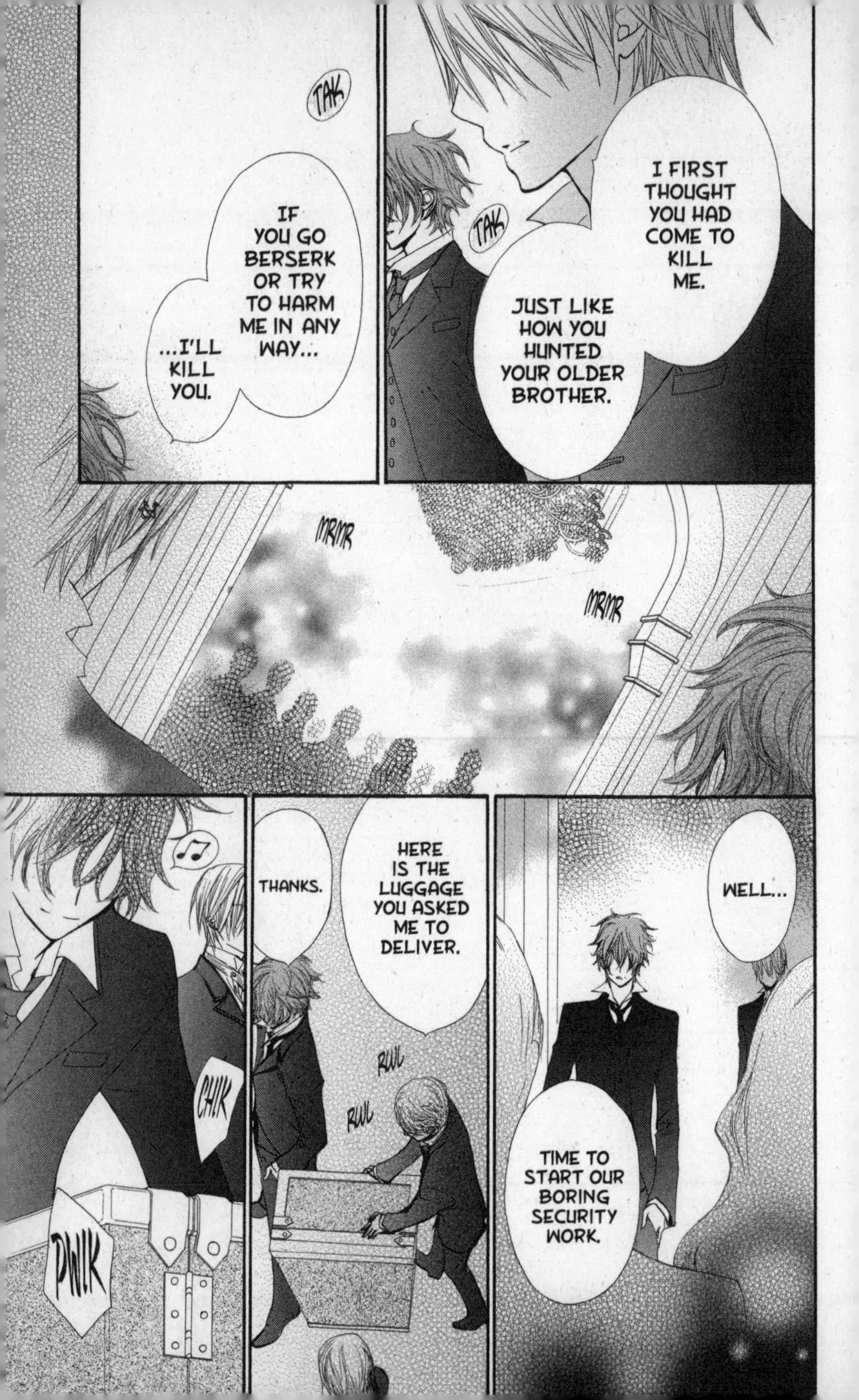
TAK
I FIRST THOUGHT YOU HAD COME TO KILL ME.
JUST LIKE HOW YOU HUNTED YOUR OLDER BROTHER.
TAK
IF YOU GO BERSERK OR TRY TO HARM ME IN ANY WAY...
...I'LL KILL YOU.
MRMR
MRMR
WELL...
TIME TO START OUR BORING SECURITY WORK.
HERE IS THE LUGGAGE YOU ASKED ME TO DELIVER.
THANKS.
RUL
RUL
CHIK
PWIK

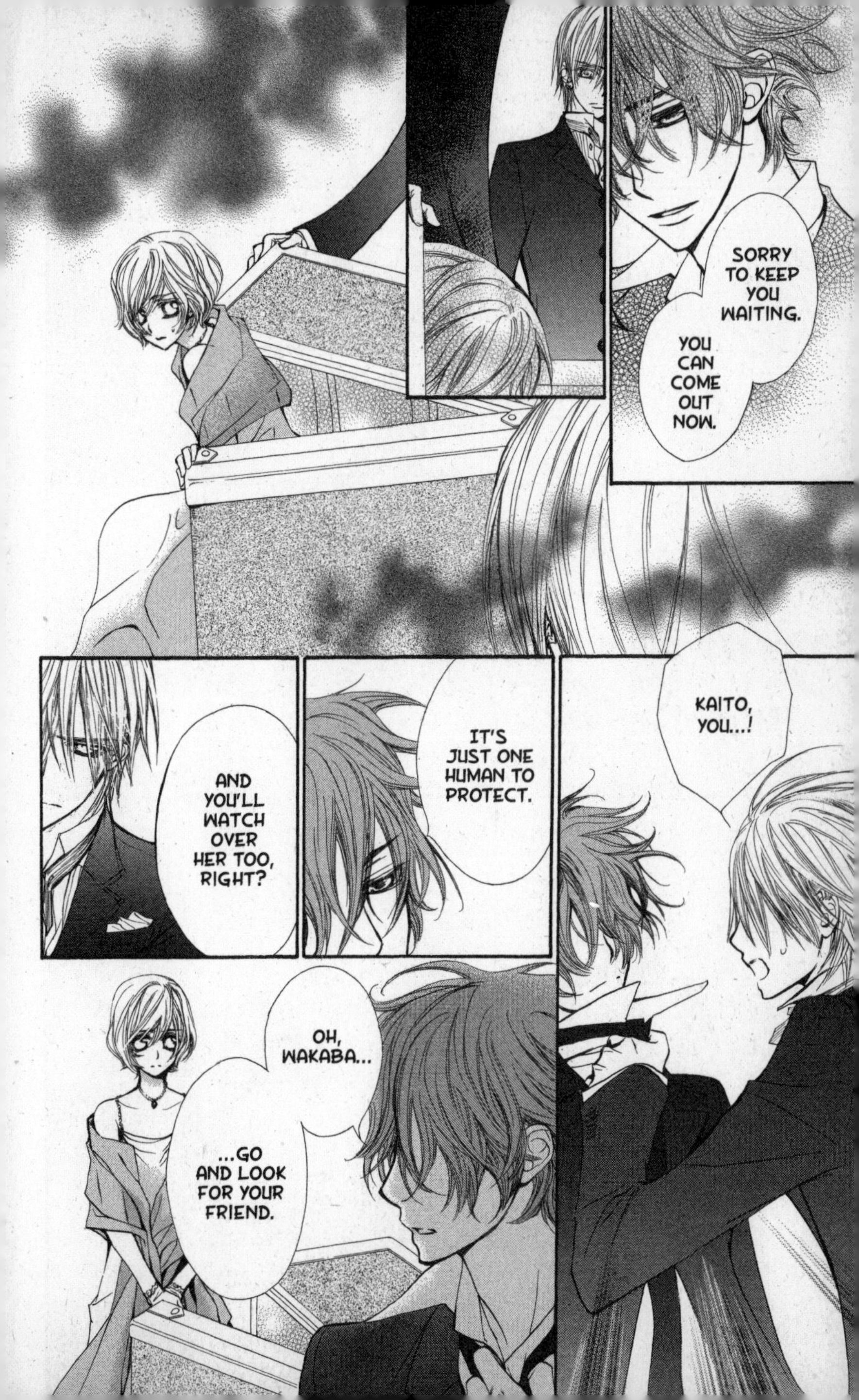
SORRY TO KEEP YOU WAITING.
YOU CAN COME OUT NOW.
KAITO, YOU...!
IT'S JUST ONE HUMAN TO PROTECT.
AND YOU'LL WATCH OVER HER TOO, RIGHT?
OH, WAKABA...
...GO AND LOOK FOR YOUR FRIEND.

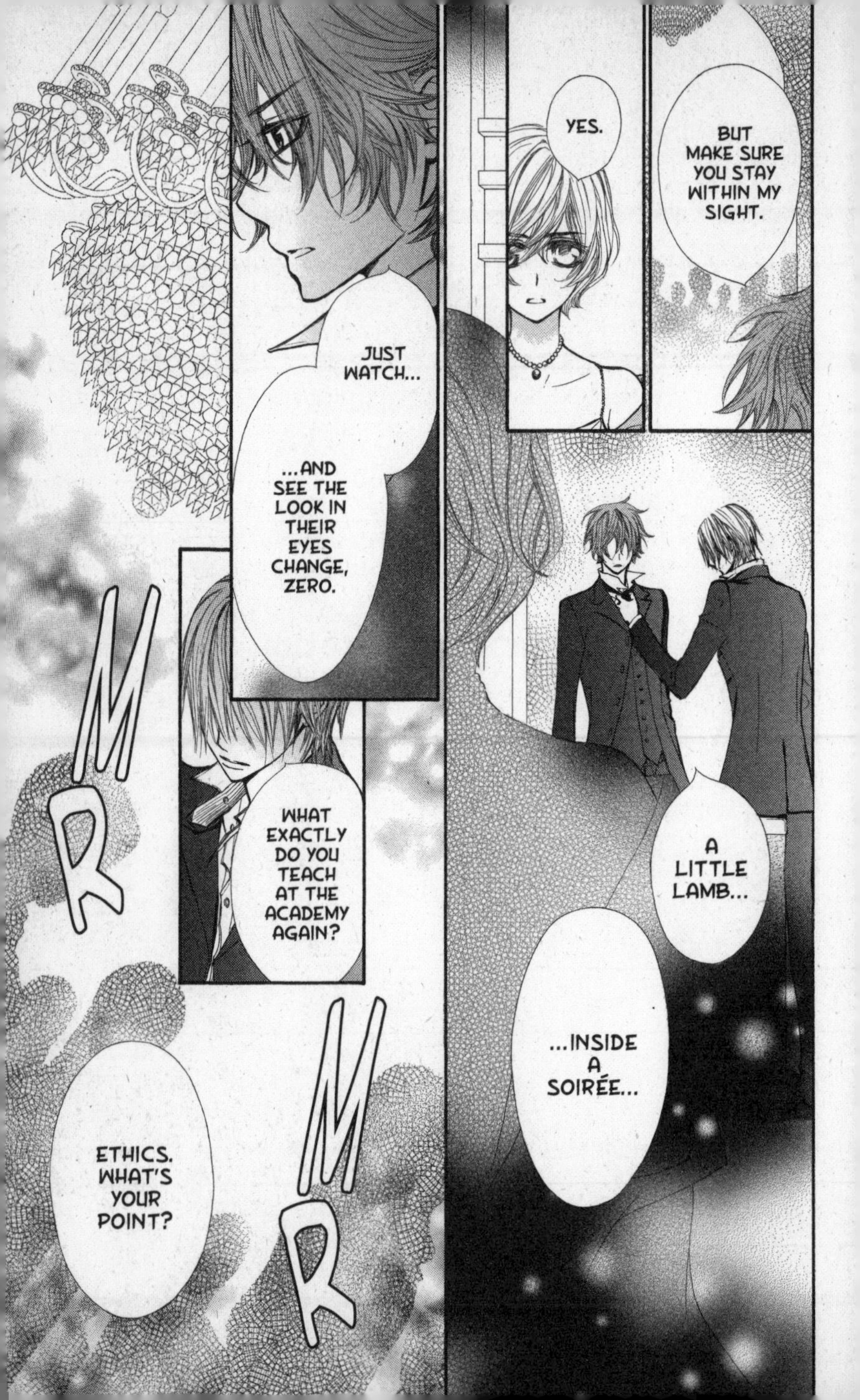
BUT MAKE SURE YOU STAY WITHIN MY SIGHT.
YES.
A LITTLE LAMB...
...INSIDE A SOIRÉE...
JUST WATCH...
...AND SEE THE LOOK IN THEIR EYES CHANGE, ZERO.
WHAT EXACTLY DO YOU TEACH AT THE ACADEMY AGAIN?
MR
ETHICS. WHAT'S YOUR POINT?
MR

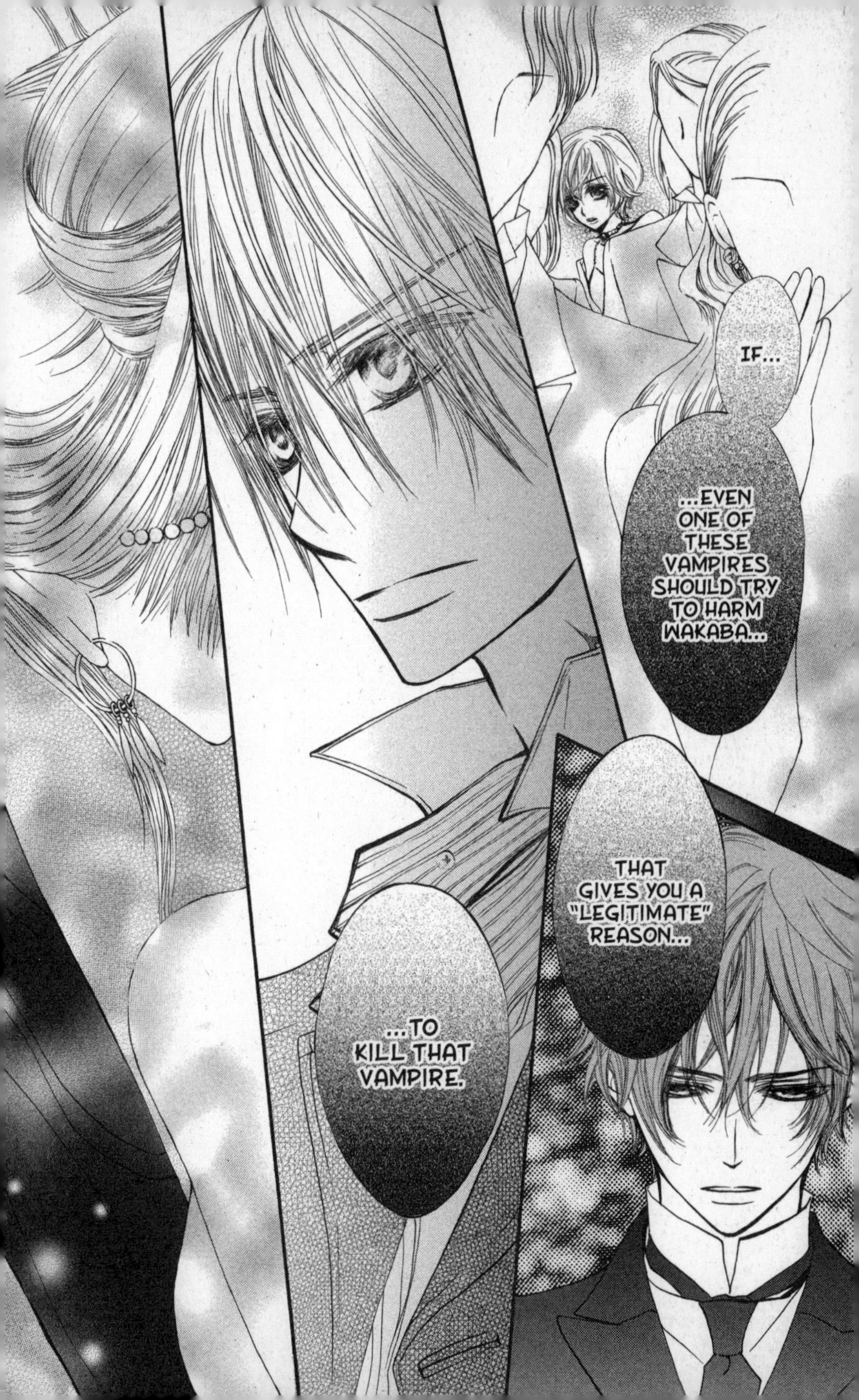
IF...
...EVEN ONE OF THESE VAMPIRES SHOULD TRY TO HARM WAKABA...
THAT GIVES YOU A "LEGITIMATE" REASON...
...TO KILL THAT VAMPIRE.

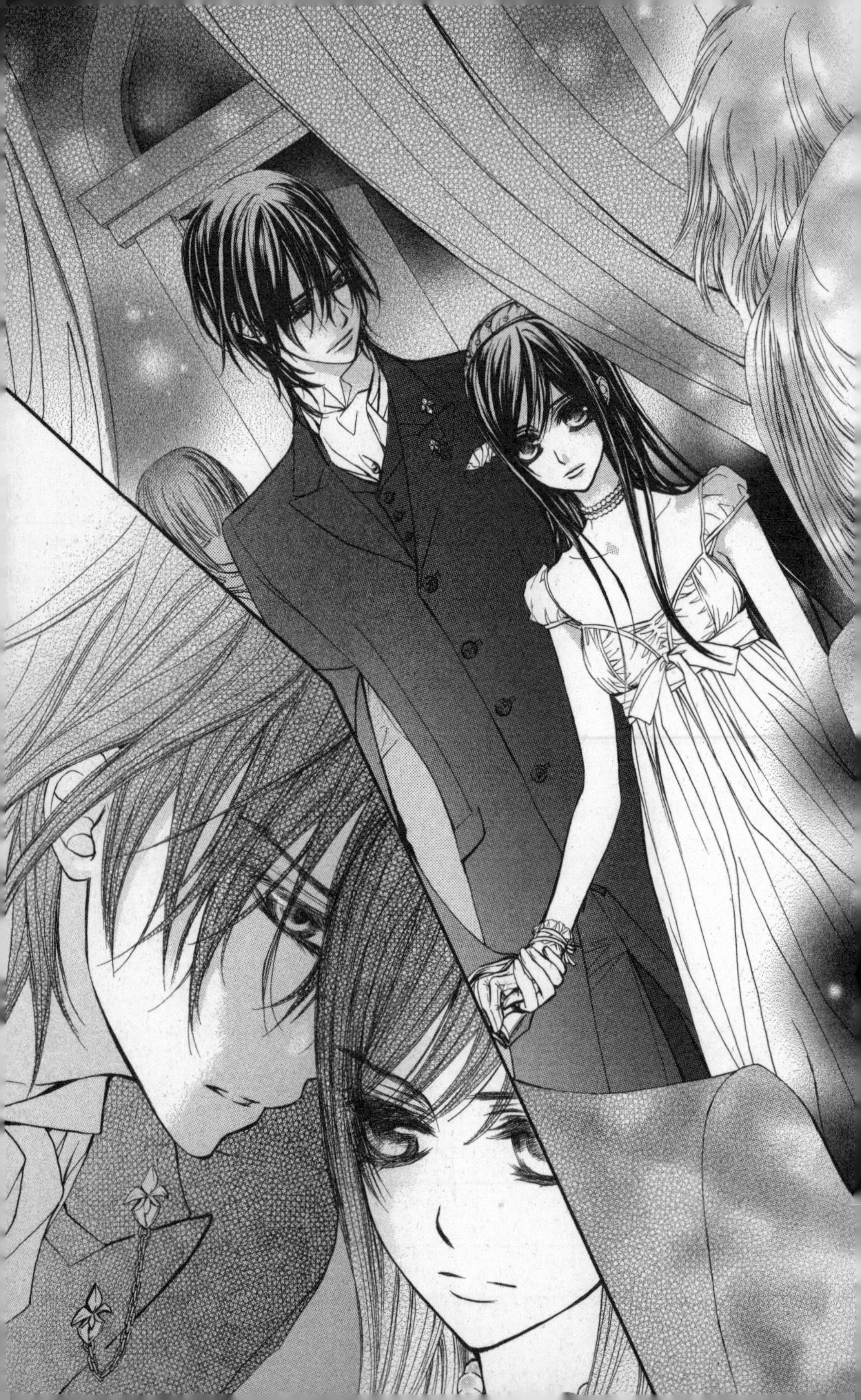

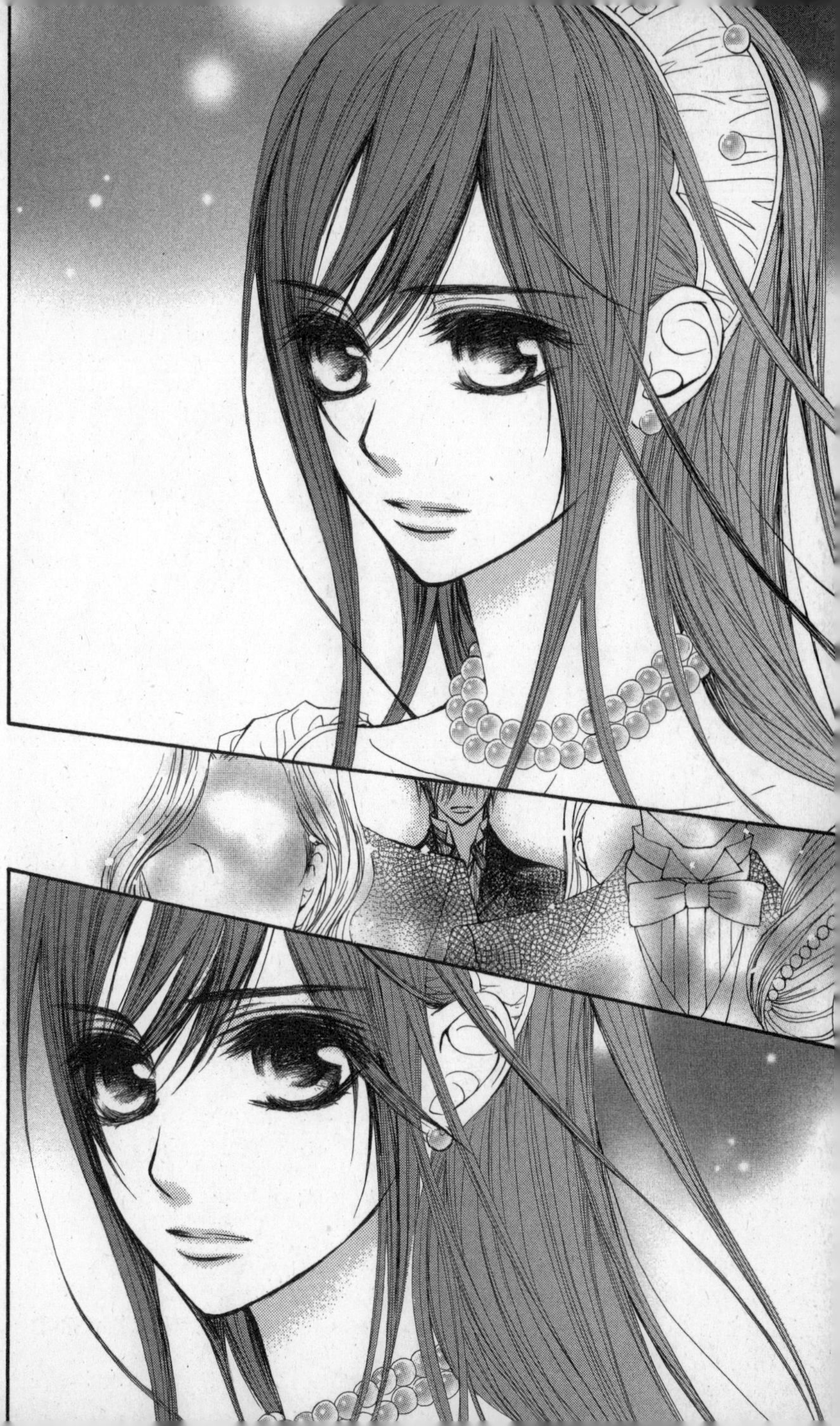

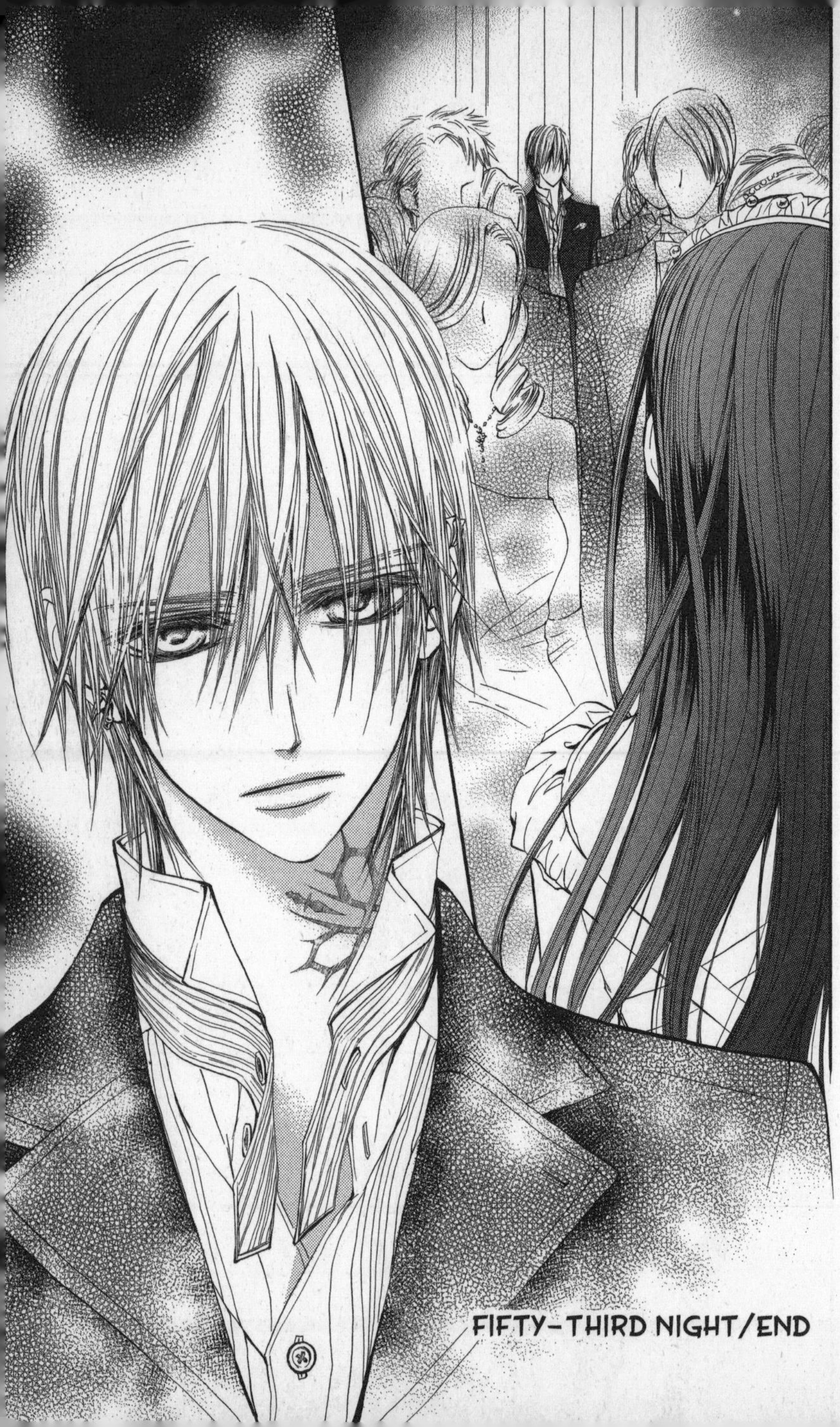
FIFTY-THIRD NIGHT/END

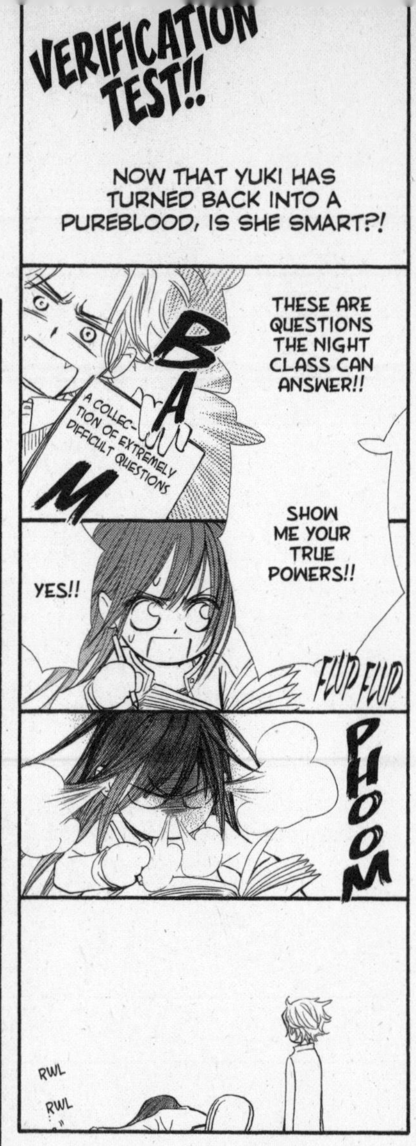
VERIFICATION TEST!!
NOW THAT YUKI HAS TURNED BACK INTO A PUREBLOOD, IS SHE SMART?!
THESE ARE QUESTIONS THE NIGHT CLASS CAN ANSWER!!
BAM
A COLLECTION OF EXTREMELY DIFFICULT QUESTIONS
SHOW ME YOUR TRUE POWERS!!
YES!!
FLIP FLIP
PHOOM
RWL
RWL

VAMPIRES COVERED IN BLOOD ARE PROHIBITED FROM ENTERING THIS PAGE!

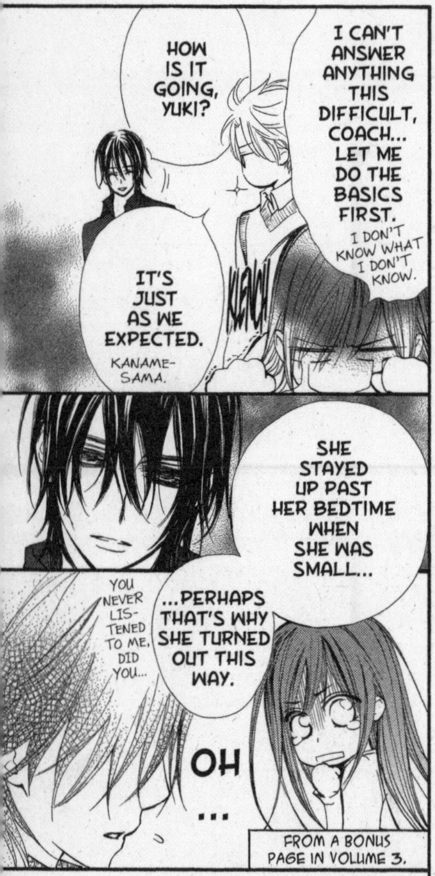
HOW IS IT GOING, YUKI?
I CAN'T ANSWER ANYTHING THIS DIFFICULT, COACH... LET ME DO THE BASICS FIRST.
I DON'T KNOW WHAT I DON'T KNOW.
IT'S JUST AS WE EXPECTED.
KANAME-SAMA.
KLENCH
SHE STAYED UP PAST HER BEDTIME WHEN SHE WAS SMALL...
...PERHAPS THAT'S WHY SHE TURNED OUT THIS WAY.
YOU NEVER LISTENED TO ME, DID YOU...
OH ...
FROM A BONUS PAGE IN VOLUME 3.

VERIFICATION TEST TO BE CONTINUED...

THE END

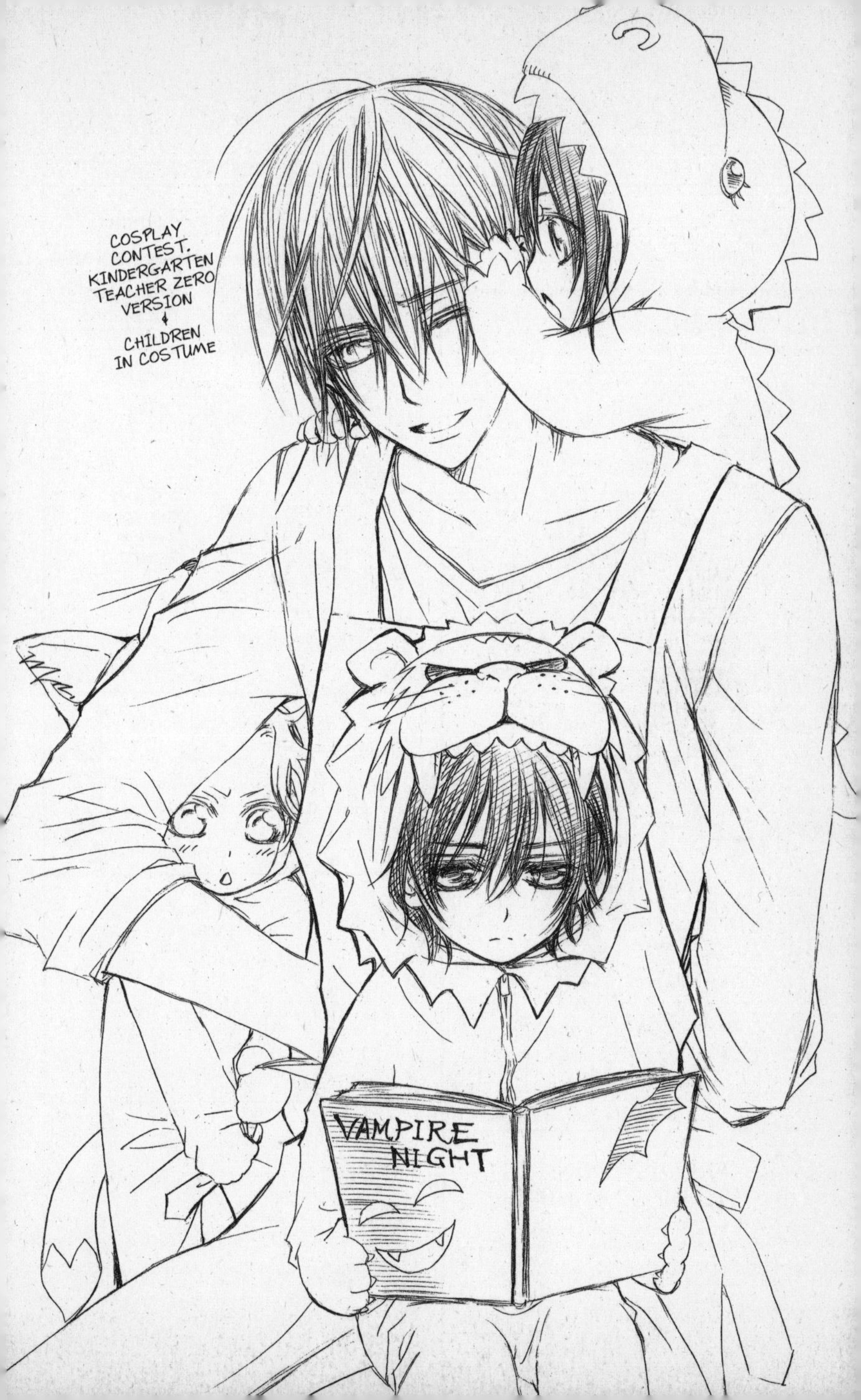
COSPLAY CONTEST. KINDERGARTEN TEACHER ZERO VERSION & CHILDREN IN COSTUME
VAMPIRE NIGHT

EDITOR'S NOTES

Characters

Matsuri Hino puts careful thought into the names of her characters in *Vampire Knight*. Below is the collection of characters through volume 11. Each character's name is presented family name first, per the kanji reading.

黒主優姫

Cross Yuki

Yuki's last name, *Kurosu*, is the Japanese pronunciation of the English word "cross." However, the kanji has a different meaning—*kuro* means "black" and *su* means "master." Her first name is a combination of *yuu*, meaning "tender" or "kind," and *ki*, meaning "princess."

錐生零

Kiryu Zero

Zero's first name is the kanji for *rei*, meaning "zero." In his last name, *Kiryu*, the *ki* means "auger" or "drill," and the *ryu* means "life."

玖蘭枢

Kuran Kaname

Kaname means "hinge" or "door." The kanji for his last name is a combination of the old-fashioned way of writing *ku*, meaning "nine," and *ran*, meaning "orchid": "nine orchids."

藍堂英

Aido Hanabusa

Hanabusa means "petals of a flower." *Aido* means "indigo temple." In Japanese, the pronunciation of *Aido* is very close to the pronunciation of the English word *idol*.

架院暁

Kain Akatsuki

Akatsuki means "dawn" or "daybreak." In *Kain, ka* is a base or support, while *in* denotes a building that has high fences around it, such as a temple or school.

早園瑠佳

Souen Ruka

In *Ruka*, the *ru* means "lapis lazuli" while the *ka* means "good-looking" or "beautiful." The *sou* in Ruka's surname, *Souen*, means "early," but this kanji also has an obscure meaning of "strong fragrance." The *en* means "garden."

一条拓麻

Ichijo Takuma

Ichijo can mean a "ray" or "streak." The kanji for *Takuma* is a combination of *taku*, meaning "to cultivate" and *ma*, which is the kanji for *asa*, meaning "hemp" or "flax," a plant with blue flowers.

支葵千里

Shiki Senri

Shiki's last name is a combination of *shi*, meaning "to support" and *ki*, meaning "mallow"—a flowering plant with pink or white blossoms. The *ri* in *Senri* is a traditional Japanese unit of measure for distance, and one *ri* is about 2.44 miles. *Senri* means "1,000 *ri*."

夜刈十牙

Yagari Toga

Yagari is a combination of *ya*, meaning "night," and *gari*, meaning "to harvest." *Toga* means "ten fangs."

一条麻遠,一翁

Ichijo Asato, aka "Ichio"

Ichijo can mean a "ray" or "streak." Asato's first name is comprised of *asa*, meaning "hemp" or "flax," and *tou*, meaning "far off." His nickname is *ichi*, or "one," combined with *ou*, which can be used as an honorific when referring to an older man.

若葉沙頼

Wakaba Sayori

Yori's full name is Sayori Wakaba. *Wakaba* means "young leaves." Her given name, *Sayori*, is a combination of *sa*, meaning "sand," and *yori*, meaning "trust."

星煉

Seiren

Sei means "star" and *ren* means "to smelt" or "refine." *Ren* is also the same kanji used in *rengoku*, or "purgatory."

遠矢莉磨

Toya Rima

Toya means a "far-reaching arrow." Rima's first name is a combination of *ri*, or "jasmine," and *ma*, which signifies enhancement by wearing away, such as by polishing or scouring.

紅まり亜

Kurenai Maria

Kurenai means "crimson." The kanji for the last *a* in Maria's first name is the same that is used in "Asia."

錐生壱縷
Kiryu Ichiru

Ichi is the old-fashioned way of writing "one," and *ru* means "thread."

緋桜閑, 狂咲姫
Hio Shizuka, Kuruizaki-hime

Shizuka means "calm and quiet." In Shizuka's family name, *hi* is "scarlet," and *ou* is "cherry blossoms." Shizuka Hio is also referred to as the "Kuruizaki-hime." *Kuruizaki* means "flowers blooming out of season," and *hime* means "princess."

藍堂月子
Aido Tsukiko

Aido means "indigo temple." *Tsukiko* means "moon child."

白蕗更
Shirabuki Sara

Shira is "white," and *buki* is "butterbur," a plant with white flowers. *Sara* means "renew."

黒主灰闇
Cross Kaien

Cross, or *Kurosu*, means "black master." Kaien is a combination of *kai*, meaning "ashes," and *en*, meaning "village gate." The kanji for *en* is also used for Enma, the ruler of the Underworld in Buddhist mythology.

玖蘭李土
Kuran Rido

Kuran means "nine orchids." In *Rido*, *ri* means "plum" and *do* means "earth."

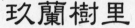

玖蘭樹里
Kuran Juri

Kuran means "nine orchids." In her first name, *ju* means "tree" and a *ri* is a traditional Japanese unit of measure for distance. The kanji for *ri* is the same as in Senri's name.

玖蘭悠
Kuran Haruka

Kuran means "nine orchids." *Haruka* means "distant" or "remote."

鷹宮海斗
Takamiya Kaito

Taka means "hawk" and *miya* means "imperial palace" or "shrine." *Kai* is "sea" and *to* means "to measure" or "grid."

Terms

-sama: The suffix *sama* is used in formal address for someone who ranks higher in the social hierarchy. The vampires call their leader "Kaname-sama" only when they are among their own kind.